# CULTURAL PLURALISM AND NATIONALIST POLITICS IN BRITISH GUIANA

by

Leo A. Despres

with a Foreword by M. G. Smith

*Rand McNally and Company* *Chicago*

# Cultural Pluralism and Nationalist Politics in British Guiana

STUDIES IN POLITICAL CHANGE

MYRON WEINER, *Editor*

Bayley, *Public Liberties in the New States*

Despres, *Cultural Pluralism and Nationalist Politics in British Guiana*

Goldrich, *Sons of the Establishment: Elite Youth in Panama and Costa Rica*

Zolberg, *Creating Political Order: The Party-States of West Africa*

RAND MCNALLY BOOKS IN COMPARATIVE GOVERNMENT AND INTERNATIONAL POLITICS

HARRY ECKSTEIN, *Advisory Editor*

Coplin, *The Functions of International Law: An Introduction to the Role of International Law in the Contemporary World*

Finlay, Holsti, & Fagen, *Enemies in Politics*

Russett, *International Regions and the International System: A Study in Political Ecology*

Singer, *Human Behavior and International Politics: Contributions from the Social-Psychological Sciences*


*Printed in U.S.A. by Rand McNally & Company*
*Library of Congress Catalog Card Number* 67-30674

FOR LORETTA AND THE CHILDREN

# FOREWORD

PROFESSOR LEO DESPRES HAS ASKED ME TO CONTRIBUTE A FOREWORD TO HIS study of pluralism in Guyana, for I have long advocated the relevance of this concept for the study of Caribbean societies. I am happy to accept this invitation, as it allows me to indicate briefly some of the monograph's merits which, being passed over lightly by the author, may escape immediate notice.

In this book Professor Despres presents an account of Guyanese society and its development during the closing years of colonial rule. These decades witnessed the rise, arrest, and fragmentation of a popular movement for local independence from British domination. The monograph accordingly provides an arresting case study of an independence movement which dissolved into bitter sectional strife before achieving its goal. Like Cyprus and India, in advance of independence, Guyana experienced those sectional hostilities that the Congo, Malaya, Uganda and Nigeria encountered thereafter. Despite this, Guyana obtained independence in May 1966; and since then the country has made brave efforts under new direction to contain the destructive forces released by its independence struggle. Dr. Despres' elegant and comprehensive study of these Guyanese developments should thus be of interest to all social scientists concerned with the processes of decolonization and the problems of emergent nationhood and unity.

The monograph also shows how anthropologists can investigate complex societies as total units and analyse them systematically by combining relevant data from institutional and community studies with others from early and recent historical periods. In this way the author combines his analyses of this complex society and its tortuous experience during the last decade of colonial rule, when the great popular movement for national independence broke into two rival blocks based on racial and cultural exclusions, with consequent uncertainty, bitterness, and bloodshed. The monograph accordingly enriches our understanding of such disintegrative movements by documenting the forces, phases, and strategies involved, and by analysing these political developments in relation to their changing societal contexts. Political scientists will readily appreciate the significance of such analysis and data for the general study of societal development from plural integration to national unity.

Professor Despres may identify himself as a cultural anthropologist; but no sociologist can overlook his central concern with the sociological implications and conditions of cultural divergence; and, throughout, the text systematically relates cultural differentiae to the systems of social relations within each of the two main ethnic blocs of Guyanese society. It is therefore excusable to regard this work as a notable union of social and cultural anthropology.

A major focus of the present analysis is the integration of Guyanese society. Excluding its peripheral Amerindians and creolized Chinese, and despite its poverty and relatively small size, this society is sharply segmented and imperfectly knit—an awkward combination of mutually exclusive ethnic groups, Anglo-Saxon, Portuguese, East Indian and Creole or Afro-Guyanese, themselves subdivided by differences of situation, culture, and colour. Together, these last two ethnic blocs account for over 90 per cent of the colonial population, and their cultures and interrelations provide the principal foci of study.

On the basis of intensive fieldwork in several Creole and East Indian communities (carefully matched for ecological and administrative variables), the author examines their social systems separately and compares them. Since Afro-Guyanese 'retire' to their native villages after working in urban and industrial fields, while East Indians for the most part remain in the country, these village descriptions indicate the differential participation of the two ethnic blocs in the urban industrial sectors of Guyanese society; and, by skilful use of census, official and other data, including field interviews, the author systematically describes the differential relations of East Indians and Afro-Guyanese to colonial institutions of government, education, religion, and economy. These data obliquely describe the general character and composition of Guyanese townships, especially Georgetown, the capital, and Mackenzie City in the bauxite belt.

To investigate societal cohesion, Professor Despres analyses the structures of these East Indian and Creole communities, separately and comparatively to determine how their characteristic institutional organisations and activities foster or impede their local, sectional, or societal integrations, by sustaining common or differential alignments with the colonial institutional system. Societal integration is thus analysed systematically and at several levels, the integration of colonial society being distinguished from that of its major ethnic components, as these sectional integrations are also distinguished from the integration of local ethnic communities.

Further, by exploiting the historical dimension at two strategic levels, the early and contemporary periods, the author shows how the integration of these ethnic segments in colonial Guyana altered in character and scope as Guyanese society underwent structural realignments linked with its changing political and economic context. Societal integration is thus shown to vary in scope, character, and intensity as an aspect of institutional articulations within and between the major ethnic divisions of the colonial society. Moreover, having isolated the forces that sustain this colonial order and identified their preconditions and implications, the account of the independence movement shows how tendencies towards polarization increased in salience and scope as decolonization proceeded. The ensuing analysis of ethnic oppositions exhibits the alternative aspects of ethnic integrations clearly. Eufunctional to its adherents, a distinctive ethnic structure may be positively dysfunctional for the society. Alternatively, once conditions have changed, such a structure may lose its functional values with minimal changes of form, or it may preserve these values despite formal changes. Such possibilities require us to discriminate the levels, ranges, units, conditions and changes of social integration and contain important suggestions for further studies of their relations. What merits particular notice is the combination of approaches, conceptions, and data that such analyses presuppose. In this monograph, Professor Despres combines diachronic and synchronic approaches with community studies and systematic controlled comparisons to investigate the integrative and divisive features of ethnic institutional patterns under similar and differing social conditions. In the process, he demonstrates the capacity of anthropological analysis to embrace complex societal structures and to illuminate their processes of change by treating them rigorously as single systems of interacting parts whose inner and reciprocal articulations are central to their integration. In this respect the present study is a pioneer attempt at macrosociological analysis of structural transformations by strictly anthropological conceptions and procedures. It demonstrates the value of ordinary field methods of social anthropology in such investigations, provided that their central problems are clearly formulated, evaluated for analytic significance, and organised in an appropriate research design. In these respects, the present monograph offers a model well worth study by all who seek a rounded sociological analysis of structural change in segmental multi-ethnic societies.

Faced with such multi-ethnic aggregates as Guyana, anthropologists have normally elected to investigate one particular ethnic segment or some characteristic institution thereof, often without restricting their observations to the problem or unit studied. Recent sociological studies of British Guiana illustrate this tendency. Thus, after studying three Afro-Guyanese communities, Raymond Smith generalised about the colonial social order (1956: 191–203), before investigating the East Indians in association with C. Jayawardena. Following these studies of the East Indians, Raymond Smith published a general account of Guyanese society that differs sharply from the findings of Professor Despres (1964: 1051–1077). According to Professor Smith, "the Indians are already assimilated to a common way of life" (1962: 141). "There is no problem of 'tribalism' in British Guiana . . . The whole society shares a common cultural equipment" (1962: 198). According to Dr. Jayawardena, "cross-cutting membership in distinct and opposed groups tends to integrate the total society. Thus class affiliations cut across industrial groups and ethnic affiliations cut across classes" (1963: 10). These statements express a view of Guyana that Professor Despres calls 'reticulated.'

In the present work, Professor Despres subjects all possible bonds of inter-ethnic assimilation in Guyana to intensive scrutiny. Having documented the differential implications of specific structures for East Indians and Creoles by comparative analysis of their ethnic milieux, he shows the limited range and scope of such inter-ethnic assimilations. Thus to determine precisely how they affect the differential incorporation of East Indian and Creole cultural sections in Guyana at differing periods of its development, he examines the mass communication media, unionism, educational arrangements, colonial land programmes, the civil service, and other societal institutions in turn. Given the colonial history and social structure, this analysis shows why it was almost inevitable that emergent political parties would also enhance the exclusive incorporations of these ethnic blocs.

Whereas 'reticulated' models of Guyanese society stress its relative cohesion and assimilation of disparate stocks within a common inclusive economic and occupational system and an inclusive, consensual stratification, Professor Despres shows that, in their divergent social contexts, such occupations as teacher, peasant, labourer, or shopkeeper have very different functional and structural implications for Creole and East Indian Guyanese. Whereas to Professor Raymond Smith, East Indian patterns of family, marriage and kinship are only "superfically" different from those he observed among rural Afro-Guyanese (1962: 131–2), by careful comparison of his own field data on these two family systems, Professor Despres demonstrates the magnitude and pivotal significance of the differences which, reinforced by other factors, effectively seal off the two ethnic blocs from interbreeding, and thus preserves their racial and social separation by segregating the ethnic contexts of family, socialization, kinship and community.

Ever since the decline of Afro-American orientations to Caribbean studies, the sociology of this region has been canvassed by three competing theoretical approaches: the 'plantation' framework of Wagley (1957), Rubin (1957, 1959) and Mintz (1959); Parsonian structural-functionalism in various modes (Braithwaite, 1953, 1960; R. T. Smith, 1956); and analyses based on the model of plural societies advanced by J. S. Furnivall (1948). Thus far, with minor exceptions, no Caribbean society has been subjected to extended analyses from two or more of these competing viewpoints. However, with this publication we can now compare monographic analyses of a single Caribbean society from two divergent theoretical perspectives. Parallel studies of societal integration in other Caribbean units may help to clarify the issues at stake, and to improve our theoretical models and analytic techniques.

Meanwhile, several features of the present study seem especially promising for social anthropological analyses of multi-ethnic societies undergoing structural change. To specify the principal dimensions and components of such units in terms of their scale, composition, situation, history, mechanisms of identity, and internal and societal articulations is clearly a primary task; and for this purpose Professor Despres' distinctions between local or minimal cultural sections and maximal or societal ones, and between local and broker institutions, are valuable instruments. This notion of broker institutions seems especially promising for operational study of complex societies focussed on the parallel, unitary, or differential integrations of their communal components. Another fertile notion for such structural analyses is the concept of isomeric social systems, which differ in their internal and external articulations despite many shared elements. Finally, to examine endogenous processes of change in the structure and articulation of multi-ethnic units, the notion of 'organizational strategy' enhances discrimination, wherever organised groups or powerful leaders are present and active.

Inevitably there remain several loose ends, unformulated distinctions, and unanswered questions in this—as in any pioneer study. Substantive issues are assured in advance of vigorous debate in Caribbean circles. Caribbean historians may also be stimulated by the present summary of Guyanese history to re-examine the evidence and to re-assess the structural relevance of different phases and elements of the colonial order for local developments since 1945. The monograph's wider implications for the general analysis of structural change in multi-ethnic societies should promote more diverse discussions among scholars.

One theoretical question of some significance concerns the cause of the split in the P.P.P. following the debacle of 1953. In guarded style, Professor Despres suggests that changes in the external context of Marxists within the P.P.P., linked with the collapse of the Caribbean Labour Congress and with the activities of American labour unions, may have served as precipitating factors. In support, he argues that we should seek exogenous determinants for this split since "we cannot invoke a constant (e.g., the plural structure of Guyanese society) to explain a variable (e.g., the success or failure of the nationalist movement to solve the organizational problems that confronted it)" (p. 281 below). This argument seems questionable on various grounds. Generalised as a methodological postulate, it directs us always to seek extrinsic 'causes' or 'precipitants' for structural change, since all social structures, plural or other, represent relatively durable and well defined milieux for such processes and events. As Marx and Durkheim perceived, such arguments are often misleading. In the present case, this postulate exaggerates the fixity of the 'plural structure of Guyanese society' despite the profound changes it underwent between 1945 and 1953. The record shows that several major changes in Guyanese institutional and sectional relations between 1950 and 1952 were wholly endogenous in origin. It should not be assumed that 'the plural structure of Guyanese society' retained an unchanging character, form, and significance throughout these developments, since the record suggests otherwise. For P.P.P. leaders at any rate, the nature, scope and composition of this plural structure varied greatly at different phases of the political struggle, as their changing organisational strategies indicate. It is advisable then to seek sociological 'explanations' of the rise, composition and split of the P.P.P. within the context of Guyanese colonial society, rather than in extrinsic conditions, influential as these undoubtedly were.

Professor Despres relates how the P.P.P. was put together by Jagan and his associates after an eligible Afro-Guyanese counterpart appeared in L. F. S. Burnham. Under the colonial regime this coalition of Creoles and East Indians, Marxists and non-Marxists, was obviously essential to mobilise the Guyanese masses in pursuit of local autonomy. Nonetheless, this union of anti-colonial forces was clearly fragile, artificial, and instrumental *ab initio*. Some of its leaders conceived the Guyanese independence struggle merely as a local theatre in the international cold war, while others regarded independence as the necessary and sufficient condition of societal unity and nationhood. Even before the elections of 1953, Burnham's destruction was being planned. It is difficult to avoid the conclusion that the split and subsequent strife had its source in those Marxist commitments that divided the popular leadership with respect to the values and implications of Guyanese independence.

The integrated analysis of the organisation, ideology, and vicissitudes of this nationalist movement is a central concern of the present work, and one of its major achievements. The study accordingly illustrates the differences and relations of 'nationalism' as ideology and as a social movement. Nationalist ideologies may be employed to mobilise and direct mass movements for local autonomy as an organisational strategy of leaders whose primary commitments and ultimate goals are far removed. Such manipulatory leadership need not be cynical in advocating nationalist ideals, if local autonomy is prerequisite for pursuit of their ultimate goals. However, insofar as these ulterior objectives diverge from nationalist ideals, the variable relations of ideology and organisation in independence movements are exposed; and by his detailed treatment of the leadership, composition, programs and history of this Guyanese independence movement, Professor Despres provides a vivid example of the ambiguous and changing roles of ideology in mass movements directed towards structural change in multi-ethnic colonial milieux.

Local and foreign observers, unaware of the detailed social composition of such popular movements or the personal alignments of their leadership, normally attempt to interpret them primarily by reference to their publicly proclaimed ideological goals and means. The present work shows clearly how superficial and misleading such interpretations are likely to be. Ideology, organisation, and public support are complementary essentials of radical mass movements in all societies; but the ideological preferences, pronouncements, interpretations, and reinterpretations of the movement's leaders should be understood as choices designed to organize and extend their movement and to increase its solidarity and power, while weakening the support and legitimacy of its immediate opponents. Those structural conditions of the social context which generate the movement also govern the recruitment of its leaders and the character and composition of its supporters and its opposition, the strategies, organisation and ideology of the contraposed groups, their divergent orientations and relative positions in subsequent affairs. For documentation of some specific mechanisms and processes at work in one case of this sort, we need only to examine the present monograph. Such data also show how inadequate analyses of multidimensional mass movements in such complex and changing situations as that of Guyana after World War II must be, if their ideological aspects are treated as transparent or decisive. This caution applies to nationalist movements in other colonial plural societies as well.

Professor Despres' conceptual analysis of the ethnic context of Guyanese 'nationalism' must also be regarded as a major contribution to our study of pluralism, using this term in Furnivall's sense to denote congruent cultural and social cleavages within politically unified aggregates. Here the author makes several refinements in conceptualisation and analytic method; to distinguish cultural sections, he employs functional analyses to determine how far and in what ways these sectional systems are isomorphic or isomeric. Linked with the important distinction between minimal and maximal cultural sections are others between local and broker institutions, and between heterogeneous and plural societies. Professor Despres distinguishes the plural society as "one that contains maximal or national cultural sections" (p. 22 below) from "a society containing local or minimal cultural sections (which) is socially and culturally heterogeneous" (p. 22). While minimal cultural sections consist of local groups that remain separate though culturally similar and distinctive, lacking a common organisation or integration at the national or territorial levels, maximal cultural sections consist of culturally similar local groups integrated by coextensive 'broker institutions'. Whereas 'local' institutions maintain the cultural differentiation and separate integration of local groups by organising activities within their community contexts, broker institutions "function to link local activities to the wider spheres of societal activity" (pp. 23, 270). Maximal cultural sections are thus identified by the integrative effect of such broker institutions on culturally similar communities throughout the society. Among broker institutions, trade unions, political parties, economic, occupational, and other special-purpose associations, religious and educational structures are especially prominent. On the other hand, within local communities, social integration generally develops through institutions of kinship, affinity, neighborhood, production, patronage, and cult. Moreover, since "maximal cultural sections presuppose the existence of minimal cultural sections" (p. 270), broker institutions likewise presuppose the operation of local institutions, and societal integration corresponds in scope and intensity with the uniform effectiveness of broker institutions.

Although these are very useful and promising conceptions, they do not distinguish clearly those 'broker' institutions which are sectionally specific, extensive and autonomous structures such as the P.P.P. and P.N.C. after 1956 from those agencies of the central government which serve to coordinate activities and regulate relations throughout the inclusive society. Broker institutions of the first type, being sectionally specific, extensive and autonomous, may integrate a sectional aggregate, diffusely, indirectly and partially, as for example Hinduism and local exogamy do among Guyanese East Indians; or they may provide representative or inclusive sectional organisations through which the cultural section is mobilised for various purposes. Under the first of these two alternatives, given its cultural and social distinctness, the 'maximal section' remains a corporate category, a bounded persisting aggregate, which, despite its distinct identity, lacks extensive autonomous organisation for management of its own affairs. Under the second alternative, the 'maximal section' possesses this extensive autonomous organisation, and constitutes a corporate group capable of effective collective action through its coordinating structures (M. G. Smith, 1966).

To illustrate his distinctions between minimal and maximal cultural sections and between plural and heterogeneous societies, Professor Despres cites Nigeria as a plural society, composed of organised maximal sections, in contrast with society in the United States, where "although many cultural groups . . . are integrated at local levels, . . . there are practically no institutional structures (e.g., labor unions, political parties, religious associations, etc.) that serve to separately integrate each of these groups at the national level of socio-cultural integration. In Nigeria, on the other hand, the Ibo, the Yoruba and the Hausa are not only culturally differentiated and locally integrated, but institutional structures exist (e.g., political parties) which serve to maintain their cultural differentiation at the national level" (p. 22).

This contrast suggests that maximal cultural sections are conceived as autonomously organised corporate groups having sectionally specific institutional structures of representative or inclusive character. This interpretation is supported by the statement that "when institutional activities serve to integrate similar cultural groups and differentiate them from other cultural groups at the national level, such groups constitute maximal or national cultural sections" (p. 22). However, Professor Despres sometimes employs his concept of maximal sections to denote aggregates of a rather different character, namely those that lack their own extensive, autonomous organisations, while maintaining differential relations with societally extensive institutional structures under external control. Such differential articulations with societal structures as these culturally distinctive aggregates exhibit must normally perpetuate their cultural distinctness; but these differential relations do not normally promote separate sectional integrations, as the following accounts of Creole and East Indian relations to the institutions of colonial Guiana indicate. Moreover, although the institutional superstructure of a plural society may provide bases for separate sectional integrations, as for example in Nigeria, Cyprus, colonial Uganda, and Morocco, this is neither necessary nor normally the case; and in Guiana before 1945, despite Professor Despres' arguments, the differential relations of East Indians and Afro-Guyanese to colonial economic, educational, religious, and bureaucratic structures, while preserving their cultural differentiations, did not integrate the various local communities in either section at a societal level. Instead these differing sectional articulations served to perpetuate sectional fragmentations. Throughout this period East Indians and Afro-Guianese remained minimal sections, unorganised aggregates of local groups, categorically distinguished by their differing cultural and racial features, diffuse intra-sectional ties, and distinct contexts and modes of subordination.

It seems desirable then to distinguish those 'maximal sections' which, despite distinctive structural and cultural features, remain unorganised corporate categories, from others that exhibit autonomous sectional organisations of a representative or inclusive kind that identify them as corporate groups. It is necessary also to distinguish those 'broker' institutions which are sectionally specific, extensive and autonomous, such as the P.P.P. and P.N.C. with their allied trade unions after 1956, from others which are societally inclusive, heteronomous and exogenous to the cultural sections whose differential subordinations, fragmentation, and segregations they maintain. Broker institutions of the first sort convert fragmented cultural sections into solidary and extensive corporate groups; broker institutions of the second sort preserve the cultural distinctness and fragmentation of these aggregates, as politically immobilised corporate categories. As presently defined, the correlative conceptions of maximal sections and broker institutions overlook the critical differences between these alternatives. Moreover this ambiguity affects the distinction between plural and heterogeneous societies, since on one reading, colonial Guyana before 1945 should be regarded as a plural society of differentially articulated cultural sections, while on the other, it should not, since neither of its massive subordinate sections were then integrated separately as corporate groups under their own extensive autonomous structures. Rather at this period, the regime exemplified the principle of 'Divide, subdivide, and rule,' and only the dominant British possessed sectionally integrative autonomous structures.

Other difficulties with these conceptions of maximal sections and broker institutions emerge in comparative analysis. For example, colonial Surinam, Congo, Algeria, South Africa, Hapsburg Austria, or Guatemala all contained subordinate populations isolated from one another and from the centres of societal control under institutions that fostered their sectional fragmentation and cultural distinctness. These societies all contained two or more culturally distinct collectivities, differentiated sharply in political and social organisation, and in their articulations with the status order. In all, one social section was organised as a ruling minority under its exclusive institutions, while the others remained fragmented, immobilised, and subordinated by the 'broker' institutions of the rulers, which preserved their fragmentation and their cultural distinctness together. Is it analytically useful or appropriate to treat such societies as heterogeneous merely because their subordinate local groups of similar culture lack any autonomous organisations to integrate them? Alternatively, is it useful or appropriate to classify these societies with others such as Nigeria, Cyprus, or India on the eve of independence in which culturally distinct sections were integrated separately by autonomous institutions, as in Guyana after 1956? To avoid these difficulties, we need only to develop the conceptions of maximal cultural sections and broker institutions to distinguish the alternatives cited above. That the author's conceptual framework can accommodate such distinctions without impairing his substantive analysis indicates the soundness of his work.

Like other scholars, Professor Despres finds the notion of 'basic institutions' an unsatisfactory tool for societal classification and analysis. However, his primary objections seem to flow from the cultural framework he prefers. Thus, he asks "If a culture is understood to be an integrated pattern of standardised social usages, then which of these usages can be considered basic or compulsory? Might not all of them be considered basic to the cultural pattern?" (p. 20). Accordingly "all institutions must be considered equally functional in the expression of culture. Therefore, as far as the expression of culture is concerned, the analytical distinction between basic, alternative and exclusive institutions is spurious, and serves no theoretical purpose" (p. 21).

On this matter, my differences with Professor Despres reflect divergence of analytic frameworks. While stressing the cultural conditions of social process and structure, my focus is on the inner organisation and external relations of social systems whereas Professor Despres apparently gives priority to the 'expression of culture.' However, although in terms of cultural expression all institutional elements may be equally functional, they are likely to differ in their significance for cultural maintenance and coherence. At the sociological level, such equivalence of institutions is also qualified by their differing significance for the maintenance of social systems. This derives from the fact that as self-perpetuating systems, societies must meet certain essential conditions. These minimum conditions of societal organisation and continuity may be isolated by logical or by comparative analysis; and the institutional arrangements that routinely fulfill these conditions may be isolated as their "basic institutional systems." This system "embraces kinship, education, religion, property, economy, recreation and certain sodalities" (M. G. Smith, 1965: 82). Such institutions are 'basic' or 'compulsory' in the sense that without them societal organisation and continuity are impossible. Whether these institutional arrangements are segregated in different structures or contained within a few functionally diffuse groupings is mainly significant for the discrimination of societal types for the comparative or internal analysis of social structure and integration. It follows then that societal similarities or differences, continuity, or change should be evident in the structures of these basic institutional systems. Societies may therefore be compared and analysed by examining the structures and internal diversity or uniformity of their basic institutional systems.

Though Professor Despres formally rejects these conceptions, his distinctions between local and broker institutions are substantively similar. His list of 'local institutional patterns' embraces the basic requisites of social life, "language (dialects), family and kinship, work, religion, socialization (and possibly education), recreational activities, associational activities, and communal activities (e.g., local governmental)" (p. 23). With due allowances for differing terminology, these local institutions correspond closely with my description of the 'basic institutional system' cited above. On the other hand, 'broker institutions' which link local communities with the wider levels of societal activity include "markets (labour and consumption), corporations, religious associations, public and/or private school associations, social and civic associations, labor unions, ethnic associations, political parties, and various governmental agencies" (p. 25). Again, except possibly for 'religious associations', these structures are all 'alternative' or 'exclusive' institutions. Moreover, since maximal sections, integrated through broker institutions, presuppose minimal ones, integrated through local institutions, the latter are prerequisites of the former and of community life as well. They may thus be appropriately described as 'basic.' Thus Professor Despres' distinction between local and broker institutions corresponds closely to that between basic institutions and others. However, his conceptions enable us to isolate these structures for field study and functional analysis more systematically and more effectively.

These remarks illustrate the cogency and fertility of Professor Despres' ideas of minimal and maximal sections, local and broker institutions, isomeric social systems and organisational strategies as elements in structural change. Whether we choose to regard the transformations of Guyanese society described in the text as conversions of previously inarticulate and immobilised corporate categories into militant and contraposed corporate groups, or as processes by which culturally similar minimal sections were integrated as maximal ones remains indifferent, provided only that we can operationalise either conceptual alternative and investigate the structures and processes involved with equal clarity and detail. Certainly in his methodical specifications of issues, criteria and procedures for the study of maximal and minimal cultural sections and their internal and external articulations in each institutional sphere, Professor Despres makes some notable contributions to the comparative and intensive analysis of plural societies in changing and stationary conditions. In demonstrating by controlled comparison the specific structural and functional differentiae of isomeric systems, and their implications for integration and change, he provides another important instrument for theoretical analysis and for field studies of social integration in plural and heterogeneous societies. Contributions of this order and variety merit general attention by social scientists.

M. G. Smith

University of California,
Los Angeles.

## REFERENCES

Braithwaite, Lloyd., 1953. "Social Stratification in Trinidad." *Social and Economic Studies*, Vol. 2, nos. 2 & 3, pp. 5–175.

——— 1960. "Social Stratification and Cultural Pluralism" in Vera Rubin (ed.), *Social and Cultural Pluralism in the Caribbean,* Annals of the New York Academy of Sciences, Vol. 83, art. 5, pp. 816–831.

Despres, Leo A., 1964. "The Implications of Nationalist Politics in British Guiana for the Development of Cultural Theory," *American Anthropologist,* Vol. 66, pp. 1051–1077.

——— 1967. *Cultural Pluralism and Nationalist Politics in British Guiana,* Rand McNally & Co., Chicago, 1967.

Furnivall, J. S., 1948. *Colonial Policy and Practice,* Cambridge University Press, London.

Jayawardena, Chandra., 1963. *Conflict and Solidarity in a Guianese Plantation.* London School of Economics Monographs on Social Anthropology, Athlone Press, London.

Mintz, Sidney W., 1959. "The Plantation as a Socio-Cultural Type" in *Plantation Systems of the New World,* Social Science Monographs VII, Pan American Union, Washington, D.C., pp. 42–49.

Rubin, Vera, 1957. "Cultural Perspectives in Caribbean Research" in V. Rubin (ed.), *Caribbean Studies: A Symposium,* Institute of Social & Economic Research, University of the West Indies, Jamaica, W.I., pp. 110–122.

———, 1959. "Introduction" in *Plantation Systems of the New World,* Social Science Monographs VII, Pan American Union, Washington, D.C., pp. 1–4.

Smith, M. G., 1965. *The Plural Society in the British West Indies.* University of California Press, Berkeley and Los Angeles.

———, 1966. "A Structural Approach to Comparative Politics" in David Easton (ed.) *Varieties of Political Theory,* Prentice-Hall, Englewood Cliffs, N.J., pp. 113–128.

Smith, Raymond T., 1956. *The Negro Family in British Guiana.* Routledge and Kegan Paul, London.

———, 1962. *British Guiana.* Oxford University Press for Royal Institute of International Affairs, London.

Wagley, Charles, 1957. "Plantation America: A Culture Sphere" in V. Rubin (ed.) *Caribbean Studies: A Symposium,* Institute of Social & Economic Research, Jamaica, W.I., pp. 3–13.

# ACKNOWLEDGMENTS

THE SUBSTANCE OF THIS BOOK IS A STUDY IN POLITICAL ANTHROPOLOGY, It presents an analysis of a nationalist political movement with special reference to the sociocultural system in which it developed. That an anthropologist might be interested in the problems of nationalist politics may come as a surprise to those who are not familiar with the discipline. Anthropologists have a self-made reputation for being interested only in preliterate societies and cultures. However, for a very long time they have also been interested in the dynamics of sociocultural change. More recently, they have given increasing attention to the transformation of sociocultural systems from one type to another. The emergence of colonial societies as nation-states falls into this class of phenomena. Among other things, nationalism is a dynamic force by which diverse peoples are creating for themselves new types of social systems. Thus, the forces of nationalism offer the anthropologist an unusual opportunity to investigate the processes of sociocultural change. It is for this reason that I undertook, in 1960–61, an intensive study of culture and nationalist politics in British Guiana (now Guyana).[1] I wish to express my gratitude to the Social Science Research Council which provided the postdoctoral research grant that made this project possible.

The methods by which data were collected for this study are numerous. Participant observation was done in both of Guiana's major political parties. Most of the important nationalist leaders were interviewed, as were many other political figures whose reputations are not so widely known outside of Guiana. Extensive field work was

[1] Since the fieldwork upon which this study is based was completed before British Guiana achieved independence, I have elected to retain the country's pre-independence title in the text.

carried out with the use of interview schedules and participant observation in a typical sugar estate community, in the major bauxite mining town, in two African villages, and in two East Indian villages. The African and Indian villages were matched to control for ecological and other factors. Data were collected on population, family and village economics, kinship patterns, land tenure and fragmentation, political attitudes, political party membership and activity, voting behavior, associational activities, and recreative patterns. Considerable data of an historical nature were also collected for each of the communities studied, for political parties, and for the society as a whole.

The methods employed to collect these data were as objective as they could be under the circumstances. Unfortunately, however, data do not speak for themselves. Their interpretation requires a point of view, and it is here that the social scientist frequently tumbles from his olympian position of objectivity. This danger always exists, but it is especially critical in a study which deals with problems involving politics and political ideologies. In this particular study, the question of communism cannot be ignored. Certainly this issue poses a serious problem of objectivity in social research. Therefore, it is only fair that I make my personal views public so that the reader can decide for himself whether or not my interpretations are biased.

Personally, I accept the principles of constitutional democracy. As I interpret these principles, it follows that individuals have the right to express views which may not be in accord with my own and that such individuals should be able to exercise this right without constraint. It also follows that individuals have the right of association and that they should not be stigmatized for associating with others who happen to share their views. At the same time, I recognize that the expression of any ideology is not always in accord with its practice. Therefore, I am inclined to judge individuals and groups in terms of heir actions rather than the ideologies they profess.

In keeping with this position, I do not consider Marxism or the expression of other styles of socialist thought to be necessarily and always inconsistent with the practice of democratic principles. And although I am fully aware of the fact that great powers such as the Soviet Union and the United States are frequently involved in international conspiracies, I am not inclined to accept every international gathering of socialists (or nonsocialists) as de facto evidence of an international conspiracy organized and controlled from Moscow (or Washington).

With respect to underdeveloped countries, I am convinced that some form of socialism is the only solution possible to correct the problems created by international inequalities. I am equally convinced that socialist values can be expressed through the institutional structures of constitutional democracy.

Many people have contributed to this study, and I sincerely regret not being able to name all of them. While in Guiana, I received only kindness and cooperation from everyone. I wish to thank the Guianese political leaders who acknowledged my presence and who, apart from their political views, displayed a deep respect for the value of social scientific research.

The Department of Local Government and the Government Information Services were of tremendous assistance in providing access to needed information and in preparing the way for field work in the villages. I am grateful for their assistance. Booker Brothers, McConnell & Company, Ltd., and the Demerara Bauxite Company facilitated my work, respectively, at Plantation Skeldon and Mackenzie City. I thank them. I also wish to thank the people of Skeldon, Eversham, Kiltairn, Cromarty, Clonbrook, Ann's Grove, and Mackenzie. They were kind, cooperative, and wonderful to work with. Therefore, to express my gratitude, I have not attempted to disguise their contribution by making their communities anonymous.

I particularly want to thank Mr. Harold B. Davis, a very close friend and fellow alumnus, for all of the assistance he provided during the twelve months I remained a guest in his country. I wish to thank him also for reading the final draft of this manuscript in order to correct any possible substantive errors that may have crept into my work.

If this study enjoys a measure of success, it is in large part due to my good friend and colleague, Professor Erika Bourguignon of The Ohio State University. While in the field, Erika graciously and critically reviewed copies of my field notes in order that the gaps in my data might be located and filled while the opportunity prevailed. I thank her for being so helpful.

This manuscript has benefited greatly from the comments and advice of several colleagues who have read portions of it at different times. I particularly want to thank Professor Alvin Wolfe and Norman Whitten of Washington University (St. Louis) and Professor Richard Schermerhorn of Western Reserve University.

In many ways, this study is indebted to M. G. Smith, a scholar whose work I have always admired but whom I have never had the pleasure of meeting. I wish to express my gratitude to him for providing this book with its foreword.

I want to thank most warmly Professor Sidney Peck of Western Reserve University. Professor Peck undertook the task of carefully reviewing the entire manuscript. If the final work does not measure up to his standards, I only wish I could have made it do so.

Last, but not least, I want to express a full measure of gratitude to my wife, Loretta A. Despres, for the assistance and understanding she has rendered me both in the field and at home. I dedicate this book to her and our children as a token of my appreciation.

L.A.D.

Cleveland, Ohio
Spring, 1967

# CONTENTS

## LIST OF FIGURES



## LIST OF TABLES

*CHAPTER 1*

# GUIANESE NATIONALISM AND THE PLURAL SOCIETY

THIS BOOK PRESENTS A STUDY OF CULTURAL PLURALISM AND NATIONALIST politics in British Guiana as they were in 1960–61. Optimistically, however, its aim is considerably broader. As a case, British Guiana is not unique. It belongs to a class of newly emerging nations that many writers have described as socially and culturally pluralistic. Like most of these nations, it has a colonial history. It also is economically underdeveloped.[1] The same forces of nationalism are at work in British Guiana as in most other underdeveloped societies. Moreover, Guiana's nationalist leaders display the same aspirations and ideological postures that tend to be displayed by nationalist leaders everywhere in the "Third World." In other words, British Guiana is caught up in the winds of change. The problems that exist there are quite similar to the problems that exist in many other emerging nations. Not the least of these is the instability which derives from the need to revamp the institutions vacated by colonial powers in order to achieve national politico-cultural integration.

It is the point of view of this book that the dynamics of nationalist politics in British Guiana, and perhaps in other new nations as well, can be most fully understood in terms of the organizational strategies nationalist leaders employ to make existing sociocultural patterns functional with respect to the changes that are taking place.

---

[1] British Guiana may be compared to other underdeveloped countries in terms of an economic development score computed by Lyle W. Shannon. According to Shannon's computations, British Guiana's level of economic development is similar to that of most of the African nations as well as most of the nations of South and Southeast Asia. It ranks below the majority of South and Central American states. See Lyle W. Shannon, *Underdeveloped Areas* (New York: Harper & Brothers, 1957), pp. 480–82. Also see Carleen O'Loughlin, "The Economy of British Guiana, 1952–56: A National Accounts Study," *Social and Economic Studies,* 8 (1959), 1–104.

If this view has any validity for the case under consideration, then possibly the theoretical framework employed to express it has wider and more significant application.

## BACKGROUND TO GUIANESE NATIONALISM

British Guiana is a small country with a relatively small population. Its total land area is approximately 83,000 square miles. The 600,000 people who inhabit this area are a product of its colonial history. According to census classifications, they are divided as follows: Amerindians or American Indians (4.0 per cent), Europeans (0.9 per cent), Portuguese (1.4 per cent), Chinese (0.6 per cent), "Mixed" or "Colored" (11.3 per cent), Africans (33.5 per cent), and East Indians (48.2 per cent). The Amerindians are the only indigenous people. All other groups were brought to British Guiana as a result of European colonial expansion in the Caribbean. The Africans, of course, were imported as slaves. With the termination of slavery, indentured workers were imported: first the Portuguese, then the Chinese, and finally the East Indians from various parts of India.

Land, resources, and people are facts of considerable importance in any discussion of British Guiana. With respect to land, the country can be divided into three major ecological zones. First, deep in the interior, there is a belt of grassy plateaus used primarily for cattle grazing. The agricultural lands in this area are limited to the foothills of the Kanuku Mountains and are used by Amerindians who continue to practice shifting cultivation. North of the savannas is a broad belt of equatorial rain forest which contains Guiana's timber and mineral resources. The economic potential of this area, except for timber and bauxite resources, is not precisely known. The development of this potential, whatever it may be, will necessitate long-range planning and very high capital investment. The immediate picture, then, is one of an agricultural economy that will gradually diversify its production mainly by the expansion of acreage and the introduction of new crops.

The third ecological zone exists along the Atlantic coast. It contains a narrow strip of rich alluvium which makes up about 4 per cent of the total land area of the country. This coastal ribbon is Guiana's agricultural region. It is also the area in which approximately 90 per cent of the population is located. Physiographically, these lands comprise a lowlying area of five to eight feet below sea level at high tide. A dual problem stems from this condition: that of preventing flooding by seawater and that of disposing the water that flows from the hinterland and accumulates in the coastal belt. The solution to this problem has necessitated an elaborate system of drainage ditches, dams, and sea walls. It has been estimated that each square mile of sugar cane cultivation requires approximately sixty-five miles of drainage canals and ditches.

The ecology of British Guiana is reflected in its present economy. In 1829, more than 80,000 African slaves were used on 404 plantations growing sugar, cotton, and coffee.[2] Emancipation and the cost of water control drove most of these plantations out of business. The remaining plantations have had to consolidate their operations in order to survive.[3] Currently, there are nineteen sugar estates. Fifteen of these are owned by Booker Brothers, McConnell & Company, a London-based firm. In 1958, sugar and sugar products made up 62 per cent of the f.o.b. value of Guiana's exports.[4] Forty-five per cent of the country's revenue from income taxes and excise duties derives from sugar. An officer of Bookers has estimated that sugar, directly or indirectly, supports nearly 80 per cent of the population.[5]

Next to sugar, bauxite mining is the largest source of national wealth. British Guiana is the third largest producer of bauxite ore in the world. In 1959, more than 1.6 million tons were exported, mainly to Canada and the United States. Two companies extract this ore, Aluminium Ltd. of Canada and Reynolds Metals of the United States. In 1958, they produced 21 per cent of the total f.o.b. value of exports. Of the two companies, Aluminium Ltd. of Canada holds the largest investment in Guianese bauxite. In addition to bauxite, diamonds and gold are also actively mined. As a source of national income, however, they have not fulfilled their early promise.[6]

---

[2] Peter Ruhomon, *Centenary History of the East Indians in British Guiana, 1838–1938* ("Guiana Edition" No. 10; Georgetown: *Daily Chronicle,* 1946), p. 9.

[3] Allan Young, *The Approaches To Local Self-Government In British Guiana* (London: Longmans, Green & Company, 1958), pp. 1–24.

[4] Sessional Paper No. 5/1959, Paper of the Second Legislative Council on British Guiana's 1960–64 Development Programme (Georgetown: B. G. Lithographic Company, 1959), p. 3.

[5] J. A. Haynes, "The Economic Importance of the Sugar Industry to British Guiana," in *Bookers Sugar;* Report of Booker Brothers, McConnell & Company, Ltd. (1954), p. 18.

[6] Raymond T. Smith, *British Guiana* (London: Oxford University Press, 1962), pp. 67–70.

Thus, British Guiana displays a typical colonial economy. Two industries produce nearly 83 per cent of the total f.o.b. value of exports. They pay approximately 60 per cent of the total revenue collected in income taxes and excise duties. Both industries are predominantly controlled by two foreign-based firms. Apart from this, the only other major source of income is rice, a crop grown primarily by East Indian peasants on small family farms. More than half of the rice produced is consumed at home, but increasing amounts are being exported to the Caribbean. While the export value of rice is not yet great, rice agriculture provides the second largest source of employment in the country. As far as employment is concerned, the sugar industry ranks first.

While a number of political associations appeared in British Guiana after the First World War, it was not until after the Second World War, when it became increasingly clear that constitutional advancement was forthcoming, that a comprehensive nationalist movement emerged. It presented itself as the Peoples Progressive Party. As a nationalist movement, the P.P.P. was comprehensive in two important respects. First, it was organized by Cheddi Jagan (an American-trained dentist of East Indian descent) and L. F. S. Burnham (a lawyer of African descent) with a view to aggregating the interests of the Indian and African masses. Second, the P.P.P. organized and maintained political cells in villages throughout the country. In terms of this grass-roots approach, the P.P.P. was the first organization with real political party credentials ever to have existed in British Guiana.

In 1953, when constitutional advancement came, the comprehensive character of the P.P.P. proved to be a great source of strength. The new constitution provided for a House of Assembly with twenty-seven seats. Twenty-four of these were open for election on the basis of universal adult suffrage. In the 1953 elections, the P.P.P. and four hastily organized political parties put up a total of fifty-one candidates. In addition, seventy-nine independents also contested seats in the House of Assembly. The P.P.P. won an overwhelming victory, capturing eighteen seats with 51 per cent of the total vote. Four independents won seats on the basis of their personal followings. The National Democratic Party won two seats. All other opposition parties lacked organization and a coherent political following.

As a comprehensive nationalist movement, the strength of the P.P.P. extended beyond its ability to win elections. It practiced the politics of dissent in the relatively static colonial society. Its ideological stance stressed interdependence and national goals rather than particularistic interests. It advocated full and immediate independence. All of these factors served to create a sense of national identity. For the first time in their history, the Guianese had something in terms of which they could perceive themselves as one people. Individual frustrations began to take on a sense of meaning within the framework of a national point of view. Disagreements existed, but for the most part they did not seem important to many Guianese in light of their newly acquired opportunity to develop a new and a free society. The momentum for change which the P.P.P. provided represented its greatest source of strength. Out of this momentum, so it seemed to many Guianese, a new nation was being born.

The birth, however, was aborted. Less than six months after the elections, the constitution was suspended and the P.P.P. government was put out of office. The details of the suspension will be considered in a later chapter. It suffices here to note that the P.P.P. government attempted to initiate too much change in too short a time. In December, 1953, a Temporary Provisions Order was issued by Her Majesty's Government. It provided for a wholly nominated Legislative Council consisting of twenty-seven members, ten of whom were to be nominated to an Executive Council. The governor, appointed by the Colonial Office, nominated the members of the Legislative Council and presided over the Executive Council. He was obliged to consult the latter, but he had the authority to act contrary to its advice.

Also in 1953, the Colonial Office appointed a commission to investigate the events leading to the suspension of the constitution and to make recommendations for constitutional advancement. Following its investigation, the Robertson Commission concluded that the most prominent leaders of the P.P.P., notably Cheddi and Janet Jagan, had "unreservedly accepted the classical communist doctrines of Marx and Lenin and were supporters of most modern communist movements." The Robertson Commission also suggested that L. F. S. Burnham was a socialist, opposed to British rule, but not a Communist. Finally, it was concluded that a new election would serve only to return the same government to office; therefore, a period of marking time in the advance toward self-government was recommended.[7] The interim government which was appointed remained in power

[7] *Report of the British Guiana Constitutional Commission,* Sir James Robertson, Chairman (London: Her Majesty's Stationery Office Report Cmd. 9274, 1954).

until 1957, when the constitution was revised and new elections were scheduled.

During the period of the interim government, the P.P.P. split into two competing political factions. The causes of the split as well as the events leading up to it will be described in another context. At this point, it suffices to note that one faction emerged under the leadership of L. F. S. Burnham and two East Indians, Dr. J. P. Lachmansingh and Jai Narine Singh. The other faction remained under the leadership of Cheddi Jagan with the support of three prominant Africans, Sidney King, Rory Westmaas, and Martin Carter. Both factions continued to claim the P.P.P. label. In 1956, a second split occurred within Jagan's faction of the P.P.P. On this occasion, Rory Westmaas and Martin Carter retired from politics, and Sidney King declared himself as an independent. Subseqeuently, in 1958, Sidney King joined forces with Burnham in opposition to Jagan.

Also during the period of the interim government, a third political party entered the picture. It called itself the United Democratic Party and represented a reorganization of the National Democratic Party (which had contested the 1953 elections) and a coalition of several independents, as well as some of the members of weaker parties which disappeared after the 1953 elections. The U.D.P. contained militant anti-Communist Catholics, equally militant African racists, and a number of Portuguese businessmen. In most respects, the U.D.P. represented an unholy alliance designed to take advantage of the split between Burnham and Jagan.

The 1957 constitution was not much of an advance beyond that of 1953. It provided for a Legislative Council consisting of a speaker, three official members, six nominated members, and fourteen members to be elected on the basis of universal adult suffrage. When the elections were held, both factions of the P.P.P., the U.D.P., two hastily organized parties, and several independents contested the fourteen seats to be elected. The major competition was between the two factions of the P.P.P. Burnham's faction won three seats with 26 per cent of the popular vote. All of them represented Georgetown districts where Burnham had a personal following among African workers. Jagan's faction, on the other hand, won nine seats with 48 per cent of the popular vote. From the 1957 election results, it is clear that the Burnham-Jagan split had not fostered a serious split between African and East Indian voters except perhaps in the urban areas. In spite of the bifurcation of the P.P.P., Jagan had managed to maintain a relatively integrated nationalist movement.

However, not long after the 1957 elections, the entire political situation changed radically. First, Burnham's faction of the P.P.P. lost its two major East Indian supporters: Lachmansingh died, and Jai Narine Singh resigned. Subsequently, his faction reorganized itself as the Peoples National Congress. This was followed by Sidney King's decision to join forces with Burnham. Then, in 1959, the U.D.P. dissolved, and most of its African membership was taken into the P.N.C. Thus, by 1960, two mass parties existed in British Guiana. One of them, the Peoples Progressive Party, was organized under the leadership of Cheddi Jagan, and its membership was predominantly East Indian. The other, the Peoples National Congress, was organized under the leadership of L. F. S. Burnham, and its membership was almost exclusively African.

In 1960, nationalist forces were progressively drawn around sectional groups. This trend received further support when Peter D'Aguiar, a prominent Portuguese businessman, organized a new third party, which called itself the United Force. The announced intentions of the U.F. were to oppose communism, to oppose socialism, to oppose the "racialism" of the P.P.P. and the P.N.C., and to offer the Guianese an economic program that featured the attraction of American and British capital as the basis for economic development. In spite of these intentions, the attempt on the part of the U.F. to mount a comprehensive nationalist movement served only to intensify sectional politics. The core of the party's leadership consisted of businessmen with a long history of colonial ties, and many of these men, particularly those who were Portuguese, had poor records in the field of race relations. Consequently, the U.F. was immediately perceived as a "white man's" party organized to defend the status quo.

This brief but rather complicated description of political party developments during the 1950's is summarized in Figure 1.

The 1961 elections demonstrated the extent to which nationalist political alignments had come to be based on sectional groups. Under the 1961 constitution, the Legislative Assembly was expanded to include thirty-five members. These seats were contested by candidates representing all three major political parties. The P.P.P. won twenty seats—all of them in rural constituencies where East Indians formed large majorities. The U.F. won four seats. Three represented Georgetown constituencies where the Portuguese are concentrated. One represented an Amerindian constituency in the interior where there is a strong Roman Catholic church influence. The P.N.C., on the other

FIGURE 1. POLITICAL PARTY DEVELOPMENTS DURING THE 1950'S

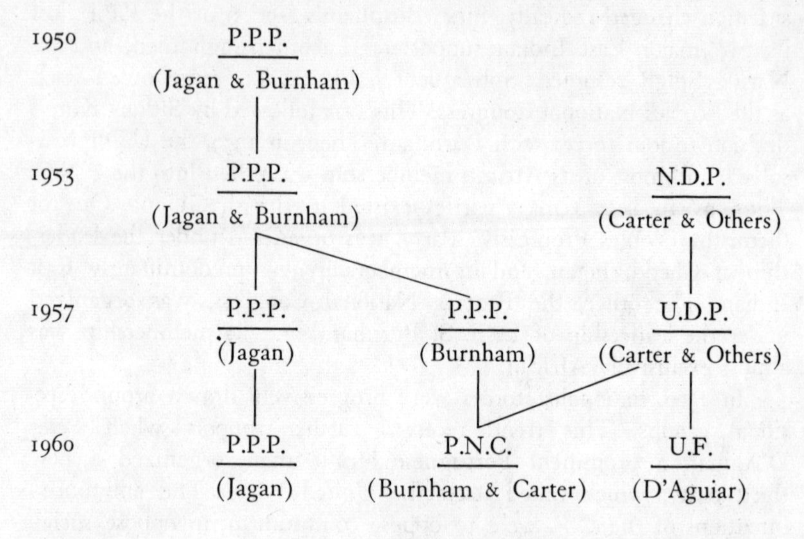


hand, won eleven seats. All of them represented urban areas where Africans or the Colored formed large majorities.

Close races between the P.N.C. and the P.P.P. developed in those areas where the distribution of Africans and Indians was close. The P.P.P. polled 46.7 per cent of the total votes cast for all three political parties. The P.N.C. polled 44.7 per cent. These percentages are almost identical to the ratio of Indians and Africans in the population when the Colored are counted with the Africans. In terms of these data, it would seem that very few voters crossed racial lines in the 1961 elections.

Voting behavior is an index of the competition for power between the major sections of British Guiana's population; it is not an index of conflict. However, less than six months after the elections, conflict broke out. On Monday, February 12, 1962, the U.F. and the P.N.C. encouraged demonstrations to protest the Jagan government's budget and tax proposals. The following day, three unions (the British Guiana Teachers' Association, the Transport Workers' Union, and the Federated Union of Government Employees) called a strike in protest against bettering the government's general budget and tax recommendations together with proposed changes in civil service benefit programs. By the end of the week, all of these forces joined in an effort to overthrow the government by forcing the elected ministers to resign their positions. Demonstrations quickly led to mob violence, and British troops had to be called in to restore order. During the disturbances, hostilities broke out between East Indians and Africans.

In October, 1962, and again in 1963, the Colonial Office convened independence conferences with the leaders of Guiana's three major political parties. On both occasions, the conferences were deadlocked over constitutional and related issues. Subsequently, the Colonial Office decided to impose its own solution. Ignoring Jagan's demands, it recommended that new elections be held before the granting of independence and that the elections be based on the system of proportional representation rather than the system of first-past-the-post. The elections, scheduled for December, 1964, were preceded by a new wave of violence. Once again, hostilities broke out between East Indians and Africans. When Jagan failed to win the elections, and when he was forcibly removed from the Prime Minister's office in order to make way for a P.N.C.-U.F. coalition, the situation continued to deteriorate.

In spite of these developments, the Colonial Office proceeded with its plans for Guiana's independence. Another conference was scheduled for November, 1965. In protest against the 1964 elections, Jagan boycotted the conference. Ignoring Jagan's absence, the Colonial Office selected May 26, 1966, as the date for granting British Guiana (to be named Guyana after independence) the status of an independent nation within the Commonwealth. However, even as this date approached, there was no reconciliation between Guiana's nationalist leaders. On Independence Day, nine members of Jagan's party continued to be forcibly detained because of their role in previous hostilities. Tensions continued to exist between the Afro-Guianese and the East Indian populations. And British troops continued to be stationed in Guyana in order to maintain the peace.

These events serve to delineate the developmental syndrome that has characterized Guiana's nationalist movement. First, in the late forties and early fifties, a comprehensive nationalist movement emerged. It represented a united front expressly organized to achieve national goals. Second, between 1953 and 1957, that front disintegrated almost completely. The sense of national identity that it had so carefully nurtured evaporated. Third, between 1957 and 1961, disparate nationalist movements developed. These have charted a course away from independence and national unity toward sectionalism, conflict, and violent power struggles. The ultimate result has been political instability and economic chaos. In all these respects, British Guiana's nationalist movement has run essentially the same course of development which Coleman and others have described for Afro-Asian countries.[8] Thus, the problems of British Guiana may be seen in a much broader perspective.

## MODERN NATIONALISM

Nationalism is a concept that has a considerable variety of meanings.[9] When the concept was first applied to the politics of western

---

[8] Gabriel A. Almond and James S. Coleman (eds.), *The Politics of The Developing Areas* (Princeton: Princeton University Press, 1960). See particularly pp. 552–57.

In Coleman's description of the developmental syndrome characteristic of the Afro-Asian countries, there is a genuine problem of distinguishing independence movements from nationalism and, at times, both of these from sectionalism. This problem appears to be widespread in the literature dealing with nationalism. Generally speaking, in the struggle for national identity and freedom, cultural nationalism has almost always preceded political nationalism (see Maurice F. Neufeld, *Poor Countries and Authoritarian Rule* [Ithaca, N.Y.: Cornell University Press, 1965], pp. 12–36). Nationalist leaders have usually insisted upon the distinctive character of their own people and the unique development of their particular "national" culture. Often, this sense of identity is extended to include culturally differentiated groups which have shared the experience of colonial oppression. Thus, a nationalist movement has as one of its distinguishing characteristics a professed ideology which makes a chauvinistic appeal to a shared tradition of one type or another. Theoretically, an independence movement may or may not display this trait. An independence movement may constitute a loose alliance of several political groups which do not share a nationalist ideology but which may develop a consensus with respect to the immediate goal of independence. On the other hand, nationalist leaders who do profess a genuine nationalist ideology may cultivate sectionalist sentiments for organizational purposes.

It is difficult at times to maintain these distinctions with respect to the analysis of the Guianese situation. When the P.P.P. first emerged, it was simultaneously an independence and a nationalist movement. Most of its leadership, particularly Jagan and Burnham, expressed a genuine nationalist ideology in terms of which they emphasized the common historical experience of Guiana's "six peoples." However, as we shall see, this did not preclude disagreement with respect to other considerations of an ideological nature. Moreover, after the nationalist movement disintegrated and organizational strategies of a sectional nature were developed, Jagan and Burnham continued to profess a genuine nationalist ideology.

[9] The body of literature dealing with nationalism is much too large to review here. A good theoretical statement on the concept "nationalism" has been made in an essay by John H. Kautsky. See John H. Kautsky (ed.), *Political Change in Underdeveloped Countries* (New York: John Wiley & Sons, 1962), pp. 30–56. Also suggestive is Bert F. Hoselitz's "Nationalism, Economic Development, and Democracy," *The Annals,* Vol. No. 305 (1956), pp. 1–11. A different approach to the problem of nationalism is presented in Karl W. Deutsch's *Nationalism and Social Communication* (Boston: M.I.T. Press, 1953). An interesting case study of nationalism and

Europe, it expressed the doctrine that the state, as a territorial entity, should be nationally homogeneous in the sense of containing a unified population with a common racial and cultural heritage. Since no objective criteria exist by which a people can determine whether or not they constitute a nation, nationalism is essentially a subjective phenomenon. A nation exists, so to speak, when the people of a state express the conviction that they constitute a nation. During the normal course of evolutionary change, this conviction emerges when individuals and groups become politically conscious of their having shared a common tradition and a common way of life for an unspecified period of time. In other words, as nationalism came to exist in Europe, it was not a fabric woven by a political act; rather, it represented a way of life nurtured by the passage of time. Modern nationalism does not display this developmental syndrome.

Modern nationalism cannot be understood apart from colonialism. Broadly defined, colonialism may be thought of as a relationship of inequality between two societies by which one is able to exploit the human and natural resources of the other.[10] European colonialism, however, took a more specific form. By the exercise of force, European countries proclaimed exclusive rights to delineated territories and their inhabitants. The colony represented a unit appended to the political structure of the colonizing nation. Its inhabitants, regardless of their specific origins and cultural traditions, became related to one another in terms of an imposed power structure. The European colonial world existed in this form until it was broken up by the forces of modern nationalism.

The developmental syndrome characteristic of modern nationalism has been described by James Coleman in a rather comprehensive comparative summary on the politics of developing areas.[11] Political parties in these areas begin as narrowly based groups. They are usually organized by members of the small Westernized elite in order to press for increased political representation. Subsequently,

---

racial politics is made by Thomas M. Franck in *Race and Nationalism: The Struggle for Power in Rhodesia-Nyasaland* (New York: Fordham University Press, 1960). The problem of nationalism and cultural minorities is given a very fine treatment in Clifford Geertz's, (ed.), *Old Societies and New States* (New York: Free Press of Glencoe, 1963).

[10] This point has been made by Vera Micheles Dean in *The Nature of the Non-Western World* (New York: New American Library, 1957), pp. 193–211.

[11] James S. Coleman, "Conclusions: The Political Systems of the Developing Areas," in Almond and Coleman, *op. cit.*, pp. 552–57. See Note 8, supra.

these groups become the nuclei of comprehensive nationalist movements which agitate for national independence. The appearance of comprehensive nationalist movements frequently serves as a stimulant to the organization of opposition forces. In the preindependence phase, as Coleman notes, the opposition tends to take one of three forms: (1) that organized with the support of colonial authorities and other conservative elements that seek to preserve the status quo; (2) that resulting from power struggles among nationalist leaders; and (3) that organized to protect minority interests following independence.

A subsequent phase of the developmental syndrome involves the disintegration of comprehensive nationalist movements. This tends to occur either in the terminal colonial period or shortly after independence has been won. Disintegration is usually accompanied by the organization of new political alignments which seek to negotiate themselves into the positions of power vacated, or about to be vacated, by the colonial government.

These new alignments manifest the centrifugal forces that exist as obstacles to politico-cultural integration in many newly emerging nations. In some cases, they represent the aggregation of ethnic, communal, or tribal interests. In other instances, they may reflect the entrance of religious leaders into politics. In India, a variety of postcolonial political groups have developed on the basis of regional or linguistic cleavages.

Regardless of the factors involved, many new nations have experienced a proliferation of particularistic political groups. Their presence in the political arena has provided fertile soil for the growth of internal power struggles. As often as not, these power struggles have been a major source of political instability.

This developmental syndrome underscores the proposition that many of the newly emerging nations are pluralistic societies. As the offspring of colonialism, they were created by a sequence of political acts. Culturally, they are not whole fabrics woven by the passage of time. The indigenous peoples within their boundaries belong to different cultural sections. Each of these cultural sections displays its own relatively distinct pattern of sociocultural integration. The national institutions that serve to integrate these different groups were manufactured by alien powers. The time during which national institutions have existed, in most instances, has been too short for the growth of traditional roots. Consequently, they are without deep meaning in the lives of those who have inherited them. Thus, even as national institutions are inherited from colonial powers, they are in the process of being changed.

These considerations add a dimension to modern nationalism which most observers have been aware of but to which few have given extensive analytic attention. Among other things, modern nationalism is a revolutionary form of sociocultural change. Old societies with old cultures are being fashioned into nation-states at an intractable rate of speed. Alien institutions and power structures are being modified in the process, and new institutions and power structures are being created. Thus, modern nationalism presents two faces to the world. One reflects the integrative forces organized on the basis of that faint sense of unity which derives from a common injustice. The integrative forces of nationalism are expressed as anticolonialism in the drive for independence and self-government. The other face of nationalism displays the divisive forces that emerge in the process of creating new forms of politico-cultural integration. It is the second face of nationalism that reflects the pluralism characteristic of many societies undergoing revolutionary change.

What, precisely, is the relationship between cultural pluralism and nationalist politics? To what extent are the forces of pluralism responsible for the political instability that tends to be associated with modern nationalism? What triggers these forces in the political arena? Presumably, most nationalist leaders have been exposed to and adopted many of the more universalistic values of Western culture. Thus, if the forces of pluralism are responsible for political instability, why is it that nationalist leaders seem incapable of containing them? The formulation of these questions raises certain theoretical issues. The analysis of the Guianese situation may proceed more meaningfully if some of these issues are discussed and a theoretical frame of reference is delineated.

## SOME THEORETICAL ISSUES

The concept "cultural pluralism" was first introduced to the analysis of change in underdeveloped areas by J. S. Furnivall, who employed it in his description of Netherlands India.[12] Observing how

[12] J. S. Furnivall, *Netherlands India: A Study of Plural Economy* (London: Cambridge University Press, 1939), pp. 446–69. Also see Furnivall's *Colonial Policy and Practice: A Comparative Study of Burma and Netherlands India* (London: Cambridge University Press, 1948).

the different cultural groups of that area lived, side by side but without much mingling, Furnivall concluded, "Nationalism within a plural society is itself a disruptive force, tending to shatter and not to consolidate its social order."[13] Subsequent researchers interested in colonial or former colonial areas have seized upon Furnivall's concept for purposes of analysis. Political scientists, particularly, have used it to explain the political convulsions which many new nations have experienced since their independence.[14] Among anthropologists, especially those who have been working with Caribbean societies, the idea of cultural pluralism has stimulated considerable theoretical debate.[15]

---

[13] Furnivall, *Netherlands India,* p. 468.

[14] Practically every contributor to the Almond and Coleman volume, *op. cit.,* uses the idea of cultural pluralism to explain political instability in underdeveloped areas. In his study of nationalism and revolution in Indonesia, George McTurnan Kahin states that the plural nature of colonial society in Indonesia constituted a major limitation in the growth of Indonesian nationalism. See Kahin's *Nationalism and Revolution in Indonesia* (Ithaca, N.Y.: Cornell University Press, 1952), p. 59. Innumerable examples can be extracted from the social science literature illustrating the use of the concept to explain a wide variety of problems in underdeveloped areas. In very few instances, however, has the concept been specifically defined and systematically employed as a theoretical model.

[15] These discussions appear in two summary volumes edited by Vera Rubin. The first, *Caribbean Studies: A Symposium,* appeared in 1957 and has been reprinted by the University of Washington Press (Seattle, 1960). The second, *Social and Cultural Pluralism in the Caribbean,* appears as a publication of the New York Academy of Sciences (Vol. 83, 1960). In the first of these two volumes, almost every paper and accompanying critical comment concerned itself with the unresolved issues of ethnohistorical research and interpretations of social structure and change in complex "pluralistic" societies. Most of the papers and critical comments included in the second volume deal more explicitly with the theoretical issues of pluralism. Other materials relevant to any theoretical discussion of pluralism would include: John Rex's "The Plural Society in Sociological Theory," *British Journal of Sociology,* 10 (1959), 114–24; Stephen Morris' "Indians in East Africa: A Study in a Plural Society," *British Journal of Sociology,* 7 (1956), 194–211; M. Nash's "The Multiple Society in Economic Development," *American Anthropologist,* 59 (1957), 825–33; D. J. Crowley's "Plural and Differential Acculturation in Trinidad," *American Anthropologist,* 59 (1957), 817–24; Maurice Freedman's "The Growth of A Plural Society in Malaya," *Pacific Affairs,* 33 (1960), 158–68; M. Freilich's "Serial Polygyny, Negro Peasants, and Model Analysis," *American Anthropologist,* 63 (1961), 955–75; Raymond T. Smith's "Review of Social and Cultural Pluralism in the Caribbean," *American Anthropologist,* 63 (1961), 155–57; B. Benedict's "Stratification in Plural Societies," *American Anthropologist,* 64 (1962), 1235–46; Lloyd A. Fallers' "Ideology and Culture in Uganda Nationalism," *American Anthropologist,* 63 (1961), 677–86; Benjamin N. Colby and Pierre van den Berghe's "Ethnic Relations in Southeastern Mexico," *American Anthropologist,* 63 (1961), 772–92; and Helen Codere's "Power in Ruanda," *Anthropologica,* 4 (1962), 45–85.

A fundamental issue of theoretical debate is whether or not the plural model, when compared to the structural-functional model of the unitary society, offers any particular research advantage for examining the problems of unity and diversity or the problems of politico-cultural change. This issue has been dealt with elsewhere.[16] However, for the purposes of clarity, a brief discussion of it is necessary in the present context.

Recently, M. G. Smith revised Furnivall's conception of pluralism and suggested that a rigorous analysis of certain types of societies is difficult, if not impossible, without making use of the plural model.[17] In developing his model, Smith takes the Malinowskian position that social institutions are the concrete isolates of organized behavior. Each institution comprises a mutually supportive set of values, rules, activities, and social relations. Institutions having to do with the same phases of life (e.g., marriage, family, extended kinship, etc.) form clusters or subsystems. These subsystems, in turn, combine to form the total institutional system. Because institutions function to define and sanction the persistent forms of social behavior, the institutions of a people's culture make up the matrix of their social structure. It follows from this that the core of a culture is its institutional system. In other words, according to Smith, institutional differences serve to differentiate differing cultures and social units.

However, not all institutional differences are of equal importance for the purpose of differentiating cultures and social units. Some institutions are more basic to a given way of life than others. For this reason, Smith, following the earlier theoretical works of Linton and Nadel, distinguishes between "compulsory," "alternative," and "exclusive" institutions.[18]

---

[16] Leo A. Despres, "The Implications of Nationalist Politics in British Guiana for the Development of Cultural Theory," *American Anthropologist,* 66 (1964), 1051–77. Also see M. G. Smith's *The Plural Society in the British West Indies* (Los Angeles: University of California Press, 1965). The analytical model which I suggest for the study of plural societies differs somewhat from Smith's conception. However, my own thinking on the concept of pluralism has been greatly influenced by his work. For a critique of Despres' paper, see H. I. McKenzie, "The Plural Society Debate, Some Comments on a Recent Contribution." *Social and Economic Studies,* Vol. 15, (1966) pp. 53–60.

[17] M. G. Smith, "Social and Cultural Pluralism," *Annals of the New York Academy of Sciences,* 83 (1960), 763–77.

[18] See Ralph Linton's *The Study of Man* (New York: Appleton-Century-Crofts, 1936), pp. 272–74. Also see S. F. Nadel's *Foundations of Social Anthropology* (Glencoe, Ill.: Free Press, 1951), p. 121.

Alternative institutions are those shared by certain individuals as a matter of choice (e.g., social class membership or community membership, etc.). Exclusive institutions are shared by individuals who belong to certain socially recognized categories (e.g., an occupational group). The basic or compulsory institutions, however, are those in which all members of a social unit must participate. Basic institutions comprise an integrated pattern embracing kinship, recreation, education, religion, property, economy, and certain types of sodalities.[19] A population that shares a basic institutional system, according to Smith, tends to form a relatively closed sociocultural unit. It is socially and culturally homogeneous.

Building upon these conceptualizations, M. G. Smith formulates his plural model. In doing so, he distinguishes three types of societies: (1) homogeneous societies, (2) heterogeneous societies, and (3) plural societies. The first of these types occurs when all the groups of a political unit share the same total institutional system. The best examples of this type are found among the preliterate societies studied by anthropologists. The heterogeneous society occurs when groups within a political unit practice and share the same system of basic institutions but, at the same time, participate in different systems of alternative and exclusive institutions. Most modern industrial societies, like the United States, display this heterogeneous character.

In contrast to the first two types, the plural society occurs when groups living within a political unit practice very different systems of compulsory or basic institutions. Under these conditions, the cultural plurality of the society corresponds to its social plurality. The culturally distinct units of the plural society are its "cultural sections." Generally, these cultural sections are highly exclusive in the sense that each displays an area of common life beyond which relationships are specific, segmental, and governed by economic and political structures. The best examples of this type of society are found among the newly emerging nations.

Thus, M. G. Smith's plural model combines conditions of cultural and social pluralism simultaneously, and both are defined in terms of the basic institutional system. However, some anthropologists have taken exception to the theory of cultural pluralism. For example, Raymond T. Smith has suggested that the concept "cultural pluralism" has little value other than summarizing in two words some very complex problems.[20] There are several aspects of the theory

[19] M. G. Smith, "Social and Cultural Pluralism," p. 769.

[20] Raymond T. Smith, "Review of Social and Cultural Pluralism in the Caribbean."

which its critics find particularly disturbing. One involves the view that cultural homogeneity is a condition of societal homogeneity. This view, Vera Rubin suggests, is utopian.[21] When it is recognized that nearly all national societies display significant regional, rural-urban, ethnic, and social class differences, from an historical point of view the homogeneous society appears to be the exception rather than the rule.[22]

Another disturbing feature of the theory of cultural pluralism, according to its critics, involves the concept "institution." If institutions are reified in a Malinowskian fashion and not defined in terms of activities analyzed in structural-functional terms, they are reduced to clusters of cultural traits about which only differences and similarities may be noted. It follows from this that society, as a social system, is defined in terms of culture. Such an approach, Braithwaite notes, is fundamentally at variance with that which stresses the viewpoint of social action.[23] As a consequence, the theory of pluralism would have little heuristic value for the analysis of social behavior.

What the critics of the plural model seem to reject most is M. G. Smith's view that, at the societal level, there is no necessary functional integration of institutional systems or cultural sections. In their view, the plural model seems to overlook the fact that there must be a minimum core of shared values if the integration of a society is to be maintained. Otherwise, they contend, the political structure of the society must be seen as essentially one of force. If this is the case, they argue, there is further difficulty with the plural model because its application would seem to be limited to the analysis of colonial societies. Furthermore, even in the case of colonial societies, it is suggested that the model emphasizes the differences between groups at the expense of ignoring those factors which serve to integrate different groups into the total system. Therefore, according to the critics, the proponents of the plural model would have us develop one type of theory for colonial societies and another type for societies that are not colonial. The effect of this would be prohibitive to the advancement of general social theory.

Thus, an alternative approach to the study of newly emerging nations may be gleaned from the writings of those who have been

[21] Vera Rubin, "Discussion of M. G. Smith's Social and Cultural Pluralism," *Annals of the New York Academy of Sciences,* 83 (1960), 780–85.

[22] L. Braithwaite, "Social Stratification and Cultural Pluralism," *Annals of the New York Academy of Sciences,* 83 (1960), 816–31.

[23] *Ibid.,* p. 823.

the most outspoken critics of the cultural pluralism theory. Many of them derive their theoretical posture from the tradition of Emile Durkheim, Max Weber, Radcliffe-Brown, and Talcott Parsons.[24] They adhere to the principle that societies are consensual normative systems. Culture, as a variable, is relevant only to the extent that it represents a system of "shared symbolic meanings which makes communication possible in an ordered social life."[25] The differentiation of cultural sections is considered to be a structural problem that may be dealt with in terms of stratification theory. Social class divisions not only distribute the members of different cultural groups with reference to social statuses, different degrees of political power, and different social functions, but they also serve to integrate different cultural groups within the overall social structure of the society. In other words, in terms of this unitary theory of society, cultural groups are structurally integrated in the total system, and to consider them as separate sections is misleading.[26]

Briefly, these are theoretical frameworks that have been used recently in a variety of studies dealing with newly emerging nations. The models provided by both frameworks employ the "systems" approach. They differ essentially in that one considers cultural groups as separately integrated sections, while the other treats them as reticulated subunits of the total system. The reticulated model minimizes the theoretical significance of historically rooted subcultures in favor of the point of view that the total system has so modified these subcultures that they no longer retain an independent identity. The plural model, on the other hand, allows for the persistence and residuality of relatively independent cultural traditions and suggests that these traditions are functionally viable not only in terms of the relationships between groups but also with reference to the overall structure of the social system.[27] This difference is illustrated more concretely by Figure 2.

---

[24] See M. G. Smith's *The Plural Society in the British West Indies,* pp. vii–xiii.

[25] Raymond T. Smith, *The Negro Family in British Guiana* (London: Routledge and Kegan Paul, Ltd., 1956), p. 253.

[26] E. P. Skinner, "Group Dynamics and Social Stratification in British Guiana," *Annals of the New York Academy of Sciences,* 83 (1960), 911.

[27] The difference which I note here is not unrelated to the disagreements between theorists who are inclined toward structural-functional analysis and those who favor ethno-historical interpretations. For a discussion of this issue, see Vera Rubin (ed.), *Caribbean Studies: A Symposium.*

FIGURE 2. COMPARISON BETWEEN THE PLURAL AND RETICULATED MODELS

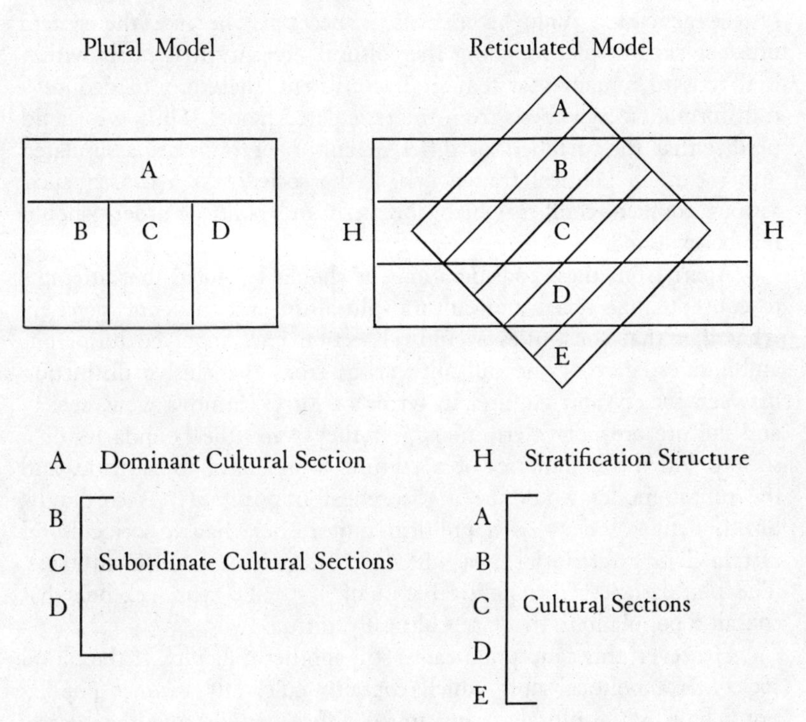


The analytical differences between these two models are extremely important to social scientists interested in the sociocultural changes resulting from the transformation of colonial societies into nation-states. Plural societies, as defined above, depend for their maintenance on the regulation of intersectional relations by one or another of the component cultural sections. When the dominant section constitutes a minority group, as is usually the case, political order is secured primarily by force or the threat of force. Changes in this structural arrangement presuppose rather extensive political changes. Thus, from the plural model we would predict that political changes of this order usually will take a violent form.

By way of contrast, the reticulated model presupposes that the individuals who belong to different cultural groups are so completely enmeshed in an overall stratification system that similar cultural groups cannot comprise separately integrated cultural sections. Political order, it seems, would emerge from the value consensus which the system generates. Value consensus is necessary because the system must be capable of containing the cultural diversity that exists within it if it is to remain a system. It is consistent, therefore, to deduce a transformation hypothesis from the reticulated model. Thus, we would predict that the members of different cultural groups are assimilated into the main political framework of the society. As a consequence, serious conflict—conflict which threatens the political order—should not be expected.

Apart from these considerations, it should be noted that attempts to conceptualize social and cultural pluralism and to define precisely what it is that constitutes a cultural section have involved numerous ambiguities. Part of the difficulty arises from the elusive distinction between society and culture. In terms of M. G. Smith's view, society and culture are not coterminous.[28] If they were, the boundaries of a society and the boundaries of a culture would have to coincide, and the plural model would be a theoretical impossibility. Accordingly, Smith defines society as a political unit rather than a sociocultural system. It is a territorial area with its own governmental institutions. The plural society is a political unit of a specific type, i.e., one that contains populations that are culturally distinct.

However, this conception raises still another difficulty. If the plural society is a political unit which contains culturally distinct populations, how is the plural society to be differentiated from the heterogeneous society? The analytical distinction between "compulsory," "alternative," and "exclusive" institutions does not provide a very systematic solution to this problem. If a culture is understood to be an integrated pattern of standardized social usages, then which of these usages can be considered basic or compulsory? Might not all of them be considered basic to the cultural pattern? Or, assuming we could isolate the "compulsory" institutional system for analytical purposes, at which point do variations become great enough to warrant the identification of separate cultural sections?

These theoretical issues cannot be easily ignored if the theory of cultural pluralism is to have any scientific utility for the analysis of politico-cultural change in newly emerging nations. However, with some modification of M. G. Smith's views, most of these issues can be dispensed with in such a way as to make possible the construction of a systematic model of the plural society.

---

[28] "Social and Cultural Pluralism," p. 768.

## THE PLURAL SOCIETY: AN ANALYTICAL MODEL

Most anthropologists have taken the position that cultural facts consist of ideas, values, symbols, and meanings existing through time (i.e., they are historically derived). As such, culture has no clearcut boundaries. By definition, however, a unit (e.g., *a culture*) must be bounded. It follows that culture can be delineated as a unit only when it is bounded by structural dimensions existing in time. Following Malinowski, social institutions are the structures through which cultural ideas and values are expressed as traditional norms regulating the affairs of individuals and groups. Thus, the author considers sound M. G. Smith's position that institutional differences serve to distinguish differing cultures and social units. How else can such distinctions be made? However, insofar as this is the case, all institutions must be considered equally functional in the expression of culture. Therefore, as far as the expression of culture is concerned, the analytical distinction between basic, alternative, and exclusive institutions is spurious and serves no theoretical purpose.

Society, in contrast to culture, is a structural unit of the most encompassing type. A society has many levels of institutional structuring, and some are more interdependent than others. For example, social activities may be institutionalized locally, regionally, or nationally. Some activities may involve horizontal structures such as castes, classes, occupational groups, professional groups, and the like. Culture is expressed through all of these different kinds of institutional structures, and the activities structured at one level need not be integrated with those structured at another level in the sense that they are interdependent.

The most inclusive structures of a society are those that have to do with its political or governmental institutions. Regardless of whether or not lower-level structures (e.g., kinship) articulate with higher-level structures (e.g., market structures), governmental institutions have as their function the integration of the social system (either through force, or value consensus, or combinations of both). Thus, the author agrees also with M. G. Smith's position that society and culture are not coterminous. However, this should not be interpreted to mean that society and culture can be entirely independent of one another (even force has to be recognized to be effective). There can be no societal structure (including the governmental) which does not mobilize some definite expression of cultural values. What, then, is the plural society, and how is it to be conceptualized?

In keeping with the systems approach, it is suggested that the definition of the plural society must take into account two related sets of facts: (1) the extent to which specified groups are culturally differentiated in terms of specific institutional activities and (2) the level at which institutional activities serve to maintain cultural differentiation as the basis for sociocultural integration. When institutional activities serve to maintain cultural differentiation between groups primarily at local levels, these groups may be identified as *minimal* or local cultural sections, for want of a better term. On the other hand, when institutional activities serve to integrate similar cultural groups and differentiate them from other cultural groups at the national level, such groups constitute *maximal* or national cultural sections.

Short of a society being homogeneous (e.g., a preliterate or tribal society), the existence of minimal cultural sections expresses the least amount of cultural variation that can exist. A society containing local or minimal cultural sections is socially and culturally heterogeneous. However, short of a society being bifurcated into two separate and independent politico-cultural systems, the existence of maximal or national cultural sections is the greatest amount of cultural variation that can be maintained within a unitary system of political activity. A plural society is one that contains maximal or national cultural sections.

The distinction between maximal and minimal cultural sections (and between the plural and heterogeneous society) may be illustrated by comparing, for example, the United States and Nigeria. The United States is a heterogeneous society. It contains within it many cultural groups that are integrated at local levels (e.g., the Irish, the Polish, the French Canadians, etc.). We usually think of these as ethnic groups. There are practically no institutional structures (e.g., labor unions, political parties, religious associations, etc.) that serve to integrate each of these groups separately at the national level of sociocultural integration. In Nigeria, on the other hand, the Ibo, the Yoruba, and the Hausa are not only culturally differentiated and locally integrated, but institutional structures exist (e.g., political parties) which serve to maintain their cultural differentiation at the national level. Compared to the United States, Nigeria is a plural society.

In these terms, the heterogeneous society and the plural society are two ideal types based on a continuum of sociocultural integration. This particular conceptualization permits the construction of analytical models which specify the criteria to be used to determine empirically the degree to which an historical society corresponds to the plural model. In order to construct such models, it is not necessary to assume that some institutions are more "basic" than others. It is useful, however, to distinguish between two broad classes of institutions: (1) those which serve to structure activities and express cultural values within the context of local communities, and (2) those which function to link local activities to the wider spheres of societal activity. The first of these types may be conveniently identified as *local institutions*. The second type may be called *broker institutions* in order to emphasize their functional character.[29]

The kinds of activities falling into each of these analytical categories may be expected to vary empirically from one society to another. Generally, however, the following kinds of activities tend to be structured in terms of local institutional patterns: language (dialects), family and kinship, religion, work, socialization (and possibly education), recreational activities, associational activities, and communal activities (e.g., local governmental). All of these kinds of activities may serve to generate institutional structures through which cultural differences may be expressed between groups in the hamlet, the village, or the neighborhood.

The question remains, By what criteria are we to judge institutional differences in order to determine the degree to which local or minimal cultural sections are apparent and viable? Three empirical questions serve to direct our attention to the data in terms of which the integration of minimal cultural sections can be ascertained. With respect to each sphere of institutional activity we may ask, Is the structure of the institutional activity valid only for particular groups? Is it valid for all groups but modified by some? Or, is the structure of the institutional activity uniformly valid for all groups?

To the extent that the structure of institutional activities is valid only for particular groups, the structures involved express different cultural values, and the groups under investigation constitute minimal cultural sections. On the other hand, if the structure of institutional activities is uniformly valid for all groups, then the groups under

---

[29] The distinction between "local" and "broker" institutions was suggested to me by a review of Julian Steward's conception of levels of sociocultural integration. Steward notes, for example, that national culture is divisible into two general kinds of features: (1) those that function at the national level and (2) those that pertain to sociocultural segments or subgroups of the population. Broker institutions, it would seem to me, function to integrate these two levels in various ways. In this sense, they are distinguishable from local institutions. See Julian Steward, *Theory of Culture Change* (Urbana: University of Illinois Press, 1955), pp. 43–63.

investigation share a common culture. Should this be the case, the minimum requirement for the theoretical relevance of the plural model has not been met, and the model will have no heuristic value for the analysis of the society in question. The first-order transformation of the plural model is illustrated by Table 1.

The separate integration of similar minimal cultural sections at the societal level of sociocultural integration is a function of broker institutional structures. Again, the type and variety of these structures will vary empirically from one society to another. However, examples

TABLE 1. CULTURAL PLURALISM: FIRST-ORDER TRANSFORMATION

| | *Invariant Points of Reference* | | |
|---|---|---|---|
| *Local Institutional Activities* | *Structure Valid for Particular Groups* | *Structure Valid for All Groups but Modified by Some* | *Structure Uniformly Valid for All Groups* |
| Language (Dialects) | X | | X |
| Family and Kinship | X | | X |
| Local Economy (Work) | X | | X |
| Religious Activities | X | | X |
| Socialization and Education | X | | X |
| Recreational Activities | X | | X |
| Associational Activities | X | | X |
| Communal Activities | X | | X |
| | Plural Model Relevant | | Plural Model Not Relevant |

of broker institutions may include markets (labor and consumption), corporations, cooperatives, religious associations, public or private school associations, social and civic associations, labor unions, ethnic associations, political parties, and various governmental agencies. This list, of course, is not exhaustive, but it will serve the purpose of illustrating the second-order transformation of the plural model.

With respect to each of these broker institutions, we may ask, Does the structure of the institutional activity reinforce the separate integration of similar local or minimal cultural sections at the national level of sociocultural integration? Or, does the structure of the institutional activity serve to mediate relationships between different cultural groups and thereby modify the expression of their different cultural values? Or, does the structure of the institutional activity serve to integrate different cultural groups by generating the expression of new cultural values? For example, in Nigeria, do Ibo, Hausa, and Yoruba belong to different labor unions? Or, do labor unions tend to cut across these local cultural sections? Or, do labor unions completely integrate individuals from these different local cultural sections?

Maximal or national cultural sections will exist when broker institutions serve to integrate, separately, similar minimal cultural sections and thereby allow for the expression of their characteristic cultural values in national spheres of social activity. When these conditions exist, the plural model accurately delineates the sociocultural patterns characteristic of the society under investigation. This second-order transformation is illustrated by Table 2.

The plural model, as defined above, has certain analytical advantages over the other two models considered earlier. For one thing, it does not require utopian assumptions about the functional integration of institutional systems. Also, it does not reify institutions by defining them exclusively in cultural terms. Institutions are treated as social structures in terms of which individuals and groups organize activities and express cultural values.

Another advantage of this particular conceptualization is that it does not dichotomize the plural society and the unified social system. The plural society is a social system with specified empirical characteristics; as such, it is no less a system than any other type of society. However, as a system, the plural society is not unitary in the sense that all of its component elements are functionally interrelated by virtue of value consensus. The cultural sections of the plural society

TABLE 2. CULTURAL PLURALISM: SECOND-ORDER TRANSFORMATION

| | *Invariant Points of Reference* | | |
|---|---|---|---|
| *Broker Institutional Activities* | *Structure Integrates Similar Local Cultural Sections* | *Structure Mediates Between Different Local Cultural Sections* | *Structure Integrates Different Local Cultural Sections* |
| Markets | X | | X |
| Corporations | X | | X |
| Labor Unions | X | | X |
| Governmental Agencies | X | | X |
| Political Parties | X | | X |
| School Associations | X | | X |
| Religious Associations | X | | X |
| Social and Civic Associations | X | | X |
| Ethnic Associations | X | | X |
| | Society Is Culturally Pluralistic | | Society Is Culturally Heterogeneous |

are subject to a common body politic. They may or may not participate in a common economy. While the relationships between individuals of different cultural sections may be segmental and instrumental, their integration into the society as an overall system is ultimately a function of governmental structures and the relative absence of conflict.

The question of conflict highlights a most important consideration: The plural model, as defined here, provides the framework for a structural and cultural analysis. It takes into account the expression of cultural differences through functioning structures, but it does not make the assumption that these differences are the sufficient and necessary conditions of conflict and instability. In other words, the plural model, by itself, is not adequate for an assessment of sociocultural change or for predictive purposes. Since this point is critical to subsequent chapters, it needs further elaboration.

## THE ORGANIZATIONAL DIMENSION

In light of the available evidence, there can be little doubt that cultural pluralism provides fertile soil for the growth of particularistic forces. It is also evident that such forces can become serious obstacles to the achievement of politico-cultural integration in new nations where colonial powers have been removed from governmental structures. However, the relative degree of integration present in the plural society is not something that can be assumed or defined apart from empirical considerations. Nor can it be assumed that maximal cultural sections, because of their different values, are incompatible and conflict-producing in terms of the transactions that occur between their respective members.

It is a fact that political change has not been violent in many societies described as pluralistic. Several newly emerging nations have achieved various degrees of political stability and national integration without serious disruptions in the prevailing social order. Moreover, the ways in which the obstacles of pluralism have been handled differ, sometimes quite markedly, from one new nation to another.

For example, several African states have dealt with the problems of pluralism in terms of comprehensive nationalist parties. This solution has been offered as justification for the one-party state by Sékou Touré of Guinea and Julius Nyerere of Tanzania.[30] Nigeria, until recently, has approached the problem differently. In Nigeria cultural sections have been maintained and given considerable autonomy within the federation. In some cases (e.g., the Malagasy Republic and

[30] For a discussion of Sékou Touré's political ideas, see L. Gray Cowan, "Guinea," in Gwendolen M. Carter (ed.), *African One-Party States* (Ithaca, N.Y.: Cornell University Press, 1962), pp. 149–236. Also see J. Nyerere, "Will Democracy Work in Africa?" in Peter R. Gould (ed.), *Africa: Continent of Change* (Belmont, Calif.: Wadsworth Publishing Company, 1961), pp. 52–55.

Sierra Leone), a relatively competitive party system has served, in part, as a vehicle for the expression of cultural differences. In Malaya, prior to independence, communal parties representing Malayan, Chinese, and Indian interests formed the Alliance. Cooperation between cultural sections is evident in Uganda. In India, centrifugal forces have been partially contained within the framework of a modified one-party system which allows for the existence of regional and minority parties.

These examples serve to illustrate the point that the plural model, when it leads to assumptions of conflict and instability, has relatively low predictive value. The reason for this limitation is that the model does not provide within its framework criteria which may be used to evaluate the probable conditions under which conflict or alternative modes of action will transpire as a result of the relationships existing between members of different cultural sections. The structural focus of the model fails to take into account what Raymond Firth has referred to as the dimension of organizational activity.[31]

In the organizational dimension, individuals are more than units related to one another by virtue of the social structures in terms of which they interact and through which they express cultural values. They may be this, but they are also conscious agents capable of calculated action with respect to themselves as well as the social universe in which they operate. To state the matter differently, cultural sections are not in themselves politically functional. They may become politically functional only when individuals and groups make them so. Therefore, in order to understand the role of cultural sections in nationalist politics, we must look at the organizational activities of

---

[31] Social organization is usually taken as a synonym for social structure. Raymond Firth has made a good case for distinguishing between them. Social structure pertains to the persisting and more ideal patterns manifested in social relations. Social organization, on the other hand, involves people getting things done. I like to think of social structure as being in the sphere of culture (e.g., institutionalized norms) and social organization as involving the sphere of social activity. The distinction, I would agree with Firth, is necessary for an analysis of change. See Raymond Firth, *Elements of Social Organization* (New York: Philosophical Library, 1951), pp. 22–40. Another source by Firth on the same subject is "Social Organization and Social Change," *Journal of the Royal Anthropological Institute of Great Britain and Ireland,* 84 (1954), 1–21. For a theoretical discussion of this distinction, see John W. Bennett and Leo A. Despres, "Kinship and Instrumental Activities: A Theoretical Inquiry," *American Anthropologist,* 62 (1960), 254–67. David F. Pocock has commented on Bennett and Despres' use of the distinction between social structure and social organization. See David F. Pocock, "Notes on Jajmani Relationships," *Contributions to Indian Sociology,* 6 (1962), 92–95.

specific individuals and groups. We must particularly look at the organizational activities of national leaders and their political parties.

In this age of planned change, national leaders often hold advanced degrees. Frequently, they have ideological commitments. Working with experts at their sides, they weigh facts, devise programs on the basis of five- and ten-year projections, calculate strategy, and elect what appears to them to be the most efficient means available to achieve their objectives. In some cases, the strategies they devise involve making cultural sections politically functional in specific ways. Whether or not this leads to conflict and instability depends upon the nature of the strategies planned and the manner of their implementation. Thus, cultural sections do not clash by chance or because their structures express incompatible values: They clash because certain individuals and groups have decided that something can be achieved by way of making them clash.

In other words, British Guiana, as well as other newly emerging nations, can be thought of as a field of social power. Within this field, social power is structured by the patterns of sociocultural integration characteristic of different groups. These patterns, in themselves, are not productive of conflict, but they are capable of being manipulated to form different types of social alignment between groups. Some of these types of social alignment are conflict-producing. The creation of social alignment for political purposes (as well as for other purposes) requires organizational strategy and organizational effort. National leaders are in a position to provide both of these elements. Whether or not the alignments they forge will lead to stability and national integration will depend, in large part, on the kinds of decisions they make. These decisions are rational in the sense that they usually derive from an evaluation of existing conditions in light of the goals they hope to achieve.

Enough by way of theoretical considerations. Having defined the problem and the frame of reference to be employed in dealing with it, it is now possible to turn to an examination of the historical foundations of cultural pluralism in British Guiana.

*CHAPTER 2*

# CULTURAL PLURALISM IN HISTORICAL PERSPECTIVE

COLONIALISM STILL EXISTS IN BRITISH GUIANA. AS A CONSEQUENCE, THE historical forces which produced Guiana and the events which shaped its character are much too immediate for them not to be dynamic in the present. The people who make up the Guianese population are the descendants of the different cultural groups that were thrown together as a result of European colonial expansion in the West Indies. Some of these people have retained much of their traditional cultural identity; others have not. What has been retained and what has been lost, and by whom, is largely a function of the kinds of colonial institutions that have existed during the past two hundred years or more. In addition, the relationships that exist today between various groups in Guiana are also related to this accumulated experience. There are, in other words, elements of diachronic determinism inherent in the present structure of Guianese society, and these need to be identified in order to comprehend the contemporary situation fully.[1]

[1] A comprehensive history of British Guiana remains to be compiled from the scattered and fragmentary materials available. This chapter relies heavily on a few standard works. These include Sir Cecil Clementi's *A Constitutional History of British Guiana* (London: Macmillan and Company, 1937); N. E. Cameron's *The Evolution of the Negro* (2 vols.; Georgetown: Argosy Company, 1934); Sir William Des Voeux's *Experiences of a Demerara Magistrate, 1865–1870* (reprinted as No. 11 in the *Daily Chronicle's* "Guiana Edition Series"; Georgetown, 1948); Dwarka Nath's *A History of Indians in British Guiana* (London: Thomas Nelson and Sons, 1950); Thomas Rain's *The Life and Labours of John Wray, Pioneer Missionary in British Guiana* (London: John Snow and Company, 1892); N. Deerr's *The History of Sugar* (2 vols.; London: Chapman and Hall, 1949); J. Rodway's *Guiana: British, Dutch and French* (London: T. Fisher Unwin, 1912); Peter Ruhomon's *Centenary History of the East Indians in British Guiana, 1838–1938* ("Guiana Edition" No. 10; Georgetown: *Daily Chronicle*, 1946); A. R. F. Webber's *Centenary History and Handbook of British Guiana* (Georgetown: Argosy Company, 1931); Allan Young's *The Approaches to Local Self-Government in British Guiana* (London: Longmans, Green & Company, 1958); R. Farley's "The Unification of British Guiana," *Social and Economic Studies*, 4 (1955): 168–83.

## EARLY SETTLEMENT

Any discussion of European colonialism in British Guiana must begin with the famous voyages of Sir Walter Raleigh. In 1595, when he charted the coast of Guiana in search of El Dorado and the mythical city of Manoa, the New World was but a Spanish claim. Apart from Spain, only Portugal had a settlement in the Americas, and Portugal, at that time, was one of the dominions of the King of Spain. The trade monopoly which Spain held in the Americas largely financed the power she enjoyed in Europe. Spanish power, perhaps more than anything else, motivated England, France, and Holland to undertake colonial adventures in the New World. It was Raleigh's extravagant claims of great wealth in the "land of waters," however, that directed their attention to the Guianas. Thus, the early history of this region is primarily a story of competition between English, French, and Dutch trading companies to establish colonies that would permit them to control the West Indian trade. As of 1665, all three nations claimed the entire territory between the Amazon and Orinoco rivers.

In spite of these territorial claims, the trading companies operating in the Guianas during the seventeeth century were unable to do more than occupy a few places with small settlements. In most instances, they were not even able to insure the survival of these settlements. This was particularly true of the English and French companies which had made repeated efforts to plant colonies in the territories now known as Surinam and French Guiana. This was not so true, however, of the Dutch West India Company (incorporated in 1621). The efforts of the Dutch West India Company were concentrated in the three territories (Essequibo, Demerara, and Berbice) that presently make up the colony of British Guiana. As a consequence, British Guiana owes much to Dutch colonialism, and some of the institutions developed there by the Dutch in the seventeenth and eighteenth centuries continued to survive for more than a hundred years after the British took full possession of these territories in 1803.

Unlike the English and French trading companies, which were small and privately organized, the Dutch West India Company was a progeny of the five "Chambers" representing the governments of Amsterdam, Zeeland, Rotterdam, the North Department (Friesland and Hoorn), and Groningen. As such, it was empowered to monopolize Dutch trade with the Americas and with the African coast between the Tropic of Cancer and the Cape of Good Hope. It was also authorized to plant colonies, to maintain armies and fleets, to build forts, to carry on war, to make treaties subject to the approval of the States-General of the Netherlands, and to secure sufficient Negro labor to develop the company's possessions. It was further authorized to legislate in its possessions subject to the laws of the Netherlands. The States-General undertook to secure the trading rights of the company, to support it by subvention, and to contribute vessels for the defense of its possessions. In return, the company provided the States-General with a share of its profits.[2]

So organized, the Dutch West India Company undertook the settlement of Essequibo in 1623. Four years later, the Zeeland Chamber of the company granted permission to Abraham van Pere to plant a colony in Berbice and to run it as a "patroon." During most of the seventeenth century, the settlers associated with these efforts were mainly occupied with the Amerindian trade. They exchanged trade goods for cotton, dyes, and wood. A few plantations were maintained but chiefly for the purpose of providing the traders with provisions. Toward the end of the century, however, the Amerindian trade was gradually supplanted by plantation agriculture and sugar cane cultivation. The first plantations were developed along the banks of the Essequibo and Berbice rivers. As these lands were taken up, new plantations were developed on the richer soils along the coast. In 1745, the Commandeur of the Dutch West India Company, Laurens Storm van's Gravesande, persuaded the company to open the Demerara region for settlement.

The administration of Essequibo, Demerara, and Berbice remained in Dutch hands until Holland joined Russia, Sweden, and Denmark in the "Armed Neutrality" pact against England during the American War of Independence. As a result of the pact, England declared war on Holland, and British ships moved against the Dutch colonies in the West Indies. In 1781, the three colonies were forced to surrender to British privateers. Less than a year later, the French, who were allied with Holland, recaptured the colonies and, in 1784, they were returned to Dutch rule. The resumption of Dutch control, however, was short-lived. When the French Revolution broke out in Europe, France invaded Holland and created the Batavian Republic. This ultimately resulted in the total ruin of Dutch commerce in the West Indies and the seizure, in 1796, of the Dutch colonies by Great

[2] Clementi, *op. cit.*, pp. 8–12.

Britain. Under the Treaty of Amiens, in 1802, the colonies were restored to the Batavian Republic. In the following year, when the peace in Europe was broken by the declaration of war between France and England, the three colonies were seized once again by Great Britain, and there was no further retrocession.

## COLONIAL POLICY AND PRACTICE

The transition from Dutch to British colonialism did not involve abrupt or far-reaching changes in the structure of Guianese society. By 1803, the plantation economy, based on the institution of chattel slavery, was firmly established. The plantations represented the functional units of colonial society as it existed around 1800. Each plantation was a structural replica of every other plantation. On the plantation, the owner, or his manager, lived in the "big house." A symbol of force and power, the "big house" was usually located within a fenced-in area called the compound. The houses nearby were occupied by overseers, bookkeepers, and other managerial staff. More distant from the "big house," but also within the compound, were located the quarters given to whites of lower status, the skilled artisans. Eventually, these were replaced by the free Colored, who were mainly the offspring of slave women and white men. The field slaves and the slaves appointed to supervise them, called "drivers," occupied huts and shacks constructed outside the compound.

As units of production, each plantation was more or less autonomous. As functional units of colonial society, however, each plantation was integrated into an overall social system. Law and government represented the basic structures of integration, and these also were laid down during Dutch rule. By virtue of the Articles of Capitulation, under which the British took possession of the three colonies in 1803, the basic elements of Dutch governmental and legal institutions were preserved. The articles provided, among other things, that

> The Laws and Usages of the Colony shall remain in force and be respected, the mode of taxation now in use be adhered to, and the inhabitants shall enjoy the public exercise of their Religion in the same manner as before Capitulation; no new establishments shall be introduced without the consent of the Court of Policy, as the Legislature of the Colony. . . .[3]

[3] *Ibid.*, pp. 411–23.

This agreement formed the basis of constitutional government and law in British Guiana until 1928, when the British Parliament provided the country with a new constitution.

Under the Articles of Capitulation, the Roman-Dutch law, rather than the English common law, became the law of the land. The significance of this fact derives from the differences between the two codes, particularly in matters pertaining to the ownership of land. The Roman-Dutch code has been less influenced by the feudal system than the English common law.[4] Thus, it deals with allodial rather than feudal tenure. Allod, as contrasted with feud, refers to land held in absolute independence without being subject to rent, service, or the acknowledgement of a superior. Under the Dutch, settlers were given large tracts of land for the purpose of developing plantations. The ownership of these lands became absolute. Even after they were abandoned, they could not be made available for settlement without the introduction of special confiscatory legislation. As a consequence, much of Guiana's best agricultural land was not accessible to peasants because it was held by absentee owners or by plantations that were not beneficially occupying it.

There are other differences between the two codes which have been important to the structure of Guianese society. Under the Roman-Dutch law, the transfer of ownership is notarial. The registration of a conveyance or deed is taken practically as complete evidence of ownership. This dispenses with the investigation of title that is required under the English common law. Because a deed need not be searched to establish the claim of ownership, groups of individuals may purchase land in the name of one or two individuals without partitioning the land with respect to the "shares" owned by specific individuals. Another difference between the two codes pertains to inheritance. The Roman-Dutch code provides that the descendants of a proprietor who dies intestate shall inherit "equal but undivided" shares of the deceased person's property. The Roman-Dutch code also provides for the acquisition of land by "prescription." A title can be secured on the basis of undisturbed possession for a specified period of time. Still another important difference pertains to leases. Under the Roman-Dutch code, all leases are considered movable property, and, unless

[4] See L. A. Freeman, "Land Tenure in British Guiana," in *Caribbean Land Tenure Symposium* (Trinidad: Caribbean Research Council, 1946), pp. 357–66. Also see the *Report of the Land Tenure and Registration of Titles Committee, 1954–1955* (Georgetown).

they are registered, they are not noted as encumbrances on the title of the lessor. Thus, a lessee whose contract is not registered has no legal claim on the land of the lessor: Regardless of how much the lessee has invested in the property, he has no security of tenure.

The Roman-Dutch code, until it was modified by legislation in the 1950's, was especially congenial to the plantocracy.[5] It protected the right of absolute ownership. It permitted groups of individuals to own undivided shares of land. These two conditions, when combined with the tenets of rational economic organization, facilitated the accumulation of large landholdings for productive or for speculative purposes. Moreover, the Roman-Dutch code made it possible for ruthless landlords to exploit tenants who, for lack of legal knowledge, failed to register leases or failed to demand registered contracts in return for rent. With respect to peasants, depending upon the special character of their institutional patterns, the Roman-Dutch code created problems of land fragmentation which, in part, account for the differential modes of economic adaptation characteristic of different cultural sections. The specific consequences of the Roman-Dutch code for particular cultural sections will be dealt with in a later context.

It would not be an exaggeration to suggest that the Articles of Capitulation affected almost every tissue of the body politic in British Guiana. They were particularly significant with respect to the structure of government. The articles, in effect, provided the plantocracy with a constitutional charter. As Clementi has shown, between 1803 and 1928 British Guiana had neither a Crown colony government (under which sovereign power resides in the Crown acting through the Principal Secretary of State for the Colonies) nor a representative government (under which the voting franchise is available to and exercised by the majority of the adult population of the country).[6] As far as legislative matters were concerned, sovereign power was vested in the Crown. At the same time, by retaining the mode of taxation existing previous to 1803, fiscal power was withheld from the Crown and vested in the Combined Court.

The Combined Court was a peculiar governmental institution that had evolved out of the circumstances of Dutch rule in British Guiana. In the seventeenth century, the administration of Essequibo was conducted by a council called the Raad van Politie en Justitie

[5] Ordinance No. 31 (Security of Tenure) of 1956 and Ordinance 18 (Land Registry Ordinance) of 1959.

[6] Clementi, *op. cit.*, pp. 326–70.

(Court of Policy and Justice). When first created, this body included only members appointed to it by the Dutch West India Company. Eventually, private planters were given representation. In 1743, a College of Kiezers (Electors) was created to elect the representatives of the private planters to the Court of Policy and Justice. Subsequently, Demerara was provided with similar governmental institutions. In 1789, the Courts of Policy for the two colonies were combined, and the representatives from each colony were elected by their respective Colleges of Kiezers. Although the number of elective or "unofficial" members varied from time to time, they never constituted a majority. Ultimate executive and legislative power remained in the hands of the Dutch West India Company and, after its demise, in the hands of the States-General of Holland.

During the confusion created by the British occupation in 1796, the Court of Policy directed that six financial representatives (three from Demerara and three from Essequibo) be elected and adjoined to the governor and the Court of Policy with the right of voting "on all matters relative to the raising of taxes and examination of accounts." The Court of Policy in session with the financial representatives was called the Combined Court. While the official members of the Court of Policy constituted a majority over the elected members, the opposite was the case in the Combined Court. As a consequence, the official majority in the Court of Policy controlled the executive and legislative powers in the colony, while the unofficial majority of the Combined Court controlled the power to raise taxes and examine the public accounts. When the British accepted this arrangement under the Articles of Capitulation, in effect they withheld fiscal power from the Crown.

Thus, the Combined Court controlled the purse in British Guiana. It determined the salaries of public officials, judges, and civil servants. It decided whether or not money would be raised to maintain roads, construct sea defenses, and extend drainage systems. It determined how much money would be available for public health, welfare, and education. Fiscal powers of this type usually generate other powers. Because it controlled the purse, the Combined Court also controlled the power to influence, shape, or obstruct both the legislative and administrative policies of the Crown acting through the governor and the Court of Policy. The question is, Who controlled the Combined Court?

When Combined Court was first established, the financial representatives, like the unofficial members of the Court of Policy, were elected by the College of Kiezers. The kiezers, in turn, were elected directly by the colonists. The franchise, however, was restricted to those who owned twenty-five slaves or more and who paid taxes on an annual income of no less than £715. Since only the planters could meet these qualifications, indirectly they controlled the election of financial representatives in the Combined Court as well as the unofficial members of the Court of Policy. As a result of the unification of British Guiana in 1831, the structure of these governmental institutions changed. The role of the kiezers was reduced to that of nominating unofficial members to the Court of Policy only when vacancies occurred. Otherwise, the unofficial members of the Court of Policy, as well as the financial representatives in the Combined Court, were elected directly by the colonists. With the abolition of slavery, the franchise was extended to include every adult male who paid taxes on an annual income of £143. In 1849, the franchise was further extended. However, these changes did not alter the position of planters with respect to government. In order to qualify for election to the Court of Policy, a man had to own eighty acres of land, half of which had to be under cultivation. The same property qualification was required of financial representatives, except that an annual income of $1,440 (B.W.I.) was accepted in lieu of the ownership of land. As a result, the voters had little choice but to vote for planters or for their representatives.

By virtue of the fiscal power vested in the Combined Court, the plantocracy occupied an interventionist position from which it controlled, almost completely, the economic structure of the colony. Representatives of the sugar oligarchy occupied positions of influence and power on such statutory boards as Drainage, the Central Board of Health, Transport and Harbours, the Civil Service Board, Public Works, Lands and Mines, and the Department of Agriculture. Thus, the decisions made at different levels of economic policy were linked to the interests of the sugar industry. For example, public works projects involving roads, railways, drainage schemes, sea defenses, and water conservancies were designed and developed primarily to benefit the plantations rather than meet the needs of the villagers. The Department of Agriculture devoted most of its attention to experimental programs designed to develop new and better varieties of sugar cane. The development of new industries, on the other hand, was controlled in relation to the economic wellbeing of the sugar industry. In 1894–

95, for example, the newly developing gold industry was required to pay direct taxes on the total value of its production in a ratio of 20 to 1 as compared with the sugar industry.[7] This money went into the colony's general revenue and was used to support the normal functions of government. At the same time, almost all of the taxes paid by the sugar industry before 1918 were diverted from the general revenue and used by the government to subsidize the immigration of indentured workers in order to provide the sugar industry with an ample supply of cheap manpower.

It should not be understood that the plantocracy ran the affairs of the colony during the nineteenth century without any form of opposition. Frequently, the interests of the planters came into direct conflict with the interests of the Crown. On such occasions, the Combined Court usually responded by refusing to vote the funds necessary for the support of the civil list or the funds necessary for governmental supplies. This occurred in 1840, when the home government disallowed the use of British Guiana's general revenues for the immigration of indentured workers. Supplies were stopped for nearly two years as a result of a dispute over the Sugar Duties Act of 1846. In 1887, the medical inspector for the colony was struck off the civil list completely when his report criticized the sanitary conditions existing on the sugar estates. At the same time, the Court of Policy was thrown into a deadlock when the elected members refused to attend sessions until the governor publicly withdrew the report of the medical inspector.[8]

As a result of the incident which occurred in 1887, the governor, Sir Henry T. Irving, undertook negotiations for constitutional changes. In a despatch, Governor Irving noted:

> A constitution, in which one interest only is represented, and in which that interest can, when it may deem proper to do so, bring about a deadlock in public affairs from which there is no constitutional mode of escape, is politically indefensible. . . . This is what has occurred now, has occurred in the past, and will recur with growing frequency in the future as other interests than those of the sugar planter increase in importance.[9]

---

[7] W. Alleyne Ireland, "Sugar and Gold," reprinted in *Demerariana, Essays: Historical, Critical, and Descriptive* (Georgetown: Baldwin and Company, 1897), p. 37.

[8] Clementi, *op. cit.*, pp. 109–27, 181.

[9] As quoted in *ibid.*, p. 299.

In the above statement, Governor Irving implicitly recognized the fact that a new elite was in the process of emerging in British Guiana. It consisted of the Colored and Negro professionals—the lawyers, doctors, teachers, and newspaper editors. It also included the Portuguese businessmen and shopkeepers who, along with many Negro workers, were beginning to turn their attention to the resources of Guiana's vast interior. Increasingly, the interests of these groups were not those of the sugar planters. At the same time, although these groups could exercise the franchise, their interests were not being represented in the affairs of government.

Constitutional reforms were finally brought about in 1891. The changes, however, were relatively minor. The College of Kiezers was abolished. An Executive Council was created, and all executive and administrative functions were removed from the Court of Policy. The Court of Policy became a purely legislative body more subject to the control of the governor. Property qualifications for election to the Court of Policy were modified to the extent of including an alternative to the ownership of eighty acres of land, namely, the possession of immovable property in the Colony to the value of $7,500 (B.W.I.). Also, the income qualification for the franchise was lowered to $480 (B.W.I.). Otherwise, the Court of Policy and the Combined Court remained intact. The Combined Court retained its fiscal powers, and, as a consequence, colonial policy and practice remained unchanged. The planters retained effective control of the affairs of the colony.

Although the constitutional reforms of 1891 did not alter the power structure in any significant way, the extension of the franchise in that year, and again in 1909, marked a definite turning point in Guianese political life. In 1850–51, the electorate consisted of only 916 persons, and almost all of these were Europeans. By 1915, this number had increased to 4,312. Table 3 presents the composition of the electorate in 1915 by racial groups.[10]

As Table 3 shows, in 1915 the people of African descent represented 62.7 per cent of the total electorate, while only 42.3 per cent of the total adult male population was African. The East Indians represented an anomaly. They comprised 51.8 per cent of the total adult male population but only 6.4 per cent of the total electorate. Under the constitution that existed at that time, the vote meant very little. How-

[10] *Ibid.*, p. 367.

TABLE 3. COMPOSITION OF ELECTORATE IN 1915

| *Race* | *Percentage of Each Race in Adult Male Population* | *Percentage of Each Race in Total Electorate (N = 4,312)* | *Percentage of Adult Males of Each Race Registered as Voters* |
|---|---|---|---|
| East Indian | 51.8 | 6.4 | 0.6 |
| African | 42.3 | 62.7 | 6.8 |
| Portuguese | 2.9 | 11.4 | 17.7 |
| British | 1.7 | 17.0 | 46.1 |
| Chinese | 0.9 | 2.4 | 12.3 |

ever, the composition of the electorate is indicative of the relative positions which various cultural sections had come to occupy within the European-dominated power structure.

Except for the extension of the franchise in 1909, no major changes were made in the constitution between 1891 and 1928. These thirty-seven years, however, are important years in Guianese history. They mark a period of economic change which ultimately generated a rather significant shift in colonial policy and practice. During this period, except for the years of the First World War when market conditions were unusually good, the sugar industry suffered a series of depressions from which it has never been able to recover the economic position it once occupied. This reversal, in part, was related to the increased competition in the world sugar market; but other factors were involved also. In 1917, indentured immigration from India was terminated, and the sugar industry's major supply of cheap labor was shut off completely. The shortage of labor which ensued was aggravated further by developments in rice agriculture. Between 1903 and 1918, the number of acres under rice cultivation increased from 17,500 to 60,432.[11] Almost all of this land was farmed by East Indians who preferred the way of life of independent peasants to that of sugar workers. Also in 1917, the Demerara Bauxite Company opened its first mining operations at Mackenzie City. The emergence of the

[11] Nath, *op. cit.*, p. 234.

bauxite industry served to reinforce the conviction of many Guianese that the vast interior contained the economic future of the country.

These economic changes served to create new business and commercial groups. The special interests of these new groups received very little attention from a government that was primarily concerned with the sugar industry. The dissatisfaction which this engendered extended to the Colonial Office in 1927, when it was noted that, as a result of seven annual budgetary deficits, British Guiana had accumulated a debt of £4.3 millions. The gravity of the situation forced the Secretary of State for the Colonies to appoint a parliamentary commission to investigate the economic condition of the colony and to recommend what measures could be taken to promote its economic development. The commission reported, among other things, that the constitution of British Guiana separated responsibility from power, that it placed the elected members in a position of opposition to the government, and that social, political, and economic development was impossible as long as the government lacked the power to enforce its own financial policy.[12]

In 1928, British Guiana was given a new constitution under which it became a Crown colony. The Court of Policy and the Combined Court were abolished. These were replaced by a Legislative Council comprised of the governor, colonial secretary, attorney-general, eight nominated officials, five nominated unofficial members, and fourteen elected members. The official members constituted a majority over the elected members. Moreover, the governor was provided with the power to veto legislation enacted by the Legislative Council in the event that he deemed such action best for the colony. An Executive Council was also provided. Two of its members were nominated by the governor from the elected members of the Legislative Council. Otherwise, the Executive Council was wholly nominated. Finally, the new constitution did not change the property qualifications for voters, but it did extend the franchise to include women.

To conclude this brief outline of colonial policy and practice, it may be emphasized that many changes occurred under British rule between 1803 and 1928. Slavery was abolished, and the free villages were founded. The institutions of local government were developed. The indenture system was organized, and with it new populations

[12] Clementi, *op. cit.*, pp. 392–93.

from different parts of the world became a part of Guianese society. A variety of social services in the field of health were initiated. Primary school education was made compulsory, and two public secondary schools were provided. From time to time, the constitution was modified and the franchise was extended. However, none of these changes altered the basic structure of colonial society in any significant way. Under the British, the plantation economy was expanded and made considerably more efficient than it had been under the Dutch. The planters were elevated to a position of power from which they shaped colonial policy to suit their own interests. As a consequence, the changes that were made during this period contributed very little to the integration of a national society. This may be seen more concretely if we briefly consider the effects which colonial policy had on the various groups that comprised the population of the country.

## AMERINDIANS

As far as the Amerindian cultures of this region are concerned, the contemporary political boundaries of British Guiana are without much significance. On the basis of archeological and early historical data, the Guianas constitute a cultural area bounded by the Amazon, Rio Negro, and Orinoco rivers. Julian Steward has suggested that this geographic area may be a center of dispersal for what anthropologists have labeled the "Tropical Forest Complex."[13] Although the prehistory of this complex is not well known, its characteristics are fairly well defined.[14] Typically, it combines hunting, fishing, and food gathering with the cultivation of manioc, pineapples, sweet potatoes, arrowgrass, cotton, tobacco, pepper, avacado, and some maize. In recent times a number of additional plants (e.g., the banana, plantain, eddoe, sugar cane, and a variety of citrus fruits) have been introduced by Europeans. Among several of the Amerindian groups, cultivation is still carried on by the slash-and-burn method. Because of this, except where reservation types of settlements have been established, Amerindian groups tend to be seminomadic.

---

[13] Julian H. Steward, "Culture Areas of the Tropical Forests," in Julian H. Steward (ed.), *Handbook of South American Indians,* 3 (1948), 886–88.

[14] John Gillen, "Tribes of the Guianas," in Julian H. Steward (ed.), *Handbook of South American Indians,* 3 (1948), 799–860.

At the present time, there is very little by way of cultural material that serves to differentiate one Amerindian group from another. In British Guiana, tribal identities have little functional significance. During early historic times, however, the Guianas did not constitute such a culturally homogeneous area. At least ten aboriginal linguistic families are known to have existed. Two of these, the Tupian and Muran, appear to have intruded into the region in post-Columbian times. In addition to linguistic differences, there is some basis for differentiating between the tribes located in the Amazon River area, those inhabiting the inland mountain-savanna regions, and those concentrated in the coastal belt. The coastal area was populated mainly by Arawakan- and Cariban-speaking peoples intermixed with some Warrau groups. The latter apparently migrated from the Orinoco Delta eastward to British Guiana and Surinam as a result of early European attempts to pacify them. The Cariban-speaking peoples, according to early accounts, were the most warlike of the tribes. However, the Acawai (one of the Cariban groups) were known everywhere as traders, and in early colonial times they assisted the Dutch in their trade with other groups. Later, the Acawai became the principal slave hunters of the interior. During the nineteenth century, they were concentrated in the Cuyuni River district of Essequibo.

For the most part, relationships between the Amerindians and the Europeans who subsequently settled in the territories of British Guiana were quite amicable. There were a few early attempts to enslave Amerindians, particularly in Berbice, but these served only to create hostilities which the Europeans could not sustain. In Essequibo, as early as 1686, a proclamation was issued which prohibited the enslavement of Amerindians without official sanction. Once the African slave trade got under way, the Dutch and English colonists made every effort to create and maintain good relations. In 1793, laws were passed which prohibited all persons from "purchasing or selling Indians, of any state or quality whatever, or from using such Indians as slaves, under penalty of the severest prosecution of the law." Rodway reports that the early planters hired Amerindians to hunt, to clear land, and to act as guides.[15] They were also employed, quite systematically, to track down runaway African slaves and, as a consequence, there has never been a development of Bush Negro

[15] Rodway, *op. cit.*, p. 224.

villages in British Guiana like those described by Herskovits for Surinam.[16]

The Amerindian policy initiated by the Dutch and subsequently adopted by the British was one of protection by segregation. During most of the eighteenth and nineteenth centuries, the Amerindians were left to themselves in the interior. In 1902, however, a reservation system was introduced. The reservation policy was further extended in 1910 by the Aboriginal Indians Protection Ordinance.[17] Among other things, this ordinance made the Commissioner of Lands and Mines the Amerindian Protector. It also prohibited unauthorized persons from entering the reservations. It provided for the protection and management of Amerindian property, and it specified the conditions regulating the employment of Amerindians and female "half-castes." These laws regulated Amerindian affairs until 1951, when a new ordinance was passed. The Amerindian Ordinance of 1951 abolished all previous legislation and adopted a long-range policy of acculturation and Westernization. It also provided for the absorption of Indian reservations into the structure of local government by the appointment of district and village councils empowered to levy taxes for local improvements in Amerindian villages.

Because of the lack of data, it is difficult to evaluate the impact of European influence on the Amerindian cultures of British Guiana. Missionary activity has been strong on the reservations in recent years, and, as a result, perhaps as much as half of the Amerindian population is now literate in English. However, the policy of protection by segregation has definitely retarded their integration into the national life of the country. The vast majority of Amerindians continue to reside in the interior, where they practice subsistence agriculture. In the Rupununi District, located on the Brazilian border, some Amerindians are employed by cattle ranchers. In the Mazaruni River District, a few Amerindians prospect for gold and diamonds. A few are employed also by the Department of Lands and Mines to guide geological surveys. Some work in the balata industry. Nevertheless, the way of life characteristic of most Amerindians hardly impinges upon that of the coastal populations. Presently, there is an Amerindian seated in the Legislative Assembly from the Northwest District in

[16] Melville J. and F. S. Herskovits, *Rebel Destiny* (New York: McGraw Hill Book Company, 1934).

[17] Young, *op. cit.*, pp. 144–49.

Essequibo. Apart from this, the Amerindians are not critical in any discussion of pluralism and nationalist politics.

## AFRO-GUIANESE

So much has been written on the subject of chattel slavery in the New World that little needs to be said about it here.[18] In Guiana, as elsewhere, slavery entailed the almost complete destruction of African institutions and customs. Of necessity, the slaves adopted the language of their masters. Their communal patterns were destroyed and replaced by the authority structure of the plantation and its managerial system. African religious beliefs and practices were suppressed, and, at the same time, most planters resisted missionary efforts to convert slaves to Christianity because of the close identification between missionary activity and the emancipation movement.[19] Similarly, kinship and family patterns were destroyed. In Guiana, the privileges of Christian marriage were denied the slaves until 1825, and the separation of slave families was not prohibited until 1831.[20] As a result of these and subsequent conditions, practically no vestiges of African culture remain in British Guiana today.

The termination of slavery in 1833 changed the entire structure of Guianese society. The most immediate effect of emancipation was economic ruin for dozens of Guianese planters. In 1829, there were approximately 100,000 slaves in the colony. More than half of these lived and worked on 230 sugar plantations and 174 coffee and cotton estates. In 1829, they produced 66,722 hogsheads of sugar, 6,778,350 pounds of coffee, and 7,272 bales of cotton for export.[21] Between 1839 and 1842, this level of production declined by three-fifths.[22] By 1849,

[18] Primary sources dealing with slavery in British Guiana are widely scattered and difficult to come by. There is very little information available on the subject in secondary sources, but what there is suggests that the situation in British Guiana was not much different from that which existed in the West Indies as a whole. A classical work dealing with slavery in the West Indies is L. J. Ragatz's *The Fall of the Planter Class in the British Caribbean 1763–1833* (London: Oxford University Press, 1928). Another important source is Eric Williams' *Capitalism and Slavery* (Chapel Hill: University of North Carolina Press, 1944).

[19] Rev. E. A. Wallbridge, *The Demerara Martyr* (Georgetown: *Daily Chronicle*, 1943). Also see Rain, *op. cit.*

[20] Clementi, *op. cit.*, p. 101.

[21] Ruhomon, *op. cit.*, p. 11.

[22] Williams, *op. cit.*, pp. 150–53.

the number of sugar plantations had been reduced to 180, and only 16 of the 174 coffee and cotton estates remained. In 1845, cotton disappeared completely from Guiana's list of exports. The sugar industry, of course, survived, but it took more than thirty years to reach the level of production it had achieved prior to emancipation.

The most direct cause of these economic changes was the emergence of a free Negro peasantry. It had been feared by some that the freed slaves would retire into the bush and develop villages with traditional patterns of African culture. This did not happen. The acculturation of the slaves had progressed much too far during the period of their bondage for them to have reconstituted their traditional ways of living. Instead, they sought land of their own in the coastal region where they also could grow crops for the market. The gravitation of former slaves away from the plantations was so rapid that the planters attempted to stop the flow of labor by adjusting the price of Crown lands beyond the reach of most. However, they could not control the sale of private lands and abandoned estates. The acquisition of these by the Negroes was made possible by the rapidly declining value of plantations as well as by the savings which the slaves had accumulated during the five-year period of apprenticeship which preceded emancipation in 1838.

Depending upon the method which the freed slaves used to purchase land, two types of villages were established. Allan Young has called these "proprietary" and "communal" villages.[23] The proprietary villages were settled by individuals who had accumulated sufficient capital to make separate purchases. Thus, each proprietor held a title to the land he had purchased. However, when individuals did not have sufficient capital to buy land, they pooled their resources with other individuals and took advantage of the provisions under the Roman-Dutch code whereby groups could own undivided lands. Thus, land titles in the communal villages were vested by way of a single deed in the names of representatives of a group of purchasers. Individual members of the group were listed on the deed as owning a specified number of shares of undivided land. In most cases, the proprietary villages developed on lands put up for sale by plantation owners in order to maintain a labor force near at hand. The communal villages, on the other hand, were usually abandoned plantations put up for sale by absentee owners. Under the conditions

---

[23] Young, *op. cit.*, pp. 10–13.

existing following emancipation, the communal village came to be the dominant form of African rural settlement.

The period between 1838 and 1848 marks the ascent of the Afro-Guianese peasantry. Before 1838, there were only two villages on the entire coast of Guiana. By 1848, there were more than a hundred. During these years, the village movement received added momentum from two prolonged strikes in the sugar industry and from the introduction of more than 23,000 indentured workers who were willing to labor for wages lower than those demanded by the freed slaves. By 1848, only 19,939 Africans remained on the sugar estates, while more than 44,000 had established themselves in villages. Of these, approximately 7,000 owned land in proprietary villages. The remainder, except for those who lived in thirteen settlements that had been established on Crown lands, were shareholders in communal villages. The total value of property acquired by the freed slaves during this ten-year period has been estimated in excess of $2 million (B.W.I.).[24] The village movement did not end in 1848, but the conditions which provided its momentum changed, and its decline became incipient.

As a cultural form, the African peasantry lacked adaptability. There are many reasons for this. For one thing, most of the plantations purchased by the villagers were in very bad repair. The buildings had deteriorated; the roads had been neglected; many of the dams had to be built anew; and much of the farmland had to be cleared of bush before it could be cultivated. These works required capital, and most of the new proprietors had used all of their savings to purchase land. Additional capital, moreover, was hard to come by. As slaves during the apprenticeship period, the Africans were fed, clothed, housed, and paid. As proprietors, they had to provide themselves with these necessities. At the same time, the wages available to those who were willing to work on the plantations were no higher than those paid during the apprenticeship period. Thus, the average villager found his resources exhausted by the purchase of land, and there was little or nothing left for development or operating costs.

Added to this was the problem of land fragmentation. Under the Dutch, when the ecological pattern for plantations was first established, each settler was granted a rectangular tract of land containing 250 acres. Typically, the estate was laid out with a facade of 412 yards

[24] *Ibid.*, p. 23.

and extended inland from the sea for a distance of approximately 3,089 yards. When this area was empoldered by the construction of sea defenses, sideline drainage trenches, and a back-dam, the owner could claim an additional 250 acres located at the rear of the "first-depth." Thus, the plantations purchased by the villagers normally consisted of tracts 412 yards in width and nearly four miles in depth. When "shares" were allocated, the new proprietors took care to provide that each shareholder occupy proportionate amounts of land containing good and bad soils. This was accomplished in one of two ways. In Demerara and Essequibo, the estates were divided into sections according to the types of soils available, and, in turn, these sections were further divided into cultivation plots according to the number of shareholders. In Berbice, the entire estates were divided into parallel strips according to the number of shareholders. Both methods resulted in fragmentation. Either the shareholder occupied plots in widely separated sections of the estate, or he occupied a strip of land twenty to forty feet in width and four miles in depth. This situation was made worse by the fact that many individuals owned half or quarter shares.

The difficulties engendered by the physical fragmentation of land were augmented further by the social fragmentation of ownership rights which resulted from the application of the Roman-Dutch law. In the case of intestacy, all the descendants of a proprietor inherited "equal but undivided shares" of the proprietor's property. Children inherited land rights from one or both parents. Sons inherited as well as daughters. Illegitimate children inherited property rights through their mothers. The property thus inherited came to be known as "children's property." It constituted an estate in which all of the "children" could participate. Since the making of wills was not a common practice among the freed slaves, it was not long before entire villages consisted of children's property. Practically anyone born in the village could claim the right to a houselot or a cultivation plot. Similarly, almost anyone could pick coconuts and other fruits from the trees on family land.

The fragmentation of ownership rights not only served to reduce the investment value of land but complicated the problem of land management. This was particularly the case with respect to the maintenance of drainage and irrigation systems. If one proprietor, for want of capital or motivation, allowed his dams and ditches to deteriorate, it affected the production of all the others. Under these ecological circumstances, cooperative effort was an absolute necessity. However, the former slaves had no tradition of social organization suitable to meet this need. The traditional patterns of African kinship that might have been functional under these conditions no longer existed. They were replaced by a bilateral kinship structure that was partly extended through the practice of serial polygyny and common-law unions.[25] The kindred associated with the inheritance of children's property did not constitute a corporate economic unit. Nuclear families and matrifocal households comprised the two major types of economic unit. Neither of these provided the organization of human resources necessary to maintain kokers or floodgates, dams, and drainage trenches.

At the same time, there was no tradition of village organization or local government to solve the problems of land management. Under slavery, small groups of individuals recognized "older heads" as leaders on the basis of their personal status. This principle of headmanship appears to have been functional in the communal villages when they were first owned by a few shareholders who had come together in a cooperative fashion to buy and work land. However, the population in most of the new villages grew rapidly beyond the bounds of this type of leadership. In New Orange Nassau, to cite one example, the number of shareholders increased from 128 to nearly 2,000 during a ten-year period.[26] Most of this increment seems to have occurred as a result of many of the original proprietors selling portions of their shares to outsiders migrating from the plantations. Others died, and their shares were inherited by descendants. Some of these, in turn, sold portions of their inheritance. Subsequently, land relationships became extremely complicated, and, apart from the central government, there was no agency to resolve disputes and fix rights and responsibilities.

The ultimate consequences of these problems have been extensively described by historians.[27] Individuals would not or could not assume cooperative responsibility for roads and sea defenses. Dams were not repaired. Drainage ditches were not cleared of new growth, and much of the farmland became useless for cultivation purposes. Without capital, without cooperation and free labor, and under the burden

[25] Raymond T. Smith, *The Negro Family in British Guiana* (London: Routledge and Kegan Paul, Ltd., 1956).

[26] Young, *op. cit.*, p. 45.

[27] *Ibid.*, pp. 24–88.

of complex land relationships, the whole system broke down. Increasingly, the villagers were forced to turn to a subsistence type of economy. Ground provisions were grown for home consumption, and, where possible, the produce from coconut and fruit trees was picked and sold in the local markets for a small cash income.

In numerous ways, the villages became a problem of major proportions to the central government. The roads that passed through them were necessary to the plantation economy. The sea defenses were equally important. Similarly, the diseases resulting from poor sanitary conditions and lack of water control could not be confined to the villages but affected the public health of the whole colony. Beginning with a series of ordinances in the 1850's, the central government became increasingly involved in village affairs. At different times, a Central Board of Villages, the Public Works Department, and the Central Board of Health represented the controlling authority for local government. In 1907, the Department of Local Government and the Local Government Board appeared. Under these, the entire country was divided into village councils (elected locally), country districts, and rural sanitary districts. In all three types of local authority, ultimate control of village affairs was vested in the Local Government Board and its field representatives.[28]

As a result of the introduction of local government, many of the communal villages were partitioned for tax purposes. These were given an elected council which, in turn, appointed an overseer who was made responsible for the maintenance of streets, dams, and internal drainage. The villages that were not partitioned (and there were many) became country districts. Except for some improvements in sanitary conditions, these villages remained essentially as they were when they were founded. They had no village councils unless the shareholders or older heads organized one voluntarily. They had no overseer unless one was temporarily appointed to supervise a project. They paid no taxes. They were not made responsible for the public road. Their streets (if they had any) and their internal drainage systems (where they existed) were matters of their own concern. Most of the communal villages that remain today are located in areas of the coastland where there are no sugar plantations and where the planters had no interest in developing permanent sea defenses.

---

[28] A. H. Marshall, *Report on Local Government in British Guiana* (Georgetown: Argosy Company, 1955), pp. 3–4.

Neither the organization of local government nor the partitioning of communal villages for tax purposes solved most of the problems of the Afro-Guianese peasantry. In a way, both added to the burdens that already existed. Most of the taxes collected in the villages were used to maintain public roads and sea defenses that were important to the sugar plantations. There was seldom enough money to put village lands in repair and develop the basis for a viable cash crop economy. As land became less productive, villagers had to seek outside employment in order to raise money for the payment of taxes. Partitioning, on the other hand, added new dimensions to the land-tenure problem. In many instances, it resulted in such extreme fragmentation that individuals elected to sell their small holdings rather than attempt to work them. In some cases, the partitioning of children's property provoked bitter disputes between relatives. The cost of settling these disputes ate up the value of the land in legal fees. At best, partitioning provided only a temporary clarification of land relationships by the distribution of new titles. As soon as these proprietors died, the titles once again devolved upon the children, and land relationships were as confused as before.

While all of these circumstances made agriculture difficult for the Afro-Guianese, there were other factors that served to divert their interests away from life in the villages. One of these was education. In 1841, there were 101 elementary schools in British Guiana.[29] At that time, education was almost completely in the hands of the London Missionary Society. The schools depended for their support primarily on fees, but money was also received from the churches, the government, and the planters. In 1852, the Teachers' Benevolent and Improvement Association was organized. Because of its efforts, in 1855 an Education Ordinance was passed which provided for teachers' certificates. This particular ordinance also settled the issue that there must be religious education in schools receiving government aid. This became the basis of the system of "dual control," whereby the schools are owned and managed by Christian churches (or private companies in some cases), but the cost of maintenance, buildings, and teachers' salaries is borne by the government.

In 1876, a Compulsory Education Ordinance was passed which required every child to attend elementary school. This particular bill also made it illegal to employ children under nine years of age or

[29] Cameron, *op. cit.*, pp. 66–82.

those over nine who did not hold a certificate of proficiency from an elementary school.

The Compulsory Education Ordinance was not equally enforced for all Guianese. The children of East Indians living on sugar estates were encouraged to maintain their own customs, and, as a consequence, they were not required to comply with the law by attending Christian schools. Since there were no Hindu or Muslim schools at the time, this meant that these children did not go to school at all.

The Afro-Guianese, more than any other group, took advantage of these developments in education. There must have been many reasons for this, and one of them most certainly involved the lack of opportunity in agriculture. The desire to live as the Europeans perhaps was important also. Another consideration involved the teachers. From the beginning of developments in education, Africans were prominent among the ranks of teachers. In the village, the headmaster occupied a position of influence and trust. He was frequently the chairman of the village council and responsible for the administration of village affairs. The young as well as the old sought his advice on many matters. There can be little doubt that the headmasters played an important role in generating a deep desire for education on the part of many Africans. In any event, educational achievement opened the door to employment opportunities not available in the village itself. By 1900, the Africans dominated every department of the civil service. They also dominated the skilled trades. In 1900, when a Guiana Scholarship was instituted, Africans were among the first to pursue higher education in England. By the First World War, Africans had organized the trade union movement, controlled the teaching profession, and were prominent in law, medicine, and government.

Quite apart from education, there were other developments that drew heavily on the African rural population. Most historians of Guiana would concur with J. Sidney McArthur's statement:

> It is beyond controversy that without the black man the gold and balata industries could not exist in the Colony. . . . It is only by working the Colony's forests that the black man can earn a living wage, and there, in the hundreds, they spend the greater part of every year where there is no imported coolie labourer.[30]

[30] J. Sydney McArthur, "Our People," *Timehri,* The Journal of the Royal Agricultural and Commercial Society of British Guiana, 7 (1921), 23–24.

It is impossible to tell precisely how many African peasants left the village farmlands to become prospectors (locally called pork knockers). During the twenty-year period from 1871 to 1891, the number of individuals employed as gold seekers and woodcutters increased from 2,131 to 6,646. Balata bleeders (men who collect balata gum in the interior) were never counted apart from "other labourers" by the census takers, but in 1891 there were 24,146 individuals listed in this category, and it seems probable that the vast majority of these were Africans. Subsequently, in 1914, the bauxite industry was organized, and its labor force was also primarily African in composition.

There can be little doubt that these new industries represented important forces for change in rural African culture. At first, in the 1880's, they provided many rural Africans with an opportunity to earn some of the money they needed to pay taxes on property that could not be easily harnessed to a cash crop economy. Subsequently, however, these industries brought rural Africans into the urban setting. Although the pork knockers and balata bleeders carried on their work in the interior, they were paid in the city, where they spent much of what they earned for European goods and pleasures. When these individuals returned to the villages, sometimes seemingly rich because of the savings they had accumulated during the long months they spent in the jungle, they excited others with stories of their exploits and good times. Eventually, working the land no longer seemed interesting and worth while. Much of the land owned by Africans was alienated to East Indians. The value of that which was retained will be discussed in a subsequent chapter.

In conclusion, the type of social system forged by British colonial policy not only produced the emergence of an African peasantry, but it also resulted in the transformation of this peasantry into an urban proletariat. Census figures provide partial evidence for the rapidity of this transformation. Between 1891 and 1921, the population of African descent (including the Colored) increased by only 2.23 per cent, while the number of Africans in urban areas increased by 10.18 per cent. This trend continued during the following twenty-five years. Between 1921 and 1946, the African population grew by 22.55 per cent, but the number of Africans in urban areas increased by 51.00 per cent. Thus, unable to earn a livelihood in the villages, pushed out of their jobs on the sugar estates by low wages and indentured workers, taking advantage of educational opportunities, rural Africans increasingly turned to urban sources of employment. Many of them became professionals and civil servants. The vast majority became prospectors, balata bleeders, lumbermen, bauxite miners, artisans, and semiskilled workers.

## EAST INDIANS

The Act of Parliament which terminated slavery in 1833 provided for a transitional period during which the freed slaves were required to serve as "apprentices" for five years and receive payment for their labor. Many of the planters, however, anticipated that once the apprenticeship period ended, the Africans would drift away in large numbers from the places of their bondage. In order to meet the impending labor shortage on the plantations, in 1835, 429 Portuguese were imported from Madeira as indentured servants. Attempts were also made to encourage the surplus Negro population in the West Indian Islands to emigrate. Between 1835 and 1837, 3,734 West Indians were imported to work on the plantations. These early experiments with imported labor, however, met with only partial success. Among the Portuguese, death rates were high, and those who survived were unwilling to suffer the hardships of plantation work. The West Indians (Africans), on the other hand, were independent and unwilling to work for low wages on the estates. The major problem, however, was that of quantity; A large supply of cheap labor was needed to replace the slaves, and this could not be provided for by the efforts of individual planters.

Out of these early experiments with imported labor, a solution to the problem of quantity emerged in the form of the indenture system. In 1836, the Court of Policy passed an ordinance providing for the introduction of servants bound by indenture. In the meantime, John Gladstone, father of the great British statesman and owner of two plantations in Guiana, opened negotiations for the importation of indentured workers from India. In 1838, 414 "hill coolies" were recruited and shipped to British Guiana from India.[31]

This first experiment with "coolies" from India proved to be an almost complete failure. Eighteen of the indentures died before reaching Guiana. The remainder, upon arrival, were allocated to plantations where the conditions under which they lived and worked

[31] Nath, *op. cit.*, pp. 8–21.

were almost identical to those from which the slaves had been liberated. Poor food, sickness, attempts to escape back to India by mythical overland routes, and brutal floggings took their toll. Within a period of fifteen months, sixty-four of the indentures died in Guiana. The Anti-Slavery Society of Great Britain, which had opposed the indenture system from the beginning, brought these dismal facts to the attention of the British public. The allegations were so serious that the governor of British Guiana was forced to appoint a commission to investigate the charges. In the meantime, a "Natives of India Protection Bill" was brought before the House of Lords and passed. Before the bill could be acted upon by the House of Commons, the Government of India suspended the emigration of indentured workers pending a complete investigation of the conditions under which the indentures were required to work.

These setbacks were only temporary. The indenture system appeared to represent the only possible solution to Guiana's labor problem, and the planters brought all the power at their command to pressure the home government into acceding to their demands. In 1841, the recruitment of indentured workers was reopened in Madeira. In the same year, indentured workers began to be recruited in Africa. By 1844, the government of India was finally persuaded to repeal its prohibition of emigration to British Guiana, Jamaica, and Trinidad. The following year, the home government agreed to provide British Guiana with a loan of £500,000 for immigration purposes. Thus began a voluminous traffic in labor from India which continued, without interruption, until 1917, when the indenture system was finally terminated. The number of individuals introduced from various countries during the existence of the indenture system is summarized in Table 4.

Population data compiled by Raymond T. Smith show that the majority of East Indian immigrants to British Guiana were Hindus from the United Provinces.[32] Approximately 16 per cent were Muslims. Less than one-third of the Hindus belonged to low-caste and outcaste groups. Most of the immigrants were from agricultural and artisan castes. It is estimated that no less than 13 per cent belonged to the highest caste groups of the "twice-born," Brahmans and Kshattryas.

[32] Raymond T. Smith, *British Guiana* (London: Oxford University Press, 1962), p. 46.

TABLE 4. NUMBER OF CONTRACT IMMIGRANTS ARRIVING IN BRITISH GUIANA: 1835–1918

| *Country of Origin* | *Dates of Immigration* | *Number of Immigrants* | *Percentage of Total* |
|---|---|---|---|
| India | 1838–1917 | 238,960 | 70.1 |
| Madeira, Azores, Cape Verde | 1835–1882 | 31,628 | 9.3 |
| Malta | 1839 | 208 | .1 |
| West Indies | 1835–1928 | 42,562 | 12.4 |
| Africa | 1838–1865 | 13,355 | 3.9 |
| China | 1853–1912 | 14,189 | 4.2 |
| Total | | 340,902 | 100 |

Source: Compiled from data presented in Dwarka Nath, *A History of Indians in British Guiana* (London: Thomas Nelson and Sons, 1950), pp. 179–180.

Several historians of Guiana have maintained that the conditions under which the indentured immigrants lived and worked were not very different from those of slavery. Ruhomon quotes a firsthand observer who described the system as follows:

> Take a large factory in Manchester or Birmingham or Belfast, build a wall around it, shut in its work-people from all intercourse, save, at rare intervals, with the outside world, keep them in absolute ignorance and get all the work you can out of them, treat them not unkindly, leave their social habits in relation to themselves as matters not concerning you who make the money from their labour and you would have constituted a little community, resembling in no small degree a sugar estate village in British Guiana.[33]

Joseph Beaumont, Chief Justice of British Guiana in 1863, described the indenture system as a "monstrous rotten system" which emulated the worst abuses of slavery.[34]

Under the immigration and labor laws, the identured worker was bound to service for a period of five years, after which he was

[33] As quoted by Ruhomon, *op. cit.*, p. 48.
[34] *Ibid.*, p. 47.

given a certificate of exemption from labor and allowed to purchase a return passage to India. Free passage to India was provided if and when the immigrant completed a ten-year period of continuous residence in the colony. The indentured worker was required to work every day except Sunday and official holidays, seven hours in the field or ten hours in the factory. In return for his labor, he received wages so low (approximately $1.50 (B.W.I.) per week) that the freed slaves refused to work for them. He also received housing (50 square feet of space to one adult or 120 square feet for a family of four), medical attention (valued by the government at twenty-five cents a day per individual), clothing, and food rations. The cost of the latter was deducted from his wages at the rate of eight cents a day for an adult and four cents for a minor. Managers who refused to provide for these necessities in accordance with the law were subject to fines.[35]

There can be little doubt that life was harsh and even cruel for the indentured worker. The immigration and labor laws provided the estates with every opportunity for exploitation. Every indentured worker was required to reside on the plantation to which he was contracted. The indenture was entitled to accumulate leave at the rate of one day and night for every two consecutive weeks of work, but he was not allowed more than seven days at any one time or more than twenty-six days in any one year. When leave was taken, the worker was given a pass indicating his exemption from labor. Immigrants absent from the estate without a pass were liable to a penalty not exceeding $10 (B.W.I.) for a male and $5 (B.W.I.) for a female. Seven days of absence without leave were taken to be desertion. Deserters were liable to fine or imprisonment. Also, any immigrant who refused to work or who failed to do his work properly, unless excused for medical reasons, was liable to a fine of $2.48 (B.W.I.) for the first offense and $10 (B.W.I.) for each subsequent offense. Similarly, the law provided penalties for drunkenness, for the use of abusive language to employers, for neglect resulting in property damage, and for hindering the work of others. Some evidence is available indicating the extent to which these laws were executed. Alleyne Ireland reported that between 1876 and 1896 a total of 209 employers were convicted for offenses against indentures under the labor and immigration laws. During the same period, no fewer than

---

[35] *Ibid.*, pp. 286–94.

67,148 indentures were convicted of offenses against employers, and 13,941 involved attempts to desert the estates.[36]

Apart from these degrading conditions, however, the indenture system differed in many important ways from the institution of chattel slavery. The indentures, unlike the slaves, were not pieces of property. They were instruments of production, to be sure, but while their labor could be used, their persons could not be owned. In theory, if not always in practice, the indentures had certain rights. One of these was the right to return to their homeland after completing their contracts. Related to this was the right to maintain their own customs and practices as long as these did not interfere with their obligation to conform to the work routine of the estate. Thus, religious beliefs and practices, the ritual observances pertaining to marriage, the social usages affecting the relationships between kin, the values associated with the education and socialization of children, and many other customary usages could be continued as far as it was possible to do so under the circumstances.

Cultural institutions and practices never remain static, even when they are isolated from external influences. There is a difference, however, between cultural transformation and cultural revolution. The rapidity with which the latter form of change occurs is such that there is very little continuity between what existed and what comes into existence. The indenture system, unlike the slave system, favored a continuity in East Indian cultural patterns. This was the case not only because the indentures had certain rights, but also because the immigration and labor laws which defined these rights served to confine the new migrants to ethnic ghettos. As new indentures arrived in one wave after another for almost three-quarters of a century, they were mixed with those who came earlier. This served to reinforce traditional habits and customs and contributed to a continuity in cultural patterning. Moreover, the indentures were relatively restricted to the estates on which they were placed. This did not prevent them from mixing with Europeans or Africans. However, the context of association with outsiders was primarily one of instrumental relationships, and this served to impede rather than facilitate the process of change.

Continuity in culture was favored also by the attitudes of the indentures with respect to sending their children to school. In 1890,

[36] W. Alleyne Ireland, "The History of the East Indian Immigrant," reprinted in *Demerariana, Essays: Historical, Critical, and Descriptive* (Georgetown: Baldwin and Company, 1897), p. 23.

the surgeon-major estimated that only approximately 10 per cent of the Indian children regularly attended school.[37] The Census Report of 1921 states that less than 50 per cent of the Indian children of school age were receiving formal instruction. The primary schools were exclusively Christian, and until 1916, when the Canadian Presbyterian Mission opened a secondary school at New Amsterdam, Hindi was not included in the curriculum of any of the schools. Indian parents did not favor sending their daughters to these schools for fear that it might make it too difficult for them to arrange suitable marriages. At the same time, they preferred to have their sons work in boys' gangs on the estates and thereby contribute ten to twelve cents per day to the savings which the family hoped to take back to India. The planters, of course, found these attitudes congenial to their interests. Thus, the compulsory education law was not enforced with respect to indentures. As a result, the stimulus to change provided by Western education did not have a widespread effect on Indian cultural patterns until the indenture system was terminated in 1917 by the government of India.

Because of their lack of education, the position of East Indians in Guianese society was relatively fixed. They filled a gap in the social system as agricultural workers, and there was little else they could do. When the indenture fulfilled his contract, illiteracy prevented him from having access to the professions, to positions in the civil service, or to many other types of employment that Africans drifted into by virtue of their schooling. Also, family obligations and kinship ties made it extremely difficult for the Indian to migrate into the interior to prospect for gold or to work in the balata fields. The choices were limited: The indenture could either reindenture himself, or he could return to India. The vast majority of indentured immigrants from India decided to remain in the colony, and this, also, has had much to do with the continuity of East Indian cultural patterns.[38]

The Indians who remained in British Guiana did not do so without persuasion. As early as 1863, James Crosby, the Immigration Agent-General, brought to the attention of the government the desirability of developing a program whereby the immigrants could be encouraged to surrender their return passage rights and remain in the colony. Subsequently, the government made Crown lands available

[37] Ruhomon, *op. cit.*, pp. 178–90.
[38] Nath, *op. cit.*, pp. 184–86.

to them for purchase. At various times, the government also attempted to organize land-settlement schemes in which the immigrants were given grants of land in lieu of return passage. In 1880, for example, Plantation Huist Dieren, an abandoned sugar estate in Essequibo, was purchased by the government for a land-settlement scheme. The head of each immigrant family received a residential lot and a cultivation lot of two acres. His wife and each child over ten years of age also received a cultivation lot, while each child under ten received half a cultivation lot.

For lack of organization, the land-settlement schemes established prior to 1900 were not very successful.[39] The government, however, did not relax its efforts to conserve the colony's labor resources by establishing an independent peasantry among the East Indians. Crown lands continued to be made available to those Indians who wished to purchase them. Plantations also continued to be purchased for organizing land-settlement schemes. The last of these were bought by the government in the early 1950's. By 1911, there were 126,517 Indians in British Guiana. Less than half of these resided on sugar estates. Only 5.7 per cent of the total lived in urban areas. This distribution has not changed a great deal over the years. By 1946, the East Indian population had increased to 163,434. A little more than one-third of these lived on sugar estates. Only 9.9 per cent resided in urban areas. The remainder lived in rural villages and land-settlement schemes.

The viability of the East Indian peasantry, as compared to the African peasantry which emerged in the 1840's, has often been explained by early writers in terms of imputed character traits. Rodway, for example, attributed the progress achieved by Indian peasants to the fact that they, in contrast to the Africans, were reliable workers, thrifty, and not easily distracted by convivialities.[40] Such an explanation overlooks the special consideration afforded the indentures under existing colonial policy.

The Indian peasantry, in effect, was created by colonial government in British Guiana. Because of governmental policies, the Indian peasants were able to avoid most of the difficulties that beset the African peasantry. The land-settlement schemes, for example, were provided with governmental aid and governmental supervision. Unlike the plantations purchased by former slaves, the land-settlement

[39] Young, *op. cit.*, pp. 152–61.
[40] Rodway, *op. cit.*, pp. 186–210.

schemes were kept in fairly good repair. Also because of governmental supervision, the problems of land fragmentation that prevented the Africans from effectively developing a cash crop economy did not exist for most Indian peasants. Land in the settlement schemes was divided into uniform lots, and these, in turn, were not allowed to be subdivided into less than half-acre lots. Tenure was secured by individual title, and the Indians learned from the government as well as from the Africans the difficulties associated with children's property. Kinship patterns also functioned to prevent land fragmentation. Under the indenture system, much of the traditional Indian kinship system remained intact. Inheritance continued to be patrilineal, and it tended to follow the principle of ultimogeniture. As a consequence, daughters and older sons frequently did not participate in the division of property.

Another factor which contributed significantly to the survival of the Indian peasantry is rice agriculture. There existed a relatively good local market for rice in British Guiana because of the large number of indentured workers imported from India. This provided the Indian peasants an economic base with a profit potential much higher than that available to Africans who mainly grew ground crops. During the First World War, British Guiana began to export large amounts of rice. The profits realized from war prices made rice agriculture even more attractive. Following the war, prices fell sharply and a depression set in. However, the depression disappeared with the outbreak of the Second World War. In order to stabilize the rice economy in keeping with the war effort, the government established a single buying and selling agency for both local and export markets. Since 1939, the rice economy has remained protected, and, as a result, the Indian peasants have been provided a degree of economic security which was never available to Africans.

In conclusion, the emergence of an independent peasantry, perhaps more than anything else, has made it possible for East Indians to preserve much of their traditional culture. Although the Indians continue to make up the major part of the labor force on the sugar estates, there tends to be a constant flow of sugar workers into the peasant villages. The vast majority of Indian peasants have tended to cluster in villages of their own on Crown lands, on lands purchased from Africans, or in official land-settlement schemes. Since approximately 1900, the expanding rice industry has provided the peasantry with its economic base. As a result of these developments, the rural

Indian population combines, in a single complex, elements of a rural proletariat with elements of a peasant culture. The institutional and structural components of this complex will be dealt with in another context. It suffices to note here that this complex has very definitely retarded the absorption of East Indians into the structure of Creole society.[41]

## PORTUGUESE

The Portuguese were among the first to come to British Guiana as indentured workers. Although they comprised 9 per cent of the total number of indentured immigrants, most of them (about 88 per cent) arrived from Madeira before 1860. It is not known precisely how many died while working on the plantations. There are perfunctory historical references to the effect that they were more subject to tropical diseases than other groups.[42] How many of them returned to their homeland after fulfilling their contracts is also unknown. There is meager evidence that a few might have migrated to Brazil.[43] In any event, it is quite certain that the vast majority of the Portuguese withdrew from the estates as soon as it was possible for them to do so.

The Portuguese, unlike the Africans and the East Indians, did not establish themselves as independent peasant farmers when they left the sugar estates. Instead, they became peddlers, hawkers, pawnbrokers, and small shopkeepers. By 1851, when an ordinance was passed providing for the licensing of all shopkeepers, the Portuguese had virtually taken over the retail trade of the colony. Fifty-eight per cent of the shops in Georgetown and 54 per cent of those in New Amsterdam were licensed to Portuguese. Portuguese merchants also owned 65 per cent of the shops licensed in rural areas.[44] Over the years, many of these small businesses were expanded into large operations. At the same time, some of the profits made in retail trade were invested in other enterprises. In the 1880's, for example, the Negro pork knockers who carried out expeditions to the goldfields were

---

[41] Creoles are natives of the Caribbean. Creole cultures vary a good deal but all of them have their historical base in slavery, plantation systems, and colonialism. See M. G. Smith, *The Plural Society in the British West Indies* (Los Angeles: University of California Press, 1965), pp. 5–9.

[42] Nath, *op. cit.*, p. 37.

[43] Ruhomon, *op. cit.*, p. 46.

[44] Smith, *British Guiana*, pp. 44–46.

primarily financed by Portuguese merchants. Similarly, Portuguese merchants also provided much of the capital needed to develop the diamond and timber industries.

The speed with which the Portuguese took over the retail trade of the colony in the 1880's was due, in large part, to the preferential treatment they received. For example, the Portuguese were able to secure credit from other Europeans, whereas Africans could not. Thus, they soon drove their African competitors out of business. This generated considerable hostility on the part of the African population. These feelings of hostility were first brought to a boil in 1856, when John Sayers Orr, an African preacher with a fanatical prejudice against Roman Catholicism, incited Africans to riot.[45] Practically every Portuguese shop in the country was destroyed before the rioting was brought under control. Following this disturbance, the government recovered the cost of compensation to Portuguese merchants by issuing a special Registration Tax. The tax was levied on the whole population, but the burden of its payment fell heaviest on the African peasants. This, needless to say, contributed little to the improvement of relationships between the two groups. In 1889, and again in 1905, similar riots took place in Georgetown.

From the time of their arrival, the Portuguese have occupied a rather ambiguous position in the structure of Guianese society. As Roman Catholics, they came to a country that was predominantly Protestant and Hindu. They are white and European, but they were imported to do the work of slaves. They became peddlers and hawkers, merchants and businessmen, in a society based on a plantation economy. Thus, economic success did not entail political power: The plantocracy controlled both the economy and the government. Because of their economic success, however, the Portuguese have had access to the plantocracy, but they have never belonged to it. Thus, they have been put in positions of influence, but seldom have they been allowed to achieve positions of power. Until recent times, the influence the Portuguese have had has been directly related to their ability to identify themselves with other Europeans. Other Europeans, however, have not reciprocated: They tend to think of the Portuguese as part of Creole society. This ambiguity of social position has not existed without being recognized by Africans and Indians. They frequently refer to the Portuguese as "Potagee," a term of derogatory description.

---

[45] Young, *op. cit.*, pp. 51–53.

## CHINESE

There is a paucity of historical material available on the Chinese in British Guiana. Perhaps the reason for this is that the number of Chinese represented but a very small percentage of the total number of immigrants introduced as indentured workers. Chinese immigration was inaugurated in 1853. It practically came to an end in 1866, when, under an Emigration Convention signed at Peking, the shipment of coolies from the mainland of China was prohibited. As of 1866, a total of 12,631 Chinese had been introduced into the colony. By 1911, only 2,622 remained. This decline was not entirely due to repatriation. The sex ratio among the indentured Chinese was more distorted than that of any other group. As a consequence, the Chinese intermarried with members of other ethnic groups to the extent that only a few retained their ethnic identity.

The Chinese were the first to make an attempt to establish an exclusively ethnic settlement in British Guiana.[46] In 1864, O. Tye Kim petitioned the government for land and financial aid in order to establish a village of Chinese Christians on the Demerara River. The petition was granted, and the following year Hopetown was founded with twenty-five settlers. When the village reached its peak of prosperity, it contained several hundred persons. However, soil exhaustion and the scarcity of women doomed the effort to failure. By 1881, Hopetown's population had declined to 222 persons, and only 81 of these were women. By 1902, it had practically disappeared as a Chinese settlement.

The Chinese were not very different from the Portuguese with respect to economic adaptation. Most of them left the plantations as soon as their contracts terminated. Those who remained in Guiana displayed very little interest in peasant agriculture. They rapidly became absorbed into a wide variety of occupations. Some became pork knockers and balata bleeders. Some worked in the timber industry. Others secured positions in the civil service. Many opened small shops in urban areas, in large rural villages, or in the vicinity of plantations. Very few of the Chinese continued to work as common laborers. By 1911, one-third of the Chinese remaining in British Guiana were located in Georgetown or New Amsterdam. Today, this number has

[46] *Ibid.*, pp. 149–52.

increased to 60 per cent. The rest are widely scattered throughout the country.

The Chinese are the least identifiable of Guiana's six ethnic groups. Racially, they are extremely mixed. They no longer retain their language. Chinese clothing is worn only on festive occasions. Food patterns have been similarly modified. As Fried has shown, in most respects the Chinese have become thoroughly anglicized.[47] About all that remains of their ethnic identity is the Chinese Association and the use of Chinese names. The Chinese Association does not display strong sentiments of ethnic exclusiveness. It is organized in Georgetown, where it sponsors parties and festivals that are attended by many people who are not Chinese.

## THE PLURAL SOCIETY IN HISTORICAL PERSPECTIVE

It has been noted that the definition of the plural society must take into account two related sets of facts: (1) the extent to which specified groups are culturally differentiated in terms of specific institutional activities, and (2) the level at which institutional activities serve to maintain cultural differentiation as a basis for sociocultural integration. When institutional activities serve to maintain culturally differentiated groups at local levels only, such groups were said to be "minimal" cultural sections. However, when institutional activities function to maintain culturally differentiated groups at the societal level, it was suggested that these groups be identified as "maximal" cultural sections. A plural society was defined as one that contained maximal cultural sections.

In terms of this conceptual framework, there can be little doubt that British Guiana has been a plural society throughout most of its history. Pluralism was rooted in the plantation system that began to take shape with the help of a few African slaves in the seventeenth century. By the time the slave trade was abolished in 1807, more than 100,000 Africans had been imported. African institutions and customs were not viable under the conditions of slavery. However, the institutions of slavery served to differentiate the Africans from the Europeans and the Amerindians. These institutions were maintained

[47] M. Fried, "The Chinese in British Guiana," *Social and Economic Studies,* 5 (1956), 54–73.

locally, on the plantations, and societally in terms of the legal and political structures which defined the status of slaves. These societal structures began to change in 1838, when slavery was abolished. The abolition of slavery opened the way for Africans to participate more fully in the institutions of European society. The process of acculturation, however, was modified by the special circumstances under which the freed Africans were forced to develop special institutions which enabled them to adapt to the existing structure of plantation society.

During the nineteenth century, the gradual evolution of a more modern plantation economy was made possible by the adoption of colonial policies designed to maintain an incessant flow of indentured workers into the colony. From a cultural point of view, the indentured workers from Madeira, India, and China were not only different from one another but also from the partially acculturated Africans and from the European plantocracy. If the Portuguese and the Chinese readily gave up their cultural identity, this was not the case with the East Indians, who arrived in larger numbers and whose experience with the indenture system was longer than that of any other group. The circumstances under which the indentures lived and worked kept them apart from other groups. The special programs designed to keep them from returning to India also kept them apart from other groups. Thus, the acculturation of East Indians to a European way of life was considerably retarded. At the communal level, whether in the villages or on the plantations, much of their traditional culture was reinforced and remained viable. At the societal level, the affairs of East Indians were regulated by the Immigration Department and the Immigration Agent-General. Their separate identity was further enhanced by such organizations as the Arya Samaj, the Sanatan Dharma, the East Indian Association, the Islamic Association, and the Sad'r Anjuman-E-Islam.

In delineating the elements of cultural history inherent in the contemporary structure of Guianese society, different sections of the population have been dealt with in terms of their cultural backgrounds and the special adaptations they made to colonial policies and practices. Accordingly, a great deal of emphasis has been placed on cultural differences at the expense of ignoring the extent to which the people of Guiana constitute one society. It would be erroneous to suggest, or even to imply, that colonial society was little more than a congeries of cultural sections held together by a European-dominated power structure. No matter how much emphasis is given to cultural differences, the fact remains that all groups were affected by the forces of unification and acculturation. For example, the plantation system has been a source of common experience in the lives of East Indians, Africans, Portuguese, and Chinese. Its rigid social structure has destroyed or modified the original cultural institutions of all these groups. The same can be said of the government, the schools, and the churches. In response to these changes, and in response to external economic and political pressures, the structure of colonial society itself has changed. Since 1917, when organized immigration ceased, the different cultural sections have become increasingly involved in a common social, economic, and political life. However, the extent to which cultural pluralism continues to be a dynamic force in Guianese society remains to be shown.

*CHAPTER 3*

# COMMUNAL PATTERNS OF SOCIOCULTURAL INTEGRATION

NOTWITHSTANDING THE FORCES OF UNIFICATION AND ACCULTURATION which have affected the various groups that make up its population, British Guiana continues to display a relatively high degree of cultural pluralism. The economic structures of colonial society have served to alienate the Afro-Guianese from the land and lodge them in the urban sector. Simultaneously, the East Indians have become more deeply entrenched in the agricultural sector. This has contributed to the persistence of those Hindu and South Asian traditions which happen to be particularly adaptive to a peasant agricultural economy. These traditions, in turn, have isolated East Indians both physically and psychologically from the larger society. The urbanization of the Africans, on the other hand, has facilitated their adoption of many European institutions and values. It also has modified, rather extensively, their rural traditions.

The differential economic adaptation of these two groups is most immediately apparent in terms of demographic data. In 1952, Africans and East Indians represented, respectively, 35.9 and 45.8 per cent of the total population.[1] Africans, however, comprised 25.4 per cent of the total number of farm operators, compared to 71.3 per cent for the East Indians. Typically, these farmers are peasants. Seventy-seven per cent of them work less than ten acres of land, and approximately one-fifth work less than two.[2] The racially mixed, a census category made up primarily of individuals of African and European ancestry, represented only 5.2 per cent of the total number of farm

[1] S. K. Fitzgerald, "Some Population and Land Aspects of British Guiana." Unpublished report of the University of Maryland United States Operations Mission to the British Guiana Land Settlement Department (1956), Table 14.

[2] *Ibid.*, Table 16.

operators. Although exact figures are not available, it is usually estimated that no more than 30 per cent of the 80,000 people who live on the sugar estates are Africans. In other words, East Indians are predominantly peasant farmers and agricultural workers, while Africans are not.

Census figures, however, do not provide the kind of data necessary to delineate the complex patterns of sociocultural integration characteristic of these two groups. For example, in 1946, the Afro-Guianese (including the mixed) comprised 74 per cent of the urban population. Still, more than half of all the Afro-Guianese (57 per cent) continued to live in rural villages. If only a small percentage of these rural Africans operate farms or work on sugar estates, how do they survive economically? If the rural-urban continuum is associated with differential acculturation, as is suggested in the case of East Indians, then how do rural Africans differ from East Indians? If rural Africans do not differ from East Indians, how do they relate to urban Africans, who, presumably, are more European in culture than East Indian peasants?

The theoretical problem underlying these questions is whether or not the Afro-Guianese, when compared to East Indians, form cultural sections and, if so, at what level are these cultural sections separately integrated? The resolution of this problem necessitates a comparative study of institutional activities and communal patterns of sociocultural integration.

## SETTLEMENT PATTERNS

In complex societies, settlement patterns can be highly variable, but local communities are usually social units of relatively limited scale. They are not self-contained social systems, and they cannot be viewed as representative of the macroscopic whole of which they form but a part. Nevertheless, these social units are critical to the analysis of institutional activities. They provide the most immediate context within which individuals interact in a multiplicity of ways as they engage in daily routine. The social structures which regulate daily routine form the building blocks for larger societal structures. Thus, the local community is a logical point of departure for the analysis of institutional activities.

Typically, the local community in British Guiana involves some type of village settlement. Sixty-eight per cent of the people who inhabit the densely populated coastal shelf live in villages. Most of these villages are strung out along the main road which runs parallel to the sea all along the coast. There are few striking differences in the physical appearance of these villages. This is due to the fact that most of them were first established as plantations, and their layout was dictated by the empoldering system which was so necessary for the cultivation of crops. Except for minor differences reflecting wealth and, perhaps, ethnic background, the houses are elevated on posts and constructed according to a uniform design that is particularly suitable to the tropics. The dwelling areas are usually located adjacent to the public road. Sometimes, these lands are separated from the road by a village pasture. Often, in Demerara, the railroad passes the front of the village and divides it from the village pasture. A few kitchen gardens may be kept near the houses in the dwelling area, but the major cultivation lands are located away from the sea and to the rear of the village. The entire layout is divided into blocks by a complicated network of drainage and irrigation trenches. In the village proper, these run parallel on both sides of every street, necessitating the use of small bridges to connect the houselots to the streets. As often as not, the only boundary which separates one village from another is a "sideline" drainage trench.

Behind these striking physical similarities lie some important differences. Some villages, for example, have populations numbering in the thousands, while others are occupied by two or three hundred people. Villages frequently go to extreme lengths to keep themselves for one ethnic group. While it is rare to find a village without a mixed population, it is also rare to find one in which the population is not predominantly either African or East Indian. Ecological differences also exist. Some villages have more cultivation lands than others. Many villages do not have sea defenses and drainage and irrigation systems. In these villages, the cultivation of crops entails considerable risk because the farmer is completely at the mercy of the elements. Organizational differences are also important. In 1955, almost 45 per cent of the rural population lived in villages organized as local authorities. An additional 30 per cent lived in villages located on lands owned or controlled by sugar estates. Finally, more than 25 per cent of the population lived in villages or land-settlement schemes without local government organization.[3]

---

[3] A. H. Marshall, *Report on Local Government in British Guiana* (Georgetown: Argosy Company, 1955), p. 105.

Most of the villages without local authorities have practically no organized system of water control. In a few exceptional cases, the lands are owned as a plantation by a family which rents them out to tenants in exchange for services. In Afro-Guianese villages without local authorities, village lands consist of undivided children's property owned by practically everyone living in the community. If a village council exists, it is a voluntary group made up of older heads, and its legal authority is extremely limited. Such a council would not be able to levy taxes on property, but it may attempt to raise funds for specific projects. Most of the services in these kinds of villages are provided by voluntary self-help groups or by some agency of the central government. In either case, there is very little continuity in the services provided. Thus, most villages without authorities have poor agricultural lands, congested housing, unkempt streets, and are directly administered by the central government as country districts. Henceforth, these villages will be parsimoniously referred to as "unorganized."

In contrast to the unorganized villages, the nuclear and extra-nuclear housing areas on the sugar estates constitute still another type.[4] The estate communities lack local authorities, but they do not lack organization. Through the British Guiana Sugar Producers' Association and the Labour Welfare Fund Committee, services are made available to the estate communities which often excel, in quantity as well as quality, those normally provided by local authorities. Included among these services are loans for building homes, health facilities, and community centers. In addition, the estate usually provides equipment, free of cost, for the maintenance of streets and internal drainage. Potable water is also supplied by the sugar industry. The community centers

[4] Following the recommendations of the West India Royal Commission (1945), estate residents are classified into essential workers (nuclear population) and nonessential workers (extra-nuclear population). It has been generally recognized that the housing of essential workers is the responsibility of the estate owners, while the rehousing of the surplus estate population is the responsibility of the government. Some estates, Plantation Skeldon for example, have decided that a special nuclear settlement is not necessary except for European personnel. However, because of government inactivity with respect to the rehousing of the surplus estate population, the Sugar Producers' Association has had to adopt policies designed to develop the extra-nuclear settlements. Consequently, most of these settlements are presently located on estate-owned land, and they have not been brought under the jurisdiction of the Department of Local Government. The efforts that have been made in this direction by the Sugar Producers' Association have been resisted by the Jagan government for certain political advantages that will be considered in a later chapter.

are organized by the residents under the supervision of trained welfare officers who, in turn, are directly responsible to the estate's personnel officer. The welfare officers also supervise the functioning of tenants' associations. While these elective groups are in charge of community affairs, the plantation manager, representing the Georgetown office of the companies represented by the S.P.A., is the ultimate source of authority. These villages may be conveniently identified as "plantation" or "industrial" communities.

Villages organized as local authorities represent a third type of settlement pattern. These communities have councils which are locally elected on the basis of a property franchise. As a consequence, the lands in these villages, including children's property, are partitioned for tax purposes. The village councils, under the Local Government Ordinance, are entrusted to discharge the functions of local government.[5] The functions of local government include the collection and expenditure of tax monies, the administration of village affairs, the appointment of overseers to supervise public works, the management of undivided lands and public property such as the village office building, the regulation of village markets and slaughterhouses, the reinforcement of public health regulations, particularly those pertaining to the construction of buildings, and the maintenance of streets and internal drainage systems. The Local Government Ordinance provides for the central control of village councils by the Local Government Board through the Department of Local Government. Practically every act of a village council is subject to the specific consent of the board, the district commissioner or, in some instances, the governor in council. The Local Government Board can, with cause, dismiss any or all members of a village council.[6]

The variables that serve to identify these settlement patterns normally bear a critical relationship to the structural dimensions of institutional activities. For example, one would expect the economy

[5] Local Government Ordinance of 1953, in *The Law of British Guiana* (London: Waterlow & Sons, 1954), chap. 150.

[6] In 1954, the Secretary of State for the British Colonies appointed Mr. A. H. Marshall to inquire into and report on all aspects of local government in both rural and urban areas and to make recommendations for reform. Marshall's report (*op. cit.*) appeared in 1955. Subsequently, in 1957, two confidential reports appeared dealing with the problem of local government reorganization. As of the time of this study, none of Marshall's recommendations for reform had been enacted into law. The major obstacle seems to involve problems of land tenure and land partitioning, particularly in the African villages. In any event, as of 1961, the Local Government Ordinance of 1953 remained the legal basis for local government organization.

of a drained village with a local authority to support social structures somewhat different from those of an unorganized and undrained village. Therefore, in any comparative analysis of East Indian and Afro-Guianese villages, it is necessary to employ a sample of village types which provides some control for such crucial variables as population size, land area, drainage and irrigation, proximity to labor markets and urban areas, and the intrusion into village affairs of such centralized governmental agencies as the Local Government Board and the Department of Local Government. In order to control these factors, three sets of matched villages were selected for study (see Table 5).[7] One village of each set is predominantly Afro-Guianese

TABLE 5. SAMPLE OF VILLAGE TYPES

| | *Population (N)* | *East Indians (Per Cent)* | *Afro-Guianese (Per Cent)* |
|---|---|---|---|
| Unorganized Villages | | | |
| Eversham | 325 | 21 | 79 |
| Cromarty | 604 | 86 | 14 |
| Plantation and Industrial | | | |
| Mackenzie City | 5,191 | 6 | 94 |
| Skeldon | 4,230 | 83 | 17 |
| Local Authorities | | | |
| Ann's Grove | 2,248 | 7 | 93 |
| Clonbrook | 1,561 | 92 | 8 |

[7] The census data presented in Table 5 are based on computations made from a sample survey of the six communities. The number of households contained in each community and the number of household heads interviewed during the course of field work are summarized in Table 6. Every effort was made to keep the sample of household heads as random as possible. In some cases, Eversham for example, it was easier to deal with the total universe because the village was too small to justify a sample.

TABLE 6. TOTAL NUMBER OF HOUSEHOLDS AND THE NUMBER OF HOUSEHOLD HEADS INTERVIEWED IN THE SAMPLE OF VILLAGE TYPES

| Villages | Total Number of Households in Each Village | | Total Number of Household Heads Interviewed in Each Village | |
|---|---|---|---|---|
| | Africans | East Indians | Africans | East Indians |
| Eversham | 37 | 9 | 27 | 6 |
| Cromarty | 12 | 67 | 3 | 29 |
| Mackenzie | 776 | 49 | 129 | 8 |
| Skeldon | 146 | 500 | 24 | 106 |
| Ann's Grove | 373 | 19 | 58 | 4 |
| Clonbrook | 24 | 179 | 0 | 41 |
| Total | 1,368 | 823 | 241 | 194 |

in racial composition, while the other is East Indian. The analysis of minimal cultural sections is based largely on the data collected in these six villages.[8]

## FAMILY AND KINSHIP NETWORKS

A minimal cultural section, as defined earlier, is a group of people organized in terms of social structures that are expressive of a relatively distinct set of cultural values. It follows from this that such a group can exist only as long as it is able to maintain institutional mechanisms by which its social heritage is transmitted to succeeding generations. In all human societies, the primary locus of social reproduction is the family. It is within the family that the facts of physical continuity and cultural heritage converge upon the individual to shape his basic social identity. If the structures in terms of which this convergence takes place do not serve to differentiate one group from another, then it is unlikely that the members of these groups will see themselves as very different kinds of people.

Anthropologists are indebted to the work of Meyer Fortes for directing their attention to the fact that the domestic group, which is essentially a housekeeping unit organized to rear children and provide for the needs of its members, goes through a developmental cycle similar to the growth cycle of living organisms.[9] Recognition of this fact is particularly important with respect to the analysis of residence patterns, because a given village may contain different types of residential units. Some consist of two individuals of the same generation who share a conjugal bond. Others are nuclear families containing a man and a woman with their offspring. In some instances, the domestic group contains members of three generations and is matrilocally or patrilocally extended. These alignments are frequently determined by instrumental and affective considerations, but, to the extent that they represent successive phases of the developmental pro-

---

[8] In the analysis that follows, only those factors relevant to the problem of pluralism will be considered. A subsequent work will deal more extensively with patterns of village life in British Guiana.

[9] See Meyer Fortes' introduction to Jack Goody (ed.), *The Developmental Cycle in Domestic Groups,* Cambridge Papers in Social Anthropology, No. 1 (Cambridge: Cambridge University Press, 1962), pp. 1–14.

cess at different points in time, it is erroneous to analyze them as discrete types. In other words, the structure of the domestic group, which should not be confused with the structure of kinship, can be isolated only when the sequence of changes that characterizes its developmental cycle is taken into account.

Table 7 presents a summary of the data collected on household composition for the four rural villages included in the study.[10] The data on household composition for Mackenzie City and Plantation Skeldon are summarized separately in Table 8. The first point of significance to note from these data is the fact that the one-generational household, regardless of the type of community involved, is not evident among East Indians. East Indian households seldom include young married couples without children or elderly people living alone. This is not true, however, of the Afro-Guianese. Almost one out of every five Afro-Guianese households contains individuals of one generation. In the rural villages of Ann's Grove and Eversham, most of these one-generational households are made up of elderly men living alone or elderly couples whose children have married and left home. In Mackenzie City, where the percentage for this type runs a bit higher than in the rural villages, most of these households contain unmarried men living alone or married men separated from families that remain in the coastal villages.

From Tables 7 and 8 it will be noted that a significant difference between Africans and Indians also exists with respect to three-generational households. Regardless of the type of community involved, almost one out of every three East Indian households contains a patrilocally extended group. Minimally, such a group consists of an elderly married couple living together with a married son and his wife and their offspring. Frequently, it includes two or more married sons with their wives and offspring. Among the Afro-Guianese, on the other hand, only one out of every five households in the rural villages is of a three-generational type. At Mackenzie City, the three-generational household is practically nonexistent. With respect to this type of household, an additional structural difference between the two groups also should be noted. Among Africans, more than 60 per cent of the three-generational households include unmarried sons

[10] Table 7 combines the data for local authorities and unorganized villages because no significant differences were found between the two types of communities with respect to household composition.

TABLE 7. HOUSEHOLD COMPOSITION: ANN'S GROVE AND EVERSHAM, CLONBROOK AND CROMARTY

| *Household Type* | *Afro-Guianese (Ann's Grove and Eversham) (N=85)* | | *East Indians (Clonbrook and Cromarty) (N=70)* | |
|---|---|---|---|---|
| I. One-Generational | | | | |
| 1. Male Heads | | | | |
| a. Living Alone | 7 | | 1 | |
| b. Living with Spouse | 5 | | 1 | |
| 2. Female Heads | | | | |
| a. Living Alone | 2 | | 0 | |
| b. Living with Spouse | 1 | | 0 | |
| Total | 15 | (17.6%) | 2 | (2.9%) |
| II. Two-Generational | | | | |
| 1. Male Heads | | | | |
| a. Nuclear Families | 39 | | 38 | |
| b. Nuclear Families with Dependent Collaterals | 6 | | 4 | |
| 2. Female Heads | | | | |
| a. Nuclear Families | 4 | | 0 | |
| b. Nuclear Families with Dependent Collaterals | 3 | | 0 | |
| Total | 52 | (61.2%) | 42 | (60.0%) |
| III. Three-Generational | | | | |
| 1. Male Heads | | | | |
| a. Patrilocally Extended | 2 | | 26 | |
| b. Includes Unmarried Children with Offspring | 10 | | 0 | |
| 2. Female Heads | | | | |
| a. Matrilocally Extended | 5 | | 0 | |
| b. Includes Unmarried Children with Offspring | 1 | | 0 | |
| Total | 18 | (21.2%) | 26 | (37.1%) |

TABLE 8. HOUSEHOLD COMPOSITION: PLANTATION SKELDON AND MACKENZIE CITY

| *Household Type* | *Afro-Guianese (Mackenzie City) (N=129)* | | *East Indians (Skeldon) (N=106)* | |
|---|---|---|---|---|
| I. One-Generational | | | | |
| 1. Male Heads | | | | |
| a. Living Alone | 22 | | 1 | |
| b. Living with Spouse | 6 | | 2 | |
| 2. Female Heads | | | | |
| a. Living Alone | 0 | | 0 | |
| b. Living with Spouse | 0 | | 0 | |
| Total | 28 | (21.7%) | 3 | (2.8%) |
| II. Two-Generational | | | | |
| 1. Male Heads | | | | |
| a. Nuclear Families | 85 | | 65 | |
| b. Nuclear Families with Dependent Collaterals | 7 | | 4 | |
| 2. Female Heads | | | | |
| a. Nuclear Families | 3 | | 0 | |
| b. Nuclear Families with Dependent Collaterals | 0 | | 0 | |
| Total | 95 | (73.6%) | 69 | (65.1%) |
| III. Three-Generational | | | | |
| 1. Male Heads | | | | |
| a. Patrilocally Extended | 2 | | 32 | |
| b. Includes Unmarried Children with Offspring | 0 | | 1 | |
| 2. Female Heads | | | | |
| a. Matrilocally Extended | 0 | | 1 | |
| b. Includes Unmarried Children with Offspring | 4 | | 0 | |
| Total | 6 | (4.7%) | 34 | (32.1%) |

or, more frequently, unmarried daughters who have moved into their parents' home with illegitimate children. In the case of unmarried daughters, the men who fathered their children are usually working away from the village on a sugar estate, in Georgetown, or at a place like Mackenzie City. This type of three-generational household exists in sharp contrast to the patrilocally extended type characteristic of East Indians, and it helps to explain, in part, the discrepancy in statistics between the African rural villages and Mackenzie City.

As is shown in Tables 7 and 8, the predominant type of household for both Africans and East Indians is a two-generational unit containing a typical nuclear family. Under particular circumstances, for both groups, collateral relatives may be added to such a unit, but they are not critical to its structure. The statistical frequency with which this type appears for each group might easily be taken as support for the conclusion that there is really very little difference between the Afro-Guianese and the East Indians with respect to family activities: In other words, the structure of the domestic unit is valid for both groups. Such a conclusion, however, fails to take into account the extent to which these different household types represent functional phases in the developmental cycle of the domestic group.

Figure 3 illustrates the developmental cycle of the East Indian domestic group. If marriage is considered as the point of initiation for the developmental cycle, it is clear that among East Indians, even among those who live in the industrial setting of Plantation Skeldon, very few married couples without children set up inde-

FIGURE 3. DEVELOPMENTAL CYCLE OF EAST INDIAN DOMESTIC GROUP

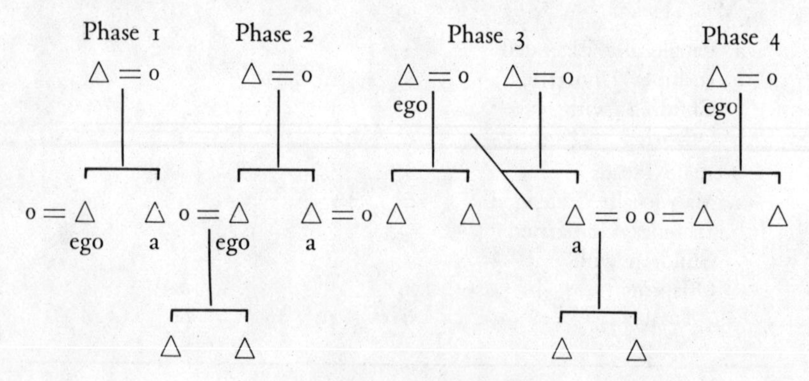

pendent households.[11] Most newlyweds continue to live in the home of the husband's parents (Phase 1). When children are born to this union, the two-generational household is transformed into a patrilocally extended unit (Phase 2). Segmentation of the patrilocally extended unit (Phase 3) varies according to a variety of circumstances. One important factor involves the quality of affective bonds between father and son and between parents-in-law and daughter-in-law. Another factor, which will be discussed later in the chapter, concerns the degree to which affective bonds are reinforced by economic cooperation between ego and his father. The number of male siblings within the household also affects segmentation because it determines the extent to which there is pressure for living space. Generally speaking, the patrilocally extended household tends to segment when one of ego's brothers, who is residing at home, has married and begins to have children. This introduces Phase 4: Ego moves into a house of his own, and his family remains a nuclear unit until his own sons begin to marry and have children.

Thus, the developmental cycle of the East Indian domestic group is one that involves an alternation between two-generational and three-generational units. Nuclear families grow into patrilocally extended groups which segment to reproduce new nuclear families. The one-generational unit emerges only when elderly persons have no issue or when, for one reason or another, married children refuse to live with their parents. In the event that a family contains only daughters, an effort is usually made to contract a marriage whereby the son-in-law will be willing to move into the home of his wife. Generally, a young man will agree to such an arrangement only when his own parents are too poor to provide him with an inheritance. Depending upon affective bonds, such an individual may or may not legally inherit property from his father-in-law. If not, it will make little difference, since his sons will more than likely inherit property from his father-in-law through their mother. We shall have

[11] African and East Indian marriage practices are extremely different in cultural content. A description has not been included here because adequate material is already available in print. For an excellent description of African practices, see Raymond T. Smith's *The Negro Family in British Guiana* (London: Routledge and Kegan Paul, 1956), pp. 167–87. For material on the East Indians, see Raymond T. Smith and C. Jayawardena's "Hindu Marriage Customs in British Guiana," *Social and Economic Studies,* 7 (1958), 178–94. Also see Raymond T. Smith and C. Jayawardena, "Marriage and the Family Amongst East Indians in British Guiana," *Social and Economic Studies,* 8 (1959), 321–76.

occasion to discuss the inheritance of property more extensively in the context of economic activities.

The developmental cycle of the Afro-Guianese domestic group, when compared to that of the East Indians, is much more difficult to describe. The reason for this is that the fundamental structures involved are complicated by pattern variations. As noted in Tables 7 and 8, household heads among the Afro-Guianese are predominantly males. However, units of all types occasionally appear with female heads. The total number of patrilocally and matrilocally extended units is not significant; but, when they do appear, they appear with equal frequency. In one way or another, these variations are related to the tendency among lower-class Africans to enter into a series of conjugal unions before contracting a legitimate marriage. In Mackenzie City, for example, 12 per cent of the household heads sampled were living in consensual unions with women. An additional 17 per cent reported that they had children by women other than the ones they eventually married. These percentages were slightly higher for the Ann's Grove and Eversham samples. The domestic group, in any society, is the major vehicle by which a child's jural status is established. It is to be expected, therefore, that the developmental cycle of the domestic group will reflect such practices as serial polygyny. However, unless these practices prevail as cultural norms, they are not likely to define the fundamental structures involved in the developmental process. Among the Afro-Guianese, serial polygyny is not accepted as a cultural norm, and its practice does not enhance the status of the individuals involved, particularly the women.

At the risk of oversimplifying the pattern variations, Figure 4 illustrates the phases more or less characteristic of the Afro-Guianese developmental cycle. The cycle is initiated (Phase 1) by a legitimate marriage. Normally, this serves to create a one-generational household unit (a type noticeably absent among the East Indians). In Mackenzie City, this rule applies equally to cases involving consensual unions. In the villages, however, there are variations on the rule. If a consensual union is involved, and if the male is absent from the village for prolonged periods because of work, the couple tend to reside in the home of the girl's parents. This creates a unit similar to the one illustrated in Phase 3, and the girl's parents generally exert pressure on their daughter to legitimize the union or terminate the relationship. On the other hand, if the couple is married, and if the husband is absent for long periods, residence with in-laws appears

FIGURE 4. DEVELOPMENTAL CYCLE OF AFRO-GUIANESE DOMESTIC GROUP

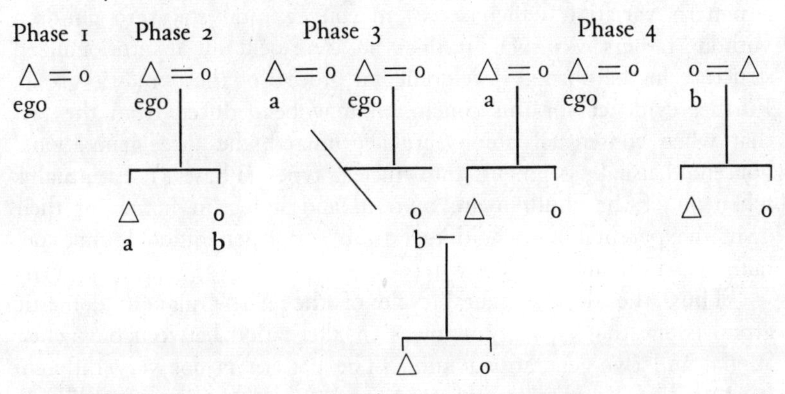


to be determined primarily on the basis of affective ties, property considerations, or the husband's jural status (i.e., whether or not he is an illegitimate child). When the husband works in the village or close to home, however, a neolocal rule applies. The one-generational household that this rule creates tends to be short-lived. As soon as children are born, the unit is transformed into a two-generational nuclear family practicing neolocal residence (Phase 2). Nuclear families of this type with female heads tend to be variations resulting from death, separation, or, in three instances, from the fact that the female has never had a husband but has children, usually by several men, living with her in a house she inherited from her parents.

The three-generational household among the Afro-Guianese (Phase 3), in contrast to the situation among East Indians, is not normally a phase in the developmental process of the domestic unit. It occurs most frequently in response to the problem of serial polygyny. No less than 62 per cent of the three-generational households contained unmarried children living at home with their illegitimate offspring. In seven out of ten cases, these unmarried children were daughters.[12] These facts would seem to suggest that among the Afro-

[12] In his study of Negro families in three Guianese villages, Raymond Smith makes much of the "matrifocal" pattern of domestic relations. There is a rather vast literature dealing with this subject matter, and in it the matrifocal pattern is reported to exist widely among New World Negroes. I must confess that I find much of this literature ambiguous and, at times, somewhat barren of theoretical value. Professor Smith takes the matrifocal pattern to mean that a woman in the status of mother is usually the de facto leader of the domestic unit (*op. cit.*, p. 223). Other researchers have suggested that matrifocality involves a three-generational domestic unit with a

Guianese the three-generational household, more often than not, is a pattern variation which serves to convey jural status to children without fathers. As such, it does not represent an institutionalized structure in the normal developmental process of the domestic group. Further evidence for this conclusion may be deduced from the fact that when consensual unions are legitimized, the three-generational household usually segments into nuclear types (Phase 4). Eventually, when all of the children are married and living in homes of their own, the parental household reverts to a one-generational unit containing a husband and his wife.

Thus, the developmental cycle of the Afro-Guianese domestic group is one that typically involves an alternation between one-generational and two-generational units. The pattern is not very different from that of Western urban societies. As a rule, nuclear families do not develop into extended households except under the circumstances resulting from consensual unions. In contrast to the East Indians, there is no pattern of patrilocal residence.

An important consideration that must be kept in mind with respect to the domestic group is the fact that it does not exist in a social vacuum. Outside of the domestic group is the politico-jural domain of the larger society. The most immediate context of the politico-jural domain, from the point of view of the domestic group, is the local community. As Fortes has emphasized, every individual is simultaneously a person in the domestic domain and a person in the politico-jural domain.[13] The status of the individual within the one is defined, in part, by the norms which prevail within the other. There exists a reciprocal relationship between the two. If close attachments are maintained between fathers and sons or between male siblings within the domestic domain, it is only because these attachments are recognized as having some kind of validity in the politico-jural domain.

---

female head (de facto and de jure). If Professor Smith's view is adopted, there would seem to be little discrepancy between his data and the findings reported here. If, on the other hand, matrifocality is taken to represent a three-generational structural type, then the data presented here do not confirm its widespread existence among lower-class Negroes in Guiana. In either case, I find it difficult to accept Professor Smith's generalization, "In the sector of Guianese society with which we are dealing, men have very little authority over household groups, or in other spheres of political and economic life" (*ibid.*, p. 143). The de facto authority of older African males with respect to children's property and the leadership they exercise in the political and economic life of the village are sufficient evidence to conclude that the authority of African females is not extended as broadly as Professor Smith appears to suggest.

[13] *Op. cit.*, p. 12.

The reverse, of course, is also true. On the other hand, if no special value is attached to the relationship between siblings of the same sex or between siblings of a different sex, it probably will be the case that such relationships have little functional validity in the politico-jural domain. In other words, the structure of the domestic group is crucial to the extension of kinship ties, and these, in turn, will help shape the character of the community.

As a function of the residence patterns associated with the domestic group, rather sharp structural differences exist between East Indian and Afro-Guianese communities with respect to the extension of consanguineal and affinal kinship ties. These structural differences may be gleaned from the data presented in Tables 9 and 10. Table 9 presents the residence of the married sons and daughters of the household heads interviewed in the villages of Clonbrook and Cromarty. Table 10 presents similar data collected in the Afro-Guianese villages of Ann's Grove and Eversham.

TABLE 9. RESIDENCE OF MARRIED SONS AND DAUGHTERS OF EAST INDIANS IN CLONBROOK AND CROMARTY

| | *Sons* | | *Daughters* | |
|---|---|---|---|---|
| | *N* | *Per Cent* | *N* | *Per Cent* |
| Home | 34 | 61.8 | 5 | 8.6 |
| Village | 10 | 18.2 | 4 | 6.9 |
| Neighboring Villages | 5 | 9.1 | 9 | 15.5 |
| Outside the District | 6 | 10.9 | 40 | 69.0 |
| Total | 55 | 100.0 | 58 | 100.0 |

TABLE 10. RESIDENCE OF MARRIED SONS AND DAUGHTERS OF AFRO-GUIANESE IN ANN'S GROVE AND EVERSHAM

| | *Sons* | | *Daughters* | |
|---|---|---|---|---|
| | *N* | *Per Cent* | *N* | *Per Cent* |
| Home | 2 | 2.8 | 6 | 10.9 |
| Village | 14 | 20.9 | 25 | 45.4 |
| Neighboring Villages | 2 | 2.8 | 4 | 7.3 |
| Outside the District | 50 | 73.5 | 20 | 36.4 |
| Total | 68 | 100.0 | 55 | 100.0 |

It may be noted in Table 9 that almost 90 per cent of the married sons of East Indian household heads live at home or very close to the homes of their fathers. Less than 11 per cent live outside of the district. The district, here, refers to an area with a radius of approximately five miles from the village. Married daughters, unlike married sons, tend to live outside of the district. Thus, with respect to the marriage of daughters, the East Indian village tends to be an exogamous unit. The situation among the Afro-Guianese is quite different. Approximately 74 per cent of the married sons of household heads live outside of the district. Most of these individuals have migrated to urban areas or into the interior in search of employment. Many of them will return to the village from time to time but will not settle there permanently until their middle or late years. On the other hand, only 36 per cent of the married daughters of Afro-Guianese household heads live outside of the district. A substantial number, 45 per cent, live in the village but not in the households of their parents.

In light of these data, it seems safe to conclude that the East Indian local community, as a domain of politico-jural relationships, tends to be comprised of related patrilocally extended households. There is little evidence to suggest that this gives rise to the organization of lineages. However, there is a strong patrilineal emphasis. Adult male siblings live close to one another and to their fathers. The bonds between fathers and sons are reinforced by the practice of village exogamy. Marriages are arranged for daughters outside of the village and, if possible, outside of the district. Conversely, the women born in the village are seldom taken as wives by the men of the village. As a consequence, patrilineal ties between households in the village are much more prevalent and much more important than affinal ties. This tends to create a situation whereby the East Indian village is divided into a series of family clusters. Within the clusters, domestic units are related to one another by consanguineal bonds between males. Between each cluster there are few, if any, relationships based on kinship. It will be shown subsequently how the relational bonds within these family clusters tend to be reinforced by inheritance patterns and by patterns of economic cooperation. However, it should be noted in passing that the low level of relational bonds between family clusters is an important factor related to the factionalism that seems to be so characteristic of East Indian villages.

By way of contrast, the Afro-Guianese village displays the characteristics of a bilateral kindred. Since the village is not an endogamous unit, it does not constitute a deme. As a consequence, kinship bonds are extremely diffuse. While practically everyone in the village is related by blood or marriage, kinship ties appear to be important only when they are affectively reinforced. Also, it must be remembered that many of the younger men and women tend to leave the village to live in Georgetown, Mackenzie City, and in other places. The ties between these individuals and their village kin are maintained in numerous ways. The homes of these individuals are almost always open to village relatives. Young men who migrate to Mackenzie City frequently live with older brothers and sisters or with uncles until they are able to obtain housing for themselves. Similarly, relatives who live away from the village often send young children to live in the village with grandparents or with others.

The closeness of relationships between relatives within the bilateral network is also expressed in terms of financial considerations. For example, 75 per cent of the workers interviewed at Mackenzie City send money on a regular basis to relatives living in coastal communities. Parents and children are the most frequent recipients, but many individuals also send money, from time to time, to siblings and collaterals when they are in need. Again, while these ties appear to be maintained primarily for affective reasons, other considerations are also important. Most individuals who live away from the village continue to have access to children's property that has been left under the stewardship of relatives. Legally, they are free to return to this property whenever they wish. However, it is always easier to return when good relationships have been maintained with those in charge. The fact of the matter is that many of the Afro-Guianese who leave the village do return to it eventually. In Ann's Grove, for example, 57 per cent of the married siblings of household heads live in the village. The percentage tends to be higher for males than it is for females, notwithstanding the fact that the former tend to migrate from the village in larger numbers during their younger years. In Eversham, the most influential proprietor in the village had spent more than forty years of his life living and working in Georgetown.

The family and kinship structures which differentiate East Indians from Afro-Guianese are necessary but insufficient conditions for the integration of minimal cultural sections. Kinship structures may explain why Africans and East Indians seldom intermarry, but they fail to explain very adequately why it is difficult for large numbers of both groups to live conveniently in the same village community. As was noted earlier, the villages tend to be either predominantly African or predominantly East Indian in population. All of the villages along the Courantyne Coast were once inhabited by Afro-Guianese. Today, most of them are almost exclusively East Indian in population. When large numbers of both groups live together in the same village, the community is usually riven by hostile factionalism. Ann's Grove and Clonbrook are cases in point. In the 1930's, these two villages were organized under the same local authority. The factionalism was so great that the Local Government Board was forced to recognize two separate and independent local authorities. The villages of Beterverwagting and Triumph were undergoing the same process of segmentation in 1960.

## THE VILLAGE ECONOMY

In order to understand why it is difficult for Africans and East Indians to live together within the same village community, it is necessary to consider certain aspects of the village economy. First, a few general comments need to be made. When discussing the economic activities carried out in Guianese villages, it must be clearly understood that these residential units are not economically self-sufficient. This is rather obvious in the case of plantations and industrial communities, but it is no less true of other types of communities. In the unorganized villages and local authorities, individuals consume a wide variety of goods that are not produced locally. Similarly, much of what these villages produce is not locally consumed. Beyond production and consumption, economic activities in the village are almost always offset by their relationship to economic activities in the larger society. This is particularly true with respect to labor. Farm operators are rarely fully occupied by their farms. When they are not planting or harvesting crops, most of them seek out some type of wage employment to supplement their incomes. Underemployment, particularly in rural areas, is a major problem in British Guiana.[14]

In order to make ends meet, peasants frequently engage in a wide variety of economic activities, including the cultivation of crops, huck-

[14] *Report to the Government of British Guiana on Employment, Unemployment and Underemployment in the Colony in 1956* (Geneva: International Labour Office, 1957).

stering, and various kinds of wage employment. This makes it impossible to classify them in terms of simple occupational categories. However, it is possible to develop general categories which can be used to describe what kinds of economic activity they typically engage in as a primary source of livelihood. Thus, for purposes of this analysis, cash crop farmers are differentiated from subsistence farmers on the basis that the former not only cultivate crops for subsistence, but, in addition, they strive to produce a surplus which can be sold for an anticipated profit. The subsistence farmer may sell crops also, but he eats most of what he produces, and he sells not for a profit but for the cash he needs to pay taxes and purchase the necessities he cannot produce. In contrast to these two types is the mixed specialist. The mixed specialist grows food for subsistence or for a little cash, but his primary source of livelihood is an income derived from some form of nonagricultural employment. Finally, the nonagriculturalist is an individual whose livelihood is dependent entirely upon such income as may be derived from nonagricultural activities. In terms of these distinctions, Table 11 presents the data collected on the primary economic activities of household heads in the four nonindustrial villages investigated.

In light of the data presented in Table 11, except for minor variations largely due to ecological factors, the economic patterns which differentiate African and East Indian villages emerge quite clearly. More than one-third of all household heads in both African villages are subsistence farmers. Only one East Indian can be counted

TABLE II. PRIMARY ECONOMIC ACTIVITY OF HOUSEHOLD HEADS IN NONINDUSTRIAL VILLAGES

| | *Afro-Guianese* | | | | *East Indian* | | | |
|---|---|---|---|---|---|---|---|---|
| | *Ann's Grove* | | *Eversham* | | *Clonbrook* | | *Cromarty* | |
| | *N* | *Per Cent* | *N* | *Per Cent* | *N* | *Per Cent* | *N* | *Per Cent* |
| Cash Crop Farmers | 2 | 3.4 | 7 | 25.9 | 22 | 53.7 | 14 | 48.3 |
| Subsistence Farmers | 20 | 34.5 | 9 | 33.3 | 0 | 0.0 | 1 | 3.4 |
| Mixed Specialists | 16 | 27.6 | 7 | 25.9 | 10 | 24.3 | 10 | 34.5 |
| Nonagricultural | 20 | 34.5 | 4 | 14.9 | 9 | 22.0 | 4 | 13.8 |
| Total | 58 | 100.0 | 27 | 100.0 | 41 | 100.0 | 29 | 100.0 |

in this category. At the same time, approximately half of all the East Indian household heads in the two villages studied are cash crop farmers. There are more cash crop farmers among the Africans in Eversham than in Ann's Grove, but this is because new land has been made available recently in that area. Even so, the percentage of cash crop farmers among Africans in Eversham does not approximate that of East Indians in the neighboring village of Cromarty. It should be noted also that the seven cash crop farmers in Eversham only cultivate a total of 59 acres of riceland, compared to the 320 acres cultivated by fourteen cash crop farmers in Cromarty. Similarly, the twenty subsistence farmers in Ann's Grove work only 39 acres of land, compared to the 204 acres cultivated by twenty-two cash crop farmers in Clonbrook. In other words, not only do more East Indians do cash crop farming than Africans, but they cultivate considerably more acreage. This generalization would appear to hold regardless of variations in village type. At Plantation Skeldon, for example, one out of every five East Indian household heads, in addition to working on the sugar estate, cultivates an average of five acres of riceland. At the same time, not a single African interviewed at Skeldon cultivates land.

The type of crops which each group prefers to cultivate is also related to these differences. As was previously noted, next to sugar, rice in British Guiana's major cash crop. It provides the second largest source of employment in the country. However, in Ann's Grove, not a single African informant cultivates rice. All of the acreage worked by African farmers of all types is given over to the cultivation of ground provisions (mainly cassava) and permanent trees (coconut, orange, mango, breadfruit, banana, etc.). The market for these crops is primarily local and generally poor. Compared to rice, the cultivation of these crops, particularly permanent trees, has one important advantage: Older people and young children may do the work with a minimum of effort. By way of contrast, 63 per cent of the acreage cultivated by East Indians in Clonbrook is given over to rice cultivation. In Eversham, most of the Africans who farm cultivate rice. However, the acreage they work is so limited that not a single one of them owns a tractor. In Cromarty, on the other hand, twelve of the fourteen Indian cash crop farmers own tractors.

The occupational histories of individuals are extremely revealing in conjunction with these comparisons. In Ann's Grove, ten of the twenty African subsistence farmers are men who have spent most of their productive years working in the diamond and gold fields. Five are men who have retired from government employment. In Eversham, practically all of the African subsistence farmers have spent the majority of their productive years working in the interior or cutting cane on the sugar plantations. The same occupational profile is manifest among the mixed specialists. Of the sixteen mixed specialists in Ann's Grove, six are diamond seekers who cultivate crops only when they are at home, three are tailors, and three are fishermen. By way of contrast, five of the ten mixed specialists in Clonbrook (Indian) are men who exchange their labor for land on the neighboring coconut estates. In Cromarty (Indian), most of the mixed specialists supplement their small farm incomes by working in rice mills. In Ann's Grove, among the Africans who are nonagriculturalists, six are artisans, six work for the government, three are cane cutters, two are teachers, two are diamond seekers, and one is a baker. In Clonbrook, of the nine nonagriculturalists, three are shopkeepers, two are artisans, one is a huckster who also operates a taxi service, one is a cane cutter, and one works for the government. In other words, East Indians tend to seek employment involving activities related to agriculture and the acquisition of land, while Africans do not.

The pattern of these economic activities is functionally related to the kinship structures described in the previous section. Rice cultivation is primarily a family proposition. This is particularly the case among sugar estate workers who combine wage employment with cash crop farming. Data collected in 1960 show that a typical farmer who cultivates five acres of rice with family labor on drained land can earn and save more money than by working as a field hand on a sugar estate. Under the same conditions, ten acres of land under rice cultivation will often suffice to finance a tractor. The tractor, however, will be profitable only if the farmer can expand his holdings and, in the meantime, rent it to others. However, because of the various tasks involved in harvesting rice, the farmer who expands his acreage must either employ agricultural workers or depend upon his relatives to help him with the work. In the event that he works with relatives who provide free labor, he can maximize his profits and invest them in more land. Thus, there tends to be a relationship between cash crop farming and the organization of extended kinship groups as corporate economic units. The strength of this relationship is indicated by the data presented in Table 12.

TABLE 12. HOUSEHOLD HEADS WHO BELONG TO EXTENDED KINSHIP GROUPS FUNCTIONING AS CORPORATE ECONOMIC UNITS IN NONINDUSTRIAL VILLAGES

| | | *East Indians* | | | *Afro-Guianese* | | |
|---|---|---|---|---|---|---|---|
| | | | *Corporate Units* | | | *Corporate Units* | |
| | *Total* | *Total Units* | *N* | *Per Cent* | *Total Units* | *N* | *Per Cent* |
| Cash Crop Farmers | 45 | 36 | 25 | 69.4 | 9 | 6 | 66.7 |
| Subsistence Farmers | 30 | 1 | 0 | 0.0 | 29 | 0 | 0.0 |
| Mixed Specialists | 43 | 20 | 6 | 30.0 | 23 | 2 | 8.7 |
| Nonagriculturalists | 37 | 13 | 3 | 23.1 | 24 | 0 | 0.0 |
| Total | 155 | 70 | 34 | 48.6 | 85 | 8 | 9.4 |

As Table 12 shows, more than two-thirds of the cash crop farmers interviewed in the East Indian villages of Clonbrook and Cromarty belong to extended kinship groups that function as corporate economic units. A similar pattern was found to exist among the few Africans who plant rice in the village of Eversham. For East Indians, rice cultivation represents a major avenue of economic mobility, and, perhaps as much as any other single factor, it has contributed to the persistence of patrilineally extended kinship structures in the Indian community. This point can best be illustrated graphically. Figure 5 shows the organization of an East Indian extended family which functions as a corporate economic group.

This family was founded in 1904, when a sugar worker completed his period of indenture and purchased a piece of land in the predominantly African village of Kiltairn. Subsequently, he leased 75 acres of undeveloped Crown land from the government for the purpose of keeping a few head of cattle and clearing some of it for rice cultivation. As his sons grew old enough to help him, the entire area was cleared of bush and put under rice cultivation. By the time the two oldest sons married, some of the profits from the original 75 acres had been used to rent Crown land for them in two neighboring villages. By 1952, when the father died, the family holdings had expanded to include 300 acres of Crown land. Of this, approximately 125 acres had been cleared and brought under cultivation. After the father's death, the land was divided among the brothers, but they continued to work it as a group and invest profits from it jointly.

FIGURE 5. EAST INDIAN CORPORATE GROUP

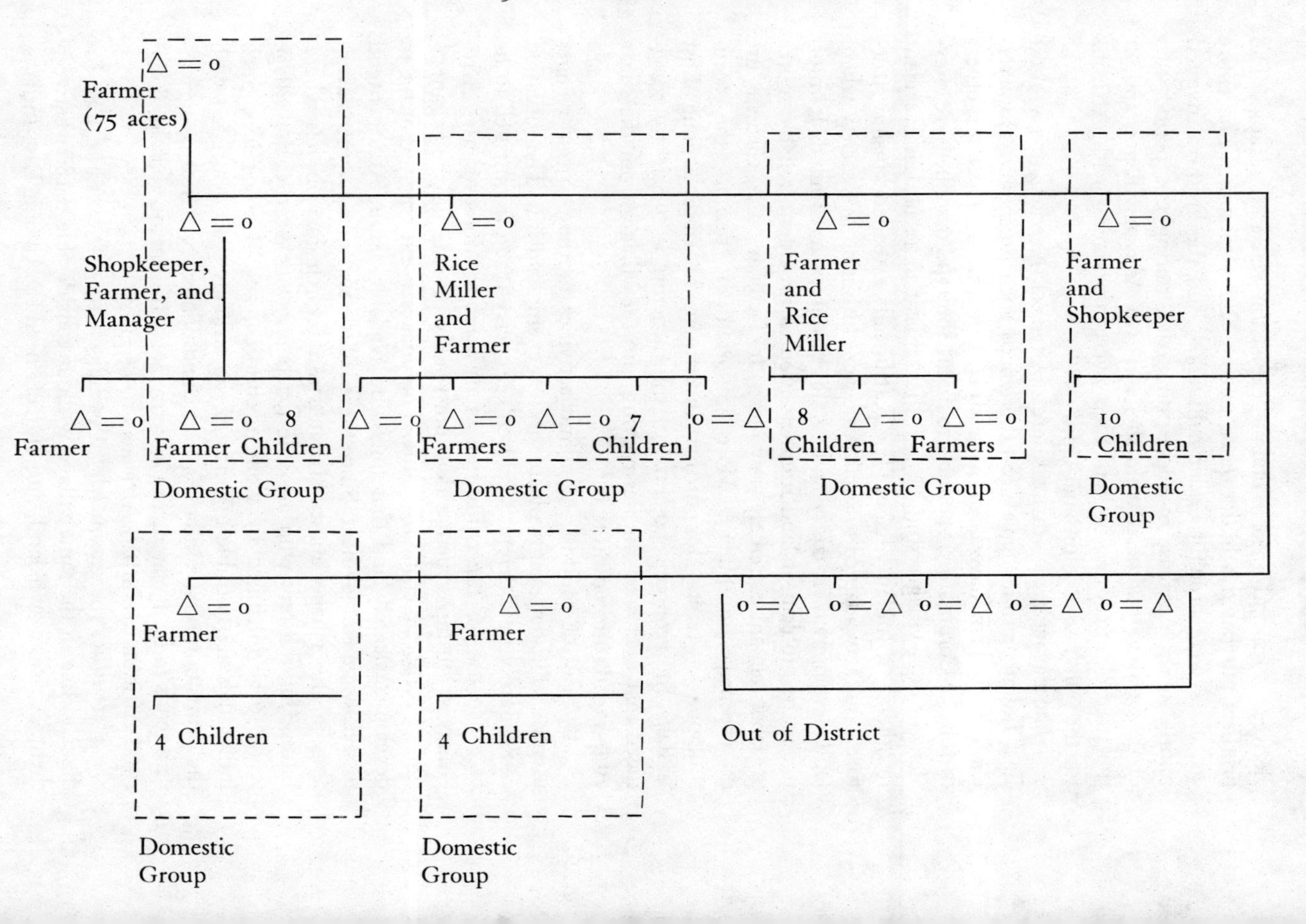

Between 1952 and 1960, economic expansion was rather rapid. The brothers purchased a bulldozer, a tractor, and a combine. The entire 300 acres were brought under cultivation, and the brothers invested jointly in the purchase of a rice mill. Also, during this period, two of the brothers purchased rum shops in two African villages, and, at the time of interview, both of them were negotiating with Africans for the purchase of additional land.

The particulars of this case are not typical. Needless to say, most East Indian families have not experienced such prosperity. However, enough of them have been successful to provide a model for others to follow. Corporate economic groups of the type described are prevalent in both villages studied, and they appear to be no less prevalent in other East Indian villages. The patrilineally extended kinship structure is suitably adapted to small-scale rice cultivation in a society where land development is costly and capital resources are limited. It minimizes the problem of land fragmentation. It provides a reliable source of labor at an extremely low cost. It facilitates the efficient use of expensive machinery. More important, it permits the accumulation of capital for further investment in land. Among East Indians, the economic potential of this structure is sufficiently recognized that nucleated families moving into the villages from the sugar estates tend to reconstitute it.

By way of contrast, economic activities in the African villages involve subsistence agriculture or wage employment. The situation could hardly be different. Children's property is too fragmented to be of much use for the cultivation of cash crops. Moreover, the Afro-Guianese kinship structure does not readily provide for the organization of corporate economic units. This makes it extremely difficult to develop uncleared land that might be available. Thus, Africans tend to seek wage employment. Since there is little wage employment available in the village, most Africans must search for jobs elsewhere. Except for the few who are able to obtain work nearby, the village tends to be inhabited by women, children, and elderly males. Such individuals are not able to perform the arduous tasks associated with the cultivation of several acres of riceland. Thus, for Africans, agriculture tends to be a way of life in retirement. In a manner of speaking, rural Africans are urban Africans out of place.

Herein lies the reason why it is difficult for Africans and East Indians to live in the same village without considerable tension between them. Africans own land, and Indians need it. Among East Indians, rice cultivation simultaneously integrates their kinship structure and provides a major avenue of economic mobility. The crucial factor in the equation is land. Without land, rice cultivation is impossible, economic mobility is difficult, the kinship structure is fragmented, and families must live in much the same way they have been forced to live on the sugar estates. On the other hand, land is also important to the Africans. It provides them with economic security. With children's property, Africans can obtain subsistence when it is most needed, i.e., when they are unemployed or too old to walk about the country in search of employment.

In this way, then, economic activities place Africans and East Indians in opposition to one another within the context of the local community. In the village, East Indians see Africans as an obstacle to their economic progress and a threat to the wellbeing of their domestic units. When the author was discussing this with Indian informants, time and again they asked, "If me dawta take up with black man, who will take she fo wife?" The implication is clear: The marriage of such a woman cannot easily be arranged, and her continued residence within the domestic group fragments what her brothers expect to share. Indians have a saying which expresses their concern about Africans in a slightly different manner, "Dey who own de land, own de country." On the other hand, village Africans also perceive a threat. An elderly African in Ann's Grove stated it in the following terms:

> Me very fearful of de coolieman taking over de whole country. Dey band themselves together to get all we own. Dey so wicked I want to cry. I cry for me children. I see the terror—the spirit of their activities. Dey rent we land and take it away. Dey loan black people money and take all dey own. Dey smart people, you know. Cunning. Dey work cheap, eat cheap, and save and save. Black people can't punish themselves so. If we punish ourselves like coolieman, we slaves again.

The opposition of Africans and East Indians in the rural sector has given rise to a series of stereotypes which further condition their relationships to one another. Generally, village Africans tend to think of East Indians as a miserly people who devote all of their time and energy to work and who are so bent upon accumulating land and money that they are not able to enjoy the fruits of their labor. East Indians, on the other hand, view Africans as a people without ambition, lazy, wasteful, and so preoccupied with sporting that they are unable to put anything aside in order to improve themselves. On the surface, there would appear to be some truth to these stereotypes. Table 13, for example, compares the six village samples with respect to the number of individuals who reported that they saved money quite regularly.

As is shown in Table 13, the percentage of Africans who save money in the villages of Ann's Grove and Eversham is considerably lower than the percentage of East Indians who save in the villages of Clonbrook and Cromarty. Moreover, the median annual savings reported by Africans who save is very much lower than that reported by East Indians. The situation is somewhat reversed when African bauxite workers at Mackenzie are compared to East Indian sugar workers at Plantation Skeldon. More bauxite workers save money than sugar workers, and they save considerably more of it. The facts reflect the differential economic status that exists between the two groups. African industrial workers, when compared to East Indian sugar workers, are rich. However, when compared to East Indian villagers, African villagers are poor. This, in part, explains the stereotypes which each group applies to the other.

However, stereotypes are not entirely founded on the misunder-

TABLE 13. COMPARISON OF EAST INDIANS AND AFRO-GUIANESE WITH RESPECT TO THE NUMBER OF INDIVIDUALS WHO REPORTED THAT THEY WERE ABLE TO SAVE MONEY

| | *Total Sample* | *Per Cent Who Save* | *Median Annual Savings (B.W.I.)* |
|---|---|---|---|
| Ann's Grove (African) | 58 | 39.7 | $100.00 |
| Clonbrook (Indian) | 41 | 80.5 | 250.00 |
| Eversham (African) | 27 | 25.9 | 250.00 |
| Cromarty (Indian) | 29 | 65.5 | 500.00 |
| Mackenzie City (African) | 129 | 81.4 | 288.00 |
| Plantation Skeldon (Indian) | 106 | 61.3 | 100.00 |

standing that derives from differential economic status. Nor can they be explained away solely in terms of the economic activities characteristic of African and Indian villages. More fundamental values are involved. The fact of the matter is that Africans, when they have money, consume conspicuously. Moreover, they tend to consume what they have when they have it. Considerable money is spent on rum, clothing, and weekly dances. The East Indians, on the other hand, also consume conspicuously, but they do so according to an entirely different set of values. The values which tend to regulate East Indian consumption are derived, in large part, from the deeply rooted beliefs which Indians hold with respect to their religious practices. These also serve to integrate minimal cultural sections.

## RELIGIOUS ACTIVITIES

Christianity, Hinduism, and Islam are the religions with which most Guianese nominally identify. Until recently, however, adherence to Christian beliefs has been accepted as the only valid and respectable form of religious worship. During the period of the indenture system, Hinduism and Islam were tolerated, but both Africans and Europeans viewed Hindus and Muslims as pagans. Marriages performed by pandits and imams were not legally valid, and this continues to be the case unless the pandit or imam has been licensed as an official marriage officer. Hindu and Muslim holidays, unlike many Christian holidays, continue to go without official recognition. Although Christian denominational schools have received government support for more than a century, it has only been within the past ten to fifteen years that the government has provided small grants for the support of approved Hindi and Arabic schools. In spite of these conditions, however, Christian influence has not made very deep inroads into the Hindu and Muslim faiths. Table 14 presents a comparison of East Indian and African informants with respect to their religious identification.

As is shown in Table 14, the Africans are almost exclusively Christian in their religious affiliation. Practically every known Christian denomination is represented among them, but the vast majority belong to the Anglican Church. A substantial number of Africans also belong to the Roman Catholic Church and the Church of Scotland. East Indians, on the other hand, are predominantly non-Christian.

TABLE 14. RELIGIOUS IDENTIFICATION OF EAST INDIAN AND AFRICAN INFORMANTS

| | *East Indians* | | *Africans* | |
|---|---|---|---|---|
| | *N* | *Per Cent* | *N* | *Per Cent* |
| Hindu Sanatan | 111 | 63.1 | 0 | 0.0 |
| Hindu-Arya Samaj | 10 | 5.7 | 0 | 0.0 |
| Muslim | 32 | 18.2 | 2 | 0.9 |
| Christian | 23 | 13.0 | 212 | 99.1 |
| Total | 176 | 100.0 | 214 | 100.0 |

Only 13 per cent of those interviewed identified themselves as Christians, and a number of these explicitly stated that they had converted to Christianity only to get ahead in their jobs. Otherwise, they continue to practice their Hindu and Muslim beliefs. Almost two-thirds of the East Indians included in the study follow the Sanatan Dharm Maha Sabha. Slightly less than 6 per cent belong to the Arya Samaj.[15]

The majority of East Indians are Sanatans who claim to subscribe to the ideals of Brahmanical Hinduism. This does not mean, however, that they scrupulously observe orthodox religious prescriptions. To be an orthodox Hindu, a man must be born into one of four castes: Brahman, Kshattriya, Vaisya, or Sudra. In addition, he must conform to the religious prescriptions of the caste into which he was born with respect to marriage, food, occupation, and the observance of domestic ceremonies pertaining to births, deaths, ancestors, the worship of household and other gods, and the offering of daily prayers and sacrifices. Needless to say, the ideals of caste stratification have been ex-

[15] The Arya Samaj is a reformist movement that was founded in India during the latter part of the nineteenth century. Its founder, Dayanand, rejected the idea of caste as well as the idea of Brahmanical authority. He preached the belief in one God who was to be worshipped without the use of images. The four Vedas were to be taken as God's knowledge, and the various deities referred to in the Vedas were to be understood as nothing more than manifestations of the Eternal Reality. Thus, the Arya Samaj strips Hinduism of its polytheistic beliefs and most of its traditional rituals, and it represents a direct attack upon Brahmanical orthodoxy. The Sanatan Dharma Sabha came into existence as a protest against the teaching of Dayanand and in defense of orthodox Hinduism. See Peter Ruhomon, *Centenary History of the East Indians in British Guiana 1838–1938* (Georgetown: Daily Chronicle, 1946), pp. 255–58. For a more extensive analysis of the continuities and discontinuities in religious beliefs among East Indians, see Chandra Jayawardena, "Religious Belief and Social Change: Aspects of the Development of Hinduism in British Guiana," *Comparative Studies in Society and History*, 8 (1966), 211–40.

tremely modified by the conditions that have existed in British Guiana.

The major restrictions pertaining to social intercourse between members of different castes have disappeared almost completely in British Guiana. Similarly, caste rituals and specialized religious ceremonies have also disappeared. Nevertheless, many elements of caste continue to persist. The ideals of high caste, particularly, are widely accepted. The Sanatan Hindu will not claim that all pandits are of Brahman origin. However, he will claim that all pandits are Brahmans. In the village of Clonbrook, several informants considered every member of the village council to be of high caste. Brahman and Kshattriya names are widely recognized by the villagers, and practically every shopkeeper in the villages studied carries a high caste name.

Elements of caste are manifested also in more subtle ways. Dark skin color, for example, tends to be associated with low caste origin. Thus, when an informant's daughter married a Madrassi, he stated, "He little dark but he good boy and he got plenty of land to make up for he darkness." Wealth is also associated with high caste origin: "When a daughter marries high the celebration is plenty big." Poverty is frequently associated with the caste known as Chamar (Untouchables in India). For example, an informant in Clonbrook stated, "Me Chamar. All de poor people of this village belong to me group." Muslims are frequently considered to be of low caste origin. As one informant stated, "The Muslims are not of we race. They low caste people. We not marry them for sure—it would not be proper for we to mix-up with them."

There are other differences between Hindu and Christian religious activities that are expressive of different cultural values. Among the Africans, as among most Christians, religious activities are primarily public events. They take place in the church where the congregation gathers for worship at prescribed times. The Hindu temple is also a public place of worship. However, except for major festivals such as Phagwah (a festival in celebration of spring), most Hindu religious ceremonies are performed in the home rather than at the temple. The congregation in attendance, if it may be called that, is made up of relatives, very close friends, and an officiating pandit. The occasions for such a gathering are quite numerous: the "Ninth Day" (when a newborn child is given his astral name by a pandit), Mooran (when the child receives his first haircut), engagement and wedding ceremonies, funerals, Sraddha ceremonies (in memory of deceased ancestors), and Yags.

In British Guiana, most Yags are given in honor of Lord Hanuman. According to Hindu belief, Lord Hanuman was a devotee of Lord Rama—the latter being an incarnation of Vishnu. Legend has it that Rama gave Hanuman a bone from his body with the instructions, "Which ever of my devotees hold with your name in any cause, you will enter into their minds and free them from their difficulties and their troubles." Thus, when in difficulty or when thankful for some blessing such as a good crop, the Hindu will set out a colored flag as a symbol of prayer to Hanuman. In addition, if the family can afford it, a Yag will be sponsored. Depending upon the wealth of the family, the affair may last from one to several days, and a bamboo tent may be constructed to accommodate a large number of guests. Regardless of the size of the affair, however, a pandit is present to officiate and recite prayers. Friends and relatives are invited, and the "jajman," the man who sponsors the Yag, must provide them with food and drink. In addition, the "jajman" must also present the pandit with a gift as a token of appreciation for his services.

As was mentioned previously, the African tends to perceive the East Indian as a miserly sort of fellow who devotes all of his time and energy to work in order to accumulate wealth. This is not quite the case. The fact of the matter is that the East Indian must devote considerable time and energy to work in order to practice his religion. Saving money is a necessary part of Hinduism. When a child is born, a man must have a little money for the "Ninth Day." If a child is sick and is restored to health, the good Hindu, if he can afford it, should sponsor a small Yag as a devotion of thanksgiving to Lord Hanuman. When a child's hair is cut for the first time, at nine months of age, the celebration of Mooran may cost a man between twenty and thirty dollars (B.W.I.). The marriage of a daughter requires the payment of a dowry in addition to other costs. When a new house is completed, or when a man harvests an exceptionally good crop, the virtuous Hindu will celebrate his progress by having a Jandhi (Yag). This also will cost money.

Hinduism represents a belief system that is woven into almost every aspect of the East Indian's economic and social life. The virtuous Hindu is simultaneously a good man and a successful man. His conformity to prescribed religious practices is taken as evidence of his virtue. At the same time, his ability to conform is evidence of his economic progress. Without some accumulation of wealth, it is extremely difficult for the Hindu to fulfill his ritual obligations. The Hindu who continuously fails to fulfill such obligations is a Chamar. For example, a pandit stated in an interview, "Every good Hindu must put aside at least one-fourth of what he earns and live off the rest no matter how little it may be. Otherwise, he cannot meet his duties according to his station in life. Only the Chamar is unable to save. He squanders what little he has on all kinds of foolishness." By this logic, the poverty of the Chamar is both an indication of his lack of status and a reflection of his lack of virtue.

Christianity, as it is practiced by the Afro-Guianese, displays a very different combination of values. In the village, the good African is not often the individual who has achieved economic success. He is not the individual who owns a lot of land or who owns an electric power plant and who lives in a large house. Such Africans are few in the village, and they do not appear to be thought of as virtuous Christians. Under colonialism, Africans have had little opportunity to associate economic status with Christian piety. In fact, the opposite is the case. The missionaries who converted the Africans were poor, helpful, and pious. The planters, on the other hand, were rich, exploitive, and not very pious in their treatment of blacks.

In the villages studied, the most successful Africans are church leaders and teachers who share both their knowledge and their material resources with others. In Ann's Grove, the most wealthy African is a man who owns and operates a bakery. When interviewed, he stated, "The black people do not look to me. Me not like them at all. I work hard, save my money, and don't sport or waste time with them on foolishness. Me more like the coolieman." It did not come as a surprise when several African and East Indian informants agreed that the baker was more like a "coolieman." By the logic of East Indian beliefs, most Africans are Chamar. By the same logic, Christianity, as Africans practice it, represents a serious threat to the cultural identity of the East Indian community. This threat is most visible in the village schools.

## EDUCATIONAL ACTIVITIES

It will be recalled from the previous chapter that the school system in British Guiana was legally established by the Education Ordinance of 1855. Under this legislation, a system of dual control was provided, whereby the government contributed to the financial support of schools that were owned and operated by Christian churches. As of 1959, there existed 327 primary schools. Of these, 298 were operated by Christian denominational bodies with the aid of governmental funds for equipment, for the maintenance of buildings, and for the payment of teachers' salaries. Only 21 primary schools were directly operated by the government. The denominational schools are controlled by governing bodies of the respective churches. Supervision with respect to standards is maintained by education officers representing the Department of Education. Thus, for more than a century, education has involved an imposed Christian standard.

In recent years, Hindu and Muslim organizations have attempted to organize schools in which East Indian children could be provided with language and religious instruction. Some government aid has been obtained for these schools, but the movement has not been very successful. The grants received from the government have been small, and the Hindi and Muslim schools are few in number. More important, these schools in no way represent a substitute for the government-aided Christian schools. The children who attend the Hindu and Muslim schools must do so on their own time after normal school hours. As a consequence, most East Indian children are required to attend Christian denominational schools in order to obtain their primary school certificates.

In view of these circumstances, it is clear that the school system functions simultaneously as a local and a broker institution. The schools exist in the villages and local communities, but they are organized externally, and they are subject to standards that are not locally defined. In this respect, both Africans and East Indians share a common set of social structures. Therefore, one would expect the schools to represent a major force contributing to the unification of the two groups. The extent to which this is the case as far as educational content and national associations are concerned will be discussed in the following chapter. Here, however, it is necessary to note that the opposite tends to be the case with respect to intergroup relations within the villages.

In the rural villages under investigation, the first thing that strikes the attention of the observer is the absence of educational facilities in those villages predominantly occupied by East Indians. Clonbrook and Cromarty have no schools—not even Hindi or Muslim schools. The children of Clonbrook attend either the Roman Catholic school or the Methodist school, both of which are located in the African village of Ann's Grove. The teaching staff at both of these schools is made up primarily of Africans who commute by train from Georgetown. Similarly, the children of Cromarty attend an Anglican school in the neighboring village of Wellington Park. Although Wellington Park is now predominantly East Indian in population, the teaching staff at the Anglican school continues to be made up primarily of Africans. Eversham, an African village much smaller than Cromarty, has a school of its own operated by the Church of Scotland.

The situation at Plantation Skeldon is not much different from that existing in the rural villages. More than 75 per cent of the population in the vicinity of Skeldon is East Indian. There are five schools in the area. Two are operated by Hindu and Muslim organizations and provide religious and language instruction after normal school hours. At the time of study, the Hindi school had an average daily enrollment of twenty-six students, a small number in light of the Hindu population of the area. The remaining three schools are denominational schools run by Christian churches. These three schools employ more East Indian teachers than those previously mentioned, but they employ very few East Indian teachers who have not converted to Christianity.

Mackenzie City, compared to Plantation Skeldon, has one of the finest educational complexes in the country. At Mackenzie, the Demerara Bauxite Company (locally referred to as Demba) constructed a primary school for the children of its employees. However, the operation of the school has been transferred completely to the government. In addition, Demba maintains a high school which it continues to operate privately primarily for the children of employees. Beyond this, Demba provides a trade school for a select number of students who are qualified by examination to attend. Finally, the company also operates a primary school exclusively for the children of senior personnel. Most of these children are Europeans or Canadians. The teachers who operate this school under the supervision of the personnel department are recruited mainly in Canada, and the standards maintained are comparable to those of Canadian schools.

In view of these facts, the structure of educational activities within the villages is a critical source of tension between Indians and Africans. During the course of field work, depth interviews were obtained from eight Indian teachers in six different villages. Of these, seven complained bitterly that it was necessary for them to become Christians in order to secure teaching positions or in order to make it possible to be considered for promotions. The only Hindu in the group stated that he had refused to become a Christian, and, as a consequence, after thirty years of teaching he had not received a promotion to the position of head teacher. Further checking revealed that this particular individual had passed his teaching examinations with unusual distinction. Moreover, an African informant who served as a member of the governing body at the school where this particular individual taught agreed that he would probably be promoted to the rank of head teacher almost immediately if he would become a member of the church.

Charges of discrimination are also frequent with respect to the treatment of students in Christian schools. Five of the eight teachers interviewed claimed that the African teachers in their schools discriminated against Indian children by not giving them the kind of special attention which they readily give to African children. Whether or not there is any truth to this accusation cannot be determined from the data collected. However, the accusation does exist as a widespread belief among Indian parents. In Clonbrook, for example, a young Indian teacher claimed that he was elected to the village council primarily because the villagers appreciated his efforts to protect Indian children from the discrimination of African teachers in the Methodist school at Ann's Grove.

Charges of discrimination and expressions of dissatisfaction over the structure of educational activities existed among East Indians in every one of the six villages studied. It would seem that these charges are symptomatic of a point of view that was first expressed in 1919 by J. A. Luckhoo, an East Indian barrister who eventually became an acting Chief Justice. In an article on the East Indians in Guiana, Lockhoo stated, "To send his boy to a denominational school to be taught English is to denationalize him and jeopardize his religious faith, and so the Indian maintains a calm indifference towards it."[16]

Village Indians are no longer indifferent toward education. At the same time, however, they are just as concerned about denationalization as they have ever been, perhaps more so. Herein lies the difficulty of the situation. The village schools not only impose Christian values, but, in addition, they place Africans in the position of being the major interpreters of these values and the primary agents of acculturation. Thus the Africans, whom most Indians consider Chamar because of their low economic status, are the very individuals to whom Indians must turn in order to achieve social status.

[16] J. A. Luckhoo, "The East Indian in British Guiana," *Timehri*, 6 (1919), 61.

The ultimate source of this structural inconsistency is twofold in nature: First, the European values which Africans have adopted are not the values which most East Indians consider important; and, second, under colonialism, the achievement of economic power has not been closely associated with the prestige that derives from educational improvement. As a consequence, the structure of educational activities within the villages not only threatens to denationalize East Indian children in the sense of modifying their Hindu and Muslim beliefs, but it also threatens to denationalize them by providing role models unrelated to the kinds of activities by which East Indians have achieved the economic status they now enjoy. Perhaps this point will emerge more clearly in the following chapter, when the school system is considered as a broker institution.

In conclusion, it should be noted that within the villages the school system contributes very little to the unification of existing minimal cultural sections. While the structure of educational activities is valid for East Indians as well as Africans, it tends to be modified by both groups according to the cultural differences existing between them.

## ASSOCIATIONAL ACTIVITIES

In Guianese villages, there exists a variety of special interest groups that may be described as voluntary associations. Some of these associations have grown out of a concern for the expression of religious values. Others have been organized specifically for the achievement of instrumental goals, e.g., land and credit cooperatives, burial societies, etc. Some associations, women's clubs and brotherhood organizations, for example, are primarily fraternal in character. Still others reflect educational interest in that they channel leisure activities in this direction. Not all of these associations are exclusively local. Some of them, political party groups, for example, are the local affiliates of national associations. Regardless of the specific groups involved, however, rather striking differences exist with respect to the associational patterns that are characteristic of African and East Indian villages. These differences pertain not only to the degree of participation in associational activities but also to the number and variety of associations represented in the social life of the villages. Table 15 presents a list of the voluntary associations that were found to exist in the four nonindustrial villages included in the study.

TABLE 15. VOLUNTARY ASSOCIATIONS IN EAST INDIAN AND AFRICAN VILLAGES

| | *Ann's Grove (African)* | *Clonbrook (East Indian)* |
|---|---|---|
| Burial Societies | All Peace Burial Society<br>Royal Crown Burial Society<br>Methodist Burial Society<br>Farmer's Burial Society | Clonbrook Burial Society |
| Religious Associations | St. Mark's Vestry<br>Anglican Synod | Hindu Temple Committee<br>Hindu Sanatan Society<br>American Aryan League<br>Anjuman-E-Islam Society |
| Educational Associations | The Reader's Club<br>Young Man's Cultural Society<br>Negroes' Improvement Association<br>A.G. Sewing Club | |
| Fraternal Associations | The Brotherhood Movement<br>The Women's Union<br>Girl Scouts<br>Boy Scouts | |
| Recreational Groups | A.G. Cricket Club<br>A.G. Community | Clonbrook Cricket Club |
| Welfare Organizations | The Red Cross | |
| Economic Organizations | Ann's Grove Land Society<br>A.G. Credit Cooperative<br>A.G. Thrift Society<br>Regional Development Committee | |
| Political Parties | Peoples National Congress<br>United Force | Peoples Progressive Party |

TABLE 15, *continued*

| | *Eversham (African)* | *Cromarty (East Indian)* |
|---|---|---|
| Burial Societies | New Burial Society<br>Eversham Burial Society | |
| Religious Associations | Christian Endeavor Society | |
| Educational Associations | Adult Education Association<br>Young Men's Improvement Association<br>Young Women's Christian Association | |
| Economic Organizations | Eversham Land Society<br>Eversham Agricultural Cooperative<br>Thrift and Credit Society | Cromarty Thrift and Credit<br>Cromarty Land Society<br>Albion Land Society<br>Canje Creek Land Society<br>Berbice River Land Society |
| Political Groups | Eversham Proprietor's Committee<br>Committee for Local Government | |

With reference to Table 15, it is quite clear that associational activities are much more varied and much more prevalent in African villages than in the East Indian villages. Ann's Grove has more than three times as many voluntary associations as Clonbrook. In Clonbrook, only 31 per cent of the East Indians interviewed (13 individuals) belong to at least one of the groups listed. Moreover, only seven of these thirteen individuals belong to some group other than the local affiliate of the Peoples Progressive Party. In Ann's Grove, on the other hand, 71 per cent of the Africans interviewed claim an active membership in at least one of the twenty-three groups listed, and 64 per cent belong to two or more of these groups. Also, no less than 60 per cent of the Africans interviewed hold a membership card in the local affiliate of the Peoples National Congress.

The types of associations existing in Ann's Grove and Clonbrook are also revealing of important differences between Africans and East Indians. In Ann's Grove, there are associations of practically every type. In Clonbrook, however, most of the voluntary groups are religious associations. Ann's Grove has four local groups concerned primarily with educational interests; Clonbrook has none. Ann's Grove has four fraternal organizations—two for adults and two for children; Clonbrook has none. Ann's Grove has a community center organized by young adults and housed in the local government office, which was constructed to have sufficient space available for community activities. Clonbrook has no community center, and its local government office was constructed exclusively to provide a place of business for the village council.

Similar differences in associational patterns were found to exist also in rural villages without local government organization. The African village of Eversham, for example, contains only 46 households, but it has no less than eleven functioning voluntary associations. Cromarty, on the other hand, has 79 households but only five voluntary associations. In Eversham, there are no fraternal associations, no organized athletic groups, no welfare associations, and no political party groups. In Cromarty, four of the five associations are land societies organized by East Indian rice farmers in order to obtain Crown land from the government. Eversham has a proprietors' committee which functions as a substitute for local government. In Cromarty, several attempts have been made to organize a proprietors' committee, but all of them have failed. Eversham has three organized groups which function primarily in the area of education. Cromarty has no associations of this type.

The industrial communities, Plantation Skeldon and Mackenzie City, must be considered separately from the rural villages as far as associational patterns are concerned, but their comparison reflects differences similar to those already described. In the vicinity of Plantation Skeldon, there exists a fairly large number of voluntary associations in which many East Indian sugar workers participate. Most of these are Hindu and Muslim religious organizations, land societies, credit cooperatives, and burial societies. There is also a strong affiliate of the Peoples Progressive Party in the area, organized under the leadership of a young Hindu priest. In the plantation community itself, however, there are practically no voluntary associations other than those organized by the estate personnel department in terms of policies advised by the British Guiana Sugar Producers' Association.

Under the welfare policy of the Sugar Producers' Association, as it pertains to estate housing, political party groups are prohibited from organizing on estate land. Tenants' associations are organized as voluntary groups in the housing schemes, and these are supervised by a community development officer who is an employee of the estate personnel department. At Skeldon, only 29 per cent of the Indians interviewed participate in the activities of the tenants' associations. The Sugar Producers' Association also provides sugar workers with community centers. While these are supposed to be maintained by the workers, they are directly supervised by community development officers who are responsible to the personnel departments of the estates. At Skeldon, the community center has a variety of committees organized to maintain activity programs. However, none of these committees functions very effectively, and the constant complaint of the community development officer there was twofold in nature: First, the authority of the personnel department is too heavy-handed in its regulation of community center activities; and, second, East Indian workers and their children have neither the time, the money, nor the interest to participate in most of the activities of the center. From observation, it would seem that the East Indians are mainly interested in the athletic events which the community center sponsored from time to time.

Mackenzie City, like Plantation Skeldon, is a company town. However, it differs from the latter in several important respects. For one thing, the bauxite workers enjoy a much higher standard of living than the sugar workers. In 1960, for example, the average weekly wage paid to bauxite workers was three times higher than that paid to sugar workers. Another difference involves company policy. The Demba Company, unlike the Sugar Producers' Association, does not exercise rigid control over the organization of community affairs. Demba permits private businesses and groups to organize in Mackenzie. It also allows political party organizations to function in the community. Still another important difference involves personnel policy. Although the Demba Company provides community facilities which it expects the workers to maintain, unlike the situation at Skeldon, the Demba personnel department is much less directly involved in the organization of groups which use these facilities.

Under these conditions, there exists a plethora of organizations and associations among the African workers who live in Mackenzie City. In addition to several credit unions, burial societies, and educational groups, there are no less than seven sports and recreational clubs, ten fraternal organizations, nine cooperative societies of various kinds, several youth organizations, two parent-teachers' associations, and the Young Men's Christian Association. Affiliates of all major political parties also exist. The level of participation in these associations is extremely high, compared to the other communities considered. Among the interviewees at Mackenzie, 81 per cent claimed a membership in at least one organization, and 51 per cent belong to more than one.

In addition to these groups and organizations which are unrelated to the operations of the Demba personnel department, the community also has a recreation hall and a sports club. These are provided by Demba, but the workers themselves are expected to maintain them with minimum supervision. This is achieved, in part, by allowing workers to keep charge accounts at the sports club for whatever costs are involved; these bills are then deducted from their pay envelopes. The recreation hall is used primarily by the Demba Band, but it is available for rent to private groups and organizations. The sports club, as a physical facility, is far more elaborate than anything available to sugar workers, containing a bar, a dancehall, and game rooms. It also has a swimming pool, an athletic field lighted for night events, and a pavilion with seating capacity for 500 people. The extensive use of these facilities reflects not only the high standard of living that prevails as a result of the bauxite industry, but also the propensity of Africans to participate more fully than East Indians in a wide range of social activities that are organized outside of the sphere of family and kinship influence.

As one views the structure of associational activities from the comparative perspective of these data, patterns emerge which clearly serve to differentiate Africans and East Indians as minimal cultural sections. Compared to Africans, East Indians are not particularly inclined to join voluntary associations or to maintain a high level of participation in associational activities. The voluntary associations which Indians do join are, more often than not, either religious in character or special groups formed to achieve particular economic goals, such as the acquisition and development of unused land. Africans, on the other hand, participate quite actively in a wide variety of groups and organizations. They appear to be particularly interested in fraternal associations, educational groups, and burial societies. They are almost equally interested in youth organizations. Political party membership is also more extensive among Africans than East Indians. Although it cannot be established conclusively from the data presented here, it would appear that the absence of voluntary associations in Indian communities is related, in part, to the fact that the East Indian family and kinship system provides for most of the activities which Africans find it necessary to organize in terms of voluntary groups and organizations.

It also should be noted that the patterns of associational activity delineated here cannot be understood apart from many of the other features of village life that differentiate the two groups. For example, the large number of associations in African villages is related to the fact that the upper stratum in these villages contains a larger number of professional people than does the upper stratum of the Indian villages. Most of the associational activities in African communities are maintained by a small but extremely active core of individuals who have assumed leadership roles. Usually, these persons are not farmers but teachers, ministers, and retired civil servants who have returned to the village to live. Frequently, the active membership in these organizations consists of older persons who have pensions or who receive money from urban-employed children and who, therefore, do not find it necessary to fully occupy themselves with cash crop farming.

Another reason for the large number of associations in African villages has to do with sex. Among Africans, females are not as confined to the home as they are among Indians. Moreover, they are not as burdened with agricultural work. Thus, they tend to be extremely active in voluntary groups—much more active even than African males. East Indian females, on the other hand, hardly ever participate in such groups.

Finally, it should be noted that many of the organizations existing in African villages derive from the influences of urban culture—influences to which East Indians have been much less subjected in personal ways than have Africans.

## SOCIAL AND RECREATIONAL ACTIVITIES

Apart from the associational patterns described above, one of the most striking features of cultural life that serves to differentiate African and Indian villages has to do with leisure activities that are not entirely related to the functioning of formally organized groups. First evidence of these differences is impressionistic. In Ann's Grove, for example, there are places where Africans gather regularly in conversation. At almost any time on any given day, one can find small groups of older men in either one of two rum shops or near the village office. These groups do not come together officially or for sport (e.g., drinking) but simply to pass the time discussing politics, discussing the affairs of friends or neighbors, or telling stories of their adventures in the diamond and gold fields of the interior. Sometimes, younger men join to listen, but generally, in Ann's Grove, the young men in the village seem to prefer the railroad station, where there is generally a game of dominoes being played. The women, on the other hand, collect at the standpipes where they draw water for the home or near the crossroads which serves as an open market for the villages of Clonbrook and Ann's Grove. In Eversham, similar groups can be found regularly at the post office, the cake shop, the rum shop, or on the bridge which links Eversham to Kiltairn. These informal groups are almost never mixed, seldom including males and females together or Africans and East Indians.

Informal groups of East Indians passing the time in idle conversation are not particularly evident in Cromarty and Clonbrook. In these villages, everyone seems to be too busy to engage in this kind of activity. Even children appear to be more frequently occupied by work than play. When Indians are seen together in these communities, more often than not they are groups of relatives working about the house or on their way to and from the rice fields or the rice mills. In Clonbrook, the village office is exclusively a place of business. Friends and neighbors do not seem to gather there to discuss politics or exchange gossip. The major rum shop in Clonbrook is patronized mainly by Africans from Ann's Grove. The situation at Plantation Skeldon is somewhat different. There, the rhythm of work and leisure is relatively fixed according to production schedules. Thus, among sugar workers who do not also maintain rice farms, there is considerably more evidence of neighboring patterns than among the village Indians.

In very general terms, the social and recreational activities of Indians differ from those of Africans. They differ particularly with respect to the kinds of values expressed, the occasions upon which they are expressed, and the manner of their expression. Among Indians, leisure activities tend to be structured in terms of the expression of religious values. Weddings, Yags, and such religious festivals as the annual Phagwah celebration represent the major occasions when Indians withdraw almost completely from normal work routines and engage in convivialities. At other times, the vast majority of Indians appear not to be very interested in what they consider to be idle pursuits. At Plantation Skeldon, for example, many Indians, particularly younger persons, enjoy going to the movies on weekend nights to see films imported from India or American westerns. During these times, only a few cliques of young men frequent the rum shops. The dances at the community center are seldom attended, particularly by females. On all occasions, parents refuse to allow their daughters to mix with Africans. During the free time which weekends and holidays provide, many sugar workers and their families engage in agricultural activities in order to supplement their incomes. In the villages, weekends and holidays pass without much special attention.

Africans also celebrate weddings and religious festivals. However, without going into detail, Christian marriages combined with African Que-que dances constitute a ceremonial complex very different from the "bamboo" weddings of East Indians. Similarly, the rituals of Christmas are not very much like those associated with Phagwah. Also, Africans do not normally engage in work on public holidays—not even in the villages. The fact of the matter is that Africans do not appear to need weddings, religious days, or holidays as occasions for engaging in social and recreational activities. With a little cash in hand, practically any weekend is an occasion for a little "sport." Thus, at Skeldon the public dances at the community center are primarily attended by Africans. At Mackenzie, dances are held almost weekly. In Ann's Grove, the village office is the locus of a party or a dance at least once or twice a month. If there are no dances, there are juke boxes in the rum shops, even in the small village of Eversham. On the whole, Africans and Indians engage in similar kinds of recreational activities, but these activities are structured differently, they occur in terms of a different time schedule, and they involve the expression of different kinds of values. More importantly, these activities seldom serve to bring Africans and Indians together in any meaningful way. Some Africans, particularly schoolteachers in the villages, are often invited to attend Indian weddings. As frequently as they are invited, however, they are expected not to show up, or, if they do, it is anticipated that they will not stay long. Informants in Ann's Grove and Eversham stated that when Indians are invited to African weddings or to Que-que dances, they almost never come. Athletic events, as a form of recreation, frequently bring the two groups together, but usually in competition against one another.

Even the Guiana Day celebrations in the schools serve to enhance the competition between the two groups by focussing attention on the cultural patterns that separate them. In 1960, the author attended these celebrations at the school in the village of Leeds on the Courantyne coast. Each group exhibited its own cultural wares in terms of its own pageants. Above the school, the Africans hoisted the flag of Ghana. Across the road, the Indians elevated the flag of India. At the conclusion of the formal ceremonies, the Africans—men, women and children—retired to the school building, where a steel band composed of African musicians played to a dance that continued long into the night. The East Indians, on the other hand, retired to the schoolyard, where Indian foods could be purchased from booths operated by Indians, and Indian musicians played traditional music on traditional instruments. Here and there, a few African and Indian village politicians mingled with one another and discussed the future of Guiana as "the land of six peoples."

## LOCAL GOVERNMENT ACTIVITIES

As was indicated earlier in this chapter, from the point of view of local government organization, there are three types of rural communities in British Guiana: (1) local authorities (e.g., Ann's Grove and Clonbrook), (2) unorganized villages (e.g., Eversham and Cromarty), and (3) plantation and industrial communities (e.g., Plantation Skeldon and Mackenzie City). Except for the latter, which are completely organized by privately owned companies, all villages are uniformly subject to the legal provisions of the Local Government Ordinance. Under the ordinance, the major difference between local authorities and unorganized villages is that the former have village councils which are two-thirds elected, while the latter come directly under the supervision of district commissioners of the Local Government Department who work through wholly nominated country authorities. In the unorganized villages, there are no legal provisions for the collection of property taxes, no local government facilities, and no village councils to provide governmental services and supervise the maintenance of building codes, roads, dams, bridges, etc.

In view of these facts, it is quite clear that local governmental institutions are not local in conception. Their legal structure is defined at the level of national government and organizationally implemented by the Department of Local Government. Local governmental institutions are broker institutions. They function to link local groups with the larger society. To some extent, a similar situation exists with respect to plantation and industrial communities. The structure of authority within the housing schemes on the sugar estates is defined by the Sugar Producers' Association, a nonlocal group, and it is organizationally implemented by the personnel departments of the individual estates. In the same way, the personnel department of the Demerara Bauxite Company implements company policy within Mackenzie City. However, apart from these considerations, there are certain structural dimensions of local governmental activity which are neither defined at the level of national government nor implemented by an agency of national government. One of these involves the orientation toward authority and its relationship to local government activities.

Among East Indians, authority is primarily defined and allocated in terms of family and kinship structures. Technically, this is not political authority. However, until very recent times East Indians have not been political. Practically all of their affairs were of such a nature that they could be regulated within the family. When, on occasion, this was not the case, feuds erupted and persisted until they were negotiated by a pandit or forgotten by the individuals involved. As a consequence, Indians have a tendency to consider external authority structures as intrusions which must be put up with because of the circumstances under which they are forced to live. Such authority structures may elicit conformity, but they do not elicit much respect. There is an exception. External authority structures elicit respect when they are implemented by agents who have a strong propensity to interpret and apply norms in a particularistic and paternal fashion.

Because of particularism, some sugar estate managers are highly respected, while others are not. Those who are respected are individuals who constantly extend personal favors to workers and their families. They are not hard on workers who absent themselves from work in order to harvest a rice crop. They provide workers' sons with employment in preference to others. They extend loans or give personal attention to individuals with problems. Indians respond in a similar fashion to village councilmen.

In Clonbrook, the most respected councilman is a moneylender who has helped dozens of villagers without being too demanding about the repayment of loans. Another councilor, a teacher, is respected because he sees to it that African teachers do not discriminate against Indian children. Councilors who are not sticklers about local governmental regulations and who do not allow these regulations to interfere too much with the personal affairs of individuals and families are highly regarded. In Clonbrook, no councilor is respected because he holds a public office. Most Indians in Clonbrook do not consider public office important, and they feel that only those individuals ought to be elected who can afford to idle away valuable time. Thus, all of the councilors in Clonbrook are either wealthy men or men who are in a position to extend favors. Needless to say, none of them are African.

The orientation toward authority among Africans is quite different. For one thing, the African kinship structure is much too equalitarian to represent an important source of authority. It places a great deal of emphasis upon the personal freedom of the individual. When a boy can leave school and support himself, he has the right to make decisions independent of the wishes of his parents. Similarly, when a young girl reaches puberty, she can decide whether or not she will leave home to live with a man. Her parents may not appreciate her decision, but there is little they can do about it other than complain. They do not give her a dowry, and they cannot alienate her from children's property should she ever want to use it. In addition to this difference, Africans, unlike Indians, have been political since the time of emancipation. Many of their affairs simply cannot be settled within the context of family and kinship structures.

As a result of these circumstances, Africans do not consider external authority structures as intrusions. History provides ample evidence of this fact. Shortly after emancipation, in the early 1840's, Africans in many villages entered into contractual agreements for the purpose of organizing committees to manage village affairs. In some cases, these contracts specified in detail rules and regulations that were to be universally applied. Penalties, in the form of fines or property confiscation, were prescribed for defaulters. When these penalties could not be enforced in some villages, the proprietors petitioned the central government to act on their behalf. In other words, Africans, unlike East Indians, have developed a tradition of communal authority which is not so closely associated with particularistic norms and which does not exist in opposition to the internal authority structure of the family and kin group.

These different orientations toward authority emerge most clearly from a comparison of local governmental activities in Eversham (African) and Cromarty (Indian). Both of these villages come under the jurisdiction of a district officer, but neither of them has a local authority under the provisions of the Local Government Ordinance. In Eversham, however, there is a proprietors' committee which functions as a local authority on the basis of a formal contractual agreement signed by the proprietors. This committee was first organized in 1857, when Eversham was purchased by a group of nineteen shareholders. At that time, the five older heads who were responsible for organizing the shareholders comprised the committee. As the estate passed into children's property, the status of older head devolved upon the oldest living descendants of the original proprietors. These individuals, whether male or female, supervised the "family buddle" (property), and allocated land to descendants who wanted to build a house or cultivate a crop. Under these conditions, the proprietors' committee was transformed into a council of seven men elected by the older heads.

By contractual agreement, the proprietors' committee is empowered by the older heads who elect it to employ an overseer for the purpose of undertaking such public works as the committee deems necessary for the welfare of the village. Costs are distributed among the proprietors according to the number of shares they own. These are collected directly from the older heads, who, in turn, collect portions from relatives using children's property. The committee is empowered to prosecute proprietors who default on their payments for public works by taking them to court if necessary. In Eversham, the committee has never found it necessary to take a proprietor to court. Perhaps the reason for this is that the extent of public works projects in Eversham is limited, and since many projects are undertaken with voluntary labor, the costs are quite nominal. The committee's operating budget has never exceeded a hundred dollars. The contractual agreement in Eversham also stipulates that no person is allowed to cut dams without the committee's approval, to tread on dams with cattle or vehicles, or to damage any fence belonging to another.

Apart from the functions stipulated in the contractual agreement, the proprietors' committee in Eversham has unofficial functions. A review of the minutes kept by the committee revealed that it was responsible for collecting and paying rent on second-depth lands leased from the Crown; it voted on applications from individuals to use Crown lands; it represented the village in all negotiations with the district commissioner; and it settled land disputes between proprietors and relatives over the use of children's property. Among informants, there was a general consensus that older heads, and then the proprietors' committee, had the responsibility of maintaining order in the village. Villagers registered complaints with the district officer or with other agents of government only when older heads, or the elected members of the committee were unable to negotiate an amicable settlement. Informants could recall only one case of a land dispute that could not be settled within the village in the past five or ten years.

The situation in Cromarty with respect to local governmental activities is very different. In fact, there are no local governmental activities in Cromarty. Cromarty has never had a proprietors' committee or anything like one. There is no group in the village, elected or self-appointed, charged with the responsibility of maintaining order or undertaking public works of any kind. There is no group or individual charged with the function of settling disputes between proprietors. Informants were asked why such a group had never been organized. They indicated that each Indian family looks out for itself and that there was too much jealousy between them to cooperate in a communal undertaking of this type. When asked what these jealousies were all about, informants stated that some families have more wealth than others; some have more land; others get better crops; some don't mind their cattle, etc.

In Cromarty, where disputes emerge between proprietors, they take the form of family feuds. Sometimes, these disputes simmer for years until they are forgotten. On occasion, they erupt into violence. For example, the father of one informant was killed by a neighbor as a result of a quarrel over land. The feud still persists between the informant in question and the sons of the neighbor who killed his father. Another informant's mother was severely beaten in a similar quarrel. As often as not, these kinds of disputes are thrown into the courts. Otherwise, individuals register complaints with the district commissioner, who usually avoids getting involved in order to make his job easier. In Cromarty, when public works are necessary, they are undertaken by the Department of Public Works, an agency of the central government. Since the village is not partitioned for tax purposes, the cost of public works cannot be charged against proprietors.

The differences in local governmental activities in Clonbrook (Indian) and Ann's Grove (African) are not quite as great as those described above. Before 1933, these two villages were organized under a single local authority. In 1933, as a result of years of quarreling between Africans and Indians over the management of village affairs, the Local Government Department decided to divide the two villages into two independent local authorities. It has been difficult to reconstruct the history of this situation but, as far as informants could remember, the numerous disputes that existed were engendered by many of the cultural differences previously described. Because of children's property, there were many more Africans with a voting franchise than Indians. As a result, Africans almost completely dominated the village council, and the Indians did not like the way the council managed village affairs.

In general, before 1933, when Africans dominated local government in Ann's Grove as well as Clonbrook, the Indians felt that the village council was wasteful and inefficient; it took too much upon itself that was unnecessary; it interfered in the lives of the people in too many ways; and it obstructed progress.

The council obstructed progress because it ignored such things as drainage and irrigation, and it spent too much money on things that were not needed, e.g., a large village office with a small hall for social affairs. The council also became involved with the administration of children's property. Rather than allow children's property to be sold for the payment of taxes (this would give Indians an opportunity to buy African land), the council paid the taxes and then allowed the proprietors to use this property (as they had always used it) on the payment of rent until such time as the rent collected was sufficient to discharge back taxes.

Indians also objected to the council's policy with respect to taxation. Before 1933, the same system of taxation existed for the two villages as presently exists in Ann's Grove. Taxes were assessed against houses, houselots, and cultivation lots. The Indians in Clonbrook maintained, as they still do, that houses and houselots constitute personal property which is not productive and which should not be taxed. Thus, in Clonbrook, taxes are assessed only against cultivation lots. In Ann's

Grove, in order to pay lower taxes, Africans build huts and leave houses unfinished and unpainted. In Clonbrook, because they are not taxed, houses are substantially constructed, finished, and painted.

The differences between the two villages that brought about a split in the local authority in 1933 still exist. In Clonbrook, as far as Indians are concerned, the local authority does not interfere too much in their private affairs. This is due, in part, to the kind of councilmen who get elected. More often than not, these councilmen are fairly wealthy men who are too busy with their private affairs to bother others. They perceive local government as nothing more than an agency organized to collect taxes. These taxes are to be used almost exclusively for the maintenance of streets, dams, and drainage ditches. In Clonbrook, elections take place without contest, unless some particular councilman has become too troublesome by meddling in things which are not considered to be the business of local government.

In Ann's Grove, on the other hand, local government is considered to be something more than an agency to maintain public works. The village council is intricately involved in the affairs of individuals as well as in the affairs of the village. The office of councilman is a prestigious position. It is usually contested for in elections. The men who get elected are almost always older heads who have an important stake in the village by virtue of their ancestry. They are men who are sought out for advice on all sorts of personal and family matters. They settle disputes when they emerge between villagers. Above all, they are men who are interested in keeping village lands in the hands of Africans. This means that the Ann's Grove council has as one of its major responsibilities the keeping of children's property out of the hands of Indians.

## THE INTEGRATION OF MINIMAL CULTURAL SECTIONS

The minimal cultural section has been operationally defined as a culturally differentiated group functioning within the context of the local community. It has been suggested that the identification of such units be predicated upon the structural analysis of local institutional activities, i.e., those activities that are more or less confined to the routine of social life in the community, whether the community be a village, a plantation, a neighborhood, or some other type of unit bounded by the social interaction of individuals as they carry on their daily affairs with one another. The logic of this approach derives from the assumption that the structures that serve to mobilize these activities also serve to express the cultural values which individuals have internalized with respect to them. It follows from this that relatively distinct social structures are expressive of equally distinct cultural values.

The question as to how culturally different particular groups have to be in order to consider them separately implies a continuum for which anthropologists have not yet devised appropriate measures. In the absence of such measures, qualitative evaluations may be made in terms of structural data. Thus, the integration of minimal cultural sections is considered to be a function of the extent to which the structure of specific institutional activities is valid (1) only for a particular group, or (2) for all groups but modified by some, or (3) uniformly valid for all groups. The analytical model for this level of sociocultural integration was summarized in Table 1 (Chapter 1). The application of this model to the data collected in a comparative study of six Guianese villages is presented in Table 16.

TABLE 16. INTEGRATION OF AFRICAN AND EAST INDIAN MINIMAL CULTURAL SECTIONS

| *Local Institutional Activities* | *Structure Is Valid Only for Particular Groups* | *Structure Is Valid for All Groups but Modified by Some* | *Structure Is Valid for All Groups* |
|---|---|---|---|
| Family and Kinship Networks | X | | |
| Economic Activities | X | | |
| Religious Activities | X | | |
| Educational Activities | | X | |
| Associational Activities | X | | |
| Social and Recreational Activities | X | | |
| Local Governmental Activities | | X | |

As is indicated in Table 16, within the social world of the local community, Africans and East Indians display markedly different patterns of sociocultural integration. Institutional structures that function with respect to the organization of a relatively wide range of social activities are valid, separately, for each group. In the sphere of educational activity, both groups share a common structure, but East Indians do not consider it suitable for the expression of cultural values which they feel are important. Similarly, local governmental structures that are uniform for both groups are extensively modified by each in accordance with the expression of very different cultural values. At the local level, there appears to be no social structure which is valid for both groups that is not extensively modified by each. Moreover, this seems to be the case regardless of variations in ecological conditions, in community size, or variations resulting from the intrusion of such external factors as those associated with industrialization. In these respects, East Indians and Africans constitute independent minimal or local cultural sections. They share no common set of social structures which serves to bind them together in such a manner as to form a single cultural group. The extent to which these two groups retain their separate cultural identity at the national level of sociocultural integration remains to be determined.

*CHAPTER 4*

# THE NATIONAL LEVEL OF SOCIOCULTURAL INTEGRATION

FROM THE EXISTENCE OF MINIMAL CULTURAL SECTIONS, IT DOES NOT FOLlow that Guianese society is pluralistic. It will be recalled that the definition of the plural society must take into account two related sets of facts: (1) the extent to which particular groups are culturally differentiated in terms of specific institutional activities, and (2) the level at which institutional activities serve to maintain cultural differentiation as the basis for sociocultural integration. In operational terms, the plural society is a unitary system of action that contains integrated groups which are culturally differentiated at the national or societal level of sociocultural integration. These groups, for want of a better term, are called maximal cultural sections. The separate integration of maximal cultural sections is largely a function of broker institutions, i.e., those institutions that serve to link the activities of individuals and groups, regardless of their communal ties, to the wider sphere of societal activity.

In Guianese society, the most important broker institutions include those involving education, the communications media, commercial and industrial organizations, markets, labor organizations, cooperatives, governmental agencies, religious and ethnic associations, and political parties.[1] With respect to these broker institutions, it should be ascer-

[1] As was indicated in Chapter 1, the list of broker institutions employed in this study is not intended as a typology. It also needs to be pointed out that broker institutions did not constitute the major focus of my field work in Guiana. Thus, this particular chapter relies rather heavily on data obtained by way of unstructured interviews with prominent Guianese political leaders, civil servants, union leaders, and business leaders. To the extent that it is possible to do so, these interview data are supplemented by information drawn from government reports and other secondary sources. I have attempted to restrict this analysis to those broker institutions on which I believe I have ample and reliable information. For example, although the law

tained the extent to which their structures (1) serve to integrate similar minimal cultural sections, or, (2) serve to mediate the relationships between individuals of different minimal cultural sections by modifying their communal values, or, (3) serve to integrate individuals of different minimal cultural sections by generating new cultural values that are in the process of being adopted by the society as a whole.

## EDUCATIONAL INSTITUTIONS

In the previous chapter, it was suggested that educational activities are carried on simultaneously in terms of both local and broker institutional structures. Schools, particularly most of the primary and secondary schools, are owned and operated by Christian denominational bodies. In varying ways, these schools are subject to the influence of local groups that are organized to carry out the educational policies of their respective denominational bodies. These denominational bodies, in turn, are not local in their organization or doctrine. At the same time, all schools receiving government aid for equipment, for the maintenance of buildings, or for the payment of teachers' salaries must comply with the educational policies and standards established by the government.

The governmental agency most directly involved in the formulation of educational policies is the Ministry of Community Development and Education (recently changed to the Ministry of Education). The issues of policy decided within this ministry involve not only budgetary considerations affecting teachers' salaries and fringe benefits, expenditures for equipment and materials, the construction of new schools, and the expansion or termination of existing programs; but they also involve the fixing of standards, curriculum development, the development of teaching materials, and the appointment of head teachers in government schools. Policy decisions are implemented by the Education Department under the supervision of the Chief Education

comprises a most important broker institution, I have not included a discussion of the law here because secondary sources are insufficient, and time did not permit me to carry out an adequate amount of primary field work among members of the legal profession to determine whether or not the law is differentially applied to Africans, East Indians, and others. I have no evidence which suggests that the law is differentially applied, but, at the same time, my data are too limited to warrant such a conclusion.

Officer. The Chief Education Officer is a civil servant in the fixed establishment. The Minister of Education, unlike the Chief Education Officer, is not a civil servant. He is nominated for his portfolio by the majority party which is elected to form the government. Thus, there exists a national institutional structure in terms of which educational policies and standards are open to political influence. The question is, How much of the educational system does this national structure encompass?

It will be recalled that, as of 1959, there were 327 primary schools in British Guiana.[2] Of these, 21 were operated directly by the government; 298 were operated by denominational bodies with the aid of government funds; and the remainder were operated by nondenominational groups also with the aid of government money. These schools enrolled a total of 118,538 children between the ages of five and sixteen years. In addition, through the Government Information Service, the government maintained a Broadcasts to Schools Unit. As of 1959, a total of 225 primary schools were known to be subscribing to these educational programs. Also in 1959, there were 2 secondary schools operated by the government, 12 secondary schools operated by private and denominational groups with government aid, and approximately 20 secondary schools known to be operating without government aid. The government-owned secondary schools enrolled 1,081 students; nine of the aided secondary schools had a total enrollment of 4,354; and it is estimated that the nonaided secondary schools enrolled approximately 3,000 students. As far as it can be determined from these figures, government-owned and government-aided schools provided for practically all of the primary education available in the country, in addition to approximately 65 per cent of the secondary education.

Apart from primary and secondary education, the government in British Guiana is also involved in much of what is available by way of advanced technical and vocational training. The Teachers Training College, which provides a two-year course for students who have passed all of the requisite teachers' certificate examinations, is owned and operated by the government, as are the Technical Institute and the Carnegie School of Home Economics. The Fredericks School of Home Economics is a privately organized institution which operates with the assistance of government funds. Apart from these, the only other

[2] This figure does not include a small number of primary schools that are privately operated by sugar estates for the children of senior staff personnel.

major educational institutions in British Guiana are the Demba Trade School, the Demba School of Nursing, the Bookers Apprenticeship Training Scheme with a school at Port Mourant, and the Extra-Mural Department of the University College of the West Indies (no longer existing because of the establishment of the University of Guyana). Neither the two schools at Demba nor the Bookers Trade School receives government aid. Similarly, as of 1959, adult education received no government aid. Programs for adults were organized by the Adult Education Association, a voluntary organization, with the cooperation of the British Council and, in some instances, the Extra-Mural Department of U.C.W.I.

Except for the few courses offered by the Extra-Mural Department of U.C.W.I., there is very little available by way of university training in British Guiana.[3] Large numbers of Guianese have gone abroad to continue their education, but not much is known about them. It is not known precisely how many have left the country to pursue higher education, where they have gone, how many have earned degrees, or what number has returned. In 1959, it was known that 587 Guianese were studying in the United Kingdom and the Irish Republic; 46 were studying in Canada; 94 in Jamaica; and 205 in the United States. Of this total group, only 101 were sponsored by government or Colonial Development and Welfare scholarships. Most of the individuals on scholarship were more or less obligated to return to Guiana after completing their course of studies. It also is known that many Guianese are pursuing higher education in Europe and in India, but not enough information is available on these students to state a precise number. Since 1961, an increasing number of Guianese have gone to East Germany and Cuba to pursue educational programs. The exact number is not known, but estimates range from 80 to 200 or more. Many of these students are privately supported by the Peoples Progressive Party.

In view of these facts, it is clear that education in Guiana involves considerably more than local social structures. Most of the schools participate in a national educational system which displays all of the features of a broker institution. The Ministry of Community Development and Education, with associated agencies of the civil service, links the activities of individuals—students, teachers, and administrators—

[3] Subsequent to the completion of field work in 1961, a national university was established by the Jagan government.

to the wider sphere of societal activity. All minimal cultural sections participate in a common educational system, even if that system is loosely integrated by virtue of its special characteristics. The questions are, What effects has this institutional complex had in generating new cultural values that serve to integrate the Guianese people as a whole? Has education contributed to the development of a Guianese national character, or has it served to maintain the differences that exist between minimal cultural sections?

Without becoming deeply involved in the philosophy of education, it is possible to distinguish between two very broad types of educational programs. On the one hand, there are those which are frequently described as "liberal" or "classical." Such programs are designed by and large to develop the intellectual faculties in order that the individual, from his study of the arts, literature, and the sciences, may internalize those values that are thought to be necessary for living the good life. On the other hand, there are those educational programs which are vocationally oriented, that is, they are designed to provide the individual with the knowledge and skills necessary to occupy specific statuses in the society within which he lives.

As Raymond T. Smith recently noted, the educational system that developed in British Guiana has always been related to a social purpose which does not seem to fit very well into either of the above categories.[4] Before emancipation, the planters were firmly convinced that any effort to make Christian gentlemen out of slaves could only produce dissatisfaction and lead to rebellion. Following emancipation, the utilitarian philosophy did not take hold, primarily because Guiana's economy was neither industrial nor independent. Professional skills were imported from the United Kingdom, while the labor skills that were necessary to grow and harvest sugar cane did not require an elaborate system of formal education. Thus, education was left to the churches, who were interested in it because of their evangelicalism.

Under the circumstances following emancipation, it was inevitable that the colonial government adopt the view held by the established churches that the primary purpose of education should consist of providing the moral and social basis for a civil society. This meant, in effect, that the language and culture of English society should be disseminated because of its civilizing value. The adoption of this view,

---

[4] Raymond T. Smith, *British Guiana* (London: Oxford University Press, 1962), pp. 145–52.

however, did not imply that the educational system was intended to alter the status quo. On the contrary, as Raymond Smith and others have noted, "the very idea of a black Englishman was thought anomalous." The structure of colonial society was such that the educated African, or any educated Guianese for that matter, could not be given access to those higher statuses that were reserved for Europeans alone. Thus, where the highest achievement was to become an English gentleman and the rewards of being an English gentlemen were denied, education could not be truly liberal. At the same time, the vocational value of British education was limited.

Nevertheless, the command of English culture provided its own rewards. The Guianese who could display the mannerisms of the English gentleman—who could emulate the standards of Christian morality, read and write, appreciate the arts, and enjoy literature—could also feel superior to those less "civilized" than himself. There was still another reward. As colonial society developed, as its economy faltered and its administrative structure expanded, there was an increasing need for "civilized" Guianese who could fill the positions that were no longer financially attractive to Europeans. English culture provided access to the civil service bureaucracy and the world of white-collar employment.

In view of these circumstances, there are many reasons why educational institutions in Guiana have not been very successful in synthesizing a value system capable of unifying, nationally, African and East Indian minimal cultural sections. It has already been noted how the Africans came to dominate the field of education, while the East Indians, during the indenture system, were neither motivated nor encouraged to send their children to school. It also has been noted how Indians feel about having their children educated by Africans who, in most instances, are considered to be Chamar (of low caste). Indian leaders have always felt that Christian schools presented a threat to their cultural identity.[5] As a consequence, they have not hesitated to be critical of the dual control of the schools by Christian churches and the government.

The criticism of dual control by Indian leaders, whether justified or not, has taken root in the Indian community, and it could not help

---

[5] Professor Philip Singer of the Albany Medical College has recently completed a study of East Indian cultural identity in British Guiana. Judging from the working papers which Professor Singer has been so kind as to provide me, there seems to be almost complete agreement between his findings and my own with respect to the persistence of Hindu cultural identity.

generating a somewhat suspicious and negative attitude toward the kind of education available to Indian children. During the course of the village surveys, informants were asked how they felt about the dual control of the schools. Of the 155 Indians who understood and responded to the question, 86.4 per cent stated a firm opposition to the system. By way of contrast 68.4 per cent of the 209 Africans who responded to the question were in favor of continuing the system. When asked to explain their opposition, most of the Indians interviewed voiced the complaints of their religious and political leaders. They felt that Indian children who were not willing to go along with ways of their Christian teachers were discriminated against, and they expressed the conviction that this was causing many Indian children to turn their backs on the Indian way of life. As one rather vociferous Indian informant put it, "If you give you child many years in these schools all he cares about when he done is sporting. Me own son I sent to high school and he na wanna work anymore." On the other hand, many of the Africans who opposed dual control felt that the government could better afford to maintain educational standards than the churches.

The truth of the matter is that the school system, until the past ten or fifteen years, has provided very little which seemed to be of value to most of the East Indian population. This is particularly the case with respect to what was being taught in terms of the curriculum. The vast majority of the East Indian population was, and still is, rural. It is comprised of sugar estate workers and rice farmers. To the people working in these industries, the values and mannerisms of the English gentleman were not very functional. And yet, the school curriculum offered little else. It did not provide a vocational education that might have been useful to farmers and agricultural workers. On the contrary, the values transmitted in the schools were largely detrimental to these occupations in terms of the aspirations they generated. Thus, until the "Swettenham Circular" was withdrawn in 1933 and education was made compulsory for Indian children, most East Indians did not consider it worth while to send their children to Christian schools.[6] In 1933, for example, there were approximately 28,980 East Indian

[6] Under the indenture system, the authorities were always reluctant to prosecute Indian parents who refused to send their children to school. The "Swettenham Circular," which addressed itself to this problem, was issued in 1904 under the direction of the governor, Sir James Alexander Swettenham. The circular contained instructions to the effect that Indian parents should not be prosecuted during the first ten years after their arrival in the colony if, on religious grounds, they objected to sending their children to Christian schools. In other words, the circular almost completely exempted Indian parents from the provisions of the Elementary Education Ordinance of 1876.

children between the ages of five and fifteen years. Only 18.7 per cent of these children were enrolled in primary schools. By 1937, four years after the "Swettenham Circular" was withdrawn, the number of East Indian children enrolled in primary schools increased by nearly 50 per cent.

If it is assumed that the educational system is a broker institution which exposes all Guianese to common cultural values, then some idea may be had concerning the extent to which certain of these values are shared by different cultural sections. Since most of the schools are operated by Christian denominational groups, consider religious values first. To what extent have Indians become Christians as a result of attending Christian schools? In 1921, no less than 91.2 per cent of the Indian population was classified as non-Christian (some of the indentures were Christian before they left India, but their number is not known). By 1946, this figure had declined to 90.3 per cent. In 1961, to the extent that the three villages studied are representative of the Indian population, 87.0 per cent of the Indians reported themselves to be non-Christian. In other words, between 1921 and 1961 there has been no appreciable change in the religious identification of East Indians as a result of the influence of Christian schools.

Another dimension of the cultural changes brought about by educational institutions, and for which some data are available, involves the matter of literacy. Most of the indentured Indians, when they first came to Guiana, spoke Hindi, Hindustani, Tamil, and Telagu. The number who were literate in these languages was probably never very large. Because of the circumstances under which the indentures had to live and work, it was inevitable that these vernaculars would disappear. However, by 1931, there were still a sizable number of Indians who not only spoke one or more of the vernaculars but who were also literate in them. The 1931 Census reports that 6.7 per cent of the Indian population was literate in Hindi; 2.2 per cent was literate in Hindustani; and less than 1 per cent was literate in Tamil and Telegu. In recent years, a number of schools have been established, mostly by private groups, which include Hindi in the curriculum. There are no data available to indicate the extent to which these efforts have been successful. The impression of most observers is that they have not been.

Since the 1930's, East Indians have become increasingly literate in English, but they still fall considerably short of the Afro-Guianese. In 1931, for example, only 25.1 per cent of the Indian population could read and write English, compared to 79.9 per cent of the Afro-

Guianese.[7] In 1946, the last year for which census data have been made available, 56 per cent of the Indians over the age of ten were literate in English, compared to 97.3 per cent of the Afro-Guianese. In 1946, there were 57,736 Guianese over the age of ten who could neither read nor write in any language. The East Indians comprised 86.3 per cent of this group, compared to 6.6 per cent for the Afro-Guianese. Undoubtedly, the educational gap between these two groups has continued to close since 1946. However, a gap still exists. In the village populations discussed in the previous chapter, the total group of East Indians interviewed averaged 3.45 years of education, compared to 5.84 years for the Africans interviewed. If East Indian attitudes toward the education of their children have been modified by educational institutions, they have not, as yet, been completely changed.

Occupational data provide still another view of the integrative effect of educational institutions. Until very recently, the highest positions in the occupational structure that have been accessible to Guianese are those which are grouped under the census categories "Public Service" and "Professional." These categories apply to officials, clerks, administrators, police officers, clergy, teachers, doctors, lawyers, engineers, and the like. These positions require a level of educational achievement, and perhaps also a level of status aspiration, beyond that of ordinary individuals. The people who fill these positions in a colonial society display a style of life that is very different from that of peasant farmers and agricultural workers. Certainly, in British Guiana the professionals and public servants reflect more of the values of the English gentleman than do the peasants and agricultural workers. To what extent have East Indians pursued these occupations?

In 1891, a total of 3,123 Guianese were classified as professionals and public servants. Of these, 181 or 5.8 per cent were East Indians.[8] While only 9 of these Indians were listed as teachers, 67 were listed "priests and mendicants." Twenty years later, in 1911, the number of East Indians classified as professionals and public servants increased to 382 or 8.2 per cent of the total number of Guianese allocated to these

[7] These rates are depressed because the 1931 figures are based on the total population of racial groups, and, consequently, they include preschool children.

[8] It is not possible to determine the exact number of Africans among professionals and public servants because the census did not list them separately from Europeans, Portuguese, Chinese, and Amerindians. However, it can be assumed that Africans comprised the vast majority of teachers and nonpensionable civil servants in 1891.

categories. During this period, however, it is interesting to note that the number of East Indian teachers increased from 9 to 25, while the number of priests and mendicants exploded from 67 to 282. In other words, during this twenty-year period, a substantial proportion of the East Indians who became professionals and public servants were priests and mendicants. By 1931, there were 6,202 Guianese professionals and public servants. Of these, 12 per cent (746) were East Indians. Only 32.3 per cent of these East Indians were in the public service. Among those classified as professionals, priests represented the largest single category (44.3 per cent of 505). In 1931, only 7.2 per cent of the 1,397 Guianese in the teaching profession were East Indians.

Unfortunately, the 1946 Census does not provide occupational data for East Indians which are comparable to those of earlier censuses. However, the progress of East Indians in the professions and the public service between 1931 and 1946 can be approximated. During this fifteen-year period, the number of professionals and public servants increased from 6,202 to 8,527. This represents an increase of 37 per cent over the 1931 figure. If it is assumed that the number of East Indians in these occupations doubled during the period, then in 1946 East Indians would have comprised approximately 17.5 per cent of the total number of Guianese professionals and public servants.[9] If anything, this figure may be a little high, considering the fact that in 1943 East Indians comprised only 10.1 per cent of the 735 Guianese on the fixed establishment of the civil service.[10]

When the period between 1891 and 1946 is considered as a whole, it represents a span of time covering almost two generations. During this period, the progress which East Indians made with respect to their entrance into the higher status occupations cannot be described as spectacular. In 1891, only 0.2 per cent of the Indian population were professionals or public servants. By 1946, the figure was still less than 1 per cent. In 1946, the East Indians represented 43.5 per cent of the total population but only 17.5 per cent of those Guianese in higher status occupations. Within two generations after emancipation, a sizable number of the Afro-Guianese were literate, and they comprised

[9] This assumption is based on the rate of increase of Indians in these occupations between 1911 and 1931. As an "outside" assumption, this rate would seem to be a safe one to use because there were no dramatic changes in Guianese society before and during the Second World War that could possibly have propelled East Indians into these occupations at an abnormal rate.

[10] Dwarka Nath, *A History of Indians in British Guiana* (London: Thomas Nelson and Sons, 1950), pp. 216–18.

the vast majority of the Guianese who were professionals and public servants. By 1946, this was still the case.

Educational institutions in British Guiana, clearly, have contributed to the development of a "national" culture. However, the values that comprise this culture are distinctly British in origin. Also, these values are not yet "national" in the sense that they have been equally adopted by the various elements of Guianese society. As of the present, British values have been adopted much more thoroughly by the Afro-Guianese than by the East Indians. In fact, a great many East Indians still consider the values maintained by educational institutions to be imposed and to represent a serious threat to their cultural identity. In this respect, educational institutions have not been able to integrate Africans and East Indians. Nevertheless, the data presented above indicate that over the years East Indians have become progressively involved in Guiana's educational institutions. Their involvement is reflected in terms of increased enrollments among Indian children in the schools. It is also reflected in terms of the increasing number of Indian professionals, public servants, and teachers. As a consequence of these changes, the expression of Indian cultural values has been modified, particularly among those Indians who occupy the kinds of statuses that tend to accompany educational achievement. The significance of this change will emerge more clearly when nationalist policies are considered.

## COMMUNICATIONS MEDIA

The mass media in British Guiana, as in most underdeveloped countries, are represented by the press and the radio broadcasting services. These communications media may be viewed as networks of social relationships which are organized to digest and disseminate information as well as to shape and influence the values expressed by publics. Such networks of social relationships constitute broker institutions because, theoretically, they are not predicated upon structures which are defined in the local community. Thus, they have an integrative capacity which is potentially national in scope. For purposes of this analysis, three questions appear to be relevant with respect to the communications media. First, what groups have organized these media? Second, what values do these groups profess? And, third, what sections of the population have availed themselves of the values of which groups?

As of 1960, four major dailies were published in British Guiana. These included the *Daily Argosy*, the *Daily Chronicle*, the *Guiana Graphic*, and the *Evening Post*. All four have been predominantly owned and controlled by a combination of big business and sugar interests. The *Daily Argosy*, for example, is almost completely owned by the family of P. C. Wight, who was a director of Plantation Enmore (one of the Booker companies), a broker, a realtor, and an insurance investor. He also was Mayor of Georgetown and a member of the Georgetown Town Council. The directors of the *Daily Chronicle* have included P. C. Wight, R. G. Humphery (R. G. Humphery & Sons, Jewelers and Pawn Brokers), and R. A. Humphery (of the Hotel Tower and Bookers Properties, Holdings and Services, Ltd.). The largest shareholders of the *Chronicle* have included P. C. Wight, Royden Nominees, Ltd. (Royal Bank of Canada), James Sanderson (banker), and Herbert Nash (banker). In 1961, the controlling interests in the *Chronicle* were purchased by Peter d'Aguiar, owner of Banks Brewery, the B. G. Bottling Company, breweries in Barbados, and founder of the United Force (a conservative party largely supported by business interests). Presently, Peter d'Aguiar is British Guiana's Minister of Finance.

The *Guiana Graphic* has had among its directors Dudley Howard (Attorney for Sandbach Parker & Company, Ltd.), R. R. Follet-Smith (Chairman of Bookers Sugar Estates, Ltd.), Guy M. Eccles (Managing Director of Blairmont Estates), and C. J. Bettencourt-Gomes (Director of Bettencourt & Company, Ltd., B. G. Mutual Fire Insurance Company, J. P. Santos, Ltd., B. G. Match Factory, Ltd., and the Rupununi Development Company, Ltd.). Controlling shares in the *Graphic* were owned by Booker Brothers, McConnell & Company, Ltd. During the course of study, the *Graphic* was sold to an independent company.

Except for the rural villages close to Georgetown or New Amsterdam, the circulation of these dailies is generally confined to the urban areas. However, the Sunday editions of the *Chronicle* and the *Argosy* are widely distributed in rural areas. Although a small number of people in a village may subscribe to the Sunday editions, after they read them, they usually pass them on to relatives or friends. In Ann's Grove, 78 per cent of the Afro-Guianese read regularly one or more of the Sunday editions. The percentage for East Indians in Clonbrook was slightly less (76 per cent). At Plantation Skeldon, 56 per cent of the Indians interviewed read a Sunday edition. At Mackenzie, among the African bauxite workers, 99 per cent read a Sunday edition. These percentages fall off sharply in the smaller villages of Eversham and Cromarty. In Eversham, 33 per cent of the Afro-Guianese regularly read a Sunday edition. In Cromarty, on the other hand, only 6 per cent (two interviewees) read a Sunday edition. From these data, it seems clear that Guiana's major newspapers are not only widely distributed but, for an underdeveloped country, widely read.

All four of the newspapers mentioned above have been maintained by editorial and news staffs which are comprised largely of educated, middle-class Afro-Guianese, who, for the most part, have been willing to accept and to communicate the editorial policies of the owners. Needless to say, editorial policies have been mostly conservative with respect to economic and political issues. Reflecting both the general and the specific interests of their owners, these papers have emphasized the economic, social, and cultural values attached to British colonial ties. They have particularly emphasized the value of private enterprise and the threat which communism poses to Guiana's freedom and economic development. At one time or another, all of these papers have been extremely critical of most of Guiana's nationalist parties and their leaders. Over the years, they have been consistently and increasingly critical of Cheddi Jagan and the Peoples Progressive Party. Between 1957 and 1961, it is extremely difficult to find in these papers any favorable comment on anything undertaken by the Jagan government.

Because of their editorial policies, particularly with respect to Jagan, the P.P.P., and the Jagan government, the Guianese dailies have inadvertently contributed to the division between East Indians and Africans. Approximately two-thirds of the Indians interviewed, when asked what they thought of the newspapers they read, claimed that these papers were anti-Indian and pro-African. When it was pointed out that the papers under discussion have been consistently critical of racialism in all of its forms, informants frequently retorted that these papers have been just as consistently critical of Cheddi Jagan. The general feeling is described in the words of one informant who stated, "Man, dey have only hate for de Indian nation in this country. Cheddi can do nothing right for dem. Dey are against he Government because he a coolieman like we." In addition to such comments, more educated Indian informants frequently noted that the papers were largely owned by sugar and business interests and they employed few Indians. These general attitudes, of course, were constantly being reinforced by the P.P.P. through its various channels of communication.

The radio broadcasting services in British Guiana represent a medium of mass communication as important as the major dailies. Broadcasting services are operated by the British Guiana United Broadcasting Company, Ltd., under the designations "Radio Demerara" and Station BGBS (British Guiana Broadcasting Service). The operations of this company are governed by an agreement executed in 1950 between the company and the government. Under the provisions of the agreement, the company was granted a fifteen-year franchise, and two government nominees were to serve on its board of directors. Among the directors of this company have been men such as J. A. Adamson (Bookers Brothers Drug Stores, Ltd.), J. St. Felix Dare (William Fogarty, Ltd.), Ernest J. Haywood (Wieting & Richter, Ltd.), and Sir Frank W. McDavid (a prominent Afro-Guianese businessman and public servant). The largest shareholders in the company include William Fogarty, Ltd., Guiana Match Factory, Ltd., C. J. Bettencourt-Gomes, Wieting & Richter, Ltd., and R. G. Humphrey & Sons, Ltd. In other words, the radio broadcasting services are owned and operated by the same colonial interests that own and operate the major newspapers.

The radio broadcasting services reach practically everyone in British Guiana. They schedule broadcasts which carry communications between friends and relatives in addition to their regular programs of news and entertainment. Perhaps because of government regulations and the influence of the Jagan government, during the period of field work, the radio broadcasting services appeared to the author to represent much more of a forum of open discussion with respect to political and economic issues. In addition to the weekly news conference conducted by Cheddi Jagan, from time to time, radio debates were scheduled between government representatives and opposition leaders. Apart from these programs, radio time was not used extensively to carry editorials except, of course, when editorials were carried as paid political advertisements.

There is some question concerning the extent to which the broadcasting medium is any more integrative with respect to existing cultural sections than the major dailies. Considerable broadcasting time was given to programs of an ethnic character, e.g., programs of Indian music or programs of West Indian music. In rural areas, where most radio sets have to be operated by relatively expensive drycell batteries, radio listening tends to be highly selective with respect to the kinds of programs tuned in. Except for news programs and programs carrying personal communications (which everyone seemed to listen to), observational data suggest that the Guianese tend to be selective in their use of radios along ethnic lines. In other words, in Indian villages, one tends to hear only Indian programs on the radio. In African villages, one seldom hears Indian music. However, in the absence of precise survey data, generalizations concerning the integrative effect of this medium of communications must be highly qualified.

In addition to the daily newspapers, there are a number of weekly publications in British Guiana. These include the *Official Gazette,* the *Labour Advocate,* the *Catholic Standard, Thunder, New Nation,* and the *Sun*. The most important of these are *Thunder, New Nation,* and *Sun*. These are published and circulated by Guiana's three major political parties. *Thunder* is the organ of the Peoples Progressive Party; the *New Nation* is published by the Peoples National Congress; and the *Sun* is issued by the United Force.

It is difficult to know precisely the circulation of these party organs. All three political parties make a concerted effort to distribute their newspapers on the streets of Georgetown and New Amsterdam.[11] In the rural areas, however, party papers are distributed by locally organized party cells. Where there are no cells operating, the distribution of party papers is either extremely sporadic or completely absent. Thus, in Eversham and Cromarty not a single informant subscribed to or read regularly a political party newspaper. In areas where there are larger concentrations of population, party cells are active, and they seem to do a pretty good job of circulating the party news organ as well as many other types of political literature.[12]

If we ignore Eversham and Cromarty and consider the larger communities discussed in the previous chapter, a better idea may be

[11] The P.P.P. and the P.N.C. also make party publications available to Guianese in New York and London.

[12] Some local cells maintain small libraries which contain an interesting variety of political literature. In one such library in the vicinity of Plantation Skeldon, one could read the English edition of the *Peking Review,* the English editions of Polish and East German newspapers, pamphlets from the Soviet Union, the *World Marxist Review,* the *Monthly Review* (published in the United States by Leo Huberman and Paul M. Sweezy), *Masses and Mainstream* (another American publication), pamphlets put out by the American Civil Liberties Union, Max Lerner's *America as a Civilization,* and *New Times* (a weekly journal published in Moscow). Although such literature was available, interview data suggest that only the most highly motivated party activists bothered to read much of it.

had of the circulation of political party newspapers. Of the 187 Africans interviewed in Ann's Grove and Mackenzie, 35 per cent subscribed to the *New Nation,* 10 per cent subscribed to *Thunder,* and only 3 per cent subscribed to the *Sun*. Since these were the individuals who actually purchased papers, it is highly probable that many more may have read them. Of the total group, only twelve Africans subscribed to two or more of these papers (most of the twelve subscribed to *Thunder* and *New Nation*). By way of contrast, among the 147 Indians interviewed in Clonbrook and Plantation Skeldon, 24 per cent subscribed to *Thunder,* 2 per cent subscribed to *Sun,* and none subscribed to the *New Nation*. The figure for Plantation Skeldon may be somewhat low because of the reluctance on the part of many sugar workers to admit the existence of P.P.P. activity in the housing schemes.

In view of these data, it would seem that political party news media are consumed fairly widely, and they are consumed pretty much along ethnic lines. Africans read the *New Nation,* and East Indians read *Thunder*. Few of them read both. As a result of these consumption patterns the attitudes which Africans and East Indians hold with respect to one another tend to be reinforced. The *New Nation* is the sharpest and most intense critic of Cheddi Jagan and the Peoples Progressive Party that exists in British Guiana. Similarly *Thunder,* in every issue, levels severe criticism at L. F. S. Burnham and the Peoples National Congress. Both papers constantly accuse one another of racial politics, and both are constantly accused of racial politics by the *Sun*. The *Sun,* of course, is largely supported by Portuguese businessmen. In light of these considerations, it is difficult to see how political party news media can serve to unify the African and Indian sections of the population.

In conclusion, the mass media do not appear to contribute much to the national integration of the Guianese population. Most of the media are owned and operated by special interest groups (i.e., planters, businessmen, and political parties). To a considerable degree these groups use the mass media to further their special interests. The values which these interests reflect are not shared in common by the Afro-Guianese and East Indian cultural sections. To the extent that these groups participate in media consumption, the attitudes they hold with respect to one another tend to be reinforced. Thus, both directly and indirectly, the communications media in British Guiana have contributed to the plural integration of Guianese society.

## COMMERCIAL AND INDUSTRIAL ORGANIZATIONS

Under most circumstances, particularly in underdeveloped countries, commercial and industrial organizations are comprised of corporate groups of a nonlocal type. That is to say, these kinds of organizations usually may be identified as perpetual groups with determinate boundaries and memberships which are extra-communal in their derivation. As corporations these groups have an internal organization, an appropriate set of regulatory procedures, a body of common affairs, and a unitary set of external relations. M. G. Smith has suggested recently that when such groups are constituted so that their continuity, identity, autonomy, organization, and exclusive affairs are not disturbed by the entrance or exit of their individual members, they have the character of a public.[13] In view of these considerations, it follows that commercial and industrial organizations must be considered as institutional structures of the broker type. Theoretically, they are capable of linking the activities of individuals to the wider sphere of societal activity.

In analyzing the structures of these particular institutions, it is useful, following Sir Henry Maine, to differentiate between "corporations aggregate" and "corporations sole."[14] Corporate groups, what Maine called "corporations aggregate," are pluralities to which an unchanging unity is ascribed; viewed externally, each group forms "one person." With respect to corporations aggregate, we want to know who, among the Guianese, have been integrated so as to comprise such a group. "Corporations sole," on the other hand, refers to the unique statuses or offices that combine to make up the corporation's structure so as to implement its procedures, carry out its functions, and insure its perpetuity. With respect to corporations sole, we want to know who, among the Guianese, have been recruited to fill these kinds of positions.

For purposes of this analysis, it is neither possible nor necessary to consider in detail all of the commercial and industrial organizations that exist in British Guiana. As was indicated in Chapter 1, Guiana has a typical colonial economy. In 1958, the f.o.b. value of exports was

---

[13] In a paper entitled "A Structural Approach to Comparative Politics," delivered at the 1963 Annual Meeting of the American Political Science Association, New York City. Published in David Easton (ed.), *Varieties of Political Theory*, pp. 113–28.

[14] Sir Henry Sumner Maine, *Ancient Law* (London: Routledge & Sons, 1904).

$97,227,547 (B.W.I.), to which agricultural products contributed 67.6 per cent (62.4 per cent for sugar and sugar preparations and 5.2 per cent for rice), minerals 23.2 per cent (21.1 per cent for bauxite and 2.1 per cent for gold and diamonds), and forest products 3.9 per cent (mainly lumber and balata). Two industries, sugar and bauxite, produced 83 per cent of the total f.o.b. value of exports and paid approximately 60 per cent of the total revenue collected by way of income taxes and excise duties. Although the export value of rice is not great, rice agriculture ranks next to sugar as the second largest source of employment in the country. Directly or indirectly, these industries generate almost 95 per cent of the income which keeps the Guianese economy going.

The colonial nature of the Guianese economy may be described more concretely in terms of Booker Brothers, McConnell & Company, Ltd. Bookers is a London-based international business cartel with holdings in Britain, Trinidad, Jamaica, Barbados, Northern Rhodesia, Nyasaland, Nigeria, Canada, India, Belgium, and British Guiana. The holdings of this company in British Guiana are so vast that many Guianese jokingly refer to their country as "Bookers' Guiana." Figure 6 graphically presents the organization of this company's holdings in Guiana.

As Figure 6 shows, the Booker group of companies is involved in practically every sector of the Guianese economy. Bookers Agricultural Holdings controls fifteen of Guiana's eighteen sugar estates, the Sugar Producers' Association, and the Kabawer Cattle Ranch Company. The Campbell Booker group of companies, on the other hand, comprises a vast network of wholesale and retail distributors dealing in groceries, furniture, household supplies, appliances, jewelry, clothing, sporting goods and equipment, office supplies, hardware, building supplies, farm equipment, and automobiles. It also operates Guiana's largest taxi service. Through Bookers Engineering and Industrial Holdings, Bookers is involved in the manufacture and sale of drugs and medical supplies, the manufacture and sale of boxes, and the publishing business. Bookers Merchants represents still another network of producers and distributors dealing in rum, stockfeed, balata, lumber, and petroleum products. Bookers Merchants is also involved in the advertising business. Booker Brothers (Liverpool) provides Bookers with its own shipping service. In conjunction with its shipping interests, Booker Brothers controls the sugar terminals in British Guiana. Somehow, this particular holding company has also involved itself with the insurance

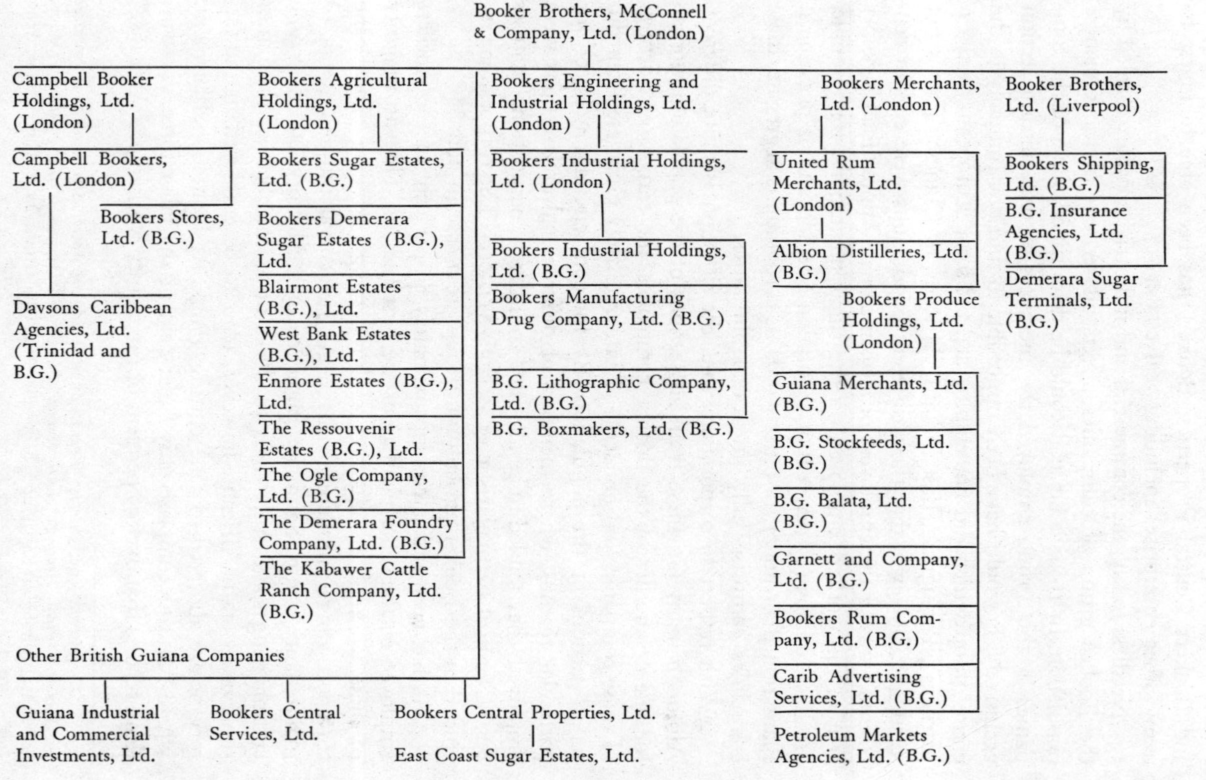


FIGURE 6. BOOKER BROTHERS, MCCONNELL & COMPANY IN BRITISH GUIANA

business. Through Guiana Industrial and Commercial Investments and Bookers Central Properties, Bookers has been able to invest in many other enterprises including real estate.

Needless to say, the commercial and industrial complex formed by the Booker group of companies affects all sections of the Guianese population. In 1960, as far as it could be determined, none of the companies in this group employed the members of one cultural section exclusively. It would have been impossible to find one company in the entire group which did not employ at least some Europeans (i.e., expatriates), Portuguese, East Indians, Africans, or Chinese. This is not to suggest, however, that these different populations were equally represented among the employees of all companies. Approximately 80 per cent of the workers employed on the sugar plantations, for example, are East Indians (73 per cent at Plantation Skeldon and 92 per cent at Plantation Blairmont). In other words, as corporations aggregate, these companies comprise fully integrated pluralities.

With respect to corporations sole, the situation is quite different. Although many Guianese from all sections of the population worked for one or another of the Booker companies, the corporate structures of these companies did not serve to integrate fully Guianese from different sections of the population. By force of circumstances, or for particular reasons, where members of different cultural sections were employed, they tended to be allocated to different occupational statuses on the basis of particularistic or ascriptive criteria. The corporations included in the Booker agricultural group are a case in point.

As has been indicated, approximately 80 per cent of the workers employed on the sugar plantations are East Indians. The vast majority of these workers are allocated to shovel gangs, weeding gangs, cane transport gangs, mechanical tillage gangs, general purpose gangs, or maintenance gangs. Some are employed in the factory, others in cane cutting gangs, and still others as clerks or as members of the junior supervisory staff. Africans, however, tend to be employed in the factory or are allocated to cane cutting gangs. At Plantation Blairmont, where Africans comprise only 8 per cent of the labor force, Jayawardena reports that over 50 per cent of the factory workers are Africans.[15]

[15] C. Jayawardena, *Interim Report on a Study of Social Structure and Processes of Social Control Amongst East Indian Sugar Workers in British Guiana* (Mona, Jamaica: Institute of Social and Economic Research, University College of the West Indies, 1957), p. 23.

At Plantation Skeldon, practically all of the Africans employed are either factory workers or cane cutters.

The allocation of Africans and East Indians to these different occupational statuses derives primarily from particularistic or ascriptive considerations. The original indentured Indians were put to work mainly as field hands, while factory operations were left to skilled African workers. Over the years, Africans have been reluctant to teach Indians the skills they need to acquire in order to work in the sugar factories. Particularly, they have been reluctant to teach them the artisan skills required of panboilers (one of the most highly rewarded occupational statuses on the plantation). Rather than force the issue, and in order to maintain industrial peace, plantation managers have gone along with these practices. Cane cutting, on the other hand, is quite another matter. Cane cutting requires heavy physical labor for which individuals are paid piecework rates. At Plantation Skeldon, Indian workers are not thought to be capable of doing what is regarded by the estate management as a full day's work. The management believes that Indians lack physical stamina. Thus, the management prefers to import African workers from coastal villages to cut cane rather than give the work to Indians. Generally these cane cutting gangs are not extensively mixed: Africans tend to work with Africans and Indians with Indians.

Certain employment policies also are based on particularistic or ascriptive criteria. At one plantation, for example, Africans are rarely employed as junior supervisory staff personnel or as clerks. Members of the senior supervisory staff indicated that this was a matter of "informal" employment policy. The Indian workers, they noted, have become increasingly troublesome over the years (particularly since the emergence of nationalist political movements). In the interests of industrial peace, it was decided to recruit clerks and junior staff personnel, as far as it was possible to do so, from among the sons of "deserving" Indian workers. As a consequence, these positions are seldom given to Africans. In the head office at this particular estate, there is not a single African male employed as a clerk. It is not known to what extent this "informal" employment policy exists on other estates but, according to several informants, it appears to be widespread.

Employment policies based on particularistic or ascriptive criteria of this type also seem to be relatively widespread among corporations outside of the Booker agricultural group. The commercial complex which comprises the Campbell Booker Holdings, for example, is another case in point. The various stores operated by Bookers in New Amsterdam and Georgetown have maintained, for years, an unofficial employment policy based on racial or color considerations. Until very recently, these stores have attempted to employ only Portuguese or "light-colored" Africans as clerks and bookkeepers. Darker Africans were usually employed to fill menial positions (e.g., stock clerks, janitors, floor sweepers, delivery boys, etc.). East Indians, because they were predominantly rural and uneducated or because African supervisors refused to consider their applications, seldom were hired to fill positions as clerks or bookkeepers. Until recently, a similar situation seems to have existed with respect to the corporations that make up the other Booker companies that operate primarily in the urban setting.

The failure of these corporations to integrate Africans and East Indians at the higher levels of the corporate structure is even more pronounced than at the lower levels. Until very recently, as a matter of policy, practically all of the senior staff personnel on the sugar estates has been recruited in Europe or from among the Portuguese or light-colored group in Guiana. As a result of the pressures generated by nationalist politicians (particularly Jagan and Burnham), this policy has been undergoing change. The Booker Group Committee (which is comprised of the board chairmen of the major Booker holding companies in Guiana) has adopted and attempted to implement a "Guianization" program. The expressed purpose of this program is to recruit Guianese on the basis of universalistic criteria and to train them to fill the positions presently occupied by Europeans. As a general observation, this program appeared to be moving ahead. However, the speed at which Bookers is able to integrate the higher levels of its corporate structure obviously depends upon the availability of Guianese with university educations and the continuation of the company's policy of providing funds for these purposes.

As one moves up the hierarchy of corporate control within the Booker group of companies, Africans and East Indians tend to disappear altogether from the corporate structure. The boards of directors of practically all of the main Booker companies are composed of Europeans. All of the members of the Booker Group Committee are Europeans. The higher levels of management are comprised almost entirely of Europeans and a few Portuguese. Technical experts and specialists throughout the complex are primarily Europeans. Most of the positions in the Sugar Producers' Association, the industrial and public relations organ for the entire sugar industry, are occupied by Europeans. The few Africans or Indians who have crept into the higher sections of the corporate structure within recent years have done so primarily because of the "Guianization" program. Thus, the corporate structures of this vast and complicated network of commercial and industrial organizations has only begun to integrate the different sections of the Guianese population.

As an international business cartel, Aluminium Limited of Canada (Alcan) is a larger but less diversified complex of corporations than Bookers. In 1960, Alcan owned the controlling equity in 38 companies located in 28 different countries. It also held investments (up to 50 per cent equity) in fifteen other companies. In British Guiana, however, Alcan's grip on the national economy is considerably less significant than Bookers'. Only two companies, the Demerara Bauxite Company (Demba) and Sprostons, are owned and operated by Alcan. Although Reynolds Metals maintains bauxite mining operations in Berbice, Demba is the largest producer of this ore in the country. Sprostons, on the other hand, is involved in shipping, construction, trading, and miscellaneous services, mainly in conjunction with Demba's operations at Mackenzie City. In 1960, based on 1959 production, Demba paid the Guianese government $6.08 millions (B.W.I.) in income taxes, rents, royalties, and import duties. For the same period, it paid Guianese workers $6.2 millions (B.W.I.) in wages. Next to Bookers, Demba represents the largest source of income in the country.

As a corporation aggregate, Demba is a less integrated plurality than most of the Booker companies, including the sugar estates. Ninety-six per cent of Demba's employees are Guianese. Although these employees are recruited from all sections of the population, approximately 95 per cent of them are African. Demba's corporate structure is almost completely lacking in integration as far as Africans and East Indians are concerned. Practically all of the East Indians employed by Demba work as gardeners and groundskeepers. Very few are allocated to the skilled occupational statuses associated with mine operations, transportation, mechanical engineering, bauxite washing, alumina production, maintenance, or administration.

In 1961, when Demba's new alumina plant was put into operation, a concerted effort was made to recruit a larger number of East Indians to train for skilled positions. The success of this effort, from Demba's point of view, was disappointing. For one thing, the number of applicants was extremely low. This was probably due to the fact that most

East Indians have no relatives in Mackenzie City and, as a consequence, are not well informed about wages and working conditions there. However, according to Demba officials, most of the Indians who did apply for jobs were simply not interested in being trained to work in the plant alongside African workers and, in some instances, under African supervisors. Finally, as a result of the few Indians who were hired and placed in the alumina plant, a serious personnel crisis developed. The African and Indian workers refused to cooperate with one another, and the situation was so bad that it actually threatened production schedules. Even the Mine Workers Union, an African-dominated organization, threatened to intervene. Ultimately, the personnel department solved the problem by retrenching, whenever possible, the Indians that were hired to initiate this new employment policy.

Demba's corporate structure, like that of the sugar estates, differentiates between junior and senior staff personnel. As far as personnel officers could determine from payroll lists, there were no East Indians among the junior staff. Except for a few Portuguese, the junior staff was comprised of African employees. The senior staff, on the other hand, was comprised of Canadians, Europeans, a few Americans, a few Portuguese, and one African. Demba, like Bookers, has initiated a "Guianization" program. However, "Guianization" in the bauxite industry will be an extremely slow process. Practically every member of Demba's senior staff is a university-trained chemist, engineer, geologist, or administrator. The rate at which Demba can recruit Guianese to fill these positions is entirely dependent upon the extent to which Guianese are able to pursue a university education in highly technical fields of scientific endeavor.

As previously indicated, rice agriculture represents the second largest source of employment in Guiana. The corporate structure of this industry, in so far as it has one, is largely governmental. It has already been noted that rice is cultivated primarily by East Indian peasants who, as independent agents, sell their produce to rice millers. These rice millers, who are also mostly East Indians, function as brokers or middlemen. By law, the only marketing agency for rice in Guiana is the government, which carries on its market activities through the Rice Marketing Board, a legally established corporate structure.[16] Rice producers and millers conduct their negotiations with

---

[16] *The Laws of British Guiana,* chap. 249.

the Rice Marketing Board through the Rice Producers' Association, an organization established by the authority of the legislature (Ordinance No. 7 of 1946) for the purpose of protecting the interests of rice producers. Thus, all farmers and millers are required by law to sell their rice crops, except for portions which are retained for domestic uses, to the Rice Marketing Board at prices which the board fixes and establishes by negotiation with the Rice Producers' Association.

Apart from these agencies, the only other corporate structures of significance in the rice industry are the British Guiana Rice Development Company, Ltd., and the various land and agricultural cooperatives which have been organized from one end of the country to the other by the Co-operative Department and the Land Settlement Department. The British Guiana Rice Development Company was established with government funds in 1953. It operates a rice factory in conjunction with a land-development scheme in the Mahaicony-Abary River area. It also operates a second factory at Anna Regina. This company was organized mainly as a result of the efforts of Sir Frank W. McDavid, a prominent civil servant and colonial administrator of African descent. Its organization, to a considerable degree, represented an effort on the part of the colonial establishment to do something for the East Indian population which might serve to wean it away from the Jagan-Burnham brand of nationalism that had erupted between 1949 and 1953.[17]

The land and agricultural cooperatives are organized as voluntary groups by the Co-operative Department under the supervision of the Commissioner for Co-operative Development. Many of these cooperatives are located in land-development schemes where agricultural activities are under the general management of the Land Settlement and the Agricultural departments. These land development schemes have been organized in recent years for the purpose of providing riceland to landless peasants (on a leasehold basis). In order to qualify for settlement in these schemes, acceptable applicants are encouraged to join an agricultural cooperative. The cooperative, with the loan of government money, provides necessary agricultural machinery and maintains a rice mill. Even if applicants do not join the cooperative, they are required to sign an agreement, attached to their lease, under

[17] When the Rice Development Company was incorporated, it issued 20,000 shares having a total face value of $2 millions (B.W.I.). Of these, 18,380 shares were allocated to the government and 1,620 shares to the Rice Marketing Board. Thus, the government controls the Rice Development Company.

which they are obligated to sell their crop to the cooperative mill rather than to private millers.[18]

Thus, almost all of the corporations involved in the rice industry are either governmental agencies or organized and controlled by governmental agencies. Theoretically, as corporation aggregates, these are integrated pluralities by virtue of the fact that the law does not specify membership on the basis of ethnic or racial criteria. In view of the corporate structure of these pluralities, however, the degree of their integration is rather limited as far as Africans are concerned. Consider the examples of the Rice Marketing Board and the Rice Producers' Association.

The Rice Marketing Board is comprised of sixteen members who are officially appointed by the governor upon the recommendation of the prime minister (Cheddi Jagan, it will be recalled, was prime minister between 1957 and 1965). The composition of the board includes two appointees from among officers in the public service, eight from among rice farmers and millers, two from among members of the Legislative Council, and two from among businessmen and merchants. The Rice Producers' Association, which nominates eight of its members to the board as representatives of farmers and millers, is organized in terms of districts (twelve in all). The district boards (which are made up of seven members) are elected every two years by rice farmers and millers. These district boards, in turn, elect two of their number to serve on the association's general council. It is the latter group, the general council, which nominates farmers and rice millers to be recommended for appointment to the Rice Marketing Board.

As far as could be determined from available records, the general council and the district boards of the Rice Producers' Association have always been overwhelmingly East Indian in terms of their membership. This is not surprising, considering the fact that the percentage of Africans who cultivate rice is relatively small compared to East Indians. Also, while a few Africans are employed in some of the larger rice mills, there are no Africans who operate rice mills. As a result of the domination of the Rice Producers' Association by East Indians, the rice farmers and millers which the association nominates for appointment to the Rice Marketing Board are almost always East

[18] These land development schemes, as we shall see, have played an important role in the organizational strategy of the Peoples Progressive Party.

Indians. Similarly, most of the individuals who have been nominated by the Jagan government to the Board are also East Indians. Thus, in terms of its corporate structure, the rice industry tends to be controlled from top to bottom by East Indians. As a consequence, this particular industry does not function as a broker institution which serves to integrate Africans and East Indians at the societal level of economic activity.

The commercial organizations which function outside of the Booker group and which are not directly involved in the sugar, bauxite, or rice industries are extremely numerous—in fact too numerous to have been thoroughly investigated during the course of field work. Although these organizations are extremely important as sources of employment and in terms of their market activities, their size precludes them from controlling a lion's share of the Guianese economy. These smaller corporations are located primarily in Georgetown and New Amsterdam. Most of them are family enterprises owned and controlled by Portuguese, Chinese, or East Indian businessmen. Many of the East Indians who own urban business houses also hold rural investments in land and rice mills.

The small business houses, whether owned by East Indians or Portuguese, are not usually integrated pluralities. Most employees are relatives of the owners. The larger business houses, however, frequently employ Africans. This is more true of the Portuguese-owned business houses than it is of those owned by East Indians. The corporate structure characteristic of these larger business houses is much the same as that described for the Booker companies. Light-colored Africans are employed as clerks. Dark-colored Africans, if employed, are given the menial tasks as janitors, floor sweepers, stock boys, delivery boys, and the like. Several of the Portuguese businessmen who were interviewed indicated that they prefer not to employ "darkies" at all except as domestics, either because they are too lazy or because they can't be trusted with responsible work. Only the very largest East Indian shops in Georgetown seem to employ a few Africans ("in order to attract the trade"), and usually these are light-colored Africans. Banks, travel agencies, and the like employ mostly Portuguese or light-colored Africans. This also seems to be true of pawnshops and jewelry shops.

In summary, commercial and industrial organizations in British Guiana create the general impression that they serve to integrate all sections of the Guianese population regardless of the cultural differences that may exist between them at the level of communal activities. To a large extent, this impression derives from the fact that a great number of these organizations constitute integrated pluralities. Because of this, Africans, Indians, Portuguese, and others are frequently seen together in similar places. However, as one begins to view these organizations in terms of their corporate structures, it becomes readily apparent that Africans, Indians, Portuguese, and others are seldom seen together doing the same things. The members of each of these groups have their place, so to speak, in the corporate structure. Their allocation to the positions they fill is based, more often than not, on particularistic or ascriptive criteria. Thus, commercial and industrial organizations may serve to mediate the differences that exist between these cultural sections but they do not, as yet, serve to integrate them.

## MARKETS AND ECONOMIC TRANSACTIONS

It is not possible to present a very extensive discussion of the social and cultural dimensions of market activity and economic transactions in British Guiana. For one thing, the data necessary for a complete analysis of these phenomena were not collected during the course of field work, and they are not available from secondary sources. Also, an adequate analysis of these phenomena would necessitate, at least from the point of view of this writer, the introduction of certain theoretical issues which are much too peripheral to the focus of the present study. At the same time, however, markets and economic transactions in Guiana do involve broker institutions, and these institutions are central to the problem of sociocultural integration. Therefore, a discussion of these phenomena is necessary, even if it must be limited by the availability of suitable data.

In view of what has been stated previously, it is rather obvious that British Guiana has a market economy. The dominant transactional principle in terms of which goods, services, and resources are distributed is the principle of market exchange. Economic units are valued in terms of a money price which is determined, in large part, by the impersonal forces of supply and demand. The market prices for these units influence economic decisions at all levels of the society. The buyers and sellers of these units are primarily dependent upon market transactions for their livelihood. In British Guiana, as in all societies with a market economy, the marketplace takes on a variety of physical and organizational forms. There are places, village markets and retail stores for example, where finished products are bought and sold. There is a labor market in which individuals negotiate for this ingredient of production. There are banks, pawnshops, cooperative societies, and individuals who service a money market by transacting loans at fixed rates of interest. And there is a market in which land and other capital goods are also bought and sold.

Some anthropological observers have emphasized the point of view that Guiana's market economy is a structural complex which has served to mold the various elements of the population into the framework of a unified society.[19] On the surface, there would seem to be some validity to this point of view. In Guiana's market economy, the price mechanism functions as an integrative device not only with respect to the allocation of goods, services, resources, and incomes, but it also functions as a common denominator for the expression of those social values which are economic in character. Since Africans and East Indians (as well as others) have to buy most of the things they consider necessary or desirable, the price mechanism serves to create a functional equivalence with respect to the expression of these values by reducing them to a monetary standard. Thus, because of their participation in the market economy, it would appear that all Guianese have a market orientation in terms of which they share a common standard of valuing.

However, apart from this common standard of valuing, there is an important difference between the principles which are operative in a market economy and the institutional structures through which these principles are implemented. Because different groups of individuals accept the rules of the game, so to speak, it does not follow that they play the game in the same way and for the same reasons. The market economy, in other words, provides a set of means in terms of which very different cultural values may be expressed and reinforced.

It has already been shown how in the Guianese villages Indians and Africans frequently want the same things (e.g., land, education, money) for very different reasons (e.g., Africans want money with which they can "sport," and Indians want it to invest in land, tractors, or dowries). It has been shown how these two groups often want dif-

[19] This point has been given particular emphasis by Raymond Smith, *op. cit.*, pp. 113–17 and 134–43.

ferent things (e.g., Africans want wage employment and Indians want land to work, or Africans want one type of local government office and Indians want another). Partly because of the market value attached to the things these groups want, it has also been shown how they have frequently come into conflict with one another in their efforts to get the things they want. In other words, at the village level of sociocultural integration, the market orientation which these two groups share is not necessarily integrative. Move often than not it tends to reinforce the cultural differences which separate them.

There is still another point that needs to be emphasized concerning the integrative functions of the market economy. Bohannan and Dalton have described the market economy as being "unicentric" rather than "multicentric" because the market principle and the price mechanism tend to integrate all sectors of the economy.[20] Multicentric economies, they note, are organized into independent spheres, each transacting different economic items and, often, according to very different transactional principles. Again, Guiana's economy is decidedly of the unicentric type—it has a market system. However, there is a difference between the market system of a developed industrial economy and the market system of an underdeveloped colonial economy. The various markets of the industrial society are extremely interdependent (e.g., the automotive industry depends upon the steel industry, and the latter depends upon other industries, etc.). This is not the case with the colonial economy.

By way of illustration, consider Guiana's two most important income-producing industries, sugar and bauxite. Each of these industries is controlled by an international business cartel. The marketing activities of these cartels, in Guiana and also in many other countries where they are located, are not very significantly interdependent. They do not process the same kinds of resources. They are dependent upon different international markets. Their sources of capital formation are not closely related. They do not use the same types of skills. In Guiana, they do not even compete in the same labor market. Each industry negotiates with completely different and entirely unrelated labor unions. And there are practically no economic transactions carried out between the companies that make up the two cartels. In Guiana, each industry can exist without the other. The principles of the market

[20] Paul Bohannan and George Dalton (eds.), *Markets in Africa* (Evanston, Ill.: Northwestern University Press, 1962). See the "Introduction" by the editors, pp. 1–26.

economy serve to integrate these sectors of market activity only in the most superficial fashion.

It also might be pointed out that a similar situation exists with respect to the rice and bauxite industries. Each of these industries tends to operate in a relatively independent sphere of Guiana's market economy. It might be suggested that the rice industry benefits from the bauxite industry in terms of the rice which bauxite workers consume. This is true, but hardly significant as a factor of integration.

By way of contrast, the sugar and rice industries are very definitely interdependent as far as marketing activities are concerned. The development of the rice industry was largely stimulated by the need to provide Indian sugar workers with a cheap diet to which they were accustomed. In the past, sugar workers were often provided with small plots of land in order that they might cultivate rice and supplement their low incomes. As has already been shown, many sugar workers still find it necessary to supplement low incomes by cultivating rice. If the sugar industry had to pay wages sufficient for its workers to consume imported rice, the industry would be very hard pressed. The sugar industry in Guiana has always depended upon an abundant supply of cheap labor and, under present conditions, such labor will be available only as long as Guiana's economy remains underdeveloped and nonindustrial.

In view of these considerations, the colonial character of Guiana's market economy imparts to it certain multicentric features.[21] The agricultural and industrial sectors of the economy comprise relatively independent spheres of market activity. To be sure, the market principle and the price mechanism are operative in both spheres but, to some extent, even these transactional principles differ in important ways. For example, the average income in the bauxite industry is three times higher than the average income in the sugar industry. And no rice farmer could match the consumption power of a typical bauxite worker without cultivating at least ten acres or more of good riceland. The major reason these two sectors of the economy do not raise havoc with one another is because they do not compete in the same markets for the same goods, services, resources, and skills. This lack of competition has been possible, in large part, because each sector of the economy has been organized in terms of two very different cultural sections of

[21] Perhaps "pluralistic" is a more appropriate term than "multicentric" to describe the character of Guiana's market economy.

the population. As with business and industrial organizations, markets and economic transactions may serve to mediate the differences that exist between these cultural sections, but they do not appear to integrate them.

## TRADE UNIONS AND LABOR ORGANIZATIONS

Trade unions and labor organizations have made a considerable contribution to the plural integration of Guianese society. This contribution stems from two sources of influence. One involves the plural character of the Guianese economy. The other involves the use of the trade union movement as a base from which union leaders have been able to launch political careers.[22] With respect to the first, the organization of trade unions has reflected, quite naturally, the differential involvement of Africans and East Indians in the urban and rural sectors of the economy. Typically, industrial unions and unions organized to represent urban workers have large African memberships. These unions are usually dominated by African leadership. Agricultural unions, on the other hand, have large East Indian memberships, and they tend to be dominated by East Indian leadership. Under these circumstances, and in conjunction with the political aspirations of union leaders, most unions have extended their activities to include the collective interests of those sections of the population from which they tend to draw their membership. Thus, they have played an important role with respect to the national integration of separate cultural sections. In order to appreciate these points, it will be useful to consider briefly the origins and the influences that have been at work in the trade union movement.

The trade union movement may be dated from 1922, when H. N. Critchlow, an African waterfront worker, organized the British Guiana Labour Union. As a general union, the B.G.L.U. was organized primarily to represent the interests of workers in Georgetown, most of whom happened to be Africans. Needless to say, the birth of this union took place in a difficult and hostile environment. In the face of hostility, the union was soon taken over by African professionals who were active in public life and whose education and connections

[22] The trade union movement has been closely linked with nationalist politics. The linkage will be discussed more fully in the following chapter.

better equipped them than the ordinary worker to guide the union's activities. Thus, according to the Venn Commission in 1949, the principle was established (and more or less accepted by workers) that the officers of a trade union, particularly the president, ought to be "big men" with knowledge and experience gained from public life.[23]

Whether for these or other reasons, the trade union movement in Guiana, as in most underdeveloped countries, has been the major platform from which political careers are launched. An early case in point is the Man Power Citizens' Association, the first union organized to represent the interests of East Indian sugar workers. The M.P.C.A. was founded in 1937 by Ayube M. Edun, an East Indian idealist with a political vision of a new world order based on a philosophy he called "Rational-Practical Idealism." After returning from a visit to England during the twenties, Edun undertook the development of this new order by publishing a weekly paper, the *Guiana Review*, in which he was extremely critical of the working conditions in the sugar industry. Subsequently he organized the M.P.C.A., which, after two years of industrial strife, received recognition as a bargaining agency by the Sugar Producers' Association. Although the M.P.C.A. fell far short of Edun's utopian vision, it did serve to provide its founder with a power base in Guiana's most important industry. Since the organization of the M.P.C.A., practically every prominent Guianese politician has made an effort to aggregate political support by becoming involved in the trade union movement.

As a consequence of these developments, there has been a proliferation of trade unions in British Guiana. By 1959, there existed no less than thirty-eight registered labor organizations to serve a population of approximately 250,000 persons of working age. Some of these unions cater to highly specialized occupational categories and have extremely small memberships. A few, for example, have less than twenty-five paid-up members. Table 17 presents a description of the most important of these unions from the point of view of size as well as political influence. Since membership data of an exact nature are not available for most of these unions, it is not possible to report precisely their membership composition. However, on the basis of interview data obtained from several prominent labor leaders, Table 17 also indicates which of these unions are predominantly African or

[23] *Report of A Commission of Inquiry into the Sugar Industry of British Guiana* (London: His Majesty's Stationery Office, 1949), p. 90.

TABLE 17. IMPORTANT LABOR ORGANIZATIONS IN BRITISH GUIANA

| *Name* | *Description* | *Leadership* |
|---|---|---|
| The British Guiana Labour Union | General, mainly dockworkers | African |
| Man Power Citizens' Association | Mainly sugar workers | Indian |
| Transport Workers Union of British Guiana | Employees of the Transport and Harbours Department | African |
| British Guiana Post Office Workers' Union | Employees of the Post Office Department | African |
| British Guiana Amalgamated Building Trade Workers Union | Employees in the building trades | Mixed |
| Government Employees' Union | Subordinate employees in government departments | African |
| British Guiana and West Indies Sugar Boilers' Union | Pan boilers on sugar estates in British Guiana and West Indies | African |
| British Guiana Headmen's Union | Headmen on sugar estates | Indian |
| Sugar Estates Clerks' Association | Clerks on sugar estates | Indian |
| British Guiana Teachers Association | Teachers in government-aided primary schools | African |
| Guiana Industrial Workers' Union | Workers in the sugar industry | Indian |
| British Guiana Civil Service Association | Civil servants | African |
| Public Works and Pure Water Supply Scheme and Sea Defense Workers Union | Subordinate employees of Public Works and other government departments | Mixed |
| British Guiana Mine Workers Union | Bauxite workers | African |

TABLE 17. IMPORTANT LABOR ORGANIZATIONS IN BRITISH GUIANA (Cont.)

| *Name* | *Description* | *Leadership* |
|---|---|---|
| Printers' Industrial Union | Employees in printing industry | African |
| Sawmill and Forest Workers' Union | Workers on sawmills and timber grants | Mixed |
| British Guiana Postmasters' Union | Postmasters | African |
| British Guiana Medical Employees' Union | Subordinate employees of Medical Department | African |
| British Guiana Seafarers' Union | Seamen | African |
| General Workers' Union | General workers | African |

East Indian in leadership. Invariably, the composition of the leadership reflects the composition of the membership.

Of the twenty unions included in Table 17, five are operative primarily in the sugar industry. These are the Man Power Citizens' Association, the Sugar Boilers' Union, the British Guiana Headmen's Union, the Sugar Estates Clerks' Association, and the Guiana Industrial Workers' Union. Of these, the smallest (114 members in 1959) and least influential is the Sugar Boilers' Union. This particular union is also the only one in the sugar industry which is predominantly African in membership and leadership.

The largest, although not the most powerful, union operating in the sugar industry is the M.P.C.A. In fact, the M.P.C.A. is the largest union in Guiana. In recent years, it has refused to make available statistics pertaining to its membership, but most estimates place it in the vicinity of 8,000 or more workers. The M.P.C.A. has never had an African or a sugar worker as its president, but it has had one African as a vice president. Ayube M. Edun, its founder, continued as the organization's president until he was succeeded, in the early fifties, by Lionel Luckhoo. Luckhoo, a successful Indian barrister who was nominated to the Legislative Council in 1952 and who organized the National Democratic Party in opposition to Jagan in 1953, was succeeded by another East Indian professional, Richard Ishmael.

During the first few years of its existence, the M.P.C.A. seems to have pursued a vigorous and sometimes militant policy in support of the sugar workers. In 1940, only a year after the union was officially recognized by the Sugar Producers' Association, the M.P.C.A. was able to report a paid-up membership of 20,970 workers. Almost immediately, however, this membership began to decline. During the war years, the union was able to accomplish little by way of improving working conditions and wages in the sugar industry. Also during these years, it seems to have developed a cordial relationship with the Sugar Producers' Association. By 1946, the compromising attitude of the M.P.C.A. was such that its treasurer, Cheddi Jagan, resigned his position and criticized the organization as having become fully identified with sugar interests. With Dr. Lachmansingh, an Indian medical practitioner and drugstore proprietor, Jagan organized the Guiana Industrial Workers' Union.

Under the leadership of Jagan and Lachmansingh, the G.I.W.U. embarked upon a program designed to wean sugar workers away from the M.P.C.A. and to replace it as a bargaining agent. In the inevitable jurisdictional conflict which ensued, the Sugar Producers' Association and the British Guiana Trades Union Council threw their support to the M.P.C.A. The Sugar Producers' Association refused to negotiate with the G.I.W.U., and the Trades Union Council, a federated organization, rejected the G.I.W.U.'s application for membership. Parenthetically, it should be noted that, except for a short period during the early fifties, the M.P.C.A., by virtue of its large membership, exercised a controlling influence in the Trades Union Council. In 1952, when it lost this influence for a time because of low membership, the M.P.C.A. resigned from the Trades Union Council.

By 1948, the G.I.W.U. claimed a membership of 4,130 (as compared to the M.P.C.A.'s claim of 5,141 in 1947). That same year, in an effort to press its case for recognition, the G.I.W.U. fomented a series of strikes on the East Coast, Demerara, estates. During the strike at Plantation Enmore, violence broke out, and the police (who happen to be Africans) shot and killed a number of East Indian workers. In spite of the strikes, the G.I.W.U. failed to win recognition from the Sugar Producers' Association. Nevertheless, the union retained the loyalty, if not always the financial support, of most of the sugar workers, and it continued to operate under Jagan's influence. In 1953, shortly after Jagan formed a new government, the G.I.W.U. once again pressed its case against the M.P.C.A. by fomenting strikes in support of the Jagan government's labor legislation, which had been vetoed by the governor. On this occasion, the strikes, together with other factors, resulted in the suspension of the constitution. As of the present, the G.I.W.U. is still functional and still without recognition from the Sugar Producers' Association.

These data support three conclusions concerning the trade unions which cater almost exclusively to the needs of sugar workers. First, the majority of these unions have predominantly East Indian memberships and are controlled by prominent East Indian leaders. Second, the largest and most influential of these unions (the M.P.C.A. and the G.I.W.U.) have been inextricably involved in national politics from the time they were first organized. And third, the political actions of these unions as well as the political activities of the men who control them have served to set Indian sugar workers apart from other sections of the Guianese labor force. Thus, the trade union movement has contributed to the reinforcement of those communal values which East Indians share by virtue of their indentured past.

Similar conclusions appear to be valid with respect to those trade unions and labor organizations that cater primarily to the needs of African workers in the urban and nonagricultural sectors of the economy. In fact, outside of the sugar industry, the trade union movement is almost completely in the hands of African politicians and workers. The British Guiana Labour Union, with over two thousand members, still serves primarily the interests of African workers in Georgetown. The British Guiana Mine Workers Union, also with over two thousand members, is completely dominated and controlled by African leaders affiliated with L. F. S. Burnham and the Peoples National Congress. The same also tends to be true of the Transport Workers' Union, the Government Employees' Union, the Post Office Workers' Union (whose president is a member of the Executive Committee of the P.N.C.), the Teachers' Association, the Civil Service Association, the Printers' Industrial Union, and the Postmasters' Union.

Thus, in response to historical circumstances and the colonial character of the Guianese economy, the trade union movement has followed a natural course of development. Unions organized to represent rural and agricultural workers, almost of necessity, have had to aggregate the economic and political interests of East Indians. Similarly, those unions which developed in the urban sectors of the economy have had to aggregate the economic and political interests of Africans. In developed countries, the economic and political interests of rural people are not normally the same as those of urban people. This is doubly the case in an underdeveloped country like British Guiana, where the rural and urban populations are differentiated in terms of their cultural origins as well as their colonial experiences. As will be shown in a subsequent chapter, such a situation cannot but affect the organizational strategies of nationalist political movements.

## THE COOPERATIVE MOVEMENT

Cooperative societies, for the most part, are voluntary associations, generally organized by groups of individuals within local communities. It has been shown that voluntary associations of this type do not contribute very significantly to the integration of Africans and East Indians in terms of their membership.[24]

The subject matter under discussion here, however, is not these local cooperative groups as such. Rather, it is the integrative features of the national cooperative movement in which these local groups participate. Although the organization of cooperative societies tends to be a voluntary undertaking, the participation of these societies in the cooperative movement is not. The cooperative movement is an institutionalized broker mechanism designed and established by the government to foster and facilitate social and economic change in Guianese society. Once a cooperative society is organized and registered, it operates under the jurisdiction of the Co-operative Department.[25]

The cooperative movement in British Guiana has a very recent origin. It began in 1943 with the creation of a Social Welfare Division within the Department of Local Government. In 1945, a Co-operative Organizer was appointed, and by the following year there were thirty-

[24] I have available considerably more data to support this conclusion than were reported in conjunction with the village studies discussed in the previous chapter. There are 552 registered cooperative societies in British Guiana. Although it was impossible to conduct a survey of all of these, a survey was made of 52 cooperative societies operating in Berbice. These data show quite conclusively that Africans are not significantly represented in cooperative societies organized by Indians. By the same token, Indians do not join in large numbers cooperative societies organized by Africans. These survey data also show that Africans are more frequently interested in thrift societies than Indians, whereas the latter are more interested in land cooperatives and agricultural credit cooperatives. The limitations of space do not permit the presentation of these data in tabular form, but they are completely supportive of the conclusions drawn in the previous chapter.

[25] Established by Ordinance No. 12 of 1948.

six savings clubs and three marketing groups with total assets of approximately $7,000 (B.W.I.). The rapidity with which the movement took hold stimulated the government to formulate legislation designed to regulate the registration of cooperative societies and to provide for their supervision by establishing a Co-operative Department with an experienced registrar at its head. The cooperative movement was further stimulated in 1954, when, as a result of a recommendation made by the International Bank for Reconstruction and Development, the government established the British Guiana Credit Corporation. During the first two years of its existence, the Credit Corporation negotiated 15,521 loans for an amount of $11,142,992 (B.W.I.). These funds represented the major source of capital for cooperative thrift and credit societies.

As a consequence of these developments, the cooperative movement has become an extremely important agency of social and economic change. In 1959, there were 552 registered cooperative societies with a membership of 36,973 persons. These societies comprised the following categories: 43 savings, 100 thrift, 133 school thrift, 103 agricultural thrift and credit, 15 consumer, 46 producer-marketing, 50 urban thrift and credit, 25 land lease–purchase, 13 farm supply, 2 transport, 12 fishermen, 1 housing, and 9 general purpose. Shares and savings were approximately $930,511 (B.W.I.), and reserve funds totaled $29,808 (B.W.I.). Guianese of all cultural sections belonged to and participated in the activities of these groups. The question is, To what extent does the cooperative movement serve to maintain cultural differentiation as the basis for sociocultural integration? In order to answer this question it is necessary to consider the national structure of the cooperative movement.

In theory, each cooperative society is spontaneously formed by a group of interested persons who come together and elect, from among their number, officers to manage the group's affairs and to register the society with the Registrar of Co-operatives. Also in theory, each cooperative society is free to manage its own affairs. In practice, however, the situation is somewhat different. Most cooperative societies are formed when individuals seeking certain types of government aid are encouraged by representatives of the Co-operative Department, or by representatives of other government departments, to organize themselves as a cooperative society in order to qualify for the aid they are seeking. It is generally a matter of indifference to the Co-operative Department whether or not these groups happen to be comprised of members of one cultural section rather than another.[26] Once organized and registered, the activities of the cooperative are closely supervised and controlled by officers of the Co-operative Department. This control is particularly evident when decisions are made that have to do with the use of government funds. Most of these decisions, as one unofficial government report states, ". . . are dependent upon the decisions of the Commissioner for Co-operative Development."

In other words, the entire cooperative movement in British Guiana tends to be organized and centrally controlled by an agency of the government. The structure through which this control is exercised is uniform for all registered cooperatives regardless of the composition of their membership. Whether it is a land society organized by a group of East Indian rice farmers or a savings society organized by a group of African teachers, the books of each are regularly inspected by field officers of the Co-operative Department. Moreover, when these societies convene business meetings, the appropriate field officer is usually notified and, if possible, attends. At these meetings, the field officer does not exercise a vote. He is there to give freely of his advice. However, because the field officer has the power to recommend or withhold government aid, his advice is not often ignored by those who make the decisions.

In these respects, the co-operative movement does not serve to maintain cultural differentiation at the national level. Cultural differentiation, to be sure, exists at local levels where minimal cultural sections exist, and this certainly influences the membership composition of particular cooperative societies. Beyond this, however, the structure of the cooperative movement is one which functions to generate new cultural values that are in the process of being adopted by the society as a whole.

## GOVERNMENTAL AGENCIES

The most inclusive structures of a society are its governmental institutions. These are broker institutions by definition. They have as their primary function the integration of the social system. There can

[26] There are important exceptions to this generalization. The relationship between the organization of cooperative groups and the existence of minimal cultural sections carries with it certain political possibilities which, as we shall see, nationalist politicians have hastened to exploit.

be little doubt that the institutions of government have served to integrate Guianese society as a whole. Since the unification of British Guiana in 1831, the country has had a centralized government, and all Guianese have led to acquiesce to its existence. However, as was noted in Chapter 2, the existence of a centralized government is not inconsistent with the plural integration of the social system. This implies, of course, that the integration of the plural society is dependent upon the regulation of its intersectional relations by one or another of the component cultural sections. As was outlined in Chapter 3, Europeans have comprised the dominant cultural section in Guiana. Until 1953, the Guianese did not have significant access to the positions of political power.

If, until recently, the Guianese have not had access to the governmental institutions which convey political power, they have had considerable access to the administrative agencies which carry on the work of government. These administrative agencies, for the most part, are the various departments of the public service. As broker institutions, they are relevant to the topic under discussion. The question to be considered is, To what extent has participation in the administrative activities of government contributed to the plural integration of Guianese society? Before attempting to provide an answer to this question, however, it is necessary to digress and briefly outline the organization of the public service in Guiana.

Before 1940, the departments of the public service were exclusively responsible to the governor through his chief secretary. Members of the legislature, both elected and appointed, had practically no involvement with the administrative functions of the public service. During the forties, under the governorship of Sir Gordon Lethem, this arrangement was slightly modified when members of the legislature were appointed to departmental advisory committees. As a result of the constitutional changes of 1953, an Executive Council was created, and the ministerial system was introduced. Members of the Executive Council were made directly responsible for those departments of the public service included in their portfolios. The ministerial system was retained even after the suspension of the 1953 constitution. The only change that resulted from the suspension was that the Executive Council became wholly appointed rather than partially elected.

Prior to the constitutional changes of 1961, when the Executive Council was replaced by a Council of Ministers, the composition of the Executive Council included three ex officio members appointed by the governor and five elected members of the majority party (i.e., the Peoples Progressive Party). The portfolios distributed by the governor to the elected ministers were Trade and Industry (including Co-operatives); Natural Resources (including Agriculture, Forests, Lands and Mines, and Geological Surveys); Labour, Health, and Housing; Communications and Works (including the Post Office, Transport and Harbours, and Civil Aviation); and Community Development and Education (which also included Local Government and Social Welfare). The portfolios of the ex officio members of the Executive Council included External Affairs, Defense, Security, Immigration, Civil Service, Administration of the Interior, Information Services, the Fire Brigade, Legal Matters and Deeds, Financial and Economic Matters, Currency Control, Banking and Credit, and Government Stores.

Although in theory the ministerial system involved elected representatives with the administrative functions of government, it did not give them the power to make political appointments to the various departments of the public service for which they were made responsible. In the British tradition, the public service is supposed to be politically neutral. Appointments to the public service are based, theoretically, on merit. Appointments are cleared through the Public Service Commission, a nonpolitical group appointed by the governor in consultation with the premier. Persons appointed to the Public Service Commission, as well as persons appointed to the public service, can neither hold public office nor be prominently active in political party organizations. However, these regulations have not prevented the public service, or for that matter the Public Service Commission, from becoming entangled in nationalist politics. This entanglement, in large part, is the logical consequence of the role which the public service has played as a broker institution in Guianese society.

During the past thirty years, the public service in Guiana has expanded considerably in response to population growth and the assumption by government of new responsibilities, particularly in the fields of welfare and economic development. In 1940, for example, there were approximately thirty-four departments of the public service, depending upon how one chooses to count them. This number had increased to fifty-seven by 1960. During the course of field work, it was not possible to make an exhaustive study of the public service. Too many people were involved, and, in many cases, historical records were not available. However, with the aid of several informants (among whom were included a number of knowledgeable departmental heads) and the *Civil Service List,* a survey was made of the ethnic backgrounds of pensionable civil servants for the years 1940 and 1960. Pensionable civil servants include departmental heads as well as those civil servants who are no longer on probation and who, as a result of their promotion, qualify to be covered by the pension provisions for civil servants. It is not known what percentage this group represents of the total number of civil service employees, but informants indicated that the percentage was sizable. The data for 1940 are summarized in Table 18; those for 1960 are presented in Table 19.

As Table 18 indicates, in 1940 the executive heads of all but seven of the thirty-four public service departments were Europeans. Most of the other Europeans included on the pensionable staff were deputy

TABLE 18. ETHNIC COMPOSITION OF PENSIONABLE CIVIL SERVANTS IN 1940

| | *Departmental or Executive Heads* | | *Pensionable Staff* | |
|---|---|---|---|---|
| | N | Per Cent | N | Per Cent |
| Europeans | 27 | 79.4 | 89 | 14.1 |
| Afro-Guianese | 5 | 14.7 | 419 | 66.6 |
| East Indians | 0 | 0.0 | 63 | 10.0 |
| Portuguese | 2 | 5.9 | 40 | 6.4 |
| Chinese and Others | 0 | 0.0 | 18 | 2.9 |
| Total | 34 | 100.0 | 629 | 100.0 |

TABLE 19. ETHNIC COMPOSITION OF PENSIONABLE CIVIL SERVANTS IN 1960

| | *Departmental or Executive Heads* | | *Pensionable Staff* | |
|---|---|---|---|---|
| | N | Per Cent | N | Per Cent |
| Europeans | 22 | 38.6 | 97 | 12.0 |
| Afro-Guianese | 26 | 45.6 | 469 | 58.0 |
| East Indians | 6 | 10.5 | 130 | 16.1 |
| Portuguese | 1 | 1.8 | 29 | 3.6 |
| Chinese and Others | 2 | 3.5 | 83 | 10.3 |
| Total | 57 | 100.0 | 808 | 100.0 |

heads or assistants. No department had as its executive head an East Indian, and only five had Afro-Guianese. The nonexecutive pensionable staff for all thirty-four departments was predominantly Afro-Guianese (66 per cent). East Indians comprised only 10 per cent of the total staff, and the vast majority of these were employed in two or three large departments such as the Medical Department and the Departments of Labour and Local Government. In fact, as of 1940, there were twenty departments of the public service which were without East Indians on their pensionable staffs. For example, none were included on the staffs of such important departments as the Colonial Secretariat, Customs, Police, Transport and Harbours, and the Treasury. In other words, in 1940, East Indians did not participate very significantly in the administrative activities of the government.

Between 1940 and 1960, twenty-three departments were added to the public service as a result of reorganization or new development. The number of pensionable civil servants increased by approximately 30 per cent over the number for 1940. These changes, however, do not appear to have extensively altered the position of East Indians with respect to their participation in the administrative activities of government. By 1960, Afro-Guianese occupied more executive positions in the public service than Europeans. The number of East Indians who occupied executive positions in 1960 was approximately the same as that for the Afro-Guianese in 1940. The percentage of East Indians included on the pensionable staff of the Public Service increased by 6.1 per cent during the twenty-year period, but in 1960 there were still twenty-one departments without East Indians on their pensionable staffs. As far as participation in the administrative activities of government is concerned, the Chinese showed more impressive gains between 1940 and 1960 than did the East Indians.

In view of these data, it would seem that the administrative agencies of government have contributed significantly to the plural integration of Guianese society. Before the Second World War, the work of government was directed almost exclusively by European personnel with the aid of a civil service largely comprised of Afro-Guianese. Since the war, the most noticeable change has been the replacement of European personnel by Afro-Guianese who have moved into executive positions. The number of East Indians in the public service today falls considerably short of being proportional to their number in the Guianese population. There are many reasons that may be adduced to explain this fact, but East Indians, by and large, attribute it to discriminatory practices and the domination of the public service by Afro-Guianese. Thus, with respect to these broker institutions, East Indians perceive themselves as a national group in competition with the Afro-Guianese. We shall have an opportunity to return to this point when nationalist politics are considered.

## RELIGIOUS AND ETHNIC ASSOCIATIONS

There are a number of religious and ethnic associations in British Guiana that have been organized specifically to further the social and, in some instances, the political interests of particular cultural sections. Examples of such groups are the East Indian Association, the Sanatana Dharma Maha Sabha, the Arya Samaj, the Hindu Society, the United Sad'r Anjuman-E-Islam, the Islamic Association, the Muslim Youth Organization, the Sword of the Spirit (Portuguese), the Chinese Association, the Afro-American Association, and the League of Coloured Peoples. All of these associations are exclusive in their membership. Africans do not belong to those which cater to East Indians, and, similarly, East Indians do not belong to those that cater to Africans.

Some of these associations are organized in terms of a national structure with affiliated groups operating in different parts of the country. This is the pattern particularly for the East Indian religious associations which have large and active memberships dispersed in villages throughout the country. Other of these associations function mainly in the urban centers and do not appear to have large memberships. The East Indian Association and the League of Coloured Peoples are of this type. The active membership of both of these groups tends to be confined to businessmen and professionals who operate in Georgetown and New Amsterdam. From time to time, however, both groups arrange to hold meetings in heavily populated rural areas where village leaders are fully cognizant of their aims and objectives.

Regardless of their organization or the size of their active membership, these religious and ethnic associations have often taken it upon themselves to speak for the cultural sections to which they cater. In fact, there are many Guianese who consider these associations to represent the views of large segments of the population. This attitude has been shared by many colonial officials. For example, whenever the Colonial Office has found it necessary to send special investigative commissions to Guiana (e.g., the constitutional commissions of 1951 and

1954), in addition to taking evidence from prominent Guinanese, these commissions usually invite written memoranda from the major religious and ethnic associations on the assumption that these associations do, in fact, speak for large sections of the population. The validity of this assumption is supported, in part, by the additional fact that practically every nationalist politician has at one time or another taken the existence of these associations into account.

The character of these associations as broker institutions may be illustrated with reference to the League of Coloured Peoples and the East Indian Association. Although the membership of both of these organizations tends to be confined to businessmen and professionals, they have been extremely active and influential among Africans and East Indians for a considerable number of years. In fact, prior to the emergence of modern political parties, each of these organizations constituted a quasi-political group which served to aggregate the political interests of the cultural sections they represented.

The League of Coloured Peoples was organized during the 1930's by Dr. C. H. Denbow, an American-trained dentist. The League seems to have developed out of the Negro Progress Convention. There are not many historical data available on the latter organization, but sporadic references indicate that it was functioning prior to the First World War. It is noted by Nath that in 1922, for example, when an effort was being made by prominent leaders of the East Indian Association to reopen immigration from India, this effort had received the support of the Negro Progress Convention on the condition that equivalent efforts would be made to introduce colonists from Africa.[27] It is also known that the Negro Progress Convention was functioning in the early thirties because in 1931 it organized a scheme whereby two Africans were sent to pursue a course of studies at Tuskegee in Alabama.[28]

When Dr. Denbow undertook the organization of the League of Coloured Peoples, it was intended to be a multiracial association. However, given the existence of the East Indian Association, it was not long before the League was reorganized ". . . to promote the social, economic, educational, and political interests of the people of African descent." In view of the fact that most of the trade unions, particularly the British Guiana Labour Union, more or less effectively represented

[27] Nath, *op. cit.*, p. 153.

[28] N. E. Cameron, *The Evolution of the Negro*, Vol. 2 (Georgetown: Argosy Company, 1934), p. 82.

the political as well as the economic interests of the African masses, the League had very little to do politically. As a consequence, during the forties it concentrated most of its attention on problems of welfare and cultural improvement among Africans in the urban areas.

The League became politically active with the emergence of nationalist politics in the 1950's. When the vast majority of the African workers followed Burnham into the Peoples Progressive Party to form, with Jagan and the East Indians, a comprehensive nationalist movement, only the League remained to express the political views held by the more conservative members of the African middle class. Thus, in opposition to Jagan and Burnham, prominent members of the League (e.g., John Carter, Dr. J. A. Nicholson, and others) organized and activated the United Democratic Party. By virtue of its relationship to the League, the U.D.P. was not only more conservative than the P.P.P. but also more racial in outlook. It drew its financial strength primarily from an organization which catered exclusively to the African cultural section. This influence, as will be shown, continued to play a role in nationalist politics after Burnham broke with the P.P.P. and, with John Carter, organized the Peoples National Congress.

The East Indian Association, as a broker institution, is very much like the League of Coloured Peoples in organization as well as in conception. That is to say, from its inception its outlook and aims have been both ethnic and political. The association was organized in 1916 by Joseph Ruhoman, a journalist. However, the man most responsible for giving life to the organization was its first president, J. A. Luckhoo. A barrister by profession, in 1916 Luckhoo had already achieved prominence as an Indian politician. He was the first Indian to be elected a financial representative in the Combined Court, and subsequently, in 1945, he became the first Indian to be appointed First Puisne Judge of the colony. Luckhoo, during most of his political life, remained active in the affairs of the association and brought to it power and prestige which it might not otherwise have had.

The aims of the East Indian Association and the scope of its activities were first defined in its original constitution. Peter Ruhomon, the East Indian historian, states some of these aims as follows:

1. To unite the members of the East Indian race in all parts of the colony for representative purposes.
2. To urge upon Government the desirability of establishing a scheme for settling time-expired East Indian immigrants on the land. . . .

3. To secure representatives of East Indian nationality in the Legislature and in all Corporations where the interests of East Indians are concerned or stand to be affected, every candidate selected, to give a pledge, beforehand, to protect and further the interests of the race, as far as it lies in his power.
4. To urge the establishment of special Government Schools under East Indian Masters for the teaching of both Hindi and English to children of East Indian parents.
5. To advocate the employment of East Indians at a much greater extent in public offices where immigrants transact business or to where they apply for various purposes.
6. To advocate and promote, by all possible legitimate means, . . . the general public interest and welfare of the East Indian community at large.[29]

In line with these objectives, the East Indian Association had a vision that Guiana might one day become "New India." One of the first projects undertaken by the association was designed to make this dream a reality by mobilizing support for reopening the immigration of Indian workers. In 1919, and again in 1924, the association deputized Luckhoo and sent him to India in an effort to sell an immigration scheme to the Indian government. Gandhi, among others, was opposed to anything which smacked of the indenture system. By 1926, after endless negotiations and investigations, the Indian government was persuaded to remove the embargo on immigration. However, the terms which were imposed were so costly that the Guianese government had to give up the project.[30] The East Indian Association failed to achieve this particular objective, but, in the process, it had succeeded in lighting the flame of Indian nationalism in Guiana. The whole enterprise had proceeded as though the Afro-Guianese were expected to disappear from the landscape. Indians, perhaps for the first time, thought of Guiana as theirs. To be sure, these thoughts did not go unnoticed among Africans.

As in the case of the League of Coloured Peoples, the political activities of the East Indian Association diminished somewhat with the organization of trade unions in the sugar industry. However, unlike the league, the association retained much of its political influence among the Indian masses. Its leaders, after all, were among the very

[29] Peter Ruhomon, *Centenary History of the East Indians in British Guiana, 1838–1938* ("Guiana Edition" No. 10; Georgetown: Daily Chronicle, 1946), pp. 228–29.

[30] Nath, *op. cit.*, pp. 141–60.

few Indians who had managed to achieve positions of prominence in Guianese society. When the Peoples Progressive Party emerged as a nationalist movement, Cheddi Jagan did not at first oppose the East Indian Association. Instead, because of its influence, he attempted to align its leaders with the movement. Thus, Dr. Lachmansingh, President of the East Indian Association between 1948 and 1951, became Senior Vice-Chairman of the Peoples Progressive Party. Jai Narine Singh, thrice President of the East Indian Association, became a member of the P.P.P. Executive Committee. It was not until after Lachmansingh and Jai Narine Singh joined Burnham in opposition to Jagan and the P.P.P. (and this unholy alliance did not persist for long either) that the East Indian Association became discredited and lost much of its political influence among the Indian masses.

Before bringing this discussion to a close, it should be noted that the religious associations (e.g., the Sanatan Dharm Maha Sabha and the Anjuman-E-Islam), unlike the League and the East Indian Association, are not ideologically racial. Nor have they been as forcefully political. Like most religious societies, these associations advocate a universal doctrine which in theory addresses itself to mankind as a whole. Needless to say, however, these doctrines have not had much appeal to Christians. As a consequence, the membership of these associations is exclusive. Thus, by aggregating the social and religious interests of East Indians, religious associations have served to integrate the East Indian cultural section and establish its national identity. Moreover, with the emergence of nationalist politics and modern political parties, the leaders of these associations (Hindu priests and Muslim moulvies) also have become important political activists. Their influence is such that no political party can afford to ignore them.

To summarize, religious and ethnic associations in British Guiana have been exclusive in their membership. For the most part, the structures of these organizations express the communal values of the groups they represent. Thus, as broker institutions, religious and ethnic associations have contributed significantly to the plural integration of Guianese society by keeping East Indians and Africans apart.

## POLITICAL PARTIES

Like other broker institutions, political parties serve to form different types of social alignment between the groups that make up a society. However, political parties differ from other types of broker institutions in one very important respect. They have as their primary function the mobilization of social power for the expressed purpose of securing the apparatus of ultimate power in society, the government. Thus, the social alignments which political parties produce are essentially power alignments. In other words, political parties bring to the process of societal integration a power dimension that most other types of broker institutions lack. It is because of this power dimension that modern political parties have contributed more to the plural integration of Guianese society than any of the broker institutions previously discussed.

The history of modern political parties was outlined briefly in Chapter 1. It will be recalled that when the Peoples Progressive Party was organized by Cheddi Jagan and L. F. S. Burnham in 1950, it presented itself as a comprehensive nationalist movement. Within the party structure Africans and Indians, together, formed political groups in villages throughout the country. In other words, when it was first organized, the P.P.P. expressed new cultural values which, judging from the 1953 elections, seemed to appeal to the majority of Indians and Africans. In 1953, no other political party was able to achieve this level of integration among Guiana's different cultural sections. The only significant opposition, the National Democratic Party, represented a hasty coalition of Indian, African, and Portuguese businessmen and professionals who were unable to associate themselves with the masses of any cultural section.

In view of the patterns of sociocultural integration described thus far, it would seem that the P.P.P. of 1953 represented an institutional innovation which Guianese society, on the whole, had not been fully prepared to receive. There was little basis for the party structure in the social fabric. The values which the P.P.P. leaders professed were but superficially understood by poorly educated East Indians and half-educated Afro-Guianese. As a consequence, these values had to be defined in terms that were more negative than positive. That is to say, they had to be defined in terms of the specific frustrations that East Indians and Afro-Guianese felt but that only a few could explain.

For example, among their many frustrations, East Indians were frustrated by low wages in the sugar industry and by the unavailability of land for rice cultivation. Africans, on the other hand, had land and cared little about the sugar industry. However, they were frustrated by unemployment in the urban sector. Neither of these two groups could relate conditions in the urban and rural sectors of the economy to institutional problems of the society any more than they could relate the process of economic development to the necessity for changes in their own ways of life. Thus, Indians and Africans accepted the P.P.P. in 1953, not because they accepted one another and defined their frustrations in mutual terms, but rather because the P.P.P. contained African and Indian leaders who addressed themselves to African and Indian problems by suggesting that national integration and independence could solve all problems.

Under these circumstances, the P.P.P. could constitute a comprehensive nationalist movement only as long as its leadership remained comprehensive with respect to existing cultural sections. Such cooperation was almost impossible to sustain. Apart from the ideological postures that divided the P.P.P. leadership, and in addition to the pressures applied to the organization when the constitution was suspended in 1953, it was extremely difficult for any P.P.P. leader to address himself to concrete African or Indian problems without appearing to be involved with sectional politics. At the same time, if concrete problems were not considered, the danger existed that a national leader might alienate himself from an important segment of the masses. Thus, it will be recalled, Guiana's comprehensive nationalist movement began to disintegrate in 1955 when Burnham broke with Jagan to form his own Peoples Progressive Party. The process of disintegration was completed in 1959, when the remnants of the United Democratic Party joined Burnham to form the Peoples National Congress.

The organizational strategies involved in these developments will be given detailed consideration in the following chapters. The problem of immediate concern is the role of political parties as broker institutions. More specifically, to what extent have political parties contributed to the plural integration of Guianese society since the disintegration of Guiana's comprehensive nationalist movement? A partial answer to this question may be derived from data on political party membership collected in the six communities discussed in the previous chapter. These data are summarized below in Table 20.

In terms of the data presented in Table 20, there is an extremely strong association between political parties and cultural sections. Of the forty-five East Indians interviewed who belonged to a political party, only one was a member of the P.N.C. Similarly, only five of the ninety-seven Africans who belonged to a political party held a membership in the P.P.P. The percentage of Africans and East Indians

TABLE 20. 1960–61 POLITICAL PARTY MEMBERSHIP OF AFRICANS AND EAST INDIANS IN SIX GUIANESE VILLAGES

| *Political Party* | *East Indians* | | *Africans* | |
|---|---|---|---|---|
| | N | Per Cent | N | Per Cent |
| Peoples Progressive Party | 40 | 88.9 | 5 | 5.1 |
| Peoples National Congress | 1 | 2.2 | 86 | 88.7 |
| United Force | 4 | 8.9 | 6 | 6.2 |
| Total | 45 | 100.0 | 97 | 100.0 |

belonging, respectively, to the P.N.C. and the P.P.P. is almost identical. Furthermore, very few of either group belonged to the United Force.

In interpreting these data, a certain amount of caution must be exercised. For one thing, these data are derived from village samples, and political party groups were not active in all of the villages studied. For example, there were no political party groups active in the villages of Eversham and Cromarty. Also, it will be recalled, political party activities were restricted in the nuclear settlement at Plantation Skeldon. Many of the sugar workers interviewed indicated that they supported the P.P.P. but would not take out a financial membership in the party for fear of being "victimized" by the estate management. Other data collected suggest that this fear was well founded. The data in Table 20 are also limited by the fact that they pertain to individuals who are financial members of political parties. In British Guiana, as in most other countries, financial members of political parties tend to be those individuals who are political activists, that is, they are people who not only contribute financially to the party but who also devote a portion of their time and energy to party work.

In other words, the membership data presented in Table 20 give some idea of how the political activists of different cultural sections align themselves with political parties, but they do not indicate fully the extent to which cultural sections, on the whole, are aligned with one political party rather than another. The political party support of cultural sections can best be shown in terms of voting data. During the course of collecting data in the villages, informants were asked what political party they expected to support in the 1961 elections. The results of this inquiry are summarized in Table 21.

TABLE 21. 1961 VOTING INTENTIONS OF AFRICANS AND EAST INDIANS IN SIX GUIANESE VILLAGES

| *Political Party* | *East Indians* | | *Africans* | |
|---|---|---|---|---|
| | N | Per Cent | N | Per Cent |
| Peoples Progressive Party | 168 | 86.6 | 15 | 6.2 |
| Peoples National Congress | 4 | 2.1 | 196 | 81.3 |
| United Force | 14 | 7.2 | 25 | 10.4 |
| Undecided | 8 | 4.1 | 5 | 2.1 |
| Total | 194 | 100.0 | 241 | 100.0 |

The findings on voting intentions in the 1961 elections do not differ very significantly from the findings on political party membership. The overwhelming majority of East Indians interviewed (86.6 per cent) indicated that they would support the Peoples Progressive Party. Very few Indians (2.1 per cent) showed any support for the Peoples National Congress. Similarly, very few Africans (6.2 per cent) indicated that they would support Cheddi Jagan and the Peoples Progressive Party. The vast majority of Africans strongly supported the Peoples National Congress. Approximately the same percentage of Africans and East Indians (10.4 and 7.2 per cent) were inclined to support the United Force.

The data collected in the villages with respect to voting intentions compare favorably with the 1961 election results. In 1961, the only political party which transversed cultural sections to any significant degree was the United Force. However, as a class-based coalition dominated by conservative Portuguese and a few Indian businessmen, the United Force received only 8.6 per cent of the total party vote. In fact, United Force candidates received so little support that they lost their election deposits in 23 of the 35 electoral districts. The 1961 election results, in combination with the data presented in Tables 20 and 21, clearly substantiate the conclusion that the P.N.C. and the P.P.P., respectively, have transformed the Afro-Guianese and East Indian cultural sections into nationally competitive power alignments.[31] Thus,

[31] For further discussion of the 1961 election results, see Paul Bradley's "The Party System in British Guiana and the General Election of 1961," *Caribbean Studies* (October, 1961).

political parties have contributed more to the plural integration of Guianese society than any other type of broker institution.

## THE INTEGRATION OF MAXIMAL CULTURAL SECTIONS

In summarizing the data presented in this chapter it is useful to recall, once again, the theoretical framework previously outlined. In terms of that framework, the plural society and the heterogeneous society were defined as two ideal type models derived from the same continuum of sociocultural phenomena. The analytical distinction between the two models was operationalized with reference to different patterns of sociocultural integration. The plural society, it was suggested, is one in which similar minimal cultural sections (i.e., local groups that are culturally differentiated) are separately integrated at the national level. The structures which function with respect to the national level of sociocultural integration are broker institutions. These are the structures that serve to link the local activities of individuals and groups to the wider sphere of societal activity. The application of the plural model to the data collected is presented in Table 22.

As Table 22 indicates, the Afro-Guianese and the East Indians constitute relatively well-integrated maximal cultural sections. Few broker institutions bring the members of these groups together in meaningful social contexts. Generally, both groups attend the same schools, but because most of these schools are operated by Christian denominational bodies, they have not been able to generate new cultural values equally acceptable to each group. Thus, educational institutions only serve to mediate relationships between existing minimal cultural sections. That is to say, the schools serve the educational needs of East Indians as well as Africans, but they are not yet the repository of a common tradition or a new national culture. Commercial and industrial organizations also bring Africans and East Indians together, but not as partners in mutual enterprises. Similarly, while both groups accept or comply with the market economy, the expression of market principles has not led them to accept other cultural values in common. The only structure which serves to unify members of both cultural sections is the cooperative movement. This structure, however, is a relatively recent innovation in Guianese society.[32]

[32] It should be noted that the cooperative movement has not been entirely successful, and one of the reasons for this is its entanglement with nationalist politics.

TABLE 22. INTEGRATION OF AFRO-GUIANESE AND EAST INDIAN MAXIMAL CULTURAL SECTIONS

| *Broker Institutions* | *Structure Integrates Similar Minimal Cultural Sections (Plural Integration)* | *Structure Mediates Between Different Minimal Cultural Sections* | *Structure Integrates Different Minimal Cultural Sections* |
|---|---|---|---|
| Educational Institutions | | X | |
| Communications Media | X | | |
| Commercial and Industrial Organizations | | X | |
| Markets and Economic Transactions | | X | |
| Trade Unions and Labor Organizations | X | | |
| Cooperative Movement | | | X |
| Governmental Agencies | X | | |
| Religious and Ethnic Associations | X | | |
| Political Parties | X | | |

In view of the data available, one may conclude that British Guiana displays the characteristics of the plural society to a marked degree. The integration of Guianese society results from a structural segmentation which tends to complement cultural differentiation. More to the point, the interdependent units of the system comprise culturally differentiated groups rather than socially differentiated persons. The relationships within these groups are relatively diffuse and predicated upon a general value consensus, whereas the relationships between them are highly specialized and segmented. The segmental relationships between Africans and East Indians derive primarily from their compliance with the instrumental norms that regulate political and economic transactions. To phrase the matter somewhat differently, in Guianese society there is an integration of culturally differentiated units which are not self-sufficient by virtue of their complementary participation in a unitary political economy. Apart from their complementary participation in the political economy, maximal cultural sections remain relatively autonomous.

*CHAPTER 5*

# PRESSURES TOWARD DISINTEGRATION

IT IS EVIDENT THAT THE CONDITIONS OF PLURALISM IN GUIANA PROVIDE fertile soil for the growth of particularistic forces. Minimal cultural sections among both the East Indians and the Afro-Guianese tend to be nationally integrated. The relationships existing between individuals belonging to these culturally differentiated groups are frequently divisive and occasionally conflict-producing. However, it cannot be assumed that these relationships present a serious obstacle to the political integration of Guianese society.

The cultural sections of the plural society are comprised of innumerable groups which are integrated at different levels of societal activity. The pattern of integration characteristic of a particular cultural section need not include social structures which function to align these groups for political purposes. However, the component groups of a cultural section do exist in a field of social power. These groups also participate in a relatively distinctive system of cultural values. Under the appropriate conditions, such groups may be rather easily mobilized for the purpose of pursuing political ends. This, of course, requires organization. And organization, of necessity, involves decision-making activities on the part of individuals.

It is true that the Afro-Guianese and the East Indian cultural sections are politically organized, respectively, by the Peoples National Congress and the Peoples Progressive Party. But this alignment of political parties with separate cultural sections is of rather recent origin. It will be recalled that when the Peoples Progressive Party was first organized, it received widespread support from Guianese of both cultural sections. Under these circumstances, cultural sections were not politically functional in any dynamic or competitive fashion. However, when Guiana's nationalist movement began to disintegrate, the entire character of the political scene altered. As new political parties were formed, the political potential of cultural sections became increasingly relevant to the struggle for power. By 1961, cultural sections provided the major bases of power on which nationalist political parties operated.

In view of these developments, the decisions taken by nationalist politicians with respect to the political integration of cultural sections were not arrived at on the spur of the moment. Rather, these decisions emerged from a complex of factors that contributed to the disintegration of Guiana's comprehensive nationalist movement. What were the pressures toward disintegration? How did Guianese nationalists respond to these pressures? What decisions were taken, and why did they seem so necessary at the time? What role did pluralism play in the disintegrative process?

## THE IDEOLOGICAL DIMENSIONS OF GUIANESE NATIONALISM

Any serious analysis of Guianese nationalism must begin with a consideration of political ideologies. Because of the cold war, British Guiana has achieved political importance out of all proportion to the size of its population or the value of its economic resources. This newly acquired status is directly related to the international struggle that is being carried on between the great power blocs for the friendship of the new nations. In the context of this struggle, British Guiana presents itself as a problem. The problem, of course, is whether or not this small British possession, when given independence, will choose to align itself with the Western powers, or the neutralist block of new states, or the ranks of the Communist nations.

As a result of the general concern for Guiana's future foreign policy, practically everything that has been written about Guianese politics has served to focus attention on the ideological postures displayed by important nationalist politicians.[1] These ideological pos-

[1] The two official documents published by Her Majesty's Government which deal with the suspension of Guiana's constitution in 1953, *The White Paper* and *The Report of The British Guiana Constitutional Commission (1954)*, focused attention primarily on the issue of whether or not Guianese nationalists were Communists. Michael Swan's book, *British Guiana: The Land of Six Peoples* (London: Her Majesty's Stationery Office, 1954), also presents an analysis of the Guianese political situation in terms of its ideological dimensions. Raymond T. Smith gives considerable emphasis to the ideological dimensions of Guianese nationalism in his book, *British Guiana* (London: Oxford University Press, 1962). More recently, Philip Reno pre-

tures, many observers seem to believe, serve to differentiate the Communists from the non-Communists. The validity of this point of view is questionable, to say the least. The accumulation of verbiage that represents the ideological pronouncements of most Guianese politicians is so devoid of style and inconsistent with their political behavior that it is difficult, if not impossible, to extract from it any sense of commitment other than a commitment to national integration and independence.

For example, several observers of the Guianese scene have found it extremely difficult to determine whether or not the leaders of the Peoples Progressive Party are international Communists or merely enthusiastic nationalists poorly versed in Marxist-Leninist doctrine. Thus, to decide the issue, they have searched the published statements of various Guianese nationalists and compared them with the classical writings of Marx, Lenin, Stalin, and others. The preoccupation with these substantive materials, it seems, has failed to settle the issue. Halperin has argued recently that the question of the Communist affiliation of Guianese nationalists cannot be solved by any amount of reasoning, analogy, or examination of political pronouncements, but only by a study of the party's actual origin and history.[2] Halperin's point of view would seem to be well taken when it is considered that since 1953 no less than fifteen prominent members of the Peoples Progressive Party have changed their party affiliation. In fact, several of this group have done so not once but two and three times.

One case in point is Sidney King. In 1953, King was a completely loyal follower of Cheddi Jagan and an extremely important leader in the Peoples Progressive Party. By his own admission, he was also a Marxist and a dedicated Communist. In 1956, King broke with Jagan and quit the Peoples Progressive Party. He ran as an independent in the 1957 elections but failed to win a seat. A year later, he joined L. F. S. Burnham and subsequently was elected a member of the Executive Committee of the Peoples National Congress. In 1961, shortly before the elections, King was thrown out of the Peoples National Congress because his "black nationalist" views were considered

---

sented a leftist interpretation of the Guianese political situation in a special issue of the *Monthly Review* (*The Ordeal of British Guiana, 1964*). Ernst Halperin's *Racism and Communism in British Guiana* (Cambridge: Massachusetts Institute of Technology Center for International Studies, 1964) deals almost exclusively with the ideological dimensions of Guianese politics.

[2] Halperin, *op. cit.*, pp. 20–30.

to be contrary to the party's position. If it is assumed that the Peoples Progressive Party is primarily Communist in its ideological posture, it would be logical to conclude that between 1953 and 1961 King moved considerably from the left to the right. In view of such cases, how are ideological pronouncements to be interpreted?

The literature dealing with the ideological dimensions of Guianese politics raises another issue that is particularly relevant to the present analysis. The issue has to do with the explanations that have been given for the disintegration of the nationalist movement. Some observers are inclined to attribute disintegration to the different ideological commitments of important nationalist leaders.[3] It is suggested, for example, that underlying the Burnham-Jagan split were ideological postures that were difficult, if not impossible, to accommodate within the framework of a unified nationalist movement.[4] This point of view implies that political ideologies have played a major role in Guianese nationalist politics.

No sensitive observer can deny that political ideologies have played an important role in Guianese politics. However, somewhat contrary to the point of view expressed above, the data available suggest that ideological commitments have not constituted a sufficient condition for the development of political factionalism and sectional politics.

For example, from its inception, the nationalist movement has included within its ranks individuals who profess ideologies that reflect capitalist, socialist, and Marxist postures. These differences did not present a serious obstacle to the movement until sometime after the Peoples Progressive Party was organized in 1950. In fact, no serious divisions occurred in the movement until the Burnham-Jagan split in 1955. This would seem to suggest that substantial changes occurred in Guiana's political climate as the movement developed momentum. It would also seem to suggest that ideological commitments took on an entirely different meaning in light of these changes. Should this be the case, it follows that ideological commitments alone are not sufficient to explain the political factionalism that erupted in 1955. These points may be made more concretely in terms of the data pertaining to the origin of the Peoples Progressive Party.

Most observers would probably agree that the Peoples Progressive

[3] This point is strongly emphasized by Halperin. Raymond Smith, on the other hand, makes a similar point (*op. cit.*, p. 179) but later seems to contradict himself (p. 182).

[4] See Halperin's analysis, *op. cit.*, pp. 46–53.

Party is the first modern political party to have emerged in British Guiana. The beginnings of the P.P.P. may be dated back to 1943. In that year, as a result of constitutional changes, the Legislative Assembly was reconstituted with a majority of elected members, and the voting franchise was expanded. In the same year, Cheddi Jagan and his wife, Janet, returned to British Guiana from the United States. Almost immediately, the Jagans became involved with political discussion groups in Georgetown and some of the neighboring villages.

These political discussion groups do not seem to have been organized for electioneering purposes. They did not take the classical form of political cells. For the most part, they were informal meetings at which interested persons gathered for the purpose of discussing the social and economic problems of Guianese society in anticipation of the struggle for independence that was expected to develop following the war. There is also no evidence to indicate that these groups were dominated by individuals who subscribed to any particular political ideology. During the first two years that these groups met, they seem to have attracted the attention of only a handful of Guianese intellectuals.

In 1945, Jagan was elected treasurer of the Man Power Citizens' Association, the largest trade union operating in the sugar industry. It was at this point that the informal discussion groups he participated in began to take on a new character. However, the changes that were about to occur cannot be understood apart from certain developments in the trade union movement. To begin with, Jagan's newly acquired position in the M.P.C.A. attracted the attention of important trade union leaders. Among these were Ashton Chase, who had replaced H. N. Critchlow as Secretary of the British Guiana Labour Union, and Jocelyn Hubbard, who was then the Secretary of the British Guiana Trades Union Council.[5] It was through Hubbard and the Trades Union Council that a direct line of communication was established between Jagan and the Caribbean Labour Congress.

The Caribbean Labour Congress was organized in 1945. Its affiliates included most of the trade unions in the Caribbean. Through the leaders of these unions, the congress also maintained close ties with the important nationalist political parties. Although its first president was Grantley Adams of Barbados, a mildly liberal nationalist, the leadership of the congress included a number of prominent trade

[5] One extremely knowledgeable informant has described Hubbard as one of the most ideologically committed Communists in British Guiana.

unionists who were closely associated with the Communist Party of Great Britain. One of these was Richard Hart, a former vice-president of the Jamaica Trades Union Congress and an executive member of Jamaica's Peoples National Party. Another was Billy Strachan, who was an active member of the British Communist Party and also the Secretary of the London Branch of the Caribbean Labour Congress. Through these connections, the British Communist Party offered to help Jagan and his associates in their efforts to establish a nationalist movement in British Guiana.

It should be noted that the organizational network which developed between Jagan's group and the British Communist Party cannot be considered a subterfuge. Contrary to Halperin's recent suggestion, the Caribbean Labour Congress was not "infiltrated" by British Communists.[6] British Communists were taken into the Congress openly and with a public knowledge of their associations and political views. Moreover, in 1945, these was nothing unusual about this.

When the Caribbean Labour Congress was founded, it, along with the British unions, the Congress of Industrial Organizations (the American Federation of Labor refused to participate), and the Communist-dominated unions of western and eastern Europe, together formed the World Federation of Trade Unions. As an international labor organization, the W.F.T.U. represented a global effort during the immediate postwar period to develop and maintain a state of co-existence between the Communist and non-Communist nations. This effort, needless to say, died with the cold war. It was buried when the Western powers created the International Confederation of Trade Unions in opposition to the leftwing groups that elected to remain with the World Federation of Trade Unions. This international schism generated splits within the trade union movement all over the Caribbean. Since trade unions were closely affiliated with nationalist political parties, quite naturally the latter were affected also.

In British Guiana, for example, the Trades Union Council retained its affiliation with the World Federation of Trade Unions for a time, but at the cost of losing its largest member, the Man Power Citizens' Association. The M.P.C.A., the British Guiana Labour Union, and the Mine Workers Union became pillars of the International Confederation of Trade Unions within the Guianese labor movement. Subsequently, as a result of the combined pressures exerted

[6] *Op. cit.*, p. 34.

by the British Trades Union Council, the M.P.C.A., the B.G.L.U., the B.G.M.W.U., and the American labor movement, the British Guiana Trades Union Council was forced to drop its affiliation with the World Federation of Trade Unions and join the International Confederation of Trade Unions. Since, in Latin America, this latter organization is dominated by the American Federation of Labor through the Inter-American Regional Workers Organization (and more recently the American Institute for Free Labor Development), this had the effect of bringing the Guianese labor movement directly under the influence (if not the control) of the American labor movement.[7]

These developments, as we shall see, had a profound effect upon Guiana's nationalist movement. The most immediate effect, however, was to force a decision upon Jagan and some of his close associates: Either they had to disassociate themselves from the established Guianese trade unions, or they had to cut themselves off from the British Communist Party. In view of the conservatism of the trade union leadership, particularly the leadership of the M.P.C.A., they decided that the nationalist movement would benefit more if they maintained their connections with the British Communist Party. Thus, Jagan resigned from his position as treasurer of the Man Power Citizens' Association.

To return to the main topic of discussion: In 1946, with the assistance of the British Communist Party, Jagan and his associates formally organized their discussion groups and created the Political Affairs Committee. The purpose of P.A.C., according to Jagan, was to integrate all of the progressive elements in Guiana within one party in preparation for demanding constitutional and other reforms.[8] The Political Affairs Committee, for the most part, adopted a Marxist-Leninist strategy. The struggle for independence was to be conducted on class lines. The working classes were to be organized in opposition to the planters and their "sugar-coated" government. Thus, P.A.C. not only gave birth to Guiana's nationalist movement, but it also pro-

---

[7] The American Institute for Free Labor Development was organized by George Meany and the A.F.L. in 1962 to keep communism out of Latin America. It was placed under the direction of Serafino Romualdi. In 1951, Romualdi was the regional director of the Inter-American Regional Workers Organization. When the B.G. Trades Union Council first applied for membership in the I.C.F.T.U., Romualdi reviewed and rejected the application, declaring that the B.G. Trades Union Council was an organization dominated by Communists.

[8] See Cheddi Jagan's *Forbidden Freedom* (London: Lawrence and Wishart, 1954), p. 44.

vided the movement with an ideological character that was to have an effect upon all subsequent developments.

From the olympian perspective of hindsight, the organizational ties that existed between the Political Affairs Committee and the British Communist Party are not too difficult to recognize. In the late forties, however, these ties were not so evident as to be easily discerned by Guianese intellectuals who were not particularly motivated to look for them. The assistance given to P.A.C. by the Communist Party was not immediately visible. It consisted mainly of organizational advice and political literature. The literature was used for educational and training purposes and came from a number of countries, including the United States. While most of it was leftist in orientation, little of it was crassly revolutionary. In fact, much of this literature presented a more realistic appraisal of the colonial situation than was available in the business-controlled Guianese press. Beyond this assistance, it is possible, but not known for certain, that the British Communist Party also provided P.A.C. with limited funds to conduct its activities. Some of these funds, if they existed, may have been used to publish a news sheet which later became known as *Thunder,* the official organ of the Peoples Progressive Party.

In 1947 Jagan contested and won a seat in the Legislative Council. As a member of the government he gave voice to the views of the Political Affairs Committee. While these views ranged over a wide variety of issues and problems, they were particularly critical of the sugar interests, the Man Power Citizens' Association, the property and income qualifications for voting, and colonialism. For the first time in Guiana's history, an elected representative of Guianese descent was openly and publicly critical of the establishment. This act of leadership, perhaps more than any previous sequence of events, served to ignite the flames of nationalism. Particularly, it excited the emerging intelligentsia. The establishment reacted immediately and in a predictable fashion. In the Legislative Council, it completely ignored Jagan by rejecting every piece of legislation he proposed. Outside of the council, it dismissed Jagan in the press as a rabble-rousing Communist.

"Nationalistic" would seem to be the most appropriate description of the ideological posture adopted by the Political Affairs Committee, particularly during the early years of its existence. Although the most important leaders of P.A.C. were relatively committed to a Marxist-

Leninist view of the Guianese situation, this view had not hardened. They did not make an issue of their commitment. In fact, they not only tolerated the expression of different views, but they actually encouraged their discussion in print and at public meetings. In other words, P.A.C. supported a policy of free and open discussion with respect to all political issues. As a consequense of this policy, P.A.C. became Guiana's major forum for political debate. As such, it attracted the attention of practically every Guianese intellectual who has subsequently become prominent in public affairs. Those who joined the organization and participated in its activities were neither required nor asked to subscribe to any particular ideological position. The members of P.A.C. were united by their common commitment to national independence and politico-cultural integration.

Ideological factionalism within the nationalist movement did not begin to develop until after Whitehall announced, in 1949, that a constitutional commission would be appointed to consider the possibility of constitutional advancement. In response to this announcement, the Political Affairs Committee increasingly concerned itself with the problem of what the Guianese ought to demand by way of constitutional changes. As the discussion of this problem was carried on, it became increasingly clear that there existed among the P.A.C. leaders a relatively hard core of Marxists who were so extreme in their views that they advocated an uncompromising policy with respect to any form of constitutional advancement short of complete and immediate independence. Among others, this core included Cheddi Jagan, Janet Jagan, Martin Carter, Rory Westmaas, Sidney King, and Brindley Benn. The policy that these individuals advocated cannot be fully appreciated apart from the convictions they shared.

By 1949, Cheddi Jagan and his close associates were convinced that Guiana's independence movement was but a part of an international movement in which all colonial peoples must join forces against the imperialist nations (including the United States). They were equally convinced that the success of the former would be directly related to the success of the latter. In addition, they believed that the development of Guiana's economy could be achieved only by the application of those socialist principles which had enabled the Soviet Union and other socialist countries to transform themselves into modern industrial nations. Accordingly, Guiana must seek support from those nations that were socialistic as well as opposed to the colonial powers, particularly from the Soviet Union and the countries of eastern Europe.[9] Among other things, these convictions implied that Guianese nationalists, including those who were not Communists, had to be prepared to sympathize, and possibly cooperate, with the international Communist movement.

Some of the Guianese intellectuals who participated in the activities of the Political Affairs Committee did not strongly object to the views expressed by Jagan and his associates. However, because of the positions they occupied in colonial society, they found these views too radical and somewhat embarrassing. Others were of a more conservative persuasion. They agreed with Jagan on many issues but they disagreed on strategy. They felt that any association between the nationalist movement and the Communist Party would serve only to postpone Guiana's independence. Still others were militantly anti-Communist and, in some cases, equally antisocialist. They perceived Jagan as a threat to capitalist investment and private enterprise. And, if it came to a choice between Jagan and the status quo, they preferred the latter. Between 1949 and 1951, individuals of all three types disassociated themselves from the nationalist movement.

The splitting which occurred between 1949 and 1951 indicated that the intelligentsia was not of one mind. Included among its members were individuals who professed ideologies of the left and individuals who professed ideologies of the right. Under the proper conditions, these differences could contribute to the growth of political factions. However, this early splitting did not present the nationalist movement with a serious problem. There are at least two reasons for this.

For one thing, the splitting resulted from disagreements that were almost purely ideological. Some of those who quit the movement could accuse it of being dominated by Communists. However,

[9] These convictions have not been modified by the P.P.P. with the passage of time. For example, in 1956 the Research and Education Committee of the P.P.P. issued a bulletin to party members. In part, it stated: "We believe that if the Labour or Communist Parties of England win an election, our country would tend to get better treatment from the Colonial Office. . . . On the other hand, the Soviet Union has always declared itself in favour of freedom for subject peoples; so we look carefully at her behaviour at home and in the United Nations. . . . With reference to other colonies, we must realize that one great vision unites us—the vision of freedom, peace and plenty. We must realize that the struggles in Kenya, Cyprus, Algeria and other colonies are part of one great movement to which we belong. We must realize that if the imperial powers are successful in holding them down, they will also hold us down."

in view of those who remained with the movement, and considering the fact that the movement did not present itself in terms of ideological doctrines, this accusation appeared ridiculous. In addition, such an accusation was politically meaningless. Jagan, as well as most other nationalists, understood perfectly well that ideological issues made very little sense to the Guianese masses. As in most underdeveloped countries, the masses in British Guiana are not accustomed to thinking about their relatively concrete needs in terms of abstract political ideas and values. They are even less accustomed to thinking about their needs with reference to international affairs. Therefore, as important as ideologies may be in comprehending the posture of political elites, ideological issues are not the fundamental context of political struggle as far as the masses are concerned.

Another reason why this early splitting did not seriously impair the nationalist movement concerns the persons who were involved. Most of them were not particularly influential with the Guianese masses. Some were middle-class Afro-Guianese who were associated with the League of Coloured Peoples. Others were East Indian businessmen who had never been very active politically and who did not want to commit themselves at this early date. Still others were trade unionists associated with the Man Power Citizens' Association, the Trades Union Council, the Teachers' Association, or the Mine Workers.

Thus, in spite of the few who broke away between 1949 and 1951, the Political Affairs Committee achieved its purpose with remarkable success. As an organization designed to aggregate the political interests of the Guianese intelligentsia, P.A.C. brought together the leadership that was needed to mobilize a comprehensive nationalist movement. When the Constitutional Commission was appointed in 1950, only a few loose ends remained to be dealt with. One of these involved the need to bring into the movement an African leader of national stature, a leader with as much influence among the African masses as Jagan had among the East Indians. Although the movement contained a number of well-known African leaders (e.g., Ashton Chase, Sidney King, Martin Carter), none of them had a national following. Such a person was needed to counteract the opposition that might be mobilized by the League of Coloured Peoples on a purely racial basis. This particular loose end was tied in 1950, when L. F. S. Burnham entered Jagan's circle of political associates.

Burnham, the son of an African head teacher, was one of Guiana's most nationally publicized scholars. At Queen's College, in Georgetown, he had won practically every academic honor available. In 1942, he was awarded the Guiana Scholarship, which took him to the University of London, where he earned the B.A. and LL.B. degrees. While in London as a student, he was President of the West Indian Students' Union and Vice-President of the London Branch of the Caribbean Labour Congress. Thus, he had political credentials which established him among the leaders in the Caribbean. When Burnham returned to British Guiana, he quickly developed a reputation as an outstanding courtroom barrister and public speaker. Burnham was exactly what the nationalist movement needed. He could solidify the support of the African cultural section and, at the same time, neutralize any opposition that might subsequently develop among the Afro-Guianese middle class.

Although Burnham quickly moved into the inner circle of the Political Affairs Committee, Jagan and his associates shared certain reservations with respect to his role in the nationalist movement. They were somewhat concerned about his independent and forceful personality. They were concerned also about his middle-class background. Because of it, Burnham had many close friends among African professionals and labor leaders who were not receptive to Jagan's ideological commitments. Another reservation concerned Burnham's politics. He was strongly committed to the federation movement in the Caribbean. In addition, although he was a burning nationalist and an outspoken socialist, while in London he had made little effort to cultivate close ties with the British Communist Party. Moreover, he did not seem to be very interested in developing such ties. As we shall see, Jagan and his associates accepted Burnham, but, because of these reservations, they never completely trusted him.

Another loose end that confronted the Political Affairs Committee as constitutional advancement approached concerned its limitations as a political organization. P.A.C. was not organized to deal with the masses. Its leadership was not defined in terms of a formal structure of authority and responsibility. It could not formulate and implement policy with respect to a definite group of followers. It had no structure in terms of which it could recruit and maintain a following in the villages and urban neighborhoods. Its sources of funds were extremely limited. And its news sheet was neither written for mass consumption nor printed for mass distribution. In other words, P.A.C. did not have the organizational credentials of a political party, and a political party was what was needed more than anything else if the nationalist movement was to develop a mass base in preparation for any national elections that might accompany constitutional change.

Late in 1950, these problems were solved by the dissolution of the Political Affairs Committee and the organization of the Peoples Progressive Party. The constitution for the P.P.P. was drafted mainly by Cheddi Jagan, Janet Jagan, L. F. S. Burnham, and a few close associates. It was ratified and adopted by the First Congress of the P.P.P. in April, 1951. This particular constitution is a rather interesting document. In spite of its simplicity, it not only defines the organizational structure of the new party but also reveals something of its ideological character.

Organizationally, the P.P.P. Constitution provides a structure in terms of which the authority vested in the Executive Committee of the party is almost absolute. The basic unit of the party is the local cell. Local cells are aggregated into larger units represented by constituency committees. The officers at both of these levels are directly elected by the membership. However, all nominations of candidates by local groups are "subject to the approval of the Executive Committee." The Executive Committee is comprised of the officers of the party and seven members of the party's General Council. These are directly elected at the Party Congress. The electors, however, are the delegates sent to the congress by local groups. Since these delegates are approved by officers who have already been approved by the Executive Committee, the possibility of unseating a member of the latter group is rather slim, short of a rebellion within the party. Therefore, the Executive Committee of the P.P.P. tends to be a self-perpetuating group responsible for all of the party's policies and political activities.[10]

With respect to ideology, among other things the 1951 Constitution of the P.P.P. committed the party to the following:

(a) To promote the interests of the subject peoples by transforming British Guiana into a Socialist Country . . .

(b) To stimulate political consciousness and guide political development by the dissemination of socialist ideas . . .

---

[10] As far as the author was able to determine, every effort that delegates have ever made to unseat a member of the Executive Committee at a party congress has resulted in the elections being declared null and void, and, in some instances, the delegates in question have been expelled from the party. In other words, it is almost impossible to change the Executive Committee of the P.P.P. without risking a split in the party.

(c) To pursue constantly a goal of national self-determination and independence.
(d) To work for the eventual political union of British Guiana with other Caribbean territories.[11]

Of the above commitments, only item (d) is relatively specific in nature. This particular item committed the P.P.P. to the support of the Caribbean Federation (the Caribbean Federation, like other federations created by the British, seemed to have been doomed from the start). With the schisms that were developing in the Caribbean at the time the P.P.P. constitution was written, it is difficult to explain the inclusion of this item. It may have represented a concession to Burnham, who strongly favored Guiana's participation in the federation, or it may have represented an effort to allay the anxieties of the Colonial Office with respect to the nationalist movement before the investigations of the Constitutional Commission. On the other hand, since the schisms in the Caribbean had not yet affected Guiana (in April, 1951, the Trades Union Council was still a member of the World Federation of Trade Unions), it may have represented a belief on Jagan's part that his alliances in the Caribbean were secure.

Interviews with various nationalists did not provide a satisfactory explanation for item (d). Nevertheless, whatever the reasons for its inclusion in the P.P.P. constitution, item (d) represented an ideological commitment that subsequently added considerable strain to the relationship existing between Burnham and Jagan. And, in addition, it also represented an issue that could have a psychological impact on cultural sections. Many East Indians, for example, equated Guiana's participation in the Caribbean Federation with "black domination."

Apart from item (d), the ideological posture adopted by the Peoples Progressive Party in 1951 was no more specific than that displayed by the Political Affairs Committee between 1946 and 1950. Thus, with respect to the role of ideology, the policies of the two organizations were almost identical. That is to say, ideological differences among nationalist leaders would not be allowed to weaken the movement. The P.P.P. welcomed the support of any nationalist committed to the goal of immediate and absolute independence for British Guiana.

---

[11] The Constitution of the Peoples Progressive Party, as ratified and adopted by the First Congress of the P.P.P. on April 1, 1951. Subsequent amendments to the constitution have not altered the party's structure in any fundamental way. The statement of goals, however, has been modified—notably by the deletion of item (d).

In view of these facts, what of a general nature can be said about the role of political ideologies in the organization of Guiana's comprehensive nationalist movement?

First, in British Guiana, as in most newly emerging nations, Communist propaganda is not designed for mass consumption by peasants and workers. Instead, it is designed to exploit the frustrations of a proletarianized intelligentsia. It has appealed most to those intellectuals who have been more or less condemned to a declassé existence as a result of the best positions being reserved for expatriates. However, in conjunction with the plural character of Guianese society, it needs to be recognized that the proletarianization of the intelligentsia has not proceeded evenly.

Light-colored Africans, for example, have had greater access to the higher positions in Guianese society than dark-colored Africans. Africans, in general, have experienced greater social mobility than the East Indians. Similarly, the sons of East Indian businessmen are found more frequently among professionals than the sons of East Indian sugar workers. In other words, not all members of the new nationalist elite are equally frustrated, and not all are equally susceptible to the appeals of Marxist-Leninist doctrines. Thus, Guianese intellectuals are not of one mind. With respect to ideological commitments, they disagree among themselves today as they have disagreed among themselves since the nationalist movement began to take shape in 1943.

Second, lines of organizational influence obviously existed between certain Guianese nationalists and the international Communist movement. These lines of influence, however, cannot readily be demonstrated from the political writings or public statements of nationalist leaders. One reason for this is that almost none of the nationalist leaders have made an effort to delineate systematically the substance of their political views. Also, up through the time of the organization of the Peoples Progressive Party, the commitment of most Guianese leaders to nationalistic goals and aspirations seems to have been more important than a commitment to any particular political doctrine. Thus, ideological styles have been in great flux, and, as we shall see, the organizational connections between certain nationalist leaders and the international Communist movement also have been in great flux.

Third, none of the more sophisticated Guianese nationalists, particularly those of a Marxist-Leninist persuasion, would entrust the fate of the nationalist movement to the propaganda appeal of political doctrines. They recognized that in countries like British Guiana, political ideologies do not make very useful instruments of mass persuasion. Most Guianese simply do not define their needs in abstract political terms.[12] The success which Guianese politicians have had in mobilizing support for the nationalist movement does not derive from their ideological commitments. Their success derives mainly from two sources: one, the widespread frustrations that all Guianese tend to share as a result of their exploitation in colonial society; and, two, the confidence that Guianese have in those leaders who, regardless of their political styles, address themselves to these frustrations.

It is evident, then, that the disagreements which existed among the nationalist elite as a result of different ideological commitments did not present a serious obstacle to the integration of a comprehensive nationalist movement. The successful organization of the Peoples Progressive Party in 1951 demonstrated that the political values associated with particular ideological perspectives could be accommodated in the cause of national independence and politico-cultural integration.

When constitutional advancement came in 1953, the Peoples Progressive Party waged an extremely successful election campaign. The party's candidates polled 51 per cent of the total vote and captured eighteen of the twenty-four seats that were up for election in the House of Assembly. On the face of this victory, the P.P.P. appeared as a dynamic and highly integrated nationalist movement. However, this was not quite the case. Even before the 1953 elections, the inner circle of the P.P.P. leadership was rife with political factionalism.

## THE PRESSURES OF PLURALISM

The factionalism that existed below the surface between 1951 and 1953 is directly related to the disintegrative pressures that began to build up once the political credentials of the Peoples Progressive Party became known. For convenience, these pressures may be con-

[12] For example, during the village studies, an effort was made to collect data on the ideological dimensions of political attitudes. To the extent that these data are accurate, it was learned that most villagers had absolutely no idea what might be involved in the nationalization of basic industries, or in the borrowing of development capital from Cuba, or in the purchase of agricultural equipment from East Germany. In fact, many villagers had no idea what might be involved in independence. I have in my field notes the comments of one informant who emphatically stated that he was in favor of immediate independence but who also insisted that British Guiana must always remain under the Queen's rule with a governor in Georgetown.

sidered in terms of three general categories. First, there were those pressures that existed simply because of the plural integration of Guianese society. Second, there were those pressures that developed as a consequence of international events over which Guianese nationalists had relatively little control. And third, there were those pressures that resulted from the development of organized opposition on the part of those Guianese who, for one reason or another, preferred to maintain the status quo. It is possible that none of these pressures alone was sufficient to create serious splits within the leadership of the Peoples Progressive Party. However, together and in combination with the ideological differences that existed in conjunction with nationalist aspirations, these pressures created centrifugal forces that became increasingly difficult to control.

Consider, first, the pressures associated with the plural integration of Guianese society. Jagan, Burnham, and most other nationalists understood that the political integration of British Guiana was not based upon a social fabric woven together by a common cultural heritage. They knew that Africans and East Indians comprised separate communities, locally as well as nationally. They also knew that the structures which served to integrate these communities were deeply rooted in Guiana's colonial past. In addition, they realized that these structures were being reinforced continuously by the communications media, by trade unions and labor organizations, by governmental agencies, by religious and ethnic associations, and by commercial and industrial organizations as well as economic transactions. Above all, Jagan and Burnham were fully cognizant of the fact that, within colonial society, Africans and East Indians did not occupy comparable positions of power.

The problems inherent in the plural structure of Guianese society were recognized also by the Constitutional Commission of 1950–51. In its report to the Secretary of State for the Colonies, the commission noted that the East Indians had "remained a community within a community with an allegiance to their motherland," while the Africans had "won their way to professional and public appointments." In recent years, the commission noted, "Indian aloofness" has given way to the realization that Indians have a permanent place in Guianese society and to a "demand for equal participation in it." This, according to the commission, presented a challenge to which other racial groups had responded by closing their ranks. Therefore, the commission warned, "race is easily identified with nationalism" and can be used as a stepping stone to political power. Moreover, the commission suggested, for the Indian peoples this identification was particularly critical, because it had already received "stimulus from the advent of independence to the Indian sub-continent."[13]

The Constitutional Commission was relatively optimistic about the conditions of pluralism in Guianese society. It perhaps was also a bit naive about these conditions. For example, comparing Guiana to the United States and Canada, the commission concluded: "If, as in these lands, the overriding loyalty is given to the community as a whole, racial distinctions, expressed in a pride in culture, tradition, and history, can be a source of enrichment and strength."[14] Most nationalists did not share the commission's optimism. In fact, they were so sensitive to the disintegrative forces of pluralism that they considered the destruction of these forces to be one of the party's more important objectives.

Thus, as previously indicated, in organizing the Peoples Progressive Party every effort was made to create a strong alliance among nationalists who also were sectional leaders in order to aggregate the support of different cultural sections. Burnham, an African, was made chairman of the party. Clinton Wong, of Chinese descent, was made senior vice-chairman. Cheddi Jagan, an East Indian, was made second vice-chairman. Rory Westmaas, an African, was made junior vice-chairman. Ram Karran, an East Indian, was made party treasurer. Janet Jagan, a former American, was made general secretary, and Sidney King, an African, was made assistant secretary. The Executive Committee of the party included such prominent East Indian leaders as Jai Narine Singh and Dr. J. P. Lachmansingh. The membership of the General Council was about evenly divided among Africans and East Indians. Ten East Indians and nine Africans were included among the candidates put up for election to the House of Assembly by the P.P.P. in 1953. After the elections, the party distributed ministerial portfolios to three Africans and three East Indians.

It is difficult to determine precisely how much this strategy of balance contributed to the P.P.P.'s 1953 election victory. For example, six of the eighteen P.P.P. candidates who were elected to the House of Assembly polled considerably fewer votes than the total number

[13] *Report of the British Guiana Constitutional Commission 1950–51*, Sir E. J. Waddington, Chairman (London: His Majesty's Stationery Office Colonial No. 280, 1951), p. 14.

[14] *Ibid.*, p. 15.

cast for independents and candidates running with opposition parties. A case in point is the election of the P.P.P. candidate Samuel M. Lachmansingh in the Western Berbice district. Lachmansingh won his seat with only 37 per cent of the total vote. The remaining vote, 63 per cent of the total, was divided among no less than ten opposing candidates. In other words, the 1953 election victory of the Peoples Progressive Party may be attributed as much to the effective organization of the party on the one hand and the lack of organized opposition on the other as to the party's strategy of balance.

Even if a measure of success can be attributed to the strategy of balance, the forces of pluralism were manifestly evident in the 1953 elections. For example, in the predominantly East Indian district of Western Essequibo, Janet Jagan won a seat with 2,523 votes. However, an East Indian opponent polled 1,452 votes, largely on the basis that Janet Jagan is not an East Indian. In the predominantly East Indian district of Demerara-Essequibo, the P.P.P. ran as its candidate Fred Bowman, an African. Bowman won the election with 3,346 votes. Four East Indian opponents, however, received a total of 3,860 votes. The East Bank Demerara district, while predominantly East Indian in population, contains a sizable African minority. The P.P.P. candidate in this district, Dr. J. P. Lachmansingh, won the seat with a huge majority vote. However, he lost the vote of most of the African minority to A. G. King, a Portuguese. In the Courantyne Coast district, which is also heavily populated by East Indians, Cheddi Jagan polled 6,233 votes. However, most of the Africans in this district voted for Loris Sharples, an African.

In other words, a district by district analysis of the 1953 election data indicates that the disintegrative forces of pluralism were at work in spite of the strategy of balance adopted by the Peoples Progressive Party. The large number of independents who polled sizable votes against P.P.P. candidates were able to do so because of particularistic considerations involving ethnicity and personal influence. The P.P.P. did not run any East Indian candidates in the predominantly African districts of Georgetown and New Amsterdam. It also did not run African candidates in the heavily populated East Indian districts of Berbice. East Indian and African candidates, respectively, had considerably more strength when they ran in East Indian and African districts. In some instances, however, the strategy of balance enabled African and East Indian candidates to carry districts which they might not have been able to carry otherwise.

In view of these considerations, the anxieties that nationalist leaders shared with respect to the plural integration of Guianese society seem to have had some basis in fact. Notwithstanding the appeals of nationalism, Africans and East Indians tended to vote in 1953 as separate national communities. The strategy of balance may have blunted the effect of this tendency somewhat, but it did not destroy it. Under these circumstances, P.P.P. leaders had to be sensitive to the danger that one of their own group, for ideological or opportunistic reasons, could cut away from the nationalist movement at practically any time and survive politically by making a direct appeal to one or the other of Guiana's major cultural sections.

## THE PRESSURE OF INTERNATIONAL EVENTS

Only a few months after the organization of the Peoples Progressive Party, the forces of pluralism took on a new and a more ominous dimension because of international developments over which Guianese nationalists had relatively little control. The developments in question involved the previously mentioned schism in the international labor movement. In 1951, the splits that had developed within the Caribbean Labour Congress because of the struggle between the World Federation of Trade Unions and the International Confederation of Trade Unions began to have an impact on the Guianese political situation. Specifically, as Guianese labor unions undertook to affiliate themselves with the International Confederation of Trade Unions, the struggles that ensued brought to the surface a complex series of factors that began to divide the leadership of the Peoples Progressive Party. In order to deal with these factors in context, it is necessary to digress for a moment and reconsider the relationship that existed between certain nationalist leaders, the trade union movement, and cultural sections.

It will be recalled that in 1946 Cheddi Jagan resigned his position as treasurer of the Man Power Citizens' Association. In his view, and, one can add, in the view of most nationalists, the M.P.C.A. had become a "company union."[15] At the same time, however, the labor

[15] The typical sugar worker considers the M.P.C.A. to be a "company union." There are many reasons why this attitude is prevalent. The union has never had a sugar worker as its president. It has not been very militant as a bargaining agency. There is also some evidence to indicate that when militant officers are elected by locals, they are quickly courted and made ineffective by plantation managers. At Plantation Skeldon, for example, very few of the East Indians who were interviewed expressed any confidence in the M.P.C.A. or its local officers.

movement was much too important to the nationalist movement for Jagan and his associates to alienate themselves from it altogether. Through the Caribbean Labour Congress, the labor movement provided organizational connections with the British Communist Party. Jagan and other leftwing nationalists considered these connections to be ideologically desirable and politically useful. The labor movement was important also because it involved power structures which could be used to mobilize the working classes in support of or in opposition to the nationalist movement. In addition, these power structures could become extremely crucial to the success of any program of socialist legislation in the event that Guiana received independence under the direction of a socialist government. For these reasons, Jagan, or any nationalist leader for that matter, had to be concerned with the control of the labor movement.

After Jagan resigned from the M.P.C.A. in 1946, he and Dr. J. P. Lachmansingh organized the Guiana Industrial Workers Union for the purpose of supplanting the M.P.C.A. in the sugar industry. In the jurisdictional struggle that ensued between the G.I.W.U. and the M.P.C.A. the latter organization received the support of the Sugar Producers' Association, the British Guiana Trades Union Council, the British Trades Union Council, and the International Confederation of Trade Unions. Because of the power of the M.P.C.A. within the British Guiana Trades Union Council, the latter organization refused to accept the G.I.W.U. as an affiliated member. As a consequence of this combined opposition, in spite of its membership claims, the G.I.W.U. failed to win recognition as a bargaining agency for the sugar workers.

As of 1950, then, Jagan's relationship to the labor movement was relatively restricted to his control of the Guiana Industrial Workers Union. However, the G.I.W.U. was largely a paper organization. If the sugar workers preferred the G.I.W.U. to the M.P.C.A., they had no way to demonstrate their support except by jurisdictional strikes. At the same time, the G.I.W.U. had no way to represent the members it claimed. It was recognized by the Sugar Producers' Association and the Guiana Trades Union Council only as a renegade organization with no legal status. It was accorded similar status by the British Trades Union Council and the International Confederation of Trade Unions. Nevertheless, the G.I.W.U. did have some legal status and recognition. It belonged to and was recognized by the Caribbean Labour Congress. It also belonged to and was recognized by the World Federation of Trade Unions.

In 1952, it appeared for a time that Jagan's efforts to link the nationalist movement to the Guianese labor movement, and his efforts to link both of these, through the Caribbean Labour Congress, to the international Communist movement, were beginning to pay off. The G.I.W.U. was admitted to the Trades Union Council. It was still considered a renegade union by the Sugar Producers' Association but, also in 1952, a labor bill was introduced to the Legislative Council which sought to alter this situation. In the case of jurisdictional disputes between two or more unions, the labor bill would empower the Commissioner of Labour to conduct elections in order to decide the issue of recognition. Needless to say, the bill failed to pass. However, it did receive the support of the Trades Union Council, and this support, among other things, resulted in the resignation of the M.P.C.A. from the council. Thus, although the G.I.W.U. could not negotiate for the sugar workers, it had at least succeeded in displacing its rival union from the Trades Union Council. In addition, since both the G.I.W.U. and the Trades Union Council were affiliated with the Caribbean Labour Congress and the World Federation of Trade Unions, the links in Jagan's organizational chain were beginning to close.

However, before these gains could be consolidated, events in the Caribbean took a turn for the worse with respect to Jagan and the Marxists within the Peoples Progressive Party. First, in Jamaica, Norman Manley expelled Richard Hart (Jagan's contact with the British Communist Party) and a number of other Marxists from the Peoples National Party. A few months later, in June, 1952, Grantley Adams of Barbados declared that the Caribbean Labour Congress should be disbanded because it was dominated by Communists. Although Jagan, Hart, and others made frantic efforts to head off the impending splits, none of their proposals were acceptable to Manley, Adams, and Bustamante, an influential Jamaican labor leader. In effect, the ideological and political hiatus between the World Federation of Trade Unions and the International Confederation of Trade Unions was simply too broad and too deep to be bridged in terms of compromises fabricated by nationalists from small colonial territories without world power or influence. Also, the Caribbean labor movement was too much in the grips of the American labor movement to expect that the World Federation of Trade Unions would be allowed to maintain its influence in opposition to the Inter-American Regional Workers Organization and the International Confederation of Trade Unions.

As a result of these developments, the Caribbean Labour Congress degenerated into a collection of small and relatively unimportant unions, largely dominated by nationalists of a Marxist persuasion and affiliated with the World Federation of Trade Unions. As an organization, the Caribbean Labour Congress was effectively isolated from the mainstream of nationalist politics by the British Trades Union Council and the American labor movement. Toward the end of 1952, the British Guiana Trades Union Council made application for membership in the International Confederation of Trade Unions. However, the application was rejected by Serafino Romualdi, then regional director of the Inter-American Regional Workers Organization and George Meany's Latin American labor ambassador.[16]

It seems that when Mr. Romualdi visited British Guiana to investigate the Trades Union Council's application, he met with Lionel Luckhoo, President of the Man Power Citizens' Association. Although it is not known for certain, it appears that Luckhoo convinced Romualdi that the Trades Union Council, because of Jagan and the G.I.-W.U., was dominated by Communists. As a result of Romualdi's decision to reject the B.G.T.U.C., the Trades Union Council continued its affiliation with the World Federation of Trade Unions and the Caribbean Labour Congress. However, the seeds of division within the Guianese labor movement were sown. Shortly after the suspension of the 1953 constitution, several Guianese labor unions, including the M.P.C.A., the Guiana Labour Union, and the Guiana Mine Workers Union, met and disbanded the Trades Union Council. They drafted new rules for a new organization which excluded from its ranks any labor union affiliated with the Caribbean Labour Congress or the World Federation of Trade Unions. All of the unions belonging to this new group affiliated with the International Confederation of Trade Unions, and all of them, except for the M.P.C.A., were dominated by Afro-Guianese labor leaders.

Needless to say, these developments placed the Marxists within the Peoples Progressive Party in a rather precarious position. Outside of the party, their most important link with the Guianese masses was

---

[16] The intervention of the American labor movement in the internal affairs of newly emerging nations, including British Guiana, is described by Sidney Lens in a recent article, "American Labor Abroad: Lovestone Diplomacy," *The Nation*, July 5, 1965, pp. 10–FF. Lens's contention that the Meanyites have given support to unionists in British Guiana in an effort to block Jagan's rise to power is fully supported by data I collected in interviews with trade union leaders in 1960–61.

the Guiana Industrial Workers Union.[17] The G.I.W.U. catered primarily to the interests of East Indian sugar workers, and most of the Marxists were Afro-Guianese. In addition, the G.I.W.U. was not recognized by the Sugar Producers' Association. It belonged to the Trades Union Council, but, in 1953, the T.U.C. was shaky and on the verge of splitting into opposing factions. Outside of British Guiana, the Caribbean Labour Congress represented the major organization with which the Marxists were connected. However, it had been split off from the mainstream of nationalist politics. At the same time, by virtue of its constitution, the Peoples Progressive Party was still committed to union with the Caribbean Federation. However, because of the domination of Caribbean politics by the more conservative nationalists, the Caribbean Federation could serve only to weaken further the position of the Guianese Marxists with respect to the nationalist movement.

To further complicate the situation, these developments did not have an adverse effect on the political position of the non-Marxists within the Peoples Progressive Party. This was particularly evident in the case of the party's chairman, L. F. S. Burnham. Although Burnham shared Jagan's views with respect to the M.P.C.A., he avoided becoming deeply involved with the jurisdictional dispute between the M.P.C.A. and the Guiana Industrial Workers Union. In 1952, Burnham was the president of the British Guiana Labour Union, one of the largest African-dominated unions in the country. In addition, Burnham had good alliances among the leadership of several other African-dominated unions. The factionalism which had erupted in the Caribbean did not disturb these alliances. Moreover, it did not alter Burnham's firm commitment to Guiana's participation in the Caribbean Federation.

Thus, under Burnham's leadership, in 1952 the British Guiana Labour Union applied for and was given membership in the International Confederation of Trade Unions. Directly and indirectly, this aligned Burnham with Manley and Bustamante of Jamaica and Grantley Adams of Barbados, all of whom Jagan considered to be

[17] Jagan was president of the Sawmill Workers Union, but this union caters to very few people. Ashton Chase was secretary of the Guiana Labour Union, but he relinquished this position when he was appointed Minister of Labour after the 1953 elections. Also, in 1953, Chase was more inclined to the non-Marxists than he was to the Marxists. Burnham was president of the Guiana Labour Union, but he was not a Marxist.

"capitalist stooges." As a consequence, Burnham was not particularly disturbed when the Caribbean Labour Congress was isolated from the Caribbean nationalist movements. To what extent did Burnham's stance on these particular matters contribute to the disintegration of the Guianese nationalist movement?

## THE ORGANIZED OPPOSITION

Added to the pressures created by international developments were the pressures generated within Guianese society when the conservative forces began to organize in opposition to the Peoples Progressive Party. While the conservative forces opposed the Peoples Progressive Party in general, much of their opposition was sharply focused upon Jagan and the leftwing elements within the party. Perhaps the most important person among the opposition forces was Lionel Luckhoo, the president of the M.P.C.A., a person of some influence within the Indian business community, a prominent barrister, and an appointed member of Guiana's Legislative Council.

Luckhoo, more than anyone else, fashioned the image of the Communist menace in Guianese political life, and he pinned it directly on Cheddi and Janet Jagan. This was the major avenue of Luckhoo's thrust against Jagan within the trade union movement. It was no less the major avenue of his thrust against the Peoples Progressive Party. In 1952, as a member of the Legislative Council, Luckhoo introduced an Undesirable Publications Bill which allowed the governor in council (i.e., the Executive Council) to ban entry into British Guiana of any literature that was deemed "subversive and contrary to the public interest." This legislation was passed and enacted into law. Its enactment was directed exclusively at the political literature which the Peoples Progressive Party imported for distribution among its political cadres around the country.

In 1951, Luckhoo joined forces with John Carter, an elected member of the Legislative Council and a barrister of African descent, and organized the National Democratic Party. The N.D.P., like the Peoples Progressive Party, employed a strategy of balance. East Indians, Africans, and Portuguese were included among its leadership. Unlike the Peoples Progressive Party, however, the N.D.P. aggregated the forces of conservatism in Guianese society. The N.D.P. candidates in the 1953 elections included Portuguese businessmen (e.g., John Fernandes and E. F. Correia), African businessmen (e.g., W. O. R. Kendall), African professionals and members of the League of Coloured Peoples (e.g., John Carter and J. A. Nicholson), East Indian professionals (e.g., Lionel Luckhoo and Balram Singh Rai), and M.P.C.A. labor leaders (e.g., Rupert Tello and Sheik M. Shakoor). As a group, these people shared but one thing in common: All of them were militant anti-Communists who were convinced that the Marxists within the Peoples Progressive Party had to be rooted out of Guianese political life.

The National Democratic Party did not present the P.P.P. with formidable opposition in the 1953 elections. The N.D.P. polled only 13 per cent of the votes (less than half the votes polled by independent candidates), and only two of its fifteen candidates (Kendall and Correia) won seats. However, with the support of the press, the N.D.P. did succeed in making communism a major issue in Guianese political life. Although its anti-Communist campaign failed to impress the Guianese masses, it did not fail to impress the colonial establishment. In fact, judging by the report of the Robertson Commission, the emphasis which the N.D.P. placed on the threat of communism in British Guiana certainly helped to prepare the way for the constitutional suspension and the removal from office of the P.P.P. government in October, 1953.

## THE CONSTITUTIONAL CRISIS

The suspension of the 1953 constitution by the executive action of the governor, Sir Alfred Savage, did not cause Guiana's comprehensive nationalist movement to disintegrate. Actually, the constitutional suspension was, in large part, the inevitable result of organizational strategies that the Peoples Progressive Party adopted in response to the pressures for disintegration. When elected to form the government, the P.P.P. ministers made efforts to implement these strategies at once. However, these efforts created a sufficient amount of political instability to provide the opposition the opportunity to remove the P.P.P. from the government in the hope that subsequent developments would result in the defeat of Jagan and his associates. Thus, the constitutional suspension served only to exacerbate the divisive tendencies that were already evident within the Peoples Progressive Party.

It is necessary to keep in mind the situation that confronted the

Marxists within the Peoples Progressive Party shortly before the 1953 elections. On the whole, they occupied an extremely precarious position with respect to the nationalist movement. While their ideological commitments were firm, the alliances that supported these commitments in the Caribbean were no longer secure and influential. Outside of the P.P.P., with very little control of the labor movement, their access to the Guianese masses was limited. Also, most of the organized opposition to the P.P.P. was focused in their direction. At the same time, the position of the non-Marxists within the P.P.P. was comparatively secure. Burnham had not alienated himself from the Guianese labor movement, and his alliances in the Caribbean were reinforced by his strong commitment to the federation.

There is ample evidence available to suggest that Jagan and his close associates were realistically apprised of the situation. They believed that if the trend of developments continued, either they would be forced to modify their ideological views considerably, or they would be forced to lead a faction out of the party. From the point of view of the Marxists, both possibilities were undesirable. They believed, on the one hand, that true independence could not be achieved if the nationalist movement aligned itself with the imperialists. On the other hand, anyone who led a faction out of the party would be forced to operate from a position of weakness, and, as things stood, this was particularly true with respect to the Marxists.

In view of these considerations, it was necessary that the Marxists develop a strategy which would enable them to re-establish their control of the nationalist movement. Such control would require that they be free to operate from a position of strength both within the P.P.P. and outside of it. With these objectives in mind, according to the author's informants, the leftwing elements of the party held a series of secret meetings before and after the 1953 elections.[18] These meetings were convened by Cheddi and Janet Jagan and were usually attended by Sidney King, Rory Westmaas, Martin Carter, Brindley Benn, Ram Karran, and Mohamed Khan, among others.

To the extent that informants could recall the particulars of these meetings, and to the extent that their memories could be checked by

[18] For reasons that are obvious, the names of informants cannot be revealed. It suffices to note that most of the data reported here and in the following section with respect to the decisions taken at these meetings were obtained, independently, in depth interviews with four knowledgeable individuals. These data were checked by the use of indirect questions in subsequent interviews with several nationalist leaders.

cross-interviewing participants, the strategy developed by the Marxists involved decisions with respect to three general areas of consideration: (1) L. F. S. Burnham, (2) the Caribbean Federation, and (3) the policies that should be pursued in the event that the P.P.P. was elected to form the government. With respect to Burnham, it was decided that either he would have to come to terms with the left wing or be forced to disassociate himself from the party. With respect to the Caribbean Federation, it was decided that British Guiana would have to insist upon complete independence before associating itself with any federation involving the Caribbean countries. Otherwise, Guiana's independence movement would be considered a domestic rather than an international affair.

With respect to the policies that should be pursued in the event that the P.P.P. was elected to form the government, it has been suggested by several observers that the leaders of the P.P.P., particularly the leaders of the left wing, considered the new constitution to be a sham, and, therefore, they committed the party to policies designed to embarrass the governor and provoke a constitutional crisis.[19] There can be no question about the fact that the Marxists considered the 1953 constitution to be a document which, in effect, perpetuated British control. This attitude was expressed on numerous occasions by Jagan and King.[20] However, it should be noted that this was an attitude which the non-Marxists also shared.[21] In view of the fact that the 1953 constitution did perpetuate British control, it is difficult to see how an expression of dissatisfaction concerning such a state of affairs can be interpreted as evidence of a policy designed to provoke a constitutional crisis.

As far as it could be determined on the basis of interview data, neither the Marxists nor the non-Marxists had any intention of provoking a constitutional crisis in the event that a P.P.P. government

[19] Raymond Smith emphasizes this explanation of the constitutional crisis (*op. cit.*, pp. 174–75). Ernst Halperin concurs with Smith's interpretation (*op. cit.*, pp. 48–49). Although Jagan has admitted, in a speech to the 1956 congress of the P.P.P., that the P.P.P. government of 1953 might have been too extreme in some of its programs, he has never admitted that it was the government's intention to provoke a constitutional crisis. Burnham also has denied that a decision was made to provoke a constitutional crisis. This particular explanation of the constitutional crisis appears to represent the point of view developed in the *Report of The British Guiana Constitutional Commission,* Sir James Robertson, Chairman, (London: Her Majesty's Stationery Office Report Cmd. 9274, 1954).

[20] *Ibid.*, pp. 32–33.

[21] *Ibid.*

was elected. What they did decide, however, was to use the limited prerogatives provided in the constitution to enact as much reform legislation as possible. If the governor elected to exercise his power of veto with respect to the legislation proposed, this would serve only to demonstrate to the Guianese that the British retained the reins of power and that the government was not a free and independent government of the people. Neither the Marxists nor the non-Marxists expected that this strategy would result in a constitutional crisis.

In order to delineate more precisely the specific strategy that the Marxists adopted for the purpose of improving their position within the nationalist movement, it is necessary to consider some of the legislation they were particularly interested in pushing when the P.P.P. government took office. Four pieces of legislation were especially relevant to their situation: (1) the Undesirable Publications (Repeal) Bill, (2) the Rice Farmers Security of Tenure (Amendment) Bill, (3) the Trade Disputes (Essential Services) (Repeal) Bill, and (4) the Labour Relations Bill.

As was previously noted, the Undesirable Publications Bill was passed in 1952 at the instigation of Lionel Luckhoo. It in effect prevented the Marxists from importing and distributing literature deemed to be subversive or "communistic." Although this bill probably did not seriously hamper the activities of the Marxists within the P.P.P., it did single them out as a special threat to the economic and political future of Guianese society. It also made it somewhat more difficult for the Marxists to communicate and defend their views in opposition to the views expressed in the mass media. Finally, the Marxists, as well as many other Guianese, were opposed to the ban as a matter of principle: It represented an encroachment upon the rights of free citizens. Although the repeal of the ordinance was passed in the House of Assembly, where the P.P.P. controlled a majority, it was amended in the State Council (where the governor controlled a majority) and returned to the House of Assembly. Before the amendment could be hammered out to everyone's satisfaction, the constitution was suspended.

For some years in British Guiana, there had been a law that attempted to provide rice farmers with security of tenure by preventing landlords from injuriously increasing rents. Even before the 1953 elections, however, it was recognized that the measures provided under the existing law were inadequate and out of date. Thus, a committee had been established by the previous legislature to go into the whole question of security of tenure. Although Jagan had served on the committee, no legislative action was proposed on the matter. After the 1953 elections, when Jagan became the Minister of Agriculture and the Leader of the House of Assembly, he proposed an amending bill with respect to existing legislation.

The amending bill went considerably beyond the question of security of tenure. It gave the district commissioner the authority to enter ricelands and to order the landlord to make improvements. If such improvements were not made, the district commissioner was to have the authority to see to it that they were made, and the costs were to be charged against the landlord. Jagan also included in the bill a provision that these costs could be recovered by "parate execution." The procedure of parate execution is unknown to English law and is a remnant of the Roman-Dutch code whereby, upon the issuance of a certificate by a public officer to the effect that money is owed the government, the court may issue a summary execution against the property of the debtor. The property may then be sold to discharge the debt.

This particular bill was especially important to Jagan and his Marxist associates. It not only provided them with an opportunity to do something concrete by way of consolidating their support among East Indian peasants, but it also conferred upon the minister and his officials wide and arbitrary powers with respect to landlords (including some sugar estates). They could, in effect, order improvements beyond the value of the land involved and force the sale of land by parate execution. Under the law pertaining to this procedure, the property is disposed to the highest bidder, and there is nothing to prevent the government from submitting the highest bid. In other words, Jagan's amending bill was designed not only to increase his political support in the Indian community but also to provide the government with a simple legal technique by which land could be alienated from landlords and rented by the government to landless peasants.

Needless to say, the Rice Farmers Security of Tenure (Amendment) Bill was passed in the House of Assembly. However, it was vigorously opposed by the ex officio members (e.g., the Chief Secretary, the Attorney General, and the Financial Secretary). When the bill came up before the State Council, it was rejected by six votes to two, only the P.P.P. members voting for the bill.

Another piece of legislation that was of considerable interest to the Marxists involved a proposal to repeal the Trades Disputes (Essential Services) Ordinance. This particular ordinance was passed as an emergency measure in 1942. It restricted the right of workers engaged in certain essential services to come out on strike. Although all of the P.P.P. ministers were in favor of repealing this ordinance, the Marxists worked particularly hard for its repeal. The reason for their special interest was that it provided them with an opportunity to develop some support among a class of urban workers with whom they had relatively little contact. Also, if the unions operating in the area of essential services could be won over to their cause, they would have an important base of power from which they could operate against any opposition government that might be elected.

The P.P.P. ministers argued that the Essential Services Ordinance was intended only for the duration of the war. They also argued that, since the war, the application of the ordinance had been extended to include a long list of industries and services that were not essential, and that the ordinance was being used to counteract unions and exploit workers. Thus, its repeal was proper and necessary. The ex-officio members of the House were vigorously opposed to a repeal of the ordinance, but they were not opposed to its modification. However, before further action could be taken, the constitution was suspended.

Of all the legislation that the P.P.P. ministers attempted to introduce during their 133 days in office, the bill that was most important to the Marxists, and also the bill that most directly precipitated a constitutional crisis, was the Labour Relations Bill. This particular bill, it seems, was drafted primarily by Cheddi Jagan and his Marxist associates. Its obvious and most immediate purpose was to provide a legal structure in terms of which the Guiana Industrial Workers Union could supplant the Man Power Citizens' Association in the sugar industry. Thus, like the labor bill that was introduced and defeated in 1952, the 1953 labor bill was designed to deal with jurisdictional disputes between rival unions.

However, the 1953 bill went far beyond the provisions of the previous labor bill.[22] The previous bill would have empowered the Commissioner of Labour to settle jurisdictional disputes by elections. The 1953 bill vested this power in the Minister of Labour. In addition, the bill empowered the minister to decide who should be classed

[22] *Ibid.*, pp. 58–63.

as a worker for the purpose of taking part in a ballot in any industry, trade, or undertaking. It also empowered the minister to make regulations prescribing the manner of holding any election as well as regulations to carry out the general provisions of the bill. In other words, the 1953 Labour Relations Bill gave the Minister of Labour indirect control of the whole trade union movement. In effect, this provided the Marxists with the access they needed to the Guianese masses in order for them to control the nationalist movement almost completely.

That the 1953 Labour Relations Bill represented an effort on the part of Jagan and the Marxists to secure control of the Guianese labor movement is well documented. In July, 1953, the newly appointed Minister of Labour, Ashton Chase, wrote to the Sugar Producers' Association asking if it would reconsider its attitude toward the Guiana Industrial Workers Union. This letter, it seems, also indicated that the P.P.P. intended to draft legislation which would enable workers to elect a union of their choice but, the letter went on to suggest, "there should hardly be need for this to apply to the sugar industry if the situation is approached realistically."[23]

In order to demonstrate the critical need for the Labour Relations Bill, on August 30, Sydney King, the P.P.P. Minister for Communications and Works, attended a meeting of the delegates and the Executive Committee of the G.I.W.U. and persuaded them to call for a strike on the sugar estates beginning on September 1. The strike was called, and by September 8, the entire sugar industry was at a standstill. In the meantime, P.P.P. ministers attempted to persuade the officials of other unions to call out their workers in sympathy with the G.I.W.U. and to extend the strike to cover the whole country. On September 23, the G.I.W.U. terminated its strike against the Sugar Producers' Association. The following day, the Labour Relations Bill was introduced to the House of Assembly, where it was passed on October 8. On October 9, the constitution was suspended, and the P.P.P. government was removed from office. The strategy adopted by the Marxists had proved to be too drastic for the governor and the organized opposition to remain unmoved.

In view of the constitutional limitations imposed on the P.P.P. government in terms of both the governor's veto and the official majority which he commanded in the State Council, the constitutional

[23] As quoted in *ibid.*, p. 60.

suspension represented an extremely drastic response, and perhaps an extremely unwise response, to the situation that had developed. To say the least, the suspension was difficult to justify in the eyes of the Guianese people and in the eyes of the world in general. The fact of the matter is that no legislation could be enacted by the P.P.P. government without the consent of the State Council and the governor. Also, the P.P.P. government was a government freely elected by the Guianese people. And at no time had the P.P.P. government violated the constitution. If the government was guilty of anything, it was guilty only of demonstrating that Guiana remained a colony of the British Crown.

In an effort to vindicate the suspension, the Crown elected to base its case on the evidence of a "communist plot." In a White Paper, Her Majesty's Government stated:

> Her Majesty's Government are quite satisfied that the elected Ministers and their Party were completely under the control of a communist clique. . . . From actions and public statements of these extremists it is clear that their objective was to turn British Guiana into a state subordinate to Moscow and a dangerous platform for extending communist influence in the Western Hemisphere.[24]

This justification was subsequently reinforced by the conclusions of the constitutional commission which was appointed to investigate the suspension and to make recommendations for further constitutional changes.[25]

To be sure, a plot did exist within the Peoples Progressive Party when it was elected to form the government in 1953. However, it would be less than accurate to describe this plot as "communist," if such a description is intended to imply that the organizational apparatus of the international Communist movement was functional with respect to the plot in question. As previously indicated, by 1953 the organizational apparatus of the international Communist movement with respect to Caribbean politics had been almost completely demolished by the schism in the international labor movement. It is even more inaccurate to attribute the plot in question to the domina-

---

[24] "Statement by Her Majesty's Government," read by the Honorable John Gutch, Chief Secretary, over Radio Demerara on October 9, 1953, and printed in the *White Paper* issued by Her Majesty's Government (1953), p. 1.

[25] Robertson Report, *op. cit.*

tion of the P.P.P. by a Marxist (or a Communist) clique. As has been shown, the plot existed precisely because the Marxist clique within the P.P.P. did not control a firm base of power, and it was rapidly losing its position of influence. And it is a complete fabrication to suggest that the objective of the plot in question was to transform British Guiana into a Soviet satellite.

If there is reason to question the validity of the explanations given by the Crown for the suspension of the constitution, there is little reason to question the impact which the suspension had on the nationalist movement. In effect, the suspension drove a wedge between the Marxists and the non-Marxists. In addition to everything else, the wedge represented the final straw. Specifically, the Marxists were discriminately singled out as "communists" and as the ringleaders who were mainly responsible for the whole crisis.

For example, Cheddi Jagan was restricted to Georgetown and subsequently imprisoned for six months for leaving the city. Janet Jagan was given four three-month sentences for holding a meeting, for demonstrating, and for being in possession of "subversive" literature. Dr. J. P. Lachmansingh, Mohamed Khan, and Fred Bowman were jailed for being in possession of "subversive" literature. Sidney King, Martin Carter, Rory Westmaas, Ajodha Singh, and Pandit Misir were imprisoned for demonstrating and for holding meetings. And Ram Karran was imprisoned for failing to report daily to the police. The non-Marxists, on the other hand, were briefly restricted in their movements. None of them violated emergency regulations as a form of protest, and none of them were imprisoned. From the point of view of the Marxists, the non-Marxists had not only betrayed the movement by refusing to protest, but they were free to mend their political fences.

## THE BURNHAM-JAGAN SPLIT

The split between L. F. S. Burnham and Cheddi Jagan occurred in 1955. It is worth while considering the nature of this split and the manner of its engineering in some detail. For one thing, it represented the culmination of the disintegrative pressures at work in the Guianese political situation. It represented a complete rupture between the Marxists and the non-Marxists. It also represented the conclusion of Guiana's comprehensive nationalist movement. The immediate effect of the split was to divide the Peoples Progressive Party into two completely independent and competitive political factions. Unlike the National Democratic Party of 1953, both factions of the P.P.P. contained dynamic, progressive leaders with national rather than sectional aspirations. However, the popularity these leaders enjoyed was sectional. Thus, the split between Burnham and Jagan marks the overt beginning of sectional politics.

It was noted in the previous section that before and immediately following the 1953 elections, the leftwing elements of the Peoples Progressive Party, specifically the Jaganites, held a number of secret meetings in order to devise a plan for the purpose of improving their position within the nationalist movement. During these meetings it was decided that whoever controlled the P.P.P. would also control British Guiana for the next twenty to thirty years, time enough to achieve a complete social revolution. The Jaganites concluded that Burnham could not be allowed to occupy this position of power. A number of considerations led to this conclusion.

First, the Jaganites felt that Burnham was too much of a deviationist. He did not accept Marxist doctrines completely and unreservedly and he did not consider such doctrines to be universally relevant to the Guianese situation. Also, Burnham did not see Guiana's independence movement as part of an international movement in which all colonial peoples must join forces against the imperialist nations. He felt that Guiana's development could be facilitated by Commonwealth membership and a friendly, but independent, attitude toward the United States. Burnham was also a gradualist. Although he was not satisfied with the 1953 constitution, he felt that the gains it represented were important enough to protect. Therefore, he did not support some of the more radical programs that the Marxists proposed. As a gradualist, Burnham believed that independence could be achieved more quickly if the P.P.P. tempered its militancy after the elections with a spirit of cooperation.

Second, as far as the Jaganites were concerned, Burnham was too much of an opportunist to be trusted. For one thing, he was under considerable pressure from middle-class African intellectuals who opposed Jagan on ideological grounds or who opposed him because they feared that, as an East Indian, he would subordinate African interests to Indian interests. The Jaganites felt that Burnham would eventually give in to this middle-class pressure and join forces with the "imperialists." As evidence of Burnham's opportunism, the Jaganites cited the position he had taken in the trade union developments of 1952. Not only had Burnham avoided becoming involved with the efforts of the Guiana Industrial Workers Union in its struggle with the Man Power Citizens' Association but, as president of the British Guiana Labour Union, he made no attempt to block that union's affiliation with the International Confederation of Trade Unions.

A third consideration involved the federation issue. Burnham favored British Guiana joining the Caribbean Federation, with or without independence. By 1953, Jagan was against the federation. He was particularly against joining the federation without independence. Jagan felt that federation membership without independence would make Guiana's independence movement a domestic rather than an international issue. He also believed that the power of the P.P.P. as a working-class movement would be submerged by the forceful leadership of the "capitalist stooges" who had taken over the leadership of the unions as well as the nationalist political parties in the Caribbean. Finally, Jagan believed that federation membership might alienate many Indian supporters who would interpret it to mean "black domination."

For these reasons, Jagan and his associates decided that Burnham either would have to come to terms with the leftwing elements or he would have to be forced out of the party. The first of these two alternatives was dismissed shortly after the 1953 elections and before the P.P.P. government took office. Shortly after the elections, a quarrel developed between the left- and rightwing elements of the party over two issues. One involved the question of parliamentary leadership, and the other concerned the question of whom the party would nominate for ministerial portfolios.

The question of parliamentary leadership (i.e., who would be the Leader of the House of Assembly) had already been settled in favor of Jagan at a party congress which was held in March, a month before the elections. Burnham argued, however, that since the congress could not have known which candidates would be elected, the decision of the congress was not valid. With respect to the nomination of ministers, the leftwing elements of the party argued that since they represented a majority among the leadership, they should decide whom the party would present for ministerial posts. Subsequently, a compromise was reached on both of these issues: Burnham gave up his bid for parliamentary leadership in exchange for three ministerial appointments.

The compromise that was reached on these issues was not a happy one for either side. As far as the left wing of the P.P.P. was concerned, Burnham had to go. One informant quoted Janet Jagan as stating, "It is now or never. If Burnham takes over this party now, he will have it forever." However, the decision to get rid of Burnham was more easily taken than implemented. Burnham had support within the party (e.g., Ashton Chase, Jai Narine Singh, Jessie Burnham, Jane Phillips-Gay, Ulric Fingal, and others). He also had considerable support among urban Africans and trade union leaders. In getting rid of Burnham, the Jaganites did not want to divert all of this support from the nationalist movement and thereby transform it into a sectional party. The situation called for tact. According to informants, a plan had to be devised whereby Burnham would be alienated simultaneously from the party and from much of his African following.

The plan that the Jaganites formulated with respect to Burnham involved, first, a stratagem designed to discredit him among his supporters. The first effort in this direction was made after the 1953 elections, when the General Council of the P.P.P. met to decide which two of its members would be nominated to the State Council. Burnham's candidate was A. Alleyne, a popular African teacher in Georgetown and a strong Burnham supporter. Alleyne, however, was not a member of the P.P.P. General Council, and he could not attend its meetings. At the meeting, Jagan nominated George Robertson (an African loyal to Jagan) as his candidate. Before Burnham had a chance to nominate Alleyne, a member of the left wing nominated Ulric Fingal, a Burnham supporter who was a member of the party's General Council and who also was present at the meeting. Although Burnham did not want Fingal, because of his presence he could not oppose his nomination. Thus, Burnham was forced to break a promise to Alleyne. According to informants, this was only one of several efforts that were made by the left wing to create quarrels between Burnham and his supporters within the party.[26]

At the same time, systematic efforts were made to discredit Burnham outside of the party. According to plan, Africans loyal to Jagan

[26] This particular move did, in fact, create a quarrel between Burnham and Alleyne. As a result of it, after the split, Alleyne became a Jagan supporter. In the 1957 elections, Alleyne ran as a candidate for Jagan's faction of the P.P.P. Although he failed to win a seat, he did succeed in polling almost 2,000 votes against Burnham's candidate in the heavily populated Afro-Guianese district of South Georgetown.

(e.g., King, Westmaas, Carter, and Benn) were to circulate rumors among the African masses to the effect that Burnham was a "racist" and a "stooge" for the sugar interests. These rumors were to be based on Burnham's association with prominent members of the League of Coloured Peoples. They were to be based also on his lack of involvement in the struggle between the Sugar Producers' Association and the Guiana Industrial Workers Union. After the suspension, Burnham unwittingly added fuel to these fires when he failed to get himself imprisoned along with other P.P.P. "martyrs." Fuel was also added to these fires unknowingly by Europeans and Portuguese who seem to have always considered Burnham a racist.

Another part of the plan to get rid of Burnham was somewhat more complicated. It involved manipulating Burnham into a situation where he could make an effort to take over the party leadership without legal justification or majority support and thereby provide just cause for his own expulsion. This was accomplished, first, by encouraging an alliance that was already developing between Burnham and two Indian nationalists, Dr. J. P. Lachmansingh and Jai Narine Singh. The Jaganites hoped that this alliance would give Burnham a false sense of security—a feeling that he had Indian support. Lachmansingh was prominent in the Guiana Industrial Workers Union, but he was not a Marxist and he did not have Jagan's influence among East Indians. Also, Lachmansingh was increasingly making things complicated for Jagan.[27] Jai Narine Singh, on the other hand, was a wealthy Indian who had once been influential in the East Indian Association. Jai Narine Singh was not trusted by Jagan. He was not a Marxist, and within the P.P.P. he displayed a marked tendency to support the right wing more often than the left.[28]

In the meantime, the Jaganites agitated in the background for the kind of split they wanted. The left wing of the party, for example, formed a permanent caucus. It convened before every meeting of the General Council to instruct members as to how they should vote on issues affecting the right wing. At almost every meeting of the General Council, Burnham was enticed into bitter arguments with King, Westmaas, and Carter. Finally, in 1955, the opportunity

---

[27] Lachmansingh was opposed to the strike which the G.I.W.U. called in 1953 when the Labour Relations Bill was introduced to the House of Assembly.

[28] Burnham nominated Jai Narine Singh as one of his three choices for a ministerial post. Singh became the Minister of Local Government and Social Welfare in 1953.

emerged for the Jaganites to make their move. At Burnham's insistence, and in opposition to members of the left wing, a party congress was convened in Georgetown. When only a few members of the left wing, including the Jagans, appeared at the congress, Burnham persuaded Clinton Wong to move a motion of no confidence in the party executive. The motion was passed, and the Jagans walked out of the congress. With primarily his supporters present, Burnham moved that elections be held. Jai Narine Singh was elected general secretary (in place of Janet Jagan), Dr. J. P. Lachmansingh was elected chairman (in place of Burnham), and Burnham, needless to say, was elected party leader (in place of Cheddi Jagan).

A few weeks after the Georgetown congress, the Jaganites convened a second party congress in the African village of Buxton. The Buxton congress was chaired by Sidney King, a Buxton schoolteacher with strong African support in the district. A motion was moved by King to declare the Georgetown elections null and void on the basis that Burnham had illegally convened the party congress. This was followed by a second motion to expel Burnham and his faction from the party. Thus, to the vast majority of Africans outside of Georgetown, it appeared that Burnham had convened an illegal congress for the purpose of securing personal power. To the East Indians, on the other hand, it appeared that Burnham was attempting to get rid of Jagan because of racial prejudice. The fact that two East Indians, Jai Narine Singh and Dr. J. P. Lachmansingh, supported Burnham did very little to diminish this attitude.

In a speech delivered to the 1956 congress of the Peoples Progressive Party, Jagan expounded the party's official position with respect to Burnham and the split in the Guianese nationalist movement. Noting Burnham's middle-class background and his close association with professionals, teachers, civil servants, and "other sections of the middle class away from the soil and away from direct contact with the toiling masses," Jagan suggested that the split was a result of middle-class opportunism. The constitutional suspension, according to Jagan, represented a barrier to the fulfillment of middle-class aspirations. It prevented members of the middle class from climbing to the top rounds of the civil service ladder. As a result, middle-class pressure forced Burnham to make a deal with the "imperialists." The "imperialists" would grant elections and thereby open the channels of middle-class opportunity if the Burnhamites would disassociate themselves from the "communist" faction and guarantee to form a "safe" government. In other words, Jagan stated, "The Burnham clique were prepared to deviate to the right, to sacrifice our proletarian working class, internationalist outlook for narrow nationalism."[29]

It is not known for certain if Burnham, as Jagan claims, actually made a deal with the "imperialists." If he did, either the "imperialists" were unaware of the actions which the Jaganites had taken to remove Burnham and his followers from the P.P.P., or, alternatively, they sadly miscalculated how these actions might affect the political stature of the Burnhamites. Judging from the results of the 1957 elections, the split almost politically emasculated Burnham.

The 1957 elections were held under a revised constitution that provided for a Legislative Council which consisted of fourteen elected and six nominated members. The fourteen seats up for election were contested by four political parties and seven independent candidates. Two of the political parties, the United Democratic Party and the National Labour Front, represented two factions of the National Democratic Party which had contested against the P.P.P. in 1953. In 1957, the United Democratic Party, under John Carter's leadership, was the political arm of the African middle class. The National Labour Front, under the leadership of Lionel Luckhoo, was the political arm of the Man Power Citizens' Association. The remaining two parties included the P.P.P. under Jagan's leadership and the P.P.P. under Burnham's leadership.

Jagan's faction of the P.P.P. won nine of the fourteen seats in the Legislative Council with 47.5 per cent of the total vote. One seat was won by each of the lesser parties, the United Democratic Party and the National Labour Front, with a combined vote of 19.7 per cent. Burnham's faction of the P.P.P. won only three seats with 25.5 per cent of the total vote. All three of the seats won by Burnham's faction were located in Georgetown constituencies that were heavily populated by working-class Africans. The seat won by the United Democratic Party was located in New Amsterdam, where Burnham did not have a personal following among the Afro-Guianese. And the only seat won by the National Labour Front was located in an Amerindian district where the N.L.F. put up an Amerindian candidate.

---

[29] Cheddi Jagan's "Address to the 1956 Congress of the Peoples Progressive Party" is reprinted in the December 22, 1956 issue of *The Daily Chronicle*, Georgetown.

Thus, as a result of the strategy outlined above, the Jaganites were able to oust Burnham and the non-Marxists from the P.P.P., maintain some semblance of an integrated national front, and win the support of a majority large enough for them to form a government with a substantial majority among the elected members. However, their plans fell considerably short of what they had hoped to achieve. The P.P.P. was strong relative to the opposition, but it was supported by less than a total majority of the Guianese voters. In addition, the number of Africans among those Guianese who voted for the P.P.P. represented an uncertain minority.

In other words, the Jaganites had succeeded in ridding the party of its rightwing elements, but in the process they had succeeded also in splitting the nationalist movement without achieving indisputable control of it. However, to the extent that their plans had failed, they had not failed because of any opposition that Burnham was capable of aggregating. Rather, they had failed because of certain unanticipated developments which followed closely upon the heels of the split.

In 1956, approximately one year after the Burnham-Jagan split, Sidney King, Martin Carter, and Rory Westmaas resigned from the Peoples Progressive Party. Since these three individuals represented the pillars of Jagan's remaining African support, their resignation came not only as a shock but also as an extreme blow to Jagan's plans for a truly integrated nationalist movement. From the very beginning of the movement, these three were the most idealistic of the Marxists. They were completely loyal to Jagan's leadership. All of them had followed Jagan to jail during the constitutional crisis. And all of them had played a prominent role in helping Jagan rid the party of its rightwing elements. More than anything else, Jagan counted on their continued loyalty to keep the nationalist movement from developing into sectional parties.

To the extent that it could be determined on the basis of documents and interviews, this unexpected split among the Jaganites resulted from a combination of circumstances that involved: (1) Khrushchev's famous speech to the 1956 congress of the Soviet Communist Party, (2) the suppression of the Hungarian Revolution by Soviet troops in 1956, and (3) Jagan's speech to the 1956 congress of the Peoples Progressive Party. The famous speech delivered by Khrushchev in 1956 not only contained a bitter condemnation of the Stalinist "cult of personality," but it also revealed the injustices that were perpetrated as a result of Stalin's rise to power. The same sort of injustices, so it seemed, were being perpetrated by the Soviet troops that put down the Hungarian Revolution. The harshness of these political realities was extremely disconcerting, to say the least, to utopian Marxists like King, Carter, and Westmaas.

If King, Carter, and Westmaas were disillusioned by these developments, their disillusionment was completed by Jagan's speech to the 1956 congress of the Peoples Progressive Party. This particular speech is an unusual political document. It represents one of the most systematic efforts that Jagan has ever made to outline his political views. It contains his analysis of the Guianese political situation, his explanation of the position that the P.P.P. was to adopt with respect to the Caribbean Federation, and his outline of the strategy that the P.P.P. was to follow in order to achieve ultimate control of the nationalist movement.

In his analysis of the Guianese political situation, Jagan quoted from and followed the teachings of "Comrade Stalin" and "Comrade Mao Tse Tung." He explicitly condemned the deviationists to the right (i.e., the Burnham clique) which threatened to ". . . degrade the revolutionary movement and submerge the Communist elements in the general welter of bourgeois nationalists." At the same time, however, he also condemned deviationism to the left. Jagan stated: ". . . up to October, 1953, we committed deviations to the left. We definitely overrated the revolutionary possibilities of our Party. . . We became bombastic. . . We were attacking everybody at the same time. . . We tended towards what Mao Tse Tung called "all struggle and no unity."[30] Since King, Carter, and Westmaas were among the most "bombastic" of the Marxists, they immediately interpreted Jagan's remarks as personal criticism. In fact, they interpreted them as an effort to clear himself of any responsibility for the constitutional suspension by projecting the blame entirely upon leftwing "dogmatists."

Because of the special circumstances associated with the Guianese political situation, King, Westmaas, and Carter began to suspect Jagan of sectional politics. The rightwing elements which they had helped to remove from the party were mainly Africans. And now they also appeared to be under attack. Their suspicions were further reinforced by Jagan's analysis of the position which the P.P.P. had to adopt with respect to the Caribbean Federation and by the strategy

---

[30] *Ibid.*

he outlined for the P.P.P. with respect to the nationalist movement. In the first instance, it appeared that Jagan was as much opposed to the federation on the grounds that it would alienate his East Indian support as he was on the grounds that it would make Guiana's nationalist movement a domestic affair. In the second instance, Jagan's proposed strategy appeared to be opportunistic in the sense that it relied rather heavily on the political integration of the East Indian cultural section. Although Jagan suggested the possibility of developing an alliance between the P.P.P. and the Burnham forces, it was clear that he did not expect such an alliance to materialize or, if it should materialize, to be more than a temporary affair.

In any event, King, Carter, and Westmaas reacted negatively to Jagan's address. From their point of view, it smacked of racialism and opportunistic politics. Carter and Westmaas were so disillusioned that they not only resigned from the P.P.P., they dropped out of politics altogether. King, on the other hand, remained in politics. In 1957, he ran as an independent in the Central Demerara district. Although his P.P.P. opponent, Balram Singh Rai (who ran as a National Democratic Party candidate in 1953), won the district with 7,125 votes, King ran a strong second with 6,285 votes. More important than who won the race is the fact that practically every one of King's votes represented an African who might have voted for the P.P.P. candidate had it not been for King's resignation.

After the 1957 elections, Jagan made efforts to maintain the semblance of a united front for the Peoples Progressive Party. Like most other Guianese nationalists, he condemned racialism whenever the opportunity presented itself. In addition, he got Brindley Benn, one of the few Africans who remained loyal, elected chairman of the Peoples Progressive Party. In subsequent party elections, Jagan even prevented East Indians from opposing Benn for the chairmanship.[31] However, the process of disintegration had proceeded too far to be

[31] Jagan's effort to maintain an integrated front by keeping Brindley Benn as the party's chairman has been costly. It has provoked at least two minor splits in the P.P.P. since 1957. In 1959, Pandit Misir, Bashir Khan, Abdul Cayum, and Karim Juman backed Balram Singh Rai for the party chairmanship. The elections were declared null and void, and Janet Jagan filed charges against Rai's backers involving "racialism" and tampering with election boxes. All but Khan were expelled. Khan was probably exonerated of charges because he not only owns a sawmill in Rosignol, but he has considerable local influence among East Indians in West Berbice. More recently, in 1962, Balram Singh Rai (who was Jagan's Minister of Home Affairs at the time) announced his candidacy in opposition to Benn for a second time. On this occasion, Rai was expelled from the party.

reversed by simple surgical techniques. It became increasingly clear to Jagan and his associates that the P.P.P. no longer could depend upon the Afro-Guianese for much support. This became especially clear in 1959, when the United Democratic Party, the political arm of the African middle class, merged with Burnham's faction of the P.P.P. to form the Peoples National Congress.

Thus, by 1959 the process of disintegration was complete. In place of Guiana's comprehensive nationalist movement, there existed two mass-based political parties. The leaders of one party, the P.N.C., were almost exclusively Afro-Guianese. The leaders of the other party, the P.P.P., were predominantly East Indian. Between 1957 and 1961, the P.P.P. formed the government. The P.N.C. represented the "loyal" opposition. However, independence had not yet been achieved; elections were scheduled for 1961; and the struggle for power was only beginning.

To conclude, while the conditions of pluralism provided fertile soil for the growth of particularistic forces, they did not present an insurmountable obstacle to the integration of a comprehensive nationalist movement. To state the matter differently, the process of disintegration required ingredients other than the conditions of pluralism. Other necessary ingredients included the ideological factionalism which existed among the nationalist elite, the political pressures that were generated by developments in the international labor movement, and the political pressures that were created by the organization of the conservative opposition. These factors produced a combination of circumstances which led nationalist politicians to associate their political survival with the forces of pluralism. Thus, the forces of pluralism became associated with the disintegration of Guiana's comprehensive nationalist movement, and the political integration of cultural sections became crucial to the struggle for power.

*CHAPTER 6*

# ORGANIZATIONAL STRATEGY AND CULTURAL SECTIONS

BEFORE 1953, THE MAJOR STRUGGLE FOR NATIONAL POWER INVOLVED A CONtest between a relatively integrated nationalist front and a deeply entrenched colonial establishment. By 1958, the nationalist front was no longer integrated, and the colonial establishment was looking for ways to disengage itself from Guianese political life in as orderly a fashion as possible. By enforcing the process of constitutional advancement, the continued British presence after 1958 precluded the necessity of revolutionary political change. Apart from this, however, the struggle for national power had shifted almost completely in its focus from the colonial establishment to the contest that was being waged between Guiana's two major political parties.

Within a constitutional framework, the only way that one or the other of these political parties could capture the positions of national power was to get its candidates elected. This required the organization of mass support. Before the disintegration of the nationalist movement, mass support could be mobilized primarily by appealing to the frustrations that most Guianese shared as a result of colonial domination. After disintegration, this approach continued to be useful, but it was no longer sufficient. The integration of the new political alignments which emerged from the collapse of the nationalist movement required a more specific appeal. Thus, the change in Guiana's political situation necessitated a change in the organizational strategy of nationalist parties.

To state the problem more precisely, by 1958, the East Indian and Afro-Guianese cultural sections appeared to represent the only bases of mass power accessible, respectively, to the Peoples Progressive Party and the Peoples National Congress. In order to integrate these cultural sections politically, however, adjustments in organizational strategies were needed. Specifically, particularistic appeals had to be made to the groups contained within each cultural section. Accordingly, the two major political parties devised and implemented plans to achieve this effect.[1]

## ORGANIZATIONAL STRATEGY OF THE P.P.P.

The disintegration of Guiana's comprehensive nationalist movement did not significantly alter the fundamental organizational structure of the Peoples Progressive Party. Complete control of the party continued to be vested in its Executive Committee and General Council. In 1958, the General Council was comprised of fifteen members, eight of whom constituted the Executive Committee. Also in 1958, two adjunct organizations were officially added to the party, a Women's Section and a Youth's Section. While both groups elected their own officers, the section officers of both groups were subordinated to the Executive Committee of the party. As the major policy-making body of the party, the Executive Committee continued to be a self-perpetuating group which included the party's most influential leaders.

Prior to the Burnham-Jagan split, a strategy of balance was main-

[1] For a discussion of the concept "organization," see the article by John W. Bennett and Leo A. Despres, "Kinship and Instrumental Activities: A Theoretical Inquiry," *American Anthropologist,* 62 (1960), 254–67. To elaborate upon the theoretical framework outlined in Chapter 2, an organizational process is essentially a decision-making process. An organizational strategy involves a complex series of decisions leading to activities which, presumably, are oriented to the achievement of particular ends. It should be noted that not all of the decisions involved in an organizational strategy are necessarily related in the sense that they are made in the context of an overall plan. Moreover, it is important to emphasize that not every decision involved need be consciously oriented to a specific organization of events. A specific organization of events may be a latent function of some decisions and a manifest function of others.

These considerations are necessary to keep in mind with respect to the subject matter dealt with in this chapter. It is not my intent to spin a conspiratorial interpretation of Guianese politics. It would be ridiculous for me to assume, and impossible to prove, that most of the organizational activities of Guianese nationalists were consciously oriented to the political integration of cultural sections. Nevertheless, conspiratorial elements are evident at times. Some of their organizational activities appeared to be manifestly oriented to the achievement of such ends. For the most part, it is these activities which I attempt to analyze here. But these should not be misinterpreted. Objectively, most leaders of the P.P.P. and the P.N.C. would have liked nothing better than the complete unification of Guianese society. However, existing circumstances and the problems of political survival precluded them from adopting unification as the immediate goal of their organizational efforts.

tained with respect to the composition of the Executive Committee and the General Council. After the split, this policy was continued. However, as a result of the split, the personnel of these two committees obviously changed. In association with older nationalists who had remained loyal to Jagan (e.g., Dr. Charles Jacob, Jr., Ashton Chase, Ram Karran, and Jocelyn Hubbard), a new cadre of young P.P.P. activists emerged. It included such men as Brindley Benn, Ranji Chandisingh, Dr. Fenton Ramsahoye, Lawrence Mann, Victor Downer, Moses Bhagwan, and Balram Singh Rai.

Until Jagan elevated these second- and third-generation nationalists from the ranks of the P.P.P. to positions of prominence, none of them were men of national stature and influence. None had significant personal followings among the Guianese masses. All depended upon Jagan for their political futures. With the possible exception of Rai, who previously had been a National Democratic Party candidate, all of these new men were completely loyal to Jagan's leadership. And, again with the exception of Rai, all of them were professed Marxists. Thus, by 1958, the Marxists were completely in charge of the P.P.P., and among them Jagan was the most influential. As a consequence, the policies which Jagan forged were the policies which the party inevitably adopted and attempted to implement.

To the extent that the organizational activities of the Peoples Progressive Party have been guided by an overall strategy, the component elements of that strategy were defined by Cheddi Jagan in his address to the 1956 party congress.[2] It is worthwhile to consider this particular address further. In it, Jagan re-evaluated the nationalist movement in light of the constitutional suspension and the Jagan-Burnham split. He also elaborated upon the revolutionary principles which appeared to be relevant to the Guianese political situation. And, finally, he outlined the courses of action which the P.P.P. was to pursue in its continued struggle for independence and national power.

Jagan viewed both the constitutional suspension and the split between himself and Burnham as the work of imperialists who wanted to forestall independence long enough to immobilize the P.P.P. and shift mass support to the conservative and reactionary elements in Guianese society. "The split," Jagan stated, "took place along racial and ideological lines, predominantly the former. Gener-

[2] Speech delivered by Cheddi Jagan to the 1956 congress of the Peoples Progressive Party, published in the December 22, 1956, issue of *The Daily Chronicle*, Georgetown.

ally, the mass of Indians came over to us, the majority of Africans, with the exception of the class conscious and the politically aware, went over to Burnham. The fact that immediately after the split, Georgetown, the 'storm centre' of our national movement, went over almost completely to the Burnham clique should be a reminder to us not to overestimate the political and ideological understanding of the masses and not to underestimate the emotional appeal of racialism."[3]

In assessing the political situation further, Jagan predicted that the reactionary forces would line up according to specific political strategies. Burnham's party, Jagan suggested, would intensify its appeal to African racialism. However, Jagan noted, in an effort to expand his support among the "toiling masses," Burnham would disguise his appeal to African racialism by the use of "leftist phraseology." Lionel Luckhoo's National Labour Front, on the other hand, would attempt to wean East Indian support away from the P.P.P. by making an appeal to East Indian racialism. Jagan reached this particular conclusion for two reasons. First, Luckhoo had broken with the African-dominated United Democratic Party over the federation issue. Second, in organizing the National Labour Front, Luckhoo had announced that it would be a "rural-based" party. Finally, Jagan concluded, other reactionary elements would attempt to destroy the P.P.P. by calling for a united "anti-communist front."

How was the P.P.P. to proceed under these circumstances? In addressing himself to this question, Jagan interpolated from the writings of Stalin, Lenin, and Mao Tse-tung. Specifically, he outlined two revolutionary principles which he considered to be particularly relevant to the Guianese political situation. These two principles may be stated as follows:

First, Marxism-Leninism is not to be interpreted as a dogma but as a guide to action: ". . . . the living soul of Marxism is the concrete analysis of concrete situations." Thus, according to Jagan, the main task of leadership was to apply Marxist-Leninist principles in such a manner as to take into consideration the national characteristics of Guianese society. Only such "opportunism" would safeguard the life of the party and facilitate the carrying out of the basic aims of the Communist movement.

Second, in the application of Marxist-Leninist principles to the Guianese situation, Jagan insisted that two deviations must be avoided.

---

[3] *Ibid.*

The first deviation, deviationism to the right, consists of underrating the revolutionary possibilities of the liberation movement (i.e., the independence movement) and overrating the value of a united national front. This form of deviationism, according to Jagan, ". . . threatens to degrade the revolutionary movement and submerge the Communist elements in the general welter of bourgeois nationalists." The second deviation which must be avoided, deviationism to the left, consists of overrating the revolutionary possibilities of the liberation movement and underrating the importance of an alliance between the working class and the revolutionary bourgeoisie against imperialism.

In discussing these principles, Jagan was particularly concerned about the dangers inherent in left deviationism. Analyzing the party's history, he stated, "While our party had the distinct advantage of left wing leadership, it suffered also from left deviationist tendencies. Some comrades of the left behaved in a mechanistic fashion; copying wholesale revolutionary tactics and slogans of left wing parties in the metropolitan, capitalistically advanced countries, without bothering to study carefully our concrete condition and historical stage of development. Some communists in our party tended to act as communists in a communist party and to make our party into a communist party of an advanced country. Therefore," Jagan continued, "this tendency towards left deviationism and adventurism must be combatted. At times it was condoned in the past in order to protect left strength and unity against the onslaught of the right. Such tendencies have had their toll on our party."

There are two reasons Jagan was particularly concerned with the dangers inherent in left deviationism. For one thing, left deviationism was no longer functional within the party. The rightwing elements of the party had been purged with the Burnham split, and the leftwing elements were no longer internally exposed to their onslaught. Secondly, Jagan had come to realize that the "bombastic" and radical behavior of certain leftwing elements had served, in part, to provoke the constitutional suspension and thereby retard Guiana's march to full independence. Under the conditions existing in 1956, leftwing deviationism could only make it more difficult for the P.P.P. to secure national power and to negotiate the independence necessary to exercise it.

It is clear from Jagan's comments on leftwing deviationism that the P.P.P. was to adjust its strategy to cope with existing conditions in a more realistic and efficient manner. The principle that Jagan had come to recognize is rather simple: The P.P.P. could not implement a social revolution without being in full possession of government. To hasten the achievement of that end, the party was to remain firmly in the control of Marxists, but it was to display a more cooperative and less radical posture.

In terms of these considerations, Jagan outlined a general plan of action for the P.P.P. to follow. Immediate and absolute independence represented the first priority. In pursuit of this objective, Jagan suggested that the P.P.P. proceed at once to the formation of a national front. "Such a front," Jagan noted, "must include the anti-imperialist parties and the party of the national capitalists."[4] In other words, it must include Burnham's party and the United Democratic Party (the latter had not yet merged with Burnham's party, and it was still under the leadership of John Carter).

In developing this stratagem further, Jagan was quite specific about the kind of national front he had in mind. It was to be a front that would not only make demands for the end of emergency regulations and the restoration of constitutional life, but the parties to the alliance would also agree to a particular course of action in support of these demands. "By this," Jagan elaborated, "is meant action such as general political strife, non-cooperation, boycott of British goods, boycott of elections under any backward constitution."

In proposing a united front for the purpose of achieving independence, it is clear that Jagan had no intention of reintegrating the nationalist movement by merging the P.P.P. with the opposition parties. For example, he deliberately warned the party about the dangers involved in entering into such an alliance. "We are primarily interested in struggle," Jagan noted, "Messrs. Burnham and Carter are primarily interested in office. If they are not really interested in struggle, in taking firm and resolute action in support of our demands, then there is no advantage in such a national front. In such a situation, we have everything to lose and nothing to gain. We will have to make concessions to them with regard to electoral seats. We will have to share our platform with them for joint meetings and expose our 'territory' to their reactionary ideas. There will be the danger of right deviationism towards all unity and no struggle."

---

[4] *Ibid*. Jagan conceded that it might be necessary for the P.P.P. to adopt a program proclaiming protection for native industries as well as the interests of native capitalists.

From the nature of Jagan's comments, it appears that he had little hope of negotiating a national front of the type he envisioned as being useful to the Peoples Progressive Party. Too many recriminations had passed between the P.P.P. and the opposition forces for such an alliance to develop. Nevertheless, Jagan did make an effort to negotiate. Talks were held with the Burnham forces in 1956. However, even as these talks were held, the "big three" (Sidney King, Rory Westmaas, and Martin Carter) broke with the P.P.P. The P.P.P. had to go it alone and adjust its strategy accordingly. However, Jagan also had made provision for this eventuality in his 1956 address.

The second part of Jagan's plan of action dealt specifically with the manner in which the P.P.P. was to consolidate its support among the Guianese masses by making the East Indian cultural section politically functional. Noting the racial, cultural, and economic differences existing between various groups in the population, Jagan compared the Portuguese native capitalist with the emerging Indian capitalist: "Whereas the Indian capitalist poses a threat to Portuguese native capitalism (mainly in commerce), he suffers from a feeling of cultural, political, and economic oppression and, consequently, is further removed from, in fact, opposed to imperialism. . . . The Indian capitalist up to this stage puts his 'national' interests before his 'class' interests. Consequently, he can be a resolute ally against imperialism within these considerations."[5]

Jagan also observed that the Indian capitalist, in many instances, displayed a "dual personality." As a landowner and a rice miller ". . . he combined the functions of feudalism (landlordism) with the functions of capitalism (rice factory, shops, etc.)." Therefore, Jagan suggested, the Indian capitalist played a "reactionary-progressive" role: reactionary because he exploited Indian peasants; progressive because, as a native capitalist, his nationalist interests were anti-imperialist. Jagan outlined what the P.P.P. was to do in regard to these structural conditions: ". . . it is our duty to split this personality, to carry out an uncompromising struggle against his reactionary, feudal, landlord tendencies in the interest of peasant farmers while, at the same time, winning him over in the struggle against our common enemy, imperialism. This," Jagan noted, "requires tact and careful handling."

There are several reasons why it was important for the P.P.P. to win the support of Indian capitalists. First, if the Indian capitalist

[5] *Ibid.*

could be weaned from his rural enterprises and made to concentrate on his urban affairs (e.g., by investing more of his capital in commerce and industry), the P.P.P. could remove a major obstacle to the reorganization of the agricultural sector of the economy. At the same time, this would make more land available to East Indian peasants. It would also increase support for the P.P.P. among East Indian peasants hostile to the East Indian landowners and rice millers that exploit them. Second, by motivating the Indian capitalists to concentrate upon their urban affairs, the P.P.P. could pit them in competition against the European and Portuguese capitalists who controlled so much of the country's commerce. Finally, East Indian capitalists were important to the P.P.P. because they represented a major source of financial support for party activity, as long as the British controlled foreign policy and as long as outside sources of financial support (e.g., the British Communist Party) were limited.

The organizational strategy outlined by Jagan in his 1956 speech provided a focus for the author's collection of data on the organizational activities of the P.P.P. in preparation for the 1961 elections. Organizational data were collected from many sources, for the most part in lengthy interviews with knowledgeable informants. Some of these informants were members of the government at the time. Others held important positions in the civil service. Some were businessmen; others were barristers or teachers. Many of the informants interviewed were P.P.P. activists. While these data are by no means exhaustive with respect to the organizational activities of the P.P.P., they do illustrate some of the ways in which a conscious effort was made to mobilize the East Indian cultural section. Taken together, these data serve to delineate the various dimensions of "apanjaht" politics.

## EAST INDIANS AND "APANJAHT" POLITICS

"Apanjaht" is a Hindi word. Translated, it means "vote for your own kind." To grasp fully the social and psychological implications of apanjaht, one should not confuse "race" with what is meant by the term "kind." Social differentiation on the basis of physical characteristics is quite common within the East Indian community. It is not unusual to hear an Indian of light complexion state that an Indian of dark complexion is not of his "jati" (caste). In similar contexts, the same person might make the same differentiation by stating that the dark Indian is not of "me race." However, regardless of their physical characteristics, all Indians tend to differentiate themselves from Africans. The basis for making such a distinction usually extends beyond a consideration of physical features. When discussing an African, an Indian will frequently state that "he is not of me kind" or "he is not of me nation."

In other words, apanjaht does not constitute an appeal based primarily on race. The reference in the slogan has very little to do with considerations of biological origin. More precisely, apanjaht represents an appeal which is made on the basis of one's cultural identity. Moreover, the reference in the slogan is diffuse in the sense that it excludes such considerations as jati. To vote for one's own kind is to vote for one who is an Indian not primarily because of his looks but because of his habits, his religion, his relationships, and his values. To vote for one's own kind is to vote for one whose way of life is similar to your own. Thus, an Indian informant in Clonbrook could say of Sidney King (an African), "When he with Cheddi he like one of we." The assumption underlying apanjaht is that the bond of cultural identity is somewhat like the bond of kinship, i.e., one's own kind of people are more likely to keep one's own interest in heart.

By 1961, apanjaht had become the unofficial slogan of the Peoples Progressive Party.[6] It had also become the election cry of East Indians from one end of British Guiana to the other. This association cannot be attributed solely to the fact that an East Indian, Cheddi Jagan, led the Peoples Progressive Party. It is important to understand that the bond of cultural identity expressed in apanjaht cannot exist without its being nurtured. For example, Lionel Luckhoo is also a prominent Indian leader, and yet large numbers of Indians have never given their support to the various political parties with which Luckhoo has been associated. This fact in itself is sufficient to indicate that the Indian support of the P.P.P. cannot be explained simply by noting that Jagan is an Indian. To explain the identification of apanjaht with the P.P.P., other factors must be taken into account. Specifically, one must take into account the various ways in which the P.P.P. has stimulated the consciousness of Indian nationalism.

The 1961 election campaign began almost immediately after the Peoples Progressive Party was elected to form the government in 1957.

[6] For example, at political rallies, P.P.P. activists would shout "apanjaht" in order to put down opposition speakers.

During the next four years, the party's organizational activities were varied and extremely incisive. They included the usual techniques of campaign politicking, but they also included more subtle techniques designed to mobilize political support by the use of legislation and the manipulation of developmental programs and governmental agencies. Not all of Jagan's organizational efforts involved apanjaht politics. However, those which did were manifest, and they indicate a concerted effort to mobilize the East Indian cultural section on several fronts. Consider, first, Jagan's efforts to secure the support of the East Indian business community.

The East Indian business community in Georgetown is made up of relatively distinct social types. These types can be differentiated in terms of their origins, the manner of their entrée into the Georgetown business world, their pattern of economic mobility, and the nature of their enterprises.

One type of Indian businessman is comprised of those individuals who moved into Georgetown twenty to thirty years ago. As a result of the boom in the rice industry during the First World War, these individuals accumulated large landholdings in rural areas. The capital which derived from these holdings was used to finance medium-sized shops in Water Street, Georgetown's main business district. As these enterprises expanded, their owners tended to buy up residences in the old, prestigious suburbs (e.g., Brickdam and Kingston), where most of the expatriates once lived. Since the end of the Second World War, businessmen of this type have been closing in on the European business houses from both ends of Water Street. Because these Indian businessmen have never been allowed to compete directly with the well-established European firms, their economic growth has been restricted. As a consequence, they continue to maintain their rural enterprises.

A second type of Indian businessman found in Georgetown does not comprise a very large group, but it is a group which has recently become extremely influential in commercial circles. The members of this group consist of a few overseas migrants who have come mainly from Trinidad and Surinam. For the most part, these men are well established in the business world. Their presence in Guiana marks an effort on their part to expand already flourishing enterprises by penetrating the Guianese market. Members of this group, most notably Thani and Kirplani, own large retail houses in the heart of the Georgetown business district. These retail houses are potentially highly competitive with the old European- and Portuguese-controlled firms.

The third type of Indian businessman found in Georgetown is also a recent migrant. The members of this group, however, predominantly come from the rural areas surrounding the city. Generally, these individuals are the sons of small rice farmers or sugar workers. Their capital is extremely limited. Some of them are attracted to the city because they need wage employment. Others have moved to the city as a result of having spent years carrying produce to the urban marketplaces. Subsequently, these individuals establish themselves in small shops or market stalls. They sell food, cakes, soft drinks, or dry goods. If they own shops, the shops are usually located in peripheral business districts (e.g., Regent and Lombard streets) or urban neighborhoods. Often, these shops may be found beneath the homes in which their owners reside.

Businessmen of this third type are "penny" capitalists, and they are hard pressed to survive. Their shops do not compete with the European firms. They are strictly family affairs, and most of their competition derives from similar kinds of shops owned by Africans or other Indians. If such enterprises manage to grow, structural modifications are made in the home, and the shop expands by adding a new line of goods. Canned goods may be added, and the cake shop becomes a small grocery store. Or dry goods may be added to the grocery store, and it becomes a general store. Frequently, these shops are maintained by women and children, while the men of the household earn wages.

In one way or another, it has been extremely important for the Peoples Progressive Party to cultivate all three types of Indian businessmen. To a large extent, they comprise the urban backbone of the party membership. Of the three types, however, the third has demanded the least amount of organizational attention. These penny capitalists exist in opposition to the African urban masses, and the nature of their existence has been sufficient to make them a hardcore group among Jagan's supporters. On the other hand, the well-established businessmen have required considerable organizational attention. As successful businessmen, they have been somewhat suspicious of Jagan's ideological views—particularly his views with respect to the role of private property and private enterprise in a developing nation. At the same time, their position in the colonial economy has given Jagan ample opportunity to attract their support and to cultivate their loyalty.

The power of the business community in Guiana, as in many other countries, tends to be expressed through such organizations as the Chamber of Commerce. There are two Chambers of Commerce in Georgetown, the Senior Chamber and the Junior Chamber. For many years, the Senior Chamber has been the important power element. Until about 1953, the important positions within the Senior Chamber were usually occupied by men who were employed by Booker companies or representatives of other large European firms. When looking for a nominated element in government, the Colonial Office invariably selected these men for appointment. On the whole, the Senior Chamber represented the European-controlled firms and the interests of the sugar industry. As such, the Senior Chamber paid very little attention to the interests of Indian businessmen.

By way of contrast, the Junior Chamber of Commerce tends to represent the interests of the Indian business community. The Junior Chamber is a comparatively new organization, founded in 1957. The initiative for its establishment came primarily from the overseas migrants. In 1960, approximately 80 per cent of the membership of the Junior Chamber was comprised of East Indians. Most of these were Water Street merchants, but even a few of the penny capitalists belonged to the group. The non-Indians who belong to the Junior Chamber are mostly Portuguese and Chinese merchants who have not been influential enough to have made their way into the Senior Chamber.

After the 1957 elections, when Jagan became the Minister of Trade and Industry, he immediately began to cultivate the interests of the East Indian business community. Specifically, he moved on two fronts. The first involved an effort to give economic support to Indian businessmen by liberalizing Guiana's trade policy. In order to delineate how this was accomplished, it is necessary to digress briefly.

During the Second World War, the colonial government established a Commodity Control Commission in order to regulate import quotas in keeping with the war effort. After the war, the commission was retained. It became an informal arm of the Chamber of Commerce, and as such, it functioned to protect the interests of the European business houses. In the 1950's, when West German and Japanese firms began to look for market outlets in British Guiana, the notices of these firms were passed around among the members of the chamber to see if anyone might be interested in their products. When none were interested in importing products that would compete with those of the firms they already represented, these trade notices died on the vine.

It is claimed that West German and Japanese trade missions were actually discouraged from looking over the Guianese market.

One of Jagan's first acts after he became Minister of Trade and Industry was to remove quota restrictions and to do away with the Commodity Control Commission. This was followed by a personal trip to West Germany in search of trade. As a result of these actions, Japanese and West German goods began to flow into the country. Quite naturally, East Indian business houses became the major outlets for these products. For example, the cheaper Japanese goods—pots, pans, cloth, etc.—are marketed by Thani, Kirplani, and other Indian business houses represented in the Junior Chamber of Commerce. The Volkswagen is sold by Sankar, a prominent member of the Junior Chamber. Majeed, a former president of the Junior Chamber, handles the Fiat. And Jardim, also a former president of the Junior Chamber, markets the Toyota, a Japanese car. (Jardim, it should be noted, is a prominent member of the P.P.P.)

In other words, Jagan's efforts to liberalize trade were directly beneficial to the East Indian business community. They gave Indian businessmen access to goods which are highly competitive with those marketed by the European-controlled firms. Thus, Indian businessmen were placed in direct competition with the "imperialist capitalists." Although figures are not available, as of 1960 Indian merchants had taken over a rather sizable share of the urban and rural retail market.

The second front on which Jagan moved involved giving political recognition to the Junior Chamber of Commerce. For example, as Minister of Trade and Industry, Jagan organized an Industrial Advisory Committee ostensibly to help him charter Guiana's course of economic development. A few of the "old guard" from Bookers, Demba, and the Senior Chamber were invited to serve on this committee. However, over half of the committee was made up of men who were prominent in the Junior Chamber of Commerce. Between 1957 and 1961, this type of recognition was extended to include other governmental committees. By 1961, when an American trade mission visited Guiana, Jagan directed the mission to the Junior Chamber and completely ignored the Senior Chamber. Finally, prior to the 1961 elections, Jagan held several meetings with Indian businessmen to assure them personally that the P.P.P. was not a Communist party and that their property would not be confiscated in the event that Guiana should receive independence under a Jagan government.

Because of Jagan's efforts, the power and influence of the Indian business community increased substantially after 1957. In an interview, one member of the Junior Chamber stated, "When the time comes we [i.e., Indian businessmen] will take over the Senior Chamber en masse." Needless to say, Jagan's power also increased. By 1961, he was in a position to practically handpick the president of the Junior Chamber. As the elections approached, the P.P.P. had the political and financial support of all but a small section of the Indian business community. The only group which did not rally to Jagan's cause was comprised of a few people who had been well established in Georgetown for many years. In some instances, these men belonged to the Senior Chamber and considered themselves to be almost part of the establishment. In other cases, they did not want to associate too openly with the P.P.P. for fear of antagonizing the Africans who contributed to the bulk of their trade.

Indian businessmen who supported the P.P.P. did so in numerous ways. They cooperated with the government and its policies. They made themselves available to serve on important committees which the government wanted to control. They also made extensive financial contributions to the party. In 1961, when Jagan proposed that the P.P.P. establish its own daily newspaper, contributions from Indian businessmen made it possible for the party to purchase the necessary printing equipment. Most importantly, Indian businessmen supported the P.P.P. by refusing to mount the anti-Communist bandwagon which the Portuguese and European business community organized and financed. This provided Jagan with an impressive source of confidence, and the opposition forces were never able to undermine it completely.

Another group that has been brought under the influence of apanjaht politics is made up of Indian professionals, most notably teachers. There are several reasons why Indian teachers have received special organizational attention from the Peoples Progressive Party since the 1957 elections. One reason has to do with numbers: Teachers now comprise the largest single group among Indian professionals.

Another reason Indian teachers have become important to the political strategy of the P.P.P. has to do with the influence they have been achieving at the communal level of sociocultural integration. This influence is particularly evident in the rural areas. It derives in part from the interest which younger Indians are now showing in education. It also derives from the fact that Indian teachers are rapidly displacing African teachers as a rural intelligentsia. Although African teachers still predominate in most of the rural schools, in villages like

Crabwood Creek, Springlands, Cromarty, Rose Hall, and around the plantations, there are enough Indian teachers so that Indians no longer seek out African teachers for counsel. Moreover, Indian teachers have become increasingly active in local government, agricultural cooperatives, religious associations, and self-help groups.[7] They also tend to be extremely active in political party groups.

Another reason Indian teachers have become important to the P.P.P. has to do with the system of dual control of the schools by Christian churches and the government (see Chapters 3 and 4). From its inception, the P.P.P. has been opposed to the system of dual control. In part, this opposition is related to ideological considerations. However, it does not necessarily derive from Marxist ideology, because it involves the question of the separation of church and state, and many Guianese who are not Marxists strongly favor such a separation. More important than ideology is the simple fact that the system of dual control cannot help being a political issue in a society as pluralistic as Guiana. The control of the schools by Christian denominational bodies has been extremely frustrating to the Hindus and Muslims who have to send their children to these schools. It has been even more frustrating to Indian teachers who feel that it has been necessary for them to compromise their values in order to hold positions in these schools.

Still another reason why Indian teachers have become important to the P.P.P. concerns the British Guiana Teachers' Association. The B.G.T.A. is the oldest and most prestigious professional association in the country. Also, within its area of influence, it is an extremely powerful organization. Ultimately, the government in British Guiana can undertake very little which is innovative in the field of education without at least the tacit cooperation of the Teachers' Association. However, the B.G.T.A. is almost exclusively dominated by Afro-Guianese who have been anything but reluctant to express their support of L. F. S. Burnham and the Peoples National Congress. Thus, in order to have access to the B.G.T.A., it has been important for Jagan to maintain the support of Indian teachers and to contribute in every way possible to their increase in numbers and influence.

The most concrete illustration of Jagan's efforts to secure the political support of Indian teachers has to do with the problem of

[7] Many Indian teachers do not give up cultivating rice after they have become teachers. It is a common complaint among Indian peasants that Indian teachers spend too much time working their farms and not enough time working with children.

dual control. As previously noted, this particular problem has been debated for years in Guiana. In 1953, when L. F. S. Burnham was the Minister of Education in the short-lived Jagan government, he declared himself and the government to be opposed to dual control. This declaration, for the most part, served only to invoke the wrath of the established churches. Thus, after the constitutional suspension, nationalist leaders were satisfied to avoid the issue by favoring a policy of continued support for existing denominational schools along with a policy of constructing new public schools under government control. This compromise seems to have worked out satisfactorily to the interests of everyone concerned except East Indians.

Contrary to the above compromise, in 1960, Balram Singh Rai, Jagan's Minister of Education, resurrected the dual control controversy and interjected it into the election campaign with the introduction of an Education Amendment Bill. This particular bill was passed only three months before the 1961 elections. It enabled the government to assume the direct control and management of fifty-one denominational schools which had been constructed with the use of governmental funds under previous administrations. The immediate effect of this legislation was to create a prolonged outcry of protest among various denominational bodies and to give weight to the charge that the Jagan government was seeking to establish the political control of education. The Education Amendment Bill also provided the opposition with an opportunity to accuse the Jagan government of following a Marxist policy of confiscation of private property and of being too incompetent to use funds that had already been allocated for the construction of new government schools.

From the point of view of organizational analysis, the 1961 Education Amendment Bill raised a number of questions. Since the bill offered little potential for aggregating election support for the P.P.P. among Amerindians, Africans, and Portuguese, and since Jagan's opposition to dual control was well known among East Indians, why did he elect to express this opposition in this particular manner and at such an inopportune moment? In other words, what did Jagan and the P.P.P. expect to gain by the introduction of legislation that provided the opposition with so much political ammunition, and why was this legislation not postponed until after the 1961 elections?

The answers to the above questions were uncovered in a series of interviews obtained from several Indian teachers three months before the Education Amendment Bill became law. Quite pointedly, they revealed another dimension of apanjaht politics. According to informants, Indian teachers had been putting considerable pressure on Jagan since 1957 to do something about the injustices associated with the system of dual control. The teachers were concerned particularly about their inability to win promotions in denominational schools. They were also concerned about unfair treatment from African head teachers in government schools. According to informants, many teachers had been notified through party channels that the government would take action to improve their situation. As of 1959, no action had been taken, and considerable unrest existed among Indian teachers because of unfulfilled promises. In 1960, when there was talk about a new political party being formed under the leadership of Peter D'Aguiar, some Indian teachers threatened to quit the P.P.P. and join the opposition.

In November, 1960, approximately one month after D'Aguiar organized the United Force, Jagan's Minister of Education announced that the government had decided to assume control of all denominational schools which had been built with public funds, including those situated on church-owned land. This announcement was not news to the Indian teachers who were interviewed. Before it was made, they had been informed that the government was planning to take over certain denominational schools. They also were informed that the government would establish a teachers' service commission which would assume the responsibility for the appointment, promotion, and discipline of teachers in government schools. In other words, the commission would take away much of the power concentrated in the hands of African head teachers and the Christian schoolboards. Two of the teachers who were interviewed also were told that they would be given positions as head teachers. In fact, they were even told the exact denominational schools to which they would be assigned.

In view of these facts, it is difficult to interpret the Education Amendment Bill as anything other than a part of Jagan's strategy of apanjaht politics. Although the Education Bill may have had certain objective merits, there can be little doubt that its introduction in an election year was designed primarily to fulfill promises which the P.P.P. had made to Indian teachers. It certainly served to aggregate the support of this particular group for the Peoples Progressive Party. However, the Education Bill also paid other political dividends.

Over a period of several months, the Education Amendment Bill provoked heated discussions in the Legislative Council, in the press, and at political rallies. During the course of these discussions, an unusual opportunity was presented to the P.P.P. leaders to demonstrate their interest in the Indian cultural section. Rai, for example, declared that religious "apartheid" was being practiced in Guianese schools to the detriment of East Indians. Ram Karran, Jagan's Minister of Communications and Works, accused the churches of trying to bully the government on the issue. Jagan announced that the bill was designed to correct the injustices that were being imposed upon the non-Christians. When Burnham opposed the bill, apparently in contradiction to his position in 1953, he was described as a racist. When the churches labeled the bill as "communist inspired," Rahman Gajraj, a nominated member of the Legislative Council, accused the churches of practicing "fascism." By the time the bill became law, practically every East Indian in the country was convinced that only the P.P.P. was interested in their education.

Although East Indian businessmen and teachers were of strategic importance to the P.P.P., these groups were not as critical to the party's immediate future as the East Indian masses. The Indian masses, for the most part, included the sugar workers and the rice farmers. They made up the vast majority of the East Indian cultural section. Without their having become involved in apanjaht politics, the P.P.P. could not have won the 1961 elections. Thus, between 1957 and 1961, the party devoted most of its organizational efforts to mobilizing the support of these two groups. Consider, first, the sugar workers.

In order to appreciate fully Jagan's strategy with respect to the sugar workers, it is necessary to consider briefly the situation that existed in the sugar industry after 1957. To begin with, the instability and the turmoil that followed Jagan's first election came as a stark warning to the sugar industry. For the first time in Guiana's history, the plantocracy, as represented by the sugar producers, seemed to realize that it needed to adopt a progressive attitude and put its house in order if it were to survive the march to independence. As a consequence of this realization, by 1957 the industry was caught up in a profound state of transition. A whole series of complex social and technological innovations were being gradually introduced. On the face of it, these innovations were designed to make the plantations more economically efficient and more responsive to the needs of workers.

Specifically, the sugar industry was seeking to rid itself of its paternalistic status vis-a-vis the sugar workers. This general policy was implemented in a variety of ways. For one thing, personnel departments were organized and introduced on all of the estates. These departments were put in charge of professional personnel officers who worked in cooperation with estate managers but who were made directly responsible to the Georgetown offices. Community centers and all of the activities associated with them were brought under the supervision of these personnel departments. In addition, all negotiations between workers and management and between unions and management were channeled through these departments. In effect, this reorganization broke the old pattern of nepotic relationships that once existed between estate managers and individual sugar workers.

In association with this new personnel policy, worker training programs were also introduced. The expressed purpose of these programs was to train Guianese to replace European personnel. Although time limitations were not specified, it was expected that eventually the entire management function on the plantations would be placed in the hands of Guianese.

Another component of this transition from paternalism involved new policies concerning the extra-nuclear settlements (i.e., the estate housing schemes). By 1960, because of population growth and the retrenchment of sugar workers as a result of technological changes, over 50 per cent of the population living in extra-nuclear settlements was comprised of people who were not employed in the sugar industry. Nevertheless, the estates continued to provide these people with drainage, sanitation, street maintenance, water, medical care, and a variety of other services. These services represented a considerable drain on profits that could be turned over, in the form of wages, to sugar workers.

In 1960, the Sugar Producers' Association undertook a program that was designed eventually to divest the industry of all responsibility for the extra-nuclear settlements. The program was simple in its conception. In effect, the S.P.A. intended to sell houselots to the people who owned houses in the extra-nuclear settlements at an extremely low cost. It was expected that by alienating these lands to the people who lived on them, the estate population would eventually be organized under local authorities. In this way, the estate population would be forced to become responsible for the management of its own affairs. As part of this policy, the S.P.A. also offered the government the opportunity to take over the ownership and management of the estate medical centers. In place of the medical centers, the S.P.A.

planned to continue to provide workers with first-aid facilities and to expand its program of industrial accident insurance.

These developments were planned to proceed simultaneously with technological changes in the industry. The technological changes under consideration included the expansion of mechanical tillage in the production of sugar cane, the replacement of obsolete equipment in the factories, the shutting down of inefficient factories and the transportation of canes to centralized plants, the construction of mechanical loading facilities, and the introduction of labor-saving devices wherever possible in the production and processing of sugar and sugar products. All of these technological changes quite naturally involved the retrenchment of workers and the development of a more skilled and more economically efficient labor force.

Changes of this order might be considered both rational and desirable from the point of view of economic development. However, they were fraught with many difficulties. For example, in many instances the introduction of personnel departments met with resistance on the part of senior staff officers as well as sugar workers. The former lacked confidence in the new procedures, while the latter could no longer receive particularistic consideration by doing favors for members of the senior staff. The changes with respect to the extranuclear settlements were even more problematic. At Skeldon, very few of the people who lived on estate land wanted to be organized under local authorities. As long as they lived on estate land, they received a variety of services, perhaps a greater variety than any local authority could provide, and they did not have to pay taxes to support these services. Similarly, the health centers operated by the estates provided better medical treatment than could be obtained in many government-operated health centers. And, needless to say, the retrenchment of workers only added to the hardships that already existed as a result of the high rates of unemployment and underemployment in Guianese society.

The frustration and insecurity that these changes generated among sugar workers provided the Peoples Progressive Party with fresh opportunities to mobilize their support. These opportunities were further compounded by problems in the labor movement. As far as sugar workers were concerned, the situation with respect to the labor movement had not changed. The Guiana Industrial Workers Union continued to exist under P.P.P. control, but the Sugar Producers' Association continued to withhold recognition of it in favor of the

Man Power Citizens' Association. The majority of sugar workers, however, had no confidence in the latter organization. At Skeldon, for example, the only workers interviewed who expressed confidence in the M.P.C.A. were either local union officers or Afro-Guianese. Most of the workers interviewed could not even recall ever having voted for an officer of the M.P.C.A., and none of them could explain how its president, Richard Ishmael, had been elected. Thus, the M.P.C.A. was in no position to mediate the changes that were taking place in the sugar industry.

Between 1957 and 1961, Jagan's strategy with respect to the sugar workers consisted of (1) fomenting labor unrest on the estates and (2) utilizing the P.P.P. apparatus, in association with Janet Jagan's position as Minister of Labour, as an unofficial union in opposition to the anti-Jagan Man Power Citizens' Association. Party cells operating in the vicinity of the sugar estates comprised the instrument by which this strategy was implemented. Judging by the cell at No. 79 Village, which is adjacent to Plantation Skeldon, these local groups were well organized and extremely active among the sugar workers. At Skeldon, for example, the chairman of the local group was a young Hindu priest who also worked as a mailman for the Post Office Department. The secretary was the proprietor of a local cinema. The treasurer owned a gasoline station and a hired car service.

All of these individuals had considerable time to devote to party activities, and all of them had extensive access to sugar workers in the area. The chairman, for example, frequently was called upon by sugar workers to officiate at weddings, funerals, and other religious ceremonies. As a mailman, he was in touch with practically every home in the extra-nuclear settlement. He also served on the educational council for the Skeldon Community Center. The secretary, on the other hand, did very little other than work for the party. As proprietor of a cinema, as a member of the No. 79 Village Council, and as a member of the board of education at Skeldon Lutheran School, he was known by almost every sugar worker in the district.

In addition to these individuals, the cell at No. 79 Village included most of the influential local Indian leaders among its members. It included, for example, several Hindu priests, almost all of the Indian schoolteachers living in the area, all of the village councilmen from the local authorities at No. 78 and No. 79 villages, many of the Indian shopkeepers, and three clerks from the assistant district commissioner's office. It also included the president of the local for the Sugar Estates

Clerks Association, several members of the Estate Joint Committee who belonged to the Man Power Citizens' Association, and practically all of the officers for the tenants' associations that were functional in the estate housing schemes. In other words, while the P.P.P. did not officially establish a party group in the extra-nuclear settlement, practically all of the local leaders in the settlement belonged to a cell which was extremely active in the area.

The activities of the local party group at Skeldon were numerous and varied. The group organized membership drives and fundraising campaigns. It organized political rallies for top party officials who delivered political speeches at Skeldon at least once or twice a month. It distributed the party newspaper, *Thunder,* and other political literature. It organized classes and provided lectures for the training of political leaders. It organized political discussion groups for party members and interested sugar workers. It unofficially, and sometimes officially, supported and campaigned for the election of candidates to village councils, tenants' associations, the estate joint committee, committees at the community center, and local union offices.

Apart from these kinds of activities, local cells in the vicinity of the estates functioned as informal labor unions. They could not negotiate for workers, but they could give them considerable moral support. At Skeldon, for example, workers were encouraged to take their problems to the party. The party, in turn, communicated these to the Georgetown headquarters and to the Minister of Labour. As Minister of Labour, Janet Jagan knew more about the dissatisfactions of sugar workers on various estates than the union that was supposed to be representing them.

On occasion, local cells would send workers directly to Georgetown to register their complaints in person at party headquarters or with the Minister of Labour. If a particular case appeared to be legitimate and serious, it would then be used by the party as the basis for an attack on the sugar industry or the Man Power Citizens' Association. Although the party could do very little for the individual involved, at least he returned home with the satisfaction that some very important people took a personal interest in his problem. On a typical afternoon at Freedom House, the P.P.P. headquarters in Georgetown, eight workers were observed registering complaints of one kind or another with party officials. Some of these had come all the way from Plantation Albion on the Courantyne Coast. When a party official was questioned about this traffic, he indicated that on some days whole delegations would be sent by workers to Freedom

House because they could obtain no satisfaction from the M.P.C.A.

There also were more direct ways in which local party cells could function as informal labor unions. At Skeldon, for example, the local group took advantage of every opportunity to support and maintain unrest on the estate. When labor disputes broke out, it intervened in every way possible. A case in point is the strike which was called by the Sugar Estate Clerks Association in November, 1960. When it appeared that the strike might be settled, the P.P.P. group encouraged some clerks to remain out until all their demands had been satisfied, regardless of what the union's officials might be willing to settle for. The P.P.P. group also encouraged other workers to support the clerks. It provided pickets and signs for picketing. It collected food and money for those clerks who needed support. And, in addition, it rehashed with workers in the area all of the traditional complaints against the sugar industry and the Man Power Citizens' Association.

To support the organizational activities of local cells, Cheddi Jagan and other top party officials worked to associate the national interests of the P.P.P. with the particular interests of the sugar workers. This was accomplished primarily by keeping certain kinds of issues boiling, particularly during the last few months preceding the 1961 elections. A few examples will suffice to illustrate the nature of the strategy.

In February, 1961, Jagan reopened the question of union representation on the estates by declaring the need for legislation which would protect the right of workers to select their own unions. In March, Jagan declared that the sugar estates should be run on a cooperative basis, starting first with the releasing of lands to sugar workers for the cultivation of cane. In May, the P.P.P. sent a delegation of retrenched workers from the Port Mourant Estate to picket the Georgetown offices of the Man Power Citizens' Association. In June, Ajodha Singh announced that sugar workers were being sacrificed for profits as a result of Bookers' efforts to mechanize the industry. In July, one month before the elections, the P.P.P. organized worker delegations and sent them to Georgetown to protest a pension scheme which the M.P.C.A. had negotiated with the Sugar Producers' Association. After a mass protest, Jagan delivered a speech and promised the workers that the government would do everything in its power to make the pension scheme operate satisfactorily. However, the pension scheme has never been implemented.

During the 1961 election campaign, apanjaht politics among Indian sugar workers was focused most sharply on the Peoples National Congress. Throughout the campaign, the P.P.P. made a concerted effort to link the P.N.C. with the sugar industry. At political rallies, for example, P.P.P. speakers outlined what appeared to be a warm relationship between Burnham's party and Bookers. They noted that the P.N.C. publication, *New Nation,* was seldom critical of the sugar industry. They also noted that the P.N.C. received much less critical attention in the business-controlled press than the P.P.P. and the Jagan government. The most substantial evidence that the P.P.P. offered in support of these accusations was based on the fact that the chairman of the P.N.C., Winifred Gaskin, also happened to be the editor of *Booker News,* a company newspaper widely circulated on the estates.

While the P.P.P. could not provide concrete evidence that Bookers actually supported the Peoples National Congress, circumstantial evidence was sufficient to engender the belief among Indian sugar workers that this was indeed the case. Consequently, a tide of Indian opposition to the P.N.C. swelled across the estates. Indian sugar workers were convinced that a P.N.C. victory at the polls would entail not only "black domination" but their continued exploitation. The opposition to Burnham was so strong among sugar workers that shortly before the 1961 elections it was almost impossible for the P.N.C. to conduct a political meeting in the vicinity of the plantations. At Skeldon, for example, Indian informants boasted that they would chase the P.N.C. leaders away if they tried to hold meetings and "lie about Cheddi" in that area. Everywhere on the plantations—e.g., Houston, Enmore, Blairmont, Albion, Port Mourant—"apanjaht" became the campaign slogan of East Indian sugar workers.

As has been shown, political party organization constituted the most important instrument of apanjaht politics on the plantations. However, this was not the case in the peasant villages. Among the peasants, the structural apparatus of the political party could not be made to function as efficiently as it was made to function on the estates. This was not due to a lack of organizational effort on the part of P.P.P. leaders. Rather, it was due to the differences that existed in the two social environments.

Sugar workers lived in compacted areas of high population density. Indian rice farmers lived in more sparsely populated villages. The daily routine of sugar workers was regulated by the conditions of their wage employment. That of the peasants was regulated by the cultivation of fields, the harvesting of crops, the milling of padi, and their engagement in supplementary forms of work. The sugar workers, in other words, were more readily available for organizational purposes than the peasants. Also, the plantation and its environs contained a larger number of potential leaders and political activists than the rural villages. In small Indian villages like Cromarty, there were no local party groups. In the larger villages like Clonbrook, party groups existed, but their membership was not large, and very few of the members were truly active. Compared to the situation at Skeldon, at Clonbrook the P.P.P. cell could hardly keep itself organized.

The major instrument of apanjaht politics with respect to Indian peasants has been economic development. In order to mobilize the support of the Indian peasants, the Jagan government catered extensively to their economic interests. It did this primarily by diverting the major portion of Guiana's economic development program to projects in the agricultural sector—particularly to projects designed to expand the rice industry.

For example, when the Jagan government took office in 1957, it inherited a development program which had been established for the period 1956–60.[8] This particular program envisaged an expenditure of $91 millions (B.W.I.) for the five-year period. Approximately 27.5 per cent of these funds was to be allocated to the agricultural sector of the economy. After the Jagan government took office, this program was revised upward to $102.5 millions. The funds allocated to the agricultural sector were increased to 33 per cent of the total available for development purposes.

Toward the end of 1958, it was decided to terminate the 1956–60 development program in 1959. When the program was concluded in 1959, only $77.4 millions of the original funds had been expended. Of this amount, 42.8 per cent was spent on the agricultural sector (including sea defenses, drainage and irrigation, land development, and agricultural credits).[9] Only 1.4 and 1.7 per cent, respectively, were spent on industrial development and education—areas of development in which Africans are primarily interested. However, 19.2 per cent

---

[8] See "Development Programme 1956–1960," Sessional Paper No. 8/1956 of the British Guiana Legislative Council.

[9] For a critical analysis of Jagan's development program by an economist, see "The Economic Future of British Guiana" by Peter Newman. The statistics quoted here are taken from Newman's unpublished manuscript. A slightly revised version appeared in *Social and Economic Studies*, 9 (1960), 263–96.

of the development budget was spent on urban housing (including public officers' housing), and this was directly beneficial to urban Afro-Guianese.

In 1959, the Jagan government introduced a new five-year development program. The new program reflected the changes that had taken place in the Guianese political situation since 1957. It reflected particularly the extent to which the Jagan government had become dependent upon the East Indian cultural section for its political support. For example, the new program envisaged an expenditure of $110.28 millions (B.W.I.) for the period 1969–64.[10] Only 3.6 and 3.8 per cent of this amount, respectively, were allocated to industrial development and education. Housing, which represented 19.2 per cent of the previous development budget, was reduced to 7.3 per cent in the new budget. At the same time, however, the funds allocated to the agricultural sector were increased to 52.5 per cent. An additional 2.5 per cent was to be spent on rural water supply. Finally, practically all of the money allocated to the agricultural sector was earmarked for the extension of existing rice acreage.[11]

The 1960–64 development program, in effect, almost completely ignored the pressing economic needs of the Afro-Guianese. In fact, this was the major criticism leveled at the program by its Afro-Guianese critics. In responding to these critics, the P.P.P. leaders argued that Guiana was primarily an agricultural country and that the development of its agricultural system was a prerequisite to the development of its industrial economy. In other words, the P.P.P. maintained that the development program was the product of rational economic planning and that it was not designed as an instrument of apanjaht politics. Undoubtedly, this point could be debated endlessly by economic planners. What cannot be debated, however, are the data that were collected on one of the large land-development schemes included in the program. These data demonstrate that if the development program was not designed as an instrument of apanjaht politics, it was certainly being used as such by the government.

The land-development scheme on which data were collected is the Black Bush Polder. Located on the Courantyne Coast, the polder

---

[10] See "Development Programme 1960–1964," Sessional Paper No. 5/1959 of the British Guiana Legislative Council.

[11] Commenting on this fact, Newman states, "By accenting the short-run palliatives of rice farming, British Guiana is piling up for itself, in the by no means distant future, a host of grave social and political problems" (*op. cit.*, unpublished draft, p. 18).

was one of the Jagan government's most publicized projects during the 1961 election campaign. The project involved the reclamation of 31,000 acres of swampland. Upon completion, it was to provide for the settlement of 1,586 families. Each family was to be given a twenty-one-year lease on fifteen acres of land to be used for the cultivation of rice. In addition, each family was to be given two acres of land for houselots and garden plots. Some idea of the magnitude of the project can be had from available statistics. It required the construction of approximately twenty miles of road, two hundred miles of drain embankments, three hundred miles of drainage and irrigation canals, the clearing of 20,000 acres of jungle bush, and the construction of numerous sluices and access bridges. Expenditures were estimated at approximately $18.67 millions (B.W.I.). This represents a capital investment of $11,800 per family. Excluding the funds spent on this project from Guiana's previous development program, the cost of the project represented 9 per cent of the 1960–64 development budget.

Peter Newman has estimated that the Black Bush Polder would provide a capital-output ratio of from 8:1 to 6:1.[12] In other words, for every six to eight dollars invested in the polder, one dollar per year would be generated in the domestic income stream. This would appear to represent a very low income return on development capital. However, the political return on this development capital appeared to be considerably more impressive.

When the polder was first conceived, prior to Jagan's election in 1957, it was to be organized as a local authority under the Department of Local Government. The families that were to be settled in the polder were to be selected on the basis of need and previous agricultural experience. However, when the polder was nearing completion, it was suggested by Jagan that it be organized as a land society under the supervision of the Department of Co-operatives, a department included in his portfolio as Minister of Trade and Industry. This modification in plan received the support of Brindley Benn, Jagan's Minister of Natural Resources and the chairman of the P.P.P. It also received the support of the Commissioner of Cooperatives, the Commissioner of Agriculture, the Commissioner of Lands and Mines, and the Commissioner of Local Government.

Subsequent to this change, a selection committee was appointed to receive applications for land in the polder and to grade the appli-

[12] *Ibid.*, p. 17.

cants suitable for settlement. The selection committee consisted of seven members. These included the Minister of Natural Resources, the Commissioner of Lands and Mines, the Commissioner of Co-operatives, or their representatives, and four unofficial members appointed at large. As of 1961, all of the unofficial members appointed to the committee were P.P.P. organizers. These, with the Minister of Natural Resources, provided the P.P.P. with a majority of five on the committee. In the event of disagreement among the members of the committee with respect to the qualifications of a particular applicant, the decision of the Minister of Natural Resources was final.

According to informants, most of whom were government officers directly involved with the settlement program, it was virtually impossible for an applicant to receive land in the polder unless the P.P.P. wanted him to receive land. As of October, 1960, the Commissioner of Lands and Mines had received more than 3,300 applications for land. Of these, less than 200 had been received from Afro-Guianese. As of February, 1961, 150 families had been settled in the polder. Of these, 147 were East Indian families. Only three families were Afro-Guianese, and informants were certain that the heads of all three were financial members of the P.P.P.

When certain party officials were asked why the Afro-Guianese were so poorly represented among the settlers in the Black Bush Polder, several explanations were given. Some suggested that the Africans were poor farmers and did not deserve to be given land. Others suggested that they were not interested in farming and, therefore, did not apply. Still others suggested that the Africans did not want to leave their villages to take up land in the polder. Perhaps these explanations are partly valid. However, they are very different from the explanations given by government officers.

The government officers who were interviewed provided two major reasons why many Africans were not applying for land in the polder. For one thing, Africans were not being encouraged to apply in large numbers. More specifically, only Africans loyal to the P.P.P. were being directed into the channels of application by party organizers who functioned as contacts between landless Indian peasants and the government agencies involved. Secondly, many Africans would not apply because it was stipulated that successful applicants must sell what little village property they might own and move into the polder's cooperative housing scheme. In other words, in order to receive property by lease from the government, it was necessary to alienate transported property or, in the case of most Africans, children's property.

Regardless of the reasons one wishes to emphasize, the Afro-Guianese did not receive very many benefits from Jagan's efforts to develop the agricultural sector of the economy. In fact, they frequently suffered from these efforts. In the African villages of Eversham and Dingwall, for example, the leases on second-depth Crown lands were taken away from the first-depth proprietors because these lands were included within the Black Bush Polder. It mattered little that these lands had been occupied by the proprietors in these villages for more than a century. It also mattered little that the first-depth lands in these villages were divided up as children's property and used primarily for houselots.

Jagan's policy with respect to the cooperative movement also produced a difficult situation for a great many rural Africans. In order to organize the agricultural sector in terms of land cooperatives made up of loyal Indian peasants, the Jagan government adopted the policy of refusing to renew leases which first-depth proprietors held to second-depth Crown lands. As these leases expired, the Crown lands were turned over to cooperative societies.

Proprietors were permitted to join these cooperatives and make application for the lands they had traditionally occupied. However, in many cases their applications were automatically disqualified on the basis of their first-depth proprietorship. When this was not the case, their applications were processed in much the same manner as those that were made for land in the Black Bush Polder. For example, an African competing with an Indian might be disqualified on the basis that he had never cultivated rice and that the land was to be used for this purpose.

In one interesting case for which data were collected, both African and Indian proprietors had been alienated from second-depth lands in favor of landless Indian peasants. Also, there were a number of locally influential P.P.P. supporters among the alienated Indian proprietors. When this situation generated static within the party, a new selection committee was appointed to review the applications. The new committee was put in charge of an African district commissioner. When many of the Indian proprietors were disqualified for a second time, they complained again to the party. On this occasion, however, local party leaders simply blamed the whole unfortunate situation on the African district commissioner and suggested that the alienated proprietors sell their first-depth property (which amounted to approximately 3.5 acres per proprietor) and apply for land in the Black Bush Polder. Satisfied that they could exchange 3.5 acres of poor land for 17 acres of new land, most of the proprietors in question continued to express confidence in the party.

As a result of Jagan's development program, between 1957 and 1961 Indian peasants were the primary recipients of more than 90,000 acres of new land. They also were the recipients of extensive agricultural credit. In the polder alone, nearly $1 million (B.W.I.) in credit was extended by the government to an agricultural cooperative which did not have enough collateral among its members to float a bank loan for a single rice combine. In association with these developments, the production of rice in British Guiana more than doubled. More importantly, the completion of the 1960–64 program held out the promise of even greater payoff because it envisaged the reclamation and distribution of an additional 110,000 acres of land.

It is difficult to determine precisely the full impact of Jagan's development program on this particular segment of the Indian cultural section. As far as apanjaht politics is concerned, its impact was certainly extensive. Practically every Indian peasant interviewed was absolutely convinced that the Jagan government represented Guiana's only hope for a prosperous future. This conviction was based on what appeared to be, for them, a social and economic revolution. As one informant put it, "If Cheddi be a bad man, a communist like Burnham call he, then why he give we people all dis land?"

To summarize, apanjaht politics contained a variety of promises which provided the East Indian population with the hope for a new and more prosperous way of life. It promised Indian businessmen new markets and economic power. It promised Indian teachers new opportunities. It promised other educated Indians access to civil service positions that were once closed to all except educated Portuguese and Afro-Guianese. It promised Indian sugar workers better representation and a larger share of the profits they produced. It promised Indian peasants more land on which they could cultivate more rice. In all of this, apanjaht politics provided the Indian way of life with a political identity which it had never had before. It symbolized economic development, progress, and power; thus, it also symbolized Indian nationalism.

Apanjaht politics also held out promises to the Peoples Progressive Party. By virtue of their numbers and their political loyalty, East

Indians could give the P.P.P. a substantial majority in any election. Thus, P.P.P. politicians expected that apanjaht politics would give them uncompromising control over the nationalist movement for years to come. However, this was not to be the case. What they had not fully considered in their organizational strategy was the way in which the Afro-Guianese might react to the political integration of the East Indian cultural section. Specifically, they had not fully considered the consequences of apanjaht politics for the Afro-Guianese.

## RACIAL POLITICS AND THE P.N.C.

Although the disintegration of Guiana's nationalist movement considerably weakened the Peoples Progressive Party, it did not destroy it. As we have seen, the Jagan-Burnham split gave Jagan complete control of what continued to be a viable political organization. In this regard, L. F. S. Burnham was not so fortunate. The split was almost disastrous to his career as a nationalist leader. To be sure, Burnham emerged from the split with a political party. However, it was little more than a personal following. In fact, because it continued to claim the P.P.P. label, it even lacked its own political identity.

More importantly, Burnham's faction of the P.P.P. lacked an organizational structure. It had an Executive Committee and a General Council, but below these there was practically nothing by way of an infrastructure. A few local groups existed, but most of them clustered in the environs of Georgetown. Outside of Georgetown the party was extremely weak. In a political sense, the African population in Central Demerara belonged to Sidney King. While King had broken with Jagan, he had not yet joined forces with Burnham. New Amsterdam was controlled by W. O. R. Kendall, and Kendall belonged to the United Democratic Party. The U.D.P. represented the somewhat conservative African middle class, a group that was still suspicious of Burnham's political views. Mackenzie City, another heavily populated African area, was divided between Burnham and the B. G. Mine Workers' Union. Although Burnham had strong union support in Georgetown, the mine workers did not completely trust him because of his former association with Jagan. Outside of these areas the country remained unorganized for Burnham or largely belonged to Jagan.

In spite of these difficulties, Burnham and his followers were extremely optimistic about the 1957 elections. They fully expected that victory would be theirs. This optimism was based on a number of erroneous considerations. For one thing, the Robertson Commission had dubbed Jagan a Communist and made him primarily responsible for the constitutional suspension. Burnham and his group were largely cleared of both these charges, and they expected to reap a harvest from the anti-Communist groups that opposed Jagan. Also, in 1956, Jagan lost the support of King, Westmaas, and Carter. Burnham, on the other hand, still retained the support of Jai Narine Singh and J. P. Lachmansingh. Thus, while apanjaht politics had reared its head, it had not yet become an alarming reality. And, finally, Burnham was confident that his association with the Guianese labor movement would provide him with widespread working-class support.

In the face of this optimism, the results of the 1957 elections came as a thunderous shock to Burnham and his followers. When they emerged from the elections with only three of the fourteen seats in the Legislative Council, it left the party in a shambles. In 1958, the situation deteriorated further. The party changed its name to the Peoples National Congress and elected Sidney King to its Executive Committee. Even at this early date, King was developing a reputation as a "black nationalist." Mainly because of Burnham's acceptance of King, Jai Narine Singh broke with the P.N.C. and formed the Guianese Independence Movement. Although Jai's departure was of little political consequence in the long run, its immediate effect was to reduce the P.N.C.'s representation in the Legislative Council to two seats. One of these was occupied by A. L. Jackson, an influential leader in the B. G. Post Office Workers' Union. The other was occupied by Burnham.

In 1958, then, the P.N.C. was not only poorly organized but it had no power and very little influence in government. At the same time, the tide of apanjaht politics was swelling rapidly on the plantations, in the land-settlement schemes, and in the rural villages. Jagan and the P.P.P. controlled the government, and with it they were welding together what appeared to be the entire East Indian population. Jagan was even making headway with respect to Indianizing such critical departments of the Civil Service as Local Government, Agriculture, Cooperatives, Lands and Mines, Education, Labor, and the Constabulary. The Government Information Services and the weekly press conference were being used by Jagan to propagandize the P.P.P. from one end of the country to the other.

In view of these developments, how could the tide of apanjaht politics be turned back? Burnham, for the first time since the split, began to realize that his survival as a nationalist leader necessitated building a new political party almost from the ground up. The 1957 elections demonstrated quite conclusively that he could not make do with what little support he had taken away from Jagan and the P.P.P. At the same time, however, the prospects of building a new nationalist party presented difficult problems. On what basis, for example, could a new party be developed? What splinter groups were available as allies? Which of these groups could be welded together behind Burnham's leadership? What kinds of compromises would have to be made? More importantly, how could these groups be mobilized before independence or in time to contest the 1961 elections?[13]

As Burnham and his followers undertook the reorganization of the P.N.C. in 1958, they surveyed the Guianese political scene for new allies. The possibilities were quite limited. In 1957, with the help of Jai Narine Singh and J. P. Lachmansingh, Burnham had failed to mobilize significant East Indian support. Considering apanjaht politics, it was obvious, or at least Burnham concluded as much, that the P.N.C. could not wean very many Indians away from Jagan and the P.P.P. This was made even more obvious by the fact that the two or three Indian intellectuals who were interested in throwing in with the P.N.C. were neither well known nor politically influential. Also, they would be considered traitors by the vast majority of the Indian people.

On the other hand, Jagan still retained some African support, particularly in the rural areas. Burnham felt that this group could be easily alienated from the P.P.P. if it were made sufficiently conscious of Indian nationalism and Jagan's apanjaht politics. There was also the United Democratic Party, the middle-class Africans in Georgetown and New Amsterdam. If this group felt threatened by apanjaht

[13] Burnham, unlike Jagan, never addressed himself to these difficult organizational problems in a public document or a published speech to a party congress. However, these problems were considered, and the solutions that were worked out for them are important because they form the framework of the P.N.C.'s organizational strategy. For the most part, the solutions for these problems emerged out of the discussions that took place at the various informal gatherings which fill the social calendar for many Afro-Guianese intellectuals in Georgetown. Thus, they only can be reconstructed from the data obtained in numerous interviews with many of the people who were directly responsible for the reorganization of the P.N.C. in 1959.

politics, as Burnham knew it would, it might be persuaded to adopt a less conservative stance and throw in with the P.N.C. As an added attraction, the P.N.C. could offer important U.D.P. leaders (e.g., Carter, Kendall, and Correia) positions of influence on the party's Executive Committee.

And then there were the Portuguese and the remnants of the National Democratic Party which opposed the P.P.P. in 1953. The Portuguese presented something of a problem. They felt extremely threatened by Jagan's Marxist-Leninist views. At the same time, because of their conservatism and their racial prejudices, they would be reluctant to throw in with a mass-based party dominated by Afro-Guianese. However, Burnham believed that if the Portuguese could be shown that their racial prejudices were a luxury which they could no longer afford, and if they could be convinced that they had nothing to fear from their former domestics, they might be persuaded to join the ranks of the P.N.C. Or, if not, at least they could be persuaded to remain on the sidelines and vote for the P.N.C. As Burnham viewed the situation, the Portuguese had no other choices. They could not survive economically under an independent Jagan government.

The Amerindians, in Burnham's view, presented no problem. As in the past, they would support their own candidate, Stephen Campbell, and he was opposed to the P.P.P. Or, alternatively, the Amerindians would follow Portuguese leadership because of Catholic church influence. In either case, they would not detract strength from the P.N.C.

Together, these groups comprised approximately 50 per cent of the Guianese population. If they could be aggregated, it would be possible to defeat the P.P.P. at the polls and stem the tide of apanjaht politics. This eventuality, as Burnham fully realized, depended also upon how the voting constituencies were drawn by the Colonial Office and the extent to which independent Indian politicians (e.g., Lionel Luckhoo and Jai Narine Singh) were successful in subtracting some of Jagan's Indian support. However, even if these contingencies should fail to materialize, a new P.N.C. organized as Burnham conceived it would be in a position to present a victorious P.P.P. with formidable opposition in the government. In fact, if it were necessary, such an opposition might even be strong enough to deny a Jagan government independence.

In broad outline, this seemed to be the organizational strategy that was generally agreed upon by the leaders of the Peoples National

Congress in 1958. Essentially, its component elements reflected an almost purely defensive adjustment to the realities of apanjaht politics. Thus, the strategy differed from that of the P.P.P. in two important respects. First, its racial overtones were intended almost exclusively for rural Afro-Guianese. In the urban area, racial politics could only endanger the entire plan of operation. Second, in order to aggregate socially divergent urban groups, the strategy displayed very little commitment to any particular political or economic ideology. For example, Burnham stated, ". . . we in the Peoples National Congress refuse to be doctrinaire, we refuse to join hands with those who believe that the state must own all the means of production or to join hands with those who contend that private enterprise must be allowed to run amok. . . ."[14]

Although this middle-of-the-road ideology may appear attractive in an economically developed society, it is a difficult perspective for a nationalist party to maintain, particularly in an underdeveloped country. On the one hand, the P.N.C. wanted to mobilize the support of the Portuguese and other economically conservative elements. On the other hand, it had to maintain the support of the Afro-Guianese labor movement. To accomplish the latter, the P.N.C. had to present itself primarily as a working-class party. This necessity, as Jagan predicted in 1956, required Burnham to employ leftist phraseology. He had to be critical of colonialism, of colonial institutions, of ascribed status, and of economic exploitation. At the same time, however, it was precisely this leftist phraseology that would make the more conservative elements suspicious of Burnham's intentions. In other words, the P.N.C.'s strategy contained certain ambiguities that would make it extremely difficult to implement.

Late in 1958, Burnham undertook negotiations with the leaders of the United Democratic Party. In March, 1959, the P.N.C. and the U.D.P. held a joint party congress in Georgetown. The two parties merged, and a new Executive Committee was created. It included Burnham as party leader. It also included such Burnham supporters as Sidney King and A. L. Jackson. John Carter, W. O. R. Kendall, Eugene Correia, and Neville Bissember, all prominent members of the U.D.P., were included on the new Executive Committee.

The P.N.C.'s new Executive Committee was a veritable hodgepodge of liberal and conservative thinking. Some of its members

---

[14] *We're No Pawn of East or West,* pamphlet issued by the P.N.C., 1960.

were strongly inclined toward some form of socialism, while others favored an opposite view. At political meetings, P.N.C. speakers often displayed a remarkable variety of conflicting views, even on relatively specific topics. John Carter, for example, might deliver a talk on how the P.N.C. intended to attract private capital and build up many new industries. The following speaker, perhaps A. L. Jackson or Jane Phillips-Gay, would emphasize the party's plans for controlling private enterprise and putting an end to the exploitation of Guianese workers. This range of views made it extremely difficult for the Executive Committee to reach an agreement on the party's official policy statement. In fact, such an agreement was not reached until only a few months before the 1961 elections, and it might not have been reached even then if Rawle Farley, a Guianese economist from the University College of the West Indies, had not been brought in by Burnham to mediate the situation and help draft a policy statement.

Although ideological problems hampered the P.N.C.'s campaign efforts vis-a-vis the opposition forces, they did not present a serious obstacle to party unity. In part, this was due to the fact that most of the Afro-Guianese intellectuals who are inclined to hold relatively rigid ideological views are also inclined to belong to the Peoples Progressive Party. More importantly, however, by 1960, the Afro-Guianese intellectuals had become acutely sensitive to the threat of Indian domination. The anxiety generated by apanjaht politics took precedence over their ideological views. As one member of the P.N.C.'s Executive Committee stated in an interview, "Burnham's outlook is too radical for me on most issues; but man, this fight is now for survival and the Afro-Guianese must stick together or lose the country to the Indians and the communists."

As of September, 1960, the P.N.C.'s organizational strategy did not call for a united front based exclusively on the African section. According to plan, the front was to include the Portuguese, the Chinese, and hopefully the Amerindians. However, in November, 1960, this plan was abruptly changed, and thereafter the P.N.C.'s organizational activities became increasingly focused along sectional lines. The factors that precipitated this turn of events had very little to do with apanjaht politics as such. Specifically, they had to do with the failure on the part of the Portuguese to throw their support behind Burnham and the P.N.C.

In 1959, when the Colonial Office entered into constitutional discussions with Guianese political leaders, a group of Portuguese businessmen and a small group of anti-Jagan East Indians, mostly labor leaders, began to meet with one another to determine what might be done to prevent another P.P.P. victory in 1961. Subsequently, Peter D'Aguiar emerged as a spokesman for this group. Recognizing their political weaknesses, they charged D'Aguiar with the responsibility of entering into negotiations with Burnham to see if a deal might be worked out whereby they could join forces with the Peoples National Congress. These negotiations with Burnham were carried on during the latter part of 1959 and most of 1960. As previously indicated, this represented the sort of move which Burnham and his associates had hoped the Portuguese would undertake. However, the P.N.C. was not quite prepared for the kind of deal that D'Aguiar and his supporters would ultimately try to negotiate.

In effect, D'Aguiar proposed the following package to the P.N.C.'s Executive Committee. D'Aguiar and his associates would join the P.N.C. and make their membership public. In addition, they would provide the P.N.C. with all the financial backing it needed to organize a massive campaign against Jagan and the P.P.P. In exchange for this support, the P.N.C. would give D'Aguiar's group nine of the fifteen seats on its Executive Committee. Burnham would remain the party leader. In the event of victory, Burnham would become Prime Minister, and D'Aguiar would become the Minister of Trade and Industry. In other words, the Portuguese business community, along with a few Indian labor leaders of little consequence, offered to purchase the Peoples National Congress. The offer did not even involve a question of merger, because D'Aguiar and his group did not represent an organized political party.

Needless to say, the leaders of the P.N.C. were insulted by D'Aguiar's offer. As Burnham stated, "He wanted to buy the party as though it were a box of empties being returned to his brewery." Nevertheless, in view of the support which D'Aguiar claimed to have, Burnham was instructed by his Executive Committee to make a counter offer. Specifically, the P.N.C. offered to give D'Aguiar six seats on its Executive Committee, providing he could fill four of these seats with the East Indian supporters he claimed to have among the members of the Rice Producers' Association. D'Aguiar accepted the offer. However, when he returned his list of nominees for the Executive Committee, it included himself, two members of the Rice Producers' Association, and three Portuguese businessmen of no political status.

The P.N.C. rejected D'Aguiar's list of candidates. Burnham's Executive Committee reasoned that unless D'Aguiar were able to bring into the party Indian leaders of political status, men capable of mustering support in areas where the P.P.P. was strong, he could contribute very little to the party's strength except by way of financial support. Moreover, if the P.N.C. accepted D'Aguiar's list of candidates, it would not only provide Jagan with substantial evidence that the party had sold out to "imperialist" capitalists, but it might also serve to alienate the support of important Afro-Guianese labor leaders. Consequently, the P.N.C. decided that it was better off proceeding without D'Aguiar's support. Considering the fact that the Portuguese had no choice but to vote for the P.N.C. or the P.P.P., and considering that they were not very likely to vote for the latter, this appeared to be a wise course of action.

As these decisions were taken, the P.N.C. did not anticipate that D'Aguiar would organize a third party. However, on October 4, 1960, D'Aguiar announced that "all connection with the P.N.C. has been severed," and the "only alternative now is to form a new party" because "all other parties are not working in the interest of the country." On the following day, the United Force was launched. Approximately fifty businessmen, mostly Portuguese, and the East Indian leaders of the Man Power Citizens' Association (e.g., Richard Ishmael, Rupert Tello, and Cleveland Charran) pledged their support to Peter D'Aguiar and the new party.

The emergence of the United Force created serious organizational problems for the P.N.C. For one thing, it diminished the possible sources of funding for the party. It also disrupted Burnham's plans for mobilizing a united non-Indian front in opposition to the P.P.P. More importantly, it opened up a second front in the election campaign—a front that the P.P.P. could largely ignore, while the P.N.C. could not.

For example, the composition of the United Force was of such a nature that it could not possibly attract support from the East Indian peasants and sugar workers. In fact, the association of M.P.C.A. leaders with D'Aguiar was an asset to the P.P.P., because it gave substance to Jagan's claim that these men were "capitalist stooges" and that the M.P.C.A. was only a "company union." Apart from the Portuguese, the Amerindians, and a few East Indian businessmen and labor leaders, the only other support that the United Force could possibly mobilize was to be found in Burnham's political camp. It was to be found in the urban areas, particularly among the middle class Afro-Guianese, or it was not to be found at all.

Even before D'Aguiar's party selected its name, an effort was made by the U.F. to split the Afro-Guianese middle class away from the P.N.C. The U.F. leaked a rumor to the *Guiana Graphic* that John Carter and other members of the P.N.C. who once belonged to the United Democratic Party were about to disassociate themselves from Burnham and join forces with D'Aguiar. Although this proved to be nothing more than a rumor, it fell sufficiently within the realm of possibility to be taken seriously by many P.N.C. supporters. Thus, at a P.N.C. meeting scheduled early in October, a motion was passed requesting the former members of the U.D.P. to reaffirm their loyalty to the party. In response to this motion, John Carter delivered a speech in which he asserted that it was not his intention, or the intention of any of his old U.D.P. associates, to join the United Force in opposition to the P.N.C.

With the emergence of the United Force, a change in attitude began to develop among the Afro-Guianese. They began to feel that they were caught up in a racial war for political survival. In the rural areas of the country, the Afro-Guianese were up against the apanjaht politics of the Jagan government and the East Indian masses. And now, in the urban areas, they were opposed by the economic power of the white Portuguese community.

Most Afro-Guianese intellectuals did not find it difficult to comprehend apanjaht politics. In many ways, it represented a national pattern of relationships between Africans and Indians that was not too different from the pattern of relationships that had existed for more than a century in the rural villages. As Afro-Guianese intellectuals perceived the situation, apanjaht politics was an unfortunate development for which the P.P.P. could be blamed, but it was also something that was to be expected once the nationalist movement had disintegrated. John Carter, for example, recognized this fact of Guianese life when he stated, "Guiana will become a nation only when this heterogeneous conglomeration of peoples becomes a homogeneous mass."[15]

By way of contrast, the Afro-Guianese intellectuals could not understand the negative response of the Portuguese to Burnham's

[15] Quoted from a recorded speech delivered by John Carter at a P.N.C. political rally in Georgetown on October 7, 1960.

political overtones. To be sure, they were aware that the Portuguese had always occupied a higher position than themselves in the structure of colonial society. They were also aware of the color barrier between the two groups. But colonial society was dying, and the color barrier was no longer fashionable. The Afro-Guianese felt that they shared a common culture with the Portuguese. Neither group participated in the traditions of South Asia. Both groups were Western in outlook and attitude. Both were Christian. Both were predominantly urban. And both were fundamentally anti-Communist. Thus, the Afro-Guianese intellectuals attributed the response of the Portuguese to class and racial prejudice. As they perceived the situation, the Portuguese were simply too prejudiced to bring themselves to associate with their former domestics.

Because of these developments, the P.N.C. leaders understood that it was no longer possible for them to mobilize a non-Indian front in opposition to the P.P.P. In addition, they understood that the P.N.C. could not win the 1961 elections. However, they did not consider themselves to be defeated. Knowing the Guianese political situation, if the P.N.C. could survive the elections with a significant vote, they also knew that they would control most of the labor unions in the urban sector as well as the majority of the government workers. If such power could be secured, Burnham believed that the P.N.C. could make demands which the Jagan government could not possibly ignore without jeopardizing its own existence.

However, the ability of the P.N.C. to survive the elections with this kind of power depended entirely upon the size of the Afro-Guianese vote. From the point of view of the party's Executive Committee, the P.N.C. had to emerge from the elections with an almost unanimous African vote if it was to secure enough support to contend with the Jagan government.[16] Thus, as other considerations receded into the background, the P.N.C. undertook the implementation of an organizational strategy designed to alienate every possible African vote from the opposition parties. Needless to say, such a strategy revolved around the issue of racial politics.

In effect, between October, 1960, and August, 1961, the P.N.C. employed a strategy of reverse racialism combined with a program of anticommunism. In other words, P.N.C. leaders did not openly and publicly call for an African vote. Instead, they devoted most of

[16] Based on interviews with members of the Executive Committee of the P.N.C.

their campaign efforts to informing the African people how the P.P.P. was practicing apanjaht politics in order to mobilize the Indian community for the purpose of bringing British Guiana under Communist rule. The purpose of this strategy was to impress upon the African people the idea that their continued freedom depended entirely upon their voting as a bloc in opposition to the P.P.P. and the East Indian population.

A similar strategy was adopted by the P.N.C. with respect to the Portuguese and the United Force. For example, in May, 1961, John Carter declared that racial integration was most desirable, but "complete integration is impossible just now. The Indians," Carter stated, "will support the P.P.P. If the P.P.P. is to be beaten the bulk of African people will have to vote as a bloc together with minorities and dissident Indians. If racial minorities are going to make any contribution to the elections they will have to throw in their lot with one or the other of the major racial groups however distasteful it might be for them to follow an Indian or African leader." Carter continued, "The mass of Africans and Indians do not trust any leadership from outside. They have too long been exploited and discriminated against by people with white skins."[17]

In summary, the Afro-Guianese cultural section shared the threat of Indian domination on several fronts. In rural areas, Indian expansion threatened the existence of villages to which urban Africans frequently retired. African workers also felt threatened because industrial development lagged at the expense of Jagan's agricultural programs. Because of Jagan's efforts to "Indianize" the civil service, African civil servants also displayed considerable anxiety. When the Jagan government mounted a program to take charge of all denominational schools that had been built with government money, African schoolteachers and headmasters were also threatened by apanjaht politics. At the same time, because of the color-class continuum, Africans also felt rejected by the Portuguese and other elements of Guianese society. It was along these lines, therefore, that the organizational activity of the P.N.C. was focused.

In the rural areas, P.N.C. politicians emphasized the threat of Indian expansion and what Jagan's agricultural program could do to their "ancestral" land. They pointed to villages in the Courantyne area where Indians were already squatting on African land, apparently

[17] As quoted in *The Daily Chronicle,* May 11, 1961.

with P.P.P. encouragement. Also in the Courantyne area, some African land had been taken over by the government for development schemes. P.N.C. politicians explained how the leasehold system in these schemes would force Africans to give up what little they had accumulated since their fathers were emancipated. They noted that even the rural health centers constructed by the government were being located in Indian villages. All of these things represented sources of fear that the P.N.C. effectively exploited in order to consolidate an African front.

In the urban areas, in addition to a vigorous anti-Communist campaign, the P.N.C. made a special effort to secure the support of the African-dominated labor unions. Particularly important were the various civil service unions (e.g., teachers, postal workers, government clerks, transportation, communications, etc.) and the industrial unions (e.g., building trades, mine workers, printers, etc.). In the event of a P.P.P. victory, these unions, being critical to the economy as well as to the normal administrative operations of government, represented major sources of power that could be used most effectively to oppose the government. Almost without exception, these unions were brought into the P.N.C. organization. Even the British Guiana Mine Workers' Union, a group that had once opposed Burnham, joined the P.N.C. camp to stem the tide of apanjaht politics.

Thus, the P.N.C. politically organized the African cultural section in opposition to Indian nationalism. The success of this strategy is measured by the results of the 1961 elections. Although the P.N.C. captured only 11 of the 35 seats contested, it emerged with a popular vote of 89,000, just 3,000 short of that received by the Peoples Progressive Party.

## PROLOGUE TO CONFLICT

Before the disintegration of Guiana's comprehensive nationalist movement, maximal cultural sections did not comprise politically organized groups competing with one another for national power. To be sure, Indians and Africans competed with one another. However, they usually competed directly as individuals or indirectly as groups separately organized to achieve particular objectives vis-à-vis the European community. Direct competition, for the most part, was limited, nonpolitical, and confined to the field of communal activities.

As a matter of fact, the differential adaptation of the two cultural sections to the institutions of colonial society precluded extensive competition between their respective members. The advent of nationalist politics and the subsequent disintegration of the nationalist movement altered this pattern of relationships.

The seeds of inevitable conflict between Africans and East Indians were sown as a result of the organizational decisions that were made by nationalist political leaders. It has been shown that these decisions were shaped by a variety of considerations and pressures. Ultimately, however, they were made with a view toward securing the positions of power about to be vacated by the British. As the 1961 elections drew to a close, the fruits of these decisions became increasingly evident.

The final months of the election campaign were marked by increased racial tension, threats of intimidation, and sporadic outbreaks of physical violence. In Bartica, for example, Cheddi Jagan was struck by a stone at a political meeting. In the African village of Buxton, P.P.P. speakers, including Janet Jagan, were forced from their platform and made to disband by an angry mob of Afro-Guianese. In the villages of Kitty and Agricola, P.P.P. speakers were pelted with rotten eggs. At Wismar, Christenburg, and Mackenzie City, P.P.P. speakers were driven from their platforms and not allowed to continue their political meetings.

Similar occurrences took place with respect to the P.N.C. In areas heavily populated by East Indians, P.N.C. supporters were frequently intimidated. In Indian villages on the Courantyne Coast, Burnham was struck with a brick and pelted with rotten eggs. In Sheet Anchor, he was struck with a broken bottle. When P.N.C. posters were put on African homes, the windows were broken and the inhabitants threatened with reprisals. At Plantation Enmore, P.N.C. speakers were forced to discontinue their meeting when the tires on their vehicles were slashed and the wires of their public address system were cut.

By August, 1961, practically every scheduled political meeting presented the risk of a racial riot. Fortunately, however, none materialized. The sporadic acts of violence that occurred were of such a nature that no one was seriously injured, and they did not become pandemic. Nevertheless, by the time of the elections, relationships between Africans and East Indians had reached a boiling point. Moreover, nationalist politicians were fully conscious of this fact. In interviews, several of them expressed a firm conviction that a wave of violence was about to sweep over Guiana, regardless of the outcome of the elections. As one nationalist put it, "Jagan will not give up Guiana and the Africans can no longer afford to let him have it."

After Jagan's election victory, the fear of racial violence was widespread in Guianese society. In fact, it was so extreme in some quarters of the African community that two of its more prominent leaders, Sidney King and H. H. Nicholson, formed a militant organization called the Society for Racial Equality. Actually, the S.R.E. did not advocate an integrated Guianese society based on racial equality. Rather, it dedicated itself to the protection of the African people. It expressed the belief that if Guiana achieved independence under Jagan, "it would be a country with Africans as slaves to East Indians." To prevent this from occurring, the S.R.E. petitioned the governments of the United States, the United Kingdom, the Soviet Union, India, Ghana, and Nigeria to establish an international commission for the purpose of partitioning Guiana into three separate but equal zones—an African Zone, an East Indian Zone, and a Free Zone in which those who wished to live with the other races could feel free to do so. Obviously, the S.R.E. was not taken seriously except by those who belonged to it.

Between 1961 and 1964, the Jagan government was confronted with one serious political crisis after another. The story of these crises is now a matter of historical record. Most of them developed out of the organizational strategies of the nationalist parties. Certainly, the first of these crises, the February crisis of 1962, represented a conscious effort on the part of the opposition parties to bring down the Jagan government before it could undertake negotiations for independence.

On this particular occasion, general strikes were called by African-dominated unions, ostensibly in opposition to Jagan's budget and tax proposals as well as to changes in the civil service benefit programs and the introduction of a compulsory savings program. When the government made an effort to prevent an outbreak of violence by placing a ban on public gatherings within a 300-yard radius of the public buildings, Peter D'Aguiar and L. F. S. Burnham led a protest demonstration which was comprised of approximately 60,000 Afro-Guianese and Portuguese. Only 150 police officers were available to control the mob. As was to be expected, a riot developed and continued intermittently for more than a week. Before the riot was quelled by British troops, the city's business district was in a shambles

Practically every East Indian shop had been gutted, several lives had been lost, and the country's economy was seriously disrupted.

Although the February riots failed to bring down the Jagan government, they did provide Burnham and D'Aguiar with sufficient causes to press Her Majesty's Government for certain changes before granting independence. Specifically, both leaders insisted that new elections be held before independence under a system of proportional representation. Under such a system, the entire country is treated as one constituency, and each voter casts a single ballot for a party list. Each party is given a number of seats in proportion to the total number of votes it represents. Thus, in order for a political party to form a government without a coalition, it must aggregate a vote in excess of 50 per cent of the total votes cast.

Clearly, the change that Burnham and D'Aguiar proposed with respect to proportional representation could only work to their own advantage. Although the P.P.P. has always managed to secure a majority under the electoral system known as first-past-the-post, it has never been able to aggregate 50 per cent of the votes.[18] One reason for this is that the East Indian population comprises something less than 50 per cent of the total Guianese population. In addition, compared to the Afro-Guianese, the East Indian population is younger and contains proportionately fewer individuals of voting age. Thus, when Burnham and D'Aguiar pressed their demands at the constitutional talks that were held in London during 1962 and 1963, Jagan countered with a plea to lower the voting age to eighteen in order to compensate for some of the losses that the new system would entail for the P.P.P.

Presented with the opportunity to rid itself of the problems of Guianese nationalism, and possibly with the view in mind that the United States was willing, if not eager, to assume the responsibility for these problems because of its posture with respect to the Caribbean and Latin America, the Colonial Office rejected Jagan's demands and decided in favor of Burnham and D'Aguiar. Elections were scheduled for December, 1964. They were to be based on proportional representation, and there was to be no lowering of the voting age.

These decisions touched off still another political crisis. In effect,

[18] Under the system of first-past-the-post a party's candidate needs to win only a majority within the constituency to be elected.

they forced Jagan to the realization that the P.P.P. could not secure power and independence on the basis of constitutional change. More specifically, he accused the opposition of having used revolutionary tactics to achieve its political objectives. The P.P.P., Jagan argued, had no alternative but to adopt a similar strategy. Thus, after Jagan returned from the London talks, a wave of terror and racial violence swept the country. It was concentrated primarily on the sugar estates and directed against the sugar industry and the Afro-Guianese. Before it was over, more than 200 persons had lost their lives, and thousands of acres of sugar cane had been destroyed. In spite of these developments, however, the Colonial Office did not alter its position with respect to the elections.

In the 1964 elections, approximately 96 per cent of the electorate voted, while British troops continued to maintain law and order. The voting followed the same pattern as in previous elections. The P.P.P. received 45.8 per cent of the total vote; the P.N.C. ran second with 40.5 per cent; and D'Aguiar's United Force received 12.4 per cent. However, under proportional representation, the results differed significantly from those of previous elections. The P.P.P.'s proportion of the vote gave Jagan twenty-four seats. The P.N.C. won twenty-two seats. The remaining seven seats were won by the United Force. Thus, only a coalition government could be formed, and it was a foregone conclusion that Jagan and the P.P.P. would be excluded from the coalition. As expected, Burnham and D'Aguiar joined forces to form the government, but their political parties continued to remain independent.

Since Burnham's election in 1964, the P.N.C. appears to have made a concerted effort to alienate the East Indian community from the P.P.P. Burnham and other P.N.C. leaders have made numerous goodwill trips to East Indian villages. East Indians also have been appointed to committees designed to redress the imbalance of race in various government departments. Three East Indians serve in Burnham's cabinet. In addition, more than $24 (U.S.) million in aid has poured into Guiana from Britain and the United States for the purpose of bolstering Burnham's government, and much of this money has been spent in East Indian districts. In spite of these efforts, however, there is little evidence to suggest that apanjaht politics is no longer a dynamic force in Guianese political life.

It may appear reckless to hazard a prediction with respect to Guiana's immediate future. Constitutional talks were held in 1965.

Although Jagan boycotted these talks, the Colonial Office proceeded to schedule independence for May, 1966.[19]

However, it does not appear that independence will substantially alter the internal political situation. The forces of pluralism cut deeply into the structure of Guianese society. Moreover, in the past ten years these forces have been extremely aggravated by nationalist politics. As a result, Guiana has not yet been able to develop new national institutions capable of integrating the various cultural sections that make up its population. Thus, the forces of pluralism are still available for those who wish to exploit them for political purposes. In the meantime, the power struggle among Guiana's nationalist leaders has neither subsided nor changed in its organizational character. In view of these conditions, it would appear that independence will launch Guiana into a new and possibly a more dangerous phase of instability and conflict.

---

[19] British Guiana received its independence May 26, 1966. Simultaneously, the country's name was changed to *Guyana*.

*CHAPTER 7*

# CULTURAL PLURALISM AND NATIONALIST POLITICS

IN THE PRECEDING CHAPTERS WE HAVE ATTEMPTED TO PRESENT A SERIES of observations in such a way as to delineate the dimensions of cultural pluralism in Guianese society. We have also attempted to relate these dimensions to the dynamics of Guianese nationalism. The investigation of the relationship between the conditions of pluralism and the dynamics of nationalism has proceeded in the nature of a case study. As a consequence, the analysis has focused primarily on substantive issues. However, because of the problem under investigation, and because of the analytical framework employed to investigate it, the analysis has not been far removed from important theoretical issues. Thus, some generalization is possible.

One theoretical problem with which this study has been concerned has to do with the conception of the plural society. In the literature of social science, the concept "cultural pluralism" has been used extensively to describe the pattern of sociocultural integration characteristic of many newly emerging nations. Edward Shils, for example, has stated that almost everywhere in Africa and Asia, ". . . the societies consist of relatively discrete collectivities—ethnic, communal, caste, religious, or linguistic—that have little sense of identity with one another or with the national whole."[1] However, efforts to conceptualize social and cultural pluralism and to define the dimensions of a plural society precisely have been both numerous and extremely ambiguous. The problem is whether or not the concept "cultural pluralism" should be dismissed as a "cliché of common-

[1] Edward Shils, "On the Comparative Study of New States," in Clifford Geertz (ed.), *Old Societies and New States* (New York: Free Press of Glencoe, 1963), p. 3.

sense sociology."[2] Can the concept be developed systematically so as to provide research advantage for examining the problems of unity and diversity in new nations? If so, what are the limitations of its use, and what explanatory value does it have?

A second theoretical issue with which this study has been concerned has to do with the problem of political instability and conflict associated with nationalism in new nations. How are instability and conflict to be explained? Following the work of Furnivall, a number of social scientists have suggested that nationalism within a plural society is a disruptive force which tends to shatter, rather than consolidate, the social order.[3] Those who are inclined to this point of view have not been too clear about the role pluralism plays in nationalist politics. Is pluralism a sufficient and necessary condition of conflict and instability? Given the conditions of pluralism and the competition for power among nationalist leaders, are political conflict and instability inevitable? Can the forces of pluralism be managed? If so, what are the sources of political instability and conflict?

With reference to these theoretical issues, the point of view expressed in this study may be stated as follows: The dynamics of nationalist politics in British Guiana, and perhaps in other new nations of a plural type, can be most fully understood in terms of the organizational strategies nationalist leaders employ to make existing sociocultural patterns functional with respect to the changes that are taking place. Most of the information needed to elaborate upon this point of view has been introduced in previous chapters, and here it will simply be reinterpreted in the context of the theoretical problems under consideration.

---

[2] Geertz prefers the concept "primordial sentiments" to such concepts as "pluralism," "tribalism," "parochialism," "communalism," "and other clichés of commonsense sociology." Apart from this preference in terms, Geertz has in mind essentially the same phenomena to which I have applied the concept "pluralism." The fact of the matter is that any concept can be construed as a commonsense cliché unless it is used in conjunction with a relatively systematic frame of reference. It is to be regretted that Geertz does not provide such a frame of reference. However, his article provides an excellent review of the plural character of new nations. See Clifford Geertz, "The Integrative Revolution," *ibid.*, pp. 103–57.

[3] For an excellent summary of Furnivall's description of the plural society, see M. G. Smith, *Stratification in Grenada* (Los Angeles: University of California Press, 1965), pp. 1–8. For additional references on the subject of pluralism and nationalist politics, see Gabriel A. Almond and James S. Coleman (eds.), *The Politics of The Developing Areas* (Princeton: Princeton University Press, 1960). Also see the article by Coleman, "Current Political Movements in Africa," *The Annals,* Vol. 298 (March, 1955), pp. 95–108.

## THE STRUCTURAL DIMENSIONS OF PLURALISM

In developing an analytical framework for the analysis of social and cultural pluralism, it has been suggested that the definition of the plural society must take into account two related sets of facts. First, it must take into account the extent to which particular groups display different systems of culture as evidenced by the activities their members engage in. Second, it must also take into account the level at which social activities serve to maintain cultural differentiation as the basis for sociocultural integration. The criteria used to determine the degree of cultural differentiation between groups are structural. It has been assumed that the institutional structures which serve to regulate the activities of individuals in groups are expressive of the cultural values characteristic of the groups in question. From this assumption, it follows that different institutional structures serve to distinguish different cultures and social units.[4]

In extending this analytical framework further, a distinction was drawn between two general types of institutional structures: (1) those that function with respect to the organization of social activities within local communities (*local institutions*); and (2) those that function to link the activities of individuals and groups to the wider sphere of societal activity (*broker institutions*). Local and broker institutional structures provide the coordinates for determining the degree of cultural differentiation between groups as well as the level of sociocultural integration that exists among groups which participate in a common cultural tradition.

To the extent that local institutional structures are valid only for particular groups, the groups in question participate in different cultural systems. Such groups constitute *minimal* or local cultural sections. On the other hand, when broker institutional structures serve to integrate nationally local groups which are culturally similar, such groups constitute *maximal* or national cultural sections. The plural society has been defined as one that contains *maximal* or national cultural sections.

As defined, the plural model establishes an order of logical priority. In other words, maximal cultural sections presuppose the existence of minimal cultural sections. If minimal cultural sections are not

[4] This conceptualization is implicit in Parsons' discussion of institutional structures. See Talcott Parsons, "The Position of Sociological Theory," *American Sociological Review*, 13 (1948), 155–64, particularly pp. 159–60.

found to exist in an empirical setting, then the plural model has little heuristic value for the analysis of the society under investigation. Thus, this analysis of Guianese society began with a comparative study of local institutional activities among Africans and East Indians, the largest and most politically significant groups in the population.

To recapitulate, it was found that Africans and East Indians form separate and comparatively different kinds of social communities. Even though many of them may live together in disproportionate numbers in particular villages or on plantations, their social worlds remain relatively autonomous. Their kinship networks are not homologous, and this, among other considerations, makes intermarriage somewhat difficult. They do not participate in the same religious traditions. They recreate separately or in competition with one another. Generally speaking, they do not form voluntary groups with one another unless pressured to do so by external governmental agencies. In the village, Africans and Indians attend the same school, but the school is usually Christian, and Indians resent this imposition. More importantly, Africans and Indians value local economic resources differently. They display different patterns of economic and social mobility. And they have markedly different orientations toward authority. In short, at the communal level of sociocultural integration, there are no social structures which serve to bring Africans and East Indians together in the expression of a common system of cultural values.

To follow the order of logical priority set forth in the definition of the plural model, the second phase of the analysis concerned itself with a comparative study of broker institutional activities. With respect to these institutional structures, the analysis revealed that the forces of unification and acculturation are at work in Guianese society. Educational institutions are one case in point. The organization of educational institutions is partially controlled by the government and relatively uniform in terms of educational content. However, the content of Guianese education is distinctly British in origin, and Christian denominational bodies exercise considerable control over the vast majority of the schools. As a consequence, educational institutions have been able to modify East Indian values and thereby mediate the relationships between Africans and East Indians, particularly in certain intellectual circles. Nevertheless, because of the system of dual control of the schools, educational institutions have not been able to generate a new national culture equally acceptable to both groups.

Commercial and industrial organizations represent another important source of unification. Almost all of the large commercial and industrial firms in Guiana employ East Indians as well as Africans. Thus, these organizations represent integrated pluralities. However, when one considers the corporate structures of most of these organizations, it is evident that East Indians and Africans tend to be allocated to different occupational statuses on the basis of ascriptive criteria. These practices are also changing, but the changes that are taking place are too recent to have generated new values capable of integrating the groups in question.

Market institutions represent still another important source of unification in Guianese society. The price mechanism, for example, is a common structural denominator for the expression of economic values. Obviously, this facilitates certain kinds of transactions between the members of different cultural groups. At the same time, however, it should be noted that the price mechanism is also a means by which the cultural values of different groups can be expressed as well as reinforced. In addition, the colonial character of Guiana's market economy imparts to it certain multicentric features. The agricultural and industrial sectors of the economy comprise relatively independent spheres of market activity, and East Indians are significantly more interested in and dependent upon the agricultural sector than are the Africans. Thus, market institutions may mediate certain types of relationships between the two groups, but they have not, as yet, contributed significantly to their unification.

Apart from these tendencies toward unification, Africans and East Indians continue to form separate and relatively well-integrated maximal cultural sections. The broker institutional structures that function to maintain cultural differentiation as the basis for social integration include the communications media, trade unions and labor organizations, agencies of the public service, religious and ethnic associations, and political parties. The communications media are owned primarily by European interests, but they are staffed mostly by Africans. While Africans and Indians belong to trade unions in overwhelming numbers, they belong to different unions operating in different sectors of the economy. Also, until very recently, the public services have displayed a racial imbalance strongly in favor of the Africans.[5] Religious and ethnic associations are exclusive in their mem-

[5] B. A. N. Collins, "Racial Imbalance in Public Services and Security Forces," *Race*, 3 (1966), 235–53.

berships and contribute significantly to the integration of similar minimal cultural sections. And, finally, since the Burnham-Jagan split, political parties have catered primarily to the interests of cultural sections.

In conclusion, the patterns of sociocultural integration that exist among the different segments of the Guianese population correspond almost completely with the structural dimensions of the plural model as defined in this book. This correspondence applies to structural forms as well as to the cultural values which these forms express. Thus, Africans comprise minimal cultural sections. The relationships that exist within these local groups in terms of family and kinship networks, children's property, religious practices, associational ties, and the like, extend outward to include relationships between individuals from similar groups. These external ties are supported and reinforced by institutional structures that bind Africans together in terms of their race, religion, education, occupational interests, mobility patterns, and organizational memberships. Such institutional structures not only integrate Africans as a national community, but they also function to express the values that provide this community with a sense of cultural identity.

A similar pattern of sociocultural integration exists with respect to the East Indians. The kinship group lies at the center of Indian sociocultural integration. Its stability is reinforced by religious beliefs, traditional marriage forms, economic functions and, to a degree, vestiges of caste. Relatives are bound together in ever widening circles of diminishing strength. The practice of village exogamy creates affinal ties between one Indian community and another. These circles of relationship are further extended by ceremonial responsibilities and friendship ties. At the periphery of these circles, broker institutions serve to relate Indians to one another in terms of religious and ethnic associations, trade union membership, economic interests, and the like. Ultimately, this pattern of sociocultural integration involves a value system which provides East Indians with a cultural identity as a national community.

## PLURALISM AND SOCIOCULTURAL CHANGE

As has been shown, British Guiana is a plural society. From the point of view of system analysis, the interdependent units of Guianese society tend to comprise culturally differentiated groups rather than socially differentiated persons. The integration of the system results primarily from the complementary participation of these groups in a unitary political economy. The institutional structures that make up the political economy were created and maintained by British colonial power. Until recent times, these structures have persisted with a minimum of change. In view of these considerations, what are the structural implications of pluralism for the process of sociocultural change? Two points need to be emphasized with respect to this question. One has to do with the functional autonomy of cultural sections. The other has to do with the structure of intersectional relations which results from functional autonomy.

Cultural sections display the characteristics of isomeric systems. That is to say, they are composed of similar organizational elements, but these elements differ in their properties because they are structured differently. Consider, for example, the differences in social stratification between village Indians and Africans.

Within the Indian village, the allocation of status and prestige is heavily weighted in favor of rice millers or large landowners; shopkeepers; pandits; certain types of salaried persons such as teachers, small shopkeepers and landowners; agricultural workers and fishermen; artisans; and unskilled workers. The prestige attached to these statuses, including the prestige attached to the status of pandit, is primarily a function of the economic differentials that obtain between them. Thus, a teacher has more prestige and influence than a small landowner or a small shopkeeper because he has a larger and more reliable source of income. A teacher who also owns land has more prestige than a teacher without land. For the same reason, a teacher has less prestige and influence than a rice miller, a large landowner, or a successful shopkeeper.

By way of contrast, among Africans, the emphasis is placed on educational differentials, age and experience, and personality traits such as a willingness to render service to others. Thus, in the African village, the allocation of status and prestige favors head teachers; older heads who are friendly, reliable, and willing to help others; younger teachers; church workers; civil servants; and good providers, regardless of how they may earn their incomes. The status of teacher is an organizational element in both the Indian and African village, but the properties attached to the status differ because it is structured differently in the stratification system of each village. This difference in structure, in turn, reflects the cultural values of each group.[6]

In summary, the functional autonomy of minimal cultural sections derives from their isomeric character. There are at least three ways in which this is evident. First, the cultural sections to which Africans and Indians belong do not reticulate, i.e., the structures that are functional in the African section do not interpenetrate those which are functional in the Indian section. Second, individual Africans or East Indians cannot easily move from one cultural section to another unless (a) the individual changes his cultural values, or (b) the cultural section into which the individual moves undergoes structural change. For example, an East Indian rice farmer cannot enhance his status among Africans by opening a shop in an African village. Similarly, an African teacher cannot enhance his status by being reassigned to a school in an Indian community. Third, different cultural sections can (and usually do) respond differently and independently to the pressures for change. For example, Indians and Africans have responded differently to the pressures for change generated by the cooperative movement.

From a structural point of view, the difference between the minimal and the maximal cultural section is primarily a difference in scale. Thus, maximal cultural sections also tend to display the characteristics of isomeric systems. This is particularly evident with respect to the differential adaptation of Africans and East Indians to Guiana's colonial economy.

For example, as rice farmers and sugar workers, East Indians comprise a rural proletarian class. Africans who live in rural areas do not belong to this class in large numbers, because they are either part of the urban unemployed or they are elderly persons engaged in subsistence agriculture. Indians do not move out of the rural areas in large numbers. When they do move into the urban sectors, however, it is usually as shopkeepers and businessmen. Those who become teachers generally remain in rural schools. Africans, on the other hand, move out of the rural areas in large numbers, but they rarely move out as businessmen and shopkeepers. For the most part, Africans who move to urban areas do so as mine workers, civil servants, teachers, clerks,

[6] For an extremely systematic treatment of stratification in a plural society, see Smith, *op. cit.*

artisans, dock workers, or domestics. Thus, Africans make up the vast majority of the urban proletariat.

To continue this analysis further, until very recent times, the sources of power in Guianese society have been lodged in the colonial establishment and those groups which implement the decisions of the establishment. As a group, the rural proletariat is more removed from these sources of power than the urban proletariat. It follows from this that Africans tend to occupy a higher position in the power structure of colonial society than Indians. In addition, the traditional patterns of social mobility characteristic of these cultural sections tend to reinforce the status differential existing between them. Thus, similar social positions within different cultural sections are not functionally equivalent, and the position that one occupies within his cultural section does not correspond to the position that one occupies in the society as a whole. The position that one occupies in the society as a whole is, at least in part, a function of the position his cultural section occupies in the power structure of the society.

In view of these considerations, what is the effect of functional autonomy on the structure of intersectional relations? Let us first examine its effect on intersectional relations in the case of minimal cultural sections.

The functional autonomy of minimal cultural sections has a direct effect upon the structure of intersectional relations within the local community. Specifically, functional autonomy tends to confine interpersonal relations between Africans and Indians to role patterns which are relatively segmental, nonaffective, and instrumental. Since competitive advantage is an important feature of such utilitarian role patterns, interpersonal relations tend to be structured in an order of superordination and subordination. Accordingly, the dimension of power is crucial to almost all intersectional relations. Thus, changes within minimal cultural sections which may affect the structure of intersectional relations invariably raise issues of power between Africans and East Indians within local settings.

By way of illustrating the above point, consider the construction of a new health center by the government. Will the government locate the facility in a predominantly African village such as Ann's Grove, or will it be constructed a short distance away in the Indian village of Clonbrook? Who will be placed in charge of the facility, an African or an East Indian? Similarly, where will the new school be located? Or, who is to be made chairman of the regional development committee? Who will process applications for loans at the district office of the cooperative savings and loan society? Ultimately, these decisions affect the competitive advantage that individuals have with respect to intersectional relations. Although the government may not consider these decisions to be political, they are political from the point of view of the Africans and Indians who are affected by them. As a result, in Guianese society, any change promulgated by an agency of the government which affects intersectional relations between minimal cultural sections will have political consequences within the local setting. What, then, is the situation with respect to maximal cultural sections?

It has been shown that the functional autonomy of maximal cultural sections largely derives from the differential status that Africans and Indians have as a result of their adaptation to the institutions of colonial society. Because of this differential status, the prestige and influence attached to the social position that an individual occupies are, in part, a function of the status attached to the cultural section with which the individual is identified. Thus, it is extremely difficult for individual Indians or Africans to improve their life chances without changing their cultural identities or, alternatively, without seeking to improve the status and power of their respective cultural sections. The structural implications of this fact may be viewed more concretely in terms of a few illustrations.

For example, in spite of their prestige and influence within their cultural section, large Indian landowners, rice millers, and businessmen have not been able to exercise as much direct control over the Guianese economy as a few very high-level public servants of African descent. Similarly, in spite of their growing numbers, Indian schoolteachers have not been able to exercise as much influence over educational institutions as African schoolteachers. Also, educated Indians have had considerably less access than educated Africans to those departments of the public service in which Africans exercise a controlling influence. Or, to cite still another example, Indian-dominated labor unions have not been able to command wages for their members comparable to the wages that have been achieved for African workers by many African-dominated labor unions. In other words, the opportunities available to individual Indians and Africans reflect the differential status which their respective cultural groups occupy in the power structure of Guianese society.

In view of these considerations, three points need to be emphasized with respect to intersectional relations between maximal cultural sections. First, at the national level, intersectional relations tend to involve transactions between organized groups rather than individuals. A case in point would be the transactions between Indian- and African-dominated labor unions within the British Guiana Trades Union Council. Second, the functional autonomy of maximal cultural sections tends to confine these intergroup transactions to a struggle for competitive advantage in the national power structure. This is most clearly evident in terms of the competition for power between such groups as the East Indian Association and the League of Coloured Peoples. And, third, any sociocultural change that can affect the structure of intersectional relations between maximal cultural sections will raise issues of national power between Africans and East Indians. The instances of this are almost too numerous to recount but, to cite one example, all of Guiana's economic development programs have raised issues of national power between Africans and East Indians.

To conclude, both minimal and maximal cultural sections display the characteristics of isomeric systems. They are composed of similar organizational elements, but these elements differ in their properties because they are structured according to different cultural values. As a consequence of these differences, cultural sections tend to comprise functionally autonomous units in the overall structure of Guianese society. The functional autonomy of these units, in turn, has certain implications for the structure of intersectional relations both nationally and within local communities.

At the level of local communities, the functional autonomy of cultural sections reduces interpersonal relations between Africans and Indians to the dimension of power. Similarly, at the national level, the functional autonomy of cultural sections tends to confine intergroup relations between Africans and Indians to a competition for national power. It follows from the structure of interpersonal relations that any sociocultural changes capable of altering the order of subordination and superordination between individual Africans and Indians will have political consequences within the local settings in which the changes occur. It follows from the structure of intergroup relations that any sociocultural changes capable of altering the position of Africans and Indians in the national power structure will have consequences for the political order of Guianese society. In other words, the conditions of pluralism in Guianese society are such that the process of sociocultural change is intrinsically a political process at all levels of the social order.

## PLURALISM AND NATIONALIST POLITICS

It has been shown how the integration of Guianese society is based upon a system of social relations between cultural units of unequal status and power. This system derives its traditional force from the differential adaptation of Africans and East Indians to the institutions of British colonialism. The core structure of this system is essentially political. Intersectional relations not only reflect the power structure of the political order under which they are subsumed, but they also serve to express the maintenance or change of that political order.

Herein lies the source of instability which the forces of nationalism are capable of aggravating. The cultural units that make up the Guianese social system enjoy a relatively high degree of functional autonomy. In order for these units to maintain their respective patterns of sociocultural integration, it is necessary that the social system continue to provide for their functional autonomy. Under present circumstances, the functional autonomy of these units is maintained by the differential status they occupy in the power structure of the society. This power structure, in turn, is reinforced by the political order under which it is subsumed. It is precisely the political order of Guianese society that the forces of nationalism seek to change. Thus, in seeking to implement changes in the political order, the forces of nationalism must inevitably pose a threat to the functional autonomy of cultural sections and create a problem of tension management between the groups that these sections represent.[7] A question to which this study has addressed itself is whether or not the nationalist movement can prevent these tensions from culminating in conflict and disrupting the social order. The findings with respect to this question may be summarized as follows.

First, in its early stages of development, the nationalist movement successfully integrated African and East Indian intellectuals as members of a new nationalist elite. The leadership which the members of this elite enjoyed was largely sectional. Moreover, they differed among themselves on issues of political ideology. However, they shared

[7] For a discussion of functional autonomy and tension management in social systems, see Alvin W. Gouldner, "Reciprocity and Autonomy in Functional Theory," in Llewellyn Gross (ed.), *Symposium on Sociological Theory* (Evanston, Ill.: Row, Peterson and Company, 1959), pp. 241–70.

a commitment to the goal of national independence. They also shared a commitment to the politico-cultural integration of Guianese society. In view of these commitments, therefore, ideological issues and the conditions of pluralism did not present an obstacle to the movement's further development.

Nevertheless, the nationalist movement could not help generating tensions between cultural sections during this early period. These tensions became increasingly apparent after 1950, when the Peoples Progressive Party was organized in preparation for constitutional change. They were most apparent in the case of the Portuguese and other Europeans who opposed the movement in favor of the status quo. They were evident also with respect to certain groups of Africans and East Indians who favored independence but who were fearful that sectional interests might be compromised in the process of achieving it.

The tensions existing between Africans and Indians during this early phase of the movement's development did not present the new nationalist elite with an insurmountable problem. As a group, it was comprehensive in its membership. It also was sufficiently committed to independence and national politico-cultural integration to meet the thrust of such sectional organizations as the League of Coloured Peoples and the East Indian Association. Thus, the new nationalist elite succeeded in achieving adequate political integration between Africans and Indians to provide the P.P.P. with a relatively impressive victory in the 1953 elections. Obviously, this display of unity did not remove all or even most of the tensions existing between cultural sections as a result of the impending changes in the Guianese political order. However, it did demonstrate the ability on the part of nationalist leaders to manage these tensions organizationally during the process of change.

Second, the disintegration of Guiana's comprehensive nationalist movement cannot be attributed exclusively to the particularistic forces of pluralism. Since this conclusion follows as much from the logic of the analysis as it does from the data presented, it needs to be elaborated upon in some detail.

As has been shown, the structure of Guianese society is such that the process of sociocultural change is intrinsically a political process at all levels of the social order. It follows from this that any change capable of altering the structure of the society carries with it the potential of stimulating the forces of pluralism, thereby creating a problem of tension management. Whether or not a particular change will create a serious problem of tension management depends upon (1) the degree to which it poses a threat to the functional autonomy of cultural sections and (2) the extent to which organizational control is exercised with respect to its introduction in order to minimize the tension it generates. In any event, these conditions are inherent in the structure of Guianese society, and they created organizational problems for the nationalist movement. However, the existence of these conditions does not explain why the movement failed to solve the organizational problems related to them.

The analytical situation, then, is as follows: Given the fact that Guiana's nationalist leaders both recognized and made a concerted organizational effort to cope with the forces of pluralism which the movement had stimulated, how is it that these forces prevailed? In other words, why did the movement disintegrate? To answer this question, one cannot invoke a constant (e.g., the plural structure of Guianese society) to explain a variable (e.g., the success or failure of the nationalist movement to solve the organizational problems that confronted it).

As we have seen, disintegration resulted from a critical conjuncture of several factors, all of which made it increasingly difficult for nationalist leaders to control organizationally the forces of pluralism. These factors included the ideological factionalism that erupted to the surface within the Peoples Progressive Party, the organization of a conservative opposition to the movement, and the internal pressures that were generated by external international developments.

It is difficult, if not impossible, to weigh these factors and to assign the decisive role of precipitant to any particular one of them. We know what happened to Guiana's nationalist movement, but we can only speculate on what might have happened had one thing or another been different. However, the fact that numerous conditions were equally necessary for disintegration to occur is, as MacIver might suggest, no ground for denying the distinctive role of the precipitant.[8] Therefore, to speculate on the conjunction of these crucial ingredients, it would appear that, more than any other complex of factors, international developments precipitated the disintegration of Guiana's comprehensive nationalist movement.

In other words, between 1952 and 1955, Guiana's comprehensive

[8] R. M. MacIver, *Social Causation* (Boston: Ginn and Company, 1942), pp. 172–84.

nationalist movement fell victim to the cold war. The ideological factionalism which ultimately resulted in the Burnham-Jagan split was directly stimulated by the efforts that were made, chiefly by the United States and the American labor movement, to alienate from hemispheric nationalist movements those nationalists who displayed a propensity for Marxist-Leninist thinking. These efforts were not made openly, and they were not carried out by American governmental intervention or through the usual channels of international diplomacy. Rather, they were made covertly and carried out by the exercise of American power and influence within the context of the international labor movement. This influence and power were so pervasive that some local unions, the British Guiana Mine Workers for example, could hardly negotiate a contract without first seeking the advice of American labor diplomats.

The splits in the Caribbean labor movement that resulted from the struggles of the cold war may not have altered the political climate in Jamaica, Trinidad, or Barbados to any significant degree, but the opposite was the case in Guiana. In Guiana, the position that the Marxists occupied within the nationalist movement was largely a function of a balance of power that existed between them and the non-Marxists. This balance of power, in turn, was based upon the relationships which members of both groups enjoyed with respect to cultural sections, Guianese labor unions, and political allies in the Caribbean. As long as this balance of power was maintained, the nationalist movement existed in a state of dynamic equilibrium. However, the divisions in the Caribbean labor movement altered this balance of political forces.

Specifically, the splits which occurred in the Caribbean labor movement made ideological issues much more critical to Guianese nationalists than organizational questions relating to political tensions between Africans and Indians or such other matters as economic development and constitutional advancement. This provided the conservative opposition with its major source of political leverage, the issue of Communism. Subsequently, these splits served to alienate the Jaganites, an important faction of the nationalist elite, from the Guianese labor movement. In addition, they interjected into Guianese politics the West Indian Federation issue with all of its racial overtones. Ultimately, these developments provoked the disagreements that culminated in the Jagan-Burnham split. In effect, this fragmented the movement's comprehensive leadership and severely impaired its organizational capacity to deal with the forces of pluralism.

Finally, the destructive forces of pluralism in Guianese society were not unleashed by the nationalist movement itself but by the competition for leadership that erupted when the movement fragmented into political factions. Once this internal power struggle emerged, its subsequent course of development was largely predetermined. For example, as long as the colonial establishment retained ultimate power for itself, even though it gave evidence of only marking time, the competition for leadership between nationalist elites had to proceed according to the constitutional and other rules which the establishment imposed. As a result, the only effective organizational adjustments that these elites could make were neocolonial in type.[9] That is to say, in order to mobilize mass support successfully, they would have to employ organizational strategies which accommodated themselves to the realities of the existing structure of colonial power.

As has been pointed out, Guiana's colonial power structure was based upon a system of social relations between cultural sections of unequal status. It follows from the nature of such a system that the major sources of power available to nationalist leaders for organizational purposes are the culturally differentiated groups of which the system is comprised. In the event of any internal power struggle which precludes revolutionary change, and therefore the destruction of the existing power structure, it is inevitable that cultural sections will become organizationally aligned in competitive opposition. This fact was fully recognized by Jagan, Burnham, and other Guianese nationalists. In what has been suggested as a type of neocolonial adjustment, these leaders adopted organizational strategies designed to make existing sociocultural patterns functional with respect to the internal struggle for constitutional power. Given a neocolonial setting in which cultural sections are politically juxtaposed in a struggle for national power, is violent conflict probable? In general, the answer is yes.

Any change resulting from a direct power struggle between cultural sections will not only reinforce their functional autonomy, but it will also tend to alter their respective positions in the power structure. Therefore, it needs to be emphasized that the political opposition of such units will increase the problem of tension management direct-

[9] I refer to this as a typical neocolonial adjustment because it is predicated upon the proposition, largely imposed by colonial power, that the status quo contains numerous elements worth preserving. Important among these elements are the existing structure of power, economic institutions, and a "rich" diversity of cultures. See Kwame Nkrumah, *Neo-Colonialism: The Last Stage of Imperialism* (New York: International Publishers, 1965).

ly in proportion to the rate and degree of sociocultural change. If such changes are extensive and occur so rapidly that compensatory mechanisms cannot be put into motion, the tensions generated between cultural sections are likely to increase to the point of explosion. However, whether or not these tensions will eventuate in violent conflict, particularly violent conflict of an organized nature, will depend largely upon the decisions that nationalist leaders take with respect to them. If nationalist leaders believe that their particular objectives can be furthered by exploiting these tensions, violent conflict will develop.

The above points may be illustrated in the case of British Guiana. When the nationalist movement disintegrated, both Jagan and Burnham were more or less compelled to accept a neocolonial adjustment to the process of sociocultural change. The political organization of cultural sections followed upon these developments. However, the subsequent election of a Jagan government in 1957, and again in 1961, brought about a relatively rapid change in the status of Indians in the power structure of Guianese society. This change not only contributed to the political integration of Africans, but it also generated explosive tensions between Africans and Indians at all levels of the social order.

It was these tensions that were organizationally exploited in 1962, when the opposition made an effort to force the resignation of the Jagan government by promoting a general strike among government workers. Conflict resulted, and it was primarily confined to outbreaks of violence between East Indians and Africans. A very similar situation developed in 1963, and again in 1964, when Jagan made the organizational decision to promote strikes on the sugar estates following his rebuff at the constitutional talks. In this instance, the decision on the part of the Colonial Office to impose a system of proportional representation not only threatened the Jagan government but also threatened the gains which East Indians felt they had achieved under the Jagan government.

Following the election of the Burnham government in 1964, the tensions existing between East Indians and Africans were hastily reduced, or at least temporarily controlled, by the use of certain compensatory mechanisms. For one thing, British troops were kept on the scene for the purpose of maintaining law and order. In addition, several influential members of the Peoples Progressive Party continued to be detained and prevented from engaging in political activities. Also, Burnham made overtures to East Indians by such devices as implementing a study ostensibly designed to correct racial imbalances in the public services. And, finally, the United States and Great Britain provided Guiana with a massive injection of funds to help Burnham restore the economy and placate East Indians by undertaking various kinds of development projects in rural areas.

Whether or not these and similar compensatory mechanisms can reduce the tensions existing between cultural sections to a level below which they are no longer explosive cannot be known for certain. However, to summarize, we can be certain of several things. First, we can be sure that, as long as Guianese society remains plural, sociocultural changes will generate tensions between cultural sections. Second, we can be sure that, as long as these cultural sections are politically juxtaposed, the tensions existing between them will be extremely difficult to manage. Third, violent conflict will result from the political juxtaposition of cultural sections whenever nationalist leaders see fit to exploit the tensions existing between them. And, finally, we can be relatively certain that these generalizations will obtain as long as Guianese nationalist elites accommodate themselves to vestiges of the colonial power structure.

## THE COMPARATIVE STUDY OF NEW NATIONS

It is always easier to understand the history we make for ourselves and others than it is to understand the history that others make for us. Those of us who have lived within the orbit of Western society for more than three centuries have been making history for ourselves as well as others. Perhaps this is no longer the case. Since the end of the Second World War, almost all of the colonies created by the expansion of European power have turned the tables. They have transformed themselves into sovereign states. Still dependent economically, burning with the fever of political instability, untutored in the ways of international politics, these new nations now stand in the world forum. Their leadership demands attention. It proclaims the dawn of a new era—a time during which the former colonial peoples will assert their right to participate with the older and economically developed nations in shaping the affairs of man.

The explosion of these new nations onto the world scene has generated an intense desire on the part of scholars and diplomats to unravel the complex patterns of their existence. Considerable progress has been made toward this objective in the short time since the new nations have come into being. We seem to comprehend the historical forces which have contributed to their origins. We also seem to understand many of the difficulties associated with their economic underdevelopment. However, we do not as yet understand their politics. The clichés of our conventional knowledge have not permitted us to fathom the minds of their politicians. What are the forces that motivate them? What factors do they take into account? How will they act upon them? What organizational tactics will they employ to achieve their objectives? Will they, or can they, achieve political stability?

What troubles us most about these new nations are the forces of instability which nationalism seems to have unleashed in them. For example, practically all of the new nations of Africa have been racked by one type of political crisis or another. Since June, 1965, no less than seven African nations have experienced military coups d'état. Almost everywhere south of the Sahara, tribalism, in one form or another, has been a problem. The situation outside of Africa is not much different. In Cyprus, the Greeks and the Turks periodically stimulate an international crisis of varying proportions. In India, serious tensions exist between Hindus and Muslims and between various regional and linguistic groups. In Ceylon, the Tamils and Sinhalese find it extremely difficult to get along. Even though the military has taken control of the government in Burma, tribalism still poses an obstacle to national unity. The forces of pluralism have disrupted the Federation of Malaysia. And, more recently, Indonesia has experienced a military coup d'état which gave vent to the animosities existing between many of the traditional groups which make up the fabric of Indonesian society. What is the relationship between nationalism and political instability in so many of these new nations?

Obviously, in the absence of detailed comparative data, it would be extremely naive to suggest an answer to the above question. Each one of these new nations differs from the other in tradition, resources, achievements, and in a hundred other particulars. However, there is much that they share in common among themselves and with other nations of the "Third World," including British Guiana.[10] To one degree or another, all of these new states are plural societies with

[10] Irving Louis Horowitz uses the term "Third World" to categorize the non-aligned nations who make up most of the underdeveloped world. See Horowitz's *Three Worlds of Development* (New York: Oxford University Press, 1966).

colonial histories.[11] All of them are economically dependent and underdeveloped—some more than others. In all of them, the impulse toward modernity is overwhelming. All of them are caught up in the struggles of the cold war—some more directly than others. And in all of them, the same forces of nationalism are at work. Thus, the new nations comprise an immensely rich field for the comparative endeavors of social scientists who seek to understand the dynamics of sociocultural change. It is appropriate, therefore, to conclude this analysis of British Guiana by drawing out some of the implications it may have for the comparative study of new nations. We shall consider, first, some specific implications for future research and then move on to more general issues of theory.

The findings with respect to the Guianese situation are conducive to the formulation of certain theoretical propositions concerning the sources of instability and conflict in new nations of the plural type. One of these propositions may be stated as follows: The structural dimensions of system integration in the plural society present a persistent problem of tension management between culturally differentiated groups at all levels of the social order. This problem of tension management is essentially a political problem. It derives its political nature from the fact that the structure of intersectional relations reflects the power structure of the political order under which they are subsumed. Thus, intersectional relationships are primarily relationships of power between culturally differentiated groups of unequal status.

Although the above proposition is valid for British Guiana, its ultimate theoretical value cannot be determined without considerable comparative research.[12] The dimensions of pluralism appear to vary tremendously from one plural society to another. To cite but one example, in Guiana, the vast majority of the population comprises two cultural sections of almost equal size. This also seems to be the case with respect to the Malays and the Chinese in Malaya. However, in Cyprus, the Greeks form the majority of the population, and the Turks comprise a small minority. In the Congo, on the other hand,

[11] See Shils, *op. cit.*, Geertz, *op. cit.*, and, in the same volume, also see McKim Marriott, "Cultural Policy in the New States," pp. 27–56.

[12] This proposition appears to be valid also for Grenada. See M. G. Smith's analysis of "Structure and Crisis in Grenada, 1950–1954," in M. G. Smith, *The Plural Society in the British West Indies* (Los Angeles: University of California Press, 1965), pp. 262–303. It should be noted that this proposition, as well as the two which follow, are fully anticipated by Smith, *ibid.*, pp. 91, 115, 157–58, 170–71, and 320.

there are some 250 separate tribal-linguistic units. Uganda presents still another situation. In Tanzania, there are a multitude of tribal units, but none of them are extremely large. How is the structure of intersectional relations affected by variations in this dimension of pluralism? It is conceivable that intersectional relationships in some plural societies will not be relationships of power and that the problem of tension management between culturally differentiated groups may exist only under special circumstances.

Another theoretical proposition implicated in the Guianese situation is that the process of sociocultural change in the plural society is intrinsically a political process at all levels of the social order. Changes capable of altering intersectional relationships will also alter the power structure in terms of which these relationships are defined. Thus, in the plural system, the process of sociocultural change will increase the problem of tension management.

Much more comparative research is needed before the above proposition can be accepted as a valid generalization. Most of the work that has been done on sociocultural change in plural societies has focused either on the problems associated with the assimilation of European values or has dealt exclusively with one cultural section or another. Very little attention has been paid to the impact of sociocultural change on intersectional relations. However, the research data available on this particular problem would appear to support the proposition that sociocultural change tends to increase the tensions existing between culturally differentiated groups in the plural society.[13]

A third proposition, closely related to the second, is that intersectional relations in the plural society not only reflect the power structure of the political order under which they are subsumed, but they also serve to express the maintenance or change of that political order. Thus, in seeking to change the political order of the society, the forces of nationalism must inevitably pose a threat to the functional autonomy

[13] See *ibid.* J. C. Mitchell refers to such tensions existing between the Bemba and the Nyanja as a result of changes in trade union policies. See J. C. Mitchell, *Tribalism and the Plural Society* (London: Oxford University Press, 1960), p. 23. The Ras Tafari movement in Jamaica would appear to represent a response to the tensions generated by sociocultural change. See G. E. Simpson, "The Ras Tafari Movement in Jamaica: A Study of Race and Class Conflict," *Social Forces,* 34 (1955), 167–70. Also see Henry L. Bretton's analysis of *Power and Stability in Nigeria* (New York: Frederick A. Praeger, 1962). A classic example of tensions generated by the process of sociocultural change in a plural society is provided in Pierre L. van den Berghe's study, *South Africa, A Study in Conflict* (Middletown, Conn., Wesleyan University Press, 1965).

of cultural sections and thereby aggravate the problem of tension management. However, as we have seen, political change of this magnitude will not produce conflict between culturally differentiated groups unless these groups are politically organized and nationalist leaders see fit to exploit the tensions existing between them.

Again, the above proposition needs the scrutiny of comparative research before it can be established as a valid generalization. As has already been noted, numerous observers have invoked the concept of pluralism to explain the instability associated with political change in an assortment of new nations. However, to the author's knowledge, none have developed the concept into an analytical framework capable of carrying the burden of systematic comparative research. Thus, it is not known to what extent intersectional relations serve to express the maintenance of or change in the political order of different plural societies. It is not known to what extent nationalist leaders have been able to manage the tensions generated by the forces of nationalism. It is also not known to what extent nationalist leaders have exploited these tensions organizationally for political purposes.

A final proposition may be phrased as follows: In the plural society, a neocolonial adjustment on the part of nationalist leaders will retard the process of modernization. Such an adjustment retains enough of the old political order to keep alive the tensions inherent in its structure. As a consequence, scarce developmental resources are diverted away from productive programs to programs designed primarily to exploit or to manage the tensions existing between culturally differentiated groups of unequal status and power. Needless to say, this proposition also requires comparative testing before its validity can be ascertained.

In sum, the application of the plural theory to the analysis of new nations would appear to pose a multitude of new and theoretically important research problems. It is not possible to discuss these problems in detail and with reference to specific societies in the present context, but it is hoped that they will be evident to specialists who are interested in pursuing them. Should this be the case, the analysis of the Guianese situation will have made a contribution to our knowledge of new nations.

This study set out to discover the patterns of sociocultural integration characteristic of Guianese society and to determine how these patterns relate to the pressures for change that have been generated by the forces of nationalism. One cannot generalize from the case of one nation to the class of new nations. However, the findings have been productive of generalizations which are in need of further research. There are several issues of a more general theoretical nature which also deserve brief attention.

In a recent statement on the comparative study of new nations, Edward Shils outlined several points which are not only relevant to the present discussion but which are also in need of greater emphasis. Shils noted, among other things, that the central concern of the study of new states is with the formation of coherent societies and polities. It follows from this, Shils suggested, that the study of new states must be "macrosociological," i.e., it must be a study of *societies* as total systems.[14]

In elaborating upon the above points, Shils emphasized that consensus is "the key phenomenon of macrosociology." In other words, the extent to which a population residing within a given territory is a society, and not just a complex of societies ruled by some system of forceful authority, is both of theoretical and practical interest. "In every instance," Shils suggested, "the problem is as follows: How does this institution or practice or belief function in the articulation of the society, in attaching or detaching or fixing each sector in its relationship to the central institutional and value systems of the society?"[15]

In light of Shils's comments, the theory of pluralism may have considerable heuristic value for the comparative study of new nations. There are several reasons for making such a suggestion. First, its analytical framework is macrosociological. It deals with the analysis of societies as total systems. In doing so, however, it does not make the assumption that some institutional structures are more basic than others. On the contrary, it assumes that all institutional structures are expressive of cultural values. Also, it does not make the equally untenable assumption that social systems are unitary in the sense that all of their institutional structures are functionally integrated. Rather, it admits of the possibility that there may be varying degrees of interdependence among social units from one system to another, and it suggests that the most effective way to ascertaining such differences is to focus attention on the functional autonomy of parts.[16]

Another reason the plural theory may prove to be extremely use-

[14] Shils, *op. cit.*, p. 20.
[15] *Ibid.*, p. 23.
[16] Gouldner, *op. cit.*, pp. 241–70.

ful for comparative analysis is that it provides a set of analytical categories in terms of which the social and cultural dimensions of system integration may be empirically delineated. Moreover, in focusing on the problem of system integration, the plural theory does not make the wholly artificial distinction that is frequently made between system integration (the orderly relationships between parts of the system) and social integration (the orderly relationships between actors). The theory deals with these two aspects of the social system simultaneously. Thus, it also avoids making many of the limiting assumptions that are frequently associated with social action theory.[17]

It specifically avoids the assumption that normative consensus, based upon a common system of cultural values, is a functional prerequisite of system integration. It also avoids the assumptions underlying the Hobbesian argument that "society based solely on force is a contradiction in terms."[18] In avoiding these particular assumptions, the comparative range of social system theory is expanded to include modern industrial societies as well as those societies of the colonial type in which elements of force are as important to system integration as are elements of normative consensus.

It should be noted, however, that the plural theory does not assume that normative consensus is an irrelevant dimension of system integration. The plural society, it will be recalled from the analysis, is comprised of culturally differentiated groups rather than socially differentiated persons. The relationships within these groups are relatively diffuse and predicated upon a general value consensus—a common culture. The relationships between these groups are highly specialized, segmented, and depend primarily upon compliance with instrumental norms which are frequently as much imposed as they are accepted. In other words, the plural society is high on consensus within culturally differentiated units and low on consensus between such units. As the functional autonomy of these units diminishes, the reverse tends to be the case.

Still another reason why the plural theory may have considerable heuristic value for the comparative study of new nations is that it

[17] For a discussion of these assumptions, see *ibid.* Also see David Lockwood, "Social Integration and System Integration," in George K. Zollschan and Walter Hirsch (eds.), *Explorations in Social Change* (Boston: Houghton Mifflin Company, 1964), pp. 244–57.

[18] For a discussion of the limitations imposed on social system theory by these assumptions, see M. G. Smith, *The Plural Society in the British West Indies,* pp. vii–xiii. Also see Gouldner, *op. cit.,* pp. 241–70.

does not reify analytical models. The homogeneous, heterogeneous, and plural societies are not postulated as historical entities but as analytical models in terms of which historical entities may be measured and compared for specific purposes. Moreover, these models employ essentially identical criteria for the purpose of delineating the structural dimensions of system integration. In short, the component elements of these models do not vary from one culture to another. Therefore, the plural theory does not implicate a scientific strategy based on the proposition that different types of theories are required in order to interpret and explain different types of historical societies.[19]

To conclude, the plural theory is not, in Shils's terms, a "general theory of society of universal comprehensiveness." However, it is an extremely useful analytical device for comparative research. Because it provides considerable insight into the dynamics of system integration and the implications these have for the process of sociocultural change, the plural theory may represent a step in the direction of a more comprehensive theory of culture and society.

---

[19] M. G. Smith has stated that the plural theory and the general theory of social action are "diametrically opposed, and yield mutually irreconcilable interpretations of societies of the type . . ." under consideration. This statement is misleading. It would appear to be valid with respect to that version of social action theory which Lockwood (*op. cit.*, p. 244) refers to as "normative functionalism," but there are other versions of social system theory, and Smith is certainly aware of this fact, as evidenced by his own work. I emphasize this point because one of the major criticisms of the plural theory, particularly Furnivall's conception, has been that it postulates a scientific strategy which would require different theories for the analysis of different types of societies. See Smith, *Stratification in Grenada,* p. 1.

# BIBLIOGRAPHY

## BOOKS

Almond, Gabriel A. and James S. Coleman (eds.), *The Politics of Developing Areas*. Princeton: Princeton University Press, 1960.

Bohannan, Paul and George Dalton (eds.), *Markets in Africa*. Evanston, Ill.: Northwestern University Press, 1962.

Bretton, Henry L., *Power and Stability in Nigeria*. New York: Frederick A. Praeger, 1962.

Cameron, N. E., *The Evolution of The Negro,* 2 Vols. Georgetown, B.G.: Argosy Co., 1934.

Carter, Gwendolen M. (ed.), *African One-Party States*. Ithaca, N.Y.: Cornell University Press, 1962.

Clementi, Sir Cecil, *A Constitutional History of British Guiana*. London: Macmillan, 1937.

Dean, Vera Micheles, *The Nature of The Non-Western World*. New York: The New American Library, 1957.

Deerr, N., *The History of Sugar,* 2 Vols. London: Chapman and Hall, 1949.

Des Voeux, Sir William, *Experiences of A Demerara Magistrate, 1865–1870*. Reprinted as No. 11 in the *Daily Chronicle's* Guiana Edition Series, Georgetown, B.G., 1948.

Deutsch, Karl W., *Nationalism and Social Communication*. Boston: M.I.T. Press, 1953.

Easton, David (ed.), *Varieties of Political Theory*. Englewood Cliffs, N.J.: Prentice-Hall, 1966.

Firth, Raymond, *Elements of Social Organization*. New York: Philosophical Library, 1951.

Fitzgerald, S. K., *Some Population and Land Aspects of British Guiana*. Unpublished report of the University of Maryland United States Operations Mission to the British Guiana Land Settlement Department, 1956.

Franck, Thomas M., *Race and Nationalism: The Struggle for Power in Rhodesia-Nyasaland*. New York: Fordham University Press, 1960.

Furnivall, J. S., *Netherlands India A Study of Plural Economy*. London: Cambridge University Press, 1939.

———, *Colonial Policy and Practice A Comparative Study of Burma and Netherlands India*. London: Cambridge University Press, 1948.

Geertz, Clifford (ed.), *Old Societies and New States*. New York: Free Press of Glencoe, 1963.

Goody, Jack (ed.), *The Developmental Cycle in Domestic Groups*. Cambridge Papers in Social Anthropology, No. 1. London: Cambridge University Press, 1962.

Gould, Peter R. (ed.), *Africa: Continent of Change*. Belmont, Calif.: Wadsworth, 1961.

Gross, Llewellyn (ed.), *Symposium on Sociological Theory*. Evanston, Ill.: Row, Peterson and Company, 1959.

Halperin, Ernst, *Racism and Communism in British Guiana*. Cambridge, Mass.: M.I.T. Center for International Studies, 1964.

Herskovits, Melville J. and F. S. Herskovits, *Rebel Destiny*. New York: McGraw Hill, 1934.

Horowitz, Irving L., *Three Worlds of Development*. New York: Oxford University Press, 1966.

Ireland, A. Alleyne, *Demerariana, Essays: Historical, Critical, and Descriptive*. Georgetown, B.G.: Baldwin and Co., 1897.

Jagan, Cheddi, *Forbidden Freedom*. London: Lawrence and Wishart, 1954.

Jaywardena, Chandra, *Interim Report on a Study of Social Structure and Processes of Social Control Amongst East Indian Sugar Workers in British Guiana*. Mona, Jamaica: Institute of Social and Economic Research, University College of the West Indies, 1957.

———, *Conflict and Solidarity in a Guianese Plantation*. London School of Economics Monographs on Social Anthropology, London: Athlone Press, 1963.

Kahin, George McTurnan, *Nationalism and Revolution in Indonesia*. Ithaca, N.Y.: Cornell University Press, 1952.

Kautsky, John H. (ed.), *Political Change in Underdeveloped Countries*. New York: John Wiley and Sons, 1962.

Linton, Ralph, *The Study of Man*. New York: Appleton-Century-Crofts, 1936.

MacIver, Robert M., *Social Causation*. New York: Ginn and Company, 1942.

Maine, Sir Henry S., *Ancient Law*. London: Routledge & Sons, 1904.

Marshall, A. H., *Report on Local Government in British Guiana*. Georgetown, B.G.: The Argosy Company, 1955.

Mitchell, J. C., *Tribalism and The Plural Society*. London: Oxford University Press, 1960.

Nadel, S. F., *The Foundations of Social Anthropology*. Glencoe, Ill.: The Free Press, 1951.

Nath, Dwarka, *A History of Indians in British Guiana*. London: Thomas Nelson & Sons, 1950.

Neufeld, Maurice F., *Poor Countries and Authoritarian Rule*. Ithaca, N.Y.: Cornell University Press, 1965.

Nkrumah, Kwame, *Neo-Colonialism The Last Stage of Imperialism*. New York: International Publishers, 1965.

Ragatz, L. J., *The Fall of The Planter Class in The British Caribbean 1763–1833*. London: Oxford University Press, 1928.

Rain, Thomas, *The Life and Labours of John Wray, Pioneer Missionary in British Guiana*. London: John Snow & Co., 1892.

Rodway, J., *Guiana: British, Dutch and French*. London: T. Fisher Unwin, 1912.

Rubin, Vera (ed.), *Caribbean Studies: A Symposium*. Mona, Jamaica: Institute of Social and Economic Research, University of the West Indies, 1957. Reprinted by the University of Washington Press, Seattle, Wash., 1960.

———, (ed.), *Social and Cultural Pluralism in The Caribbean*. Annals of the New York Academy of Sciences, Vol. 83, 1960.

Ruhomon, Peter, *Centenary History of The East Indians in British Guiana, 1838–1938*. Georgetown, B.G.: The Daily Chronicle's Guiana Edition, 1946.

Shannon, Lyle W. *Underdeveloped Areas*. New York: Harper & Brothers, 1957.

Smith, M. G., *Stratification in Grenada*. Los Angeles: University of California Press, 1965.

———, *The Plural Society in The British West Indies*. Los Angeles: University of California Press, 1965.

Smith, Raymond T., *The Negro Family in British Guiana*. London: Routledge and Kegan Paul, Ltd., 1956.

———, *British Guiana*. London: Oxford University Press, 1962.

Steward, Julian H. (ed.), *Handbook of South American Indians,* 6 Vols. Washington, D.C.: Smithsonian Institution, Bureau of American Ethnology, 1946–50.

Steward, Julian H., *Theory of Culture Change*. Urbana, Ill.: University of Illinois Press, 1955.

Swan, Michael, *British Guiana The Land of Six Peoples*. London: H.M.S.O., 1957.

van den Berghe, Pierre L., *South Africa, A Study in Conflict*. Middletown, Conn.: Wesleyan University Press, 1965.

Wallbridge, Rev. E. A., *The Demerara Martyr*. Georgetown, B.G.: Daily Chronicle, 1943.

Webber, A. R. F., *Centenary History and Handbook of British Guiana*. Georgetown, B.G.: Argosy Co., 1931.

Williams, Eric, *Capitalism and Slavery*. Chapel Hill, N.C.: University of North Carolina Press, 1944.

Young, Allan, *The Approaches to Local Self-Government in British Guiana*. London: Longmans, Green & Company, Ltd., 1958.

Zollschan, George K. and Walter Hirsch (eds.), *Explorations in Social Change*. New York: Houghton, Mifflin, 1964.

## ARTICLES AND PERIODICALS

Benedict, B., "Stratification in Plural Societies," *American Anthropologist,* 64, (1962), 1235–46.

Bennett, John W. and Leo A. Despres, "Kinship and Instrumental Activities," *American Anthropologist,* 62, (1960), 254–67.

Bradley, P., "The Party System in British Guiana and the General Election of 1961," *Caribbean Studies,* October, 1961.

Braithwaite, Lloyd, "Social Stratification in Trinidad," *Social and Economic Studies,* 2, nos. 2 & 3, (1953), 5–175.

———, "Social Stratification and Cultural Pluralism" in Vera Rubin (ed.), *Social and Cultural Pluralism in the Caribbean.* Annals of the New York Academy of Sciences, 83, (1960), 816–31.

Codere, Helen, "Power in Ruanda," *Anthropologica,* 4, (1962), 45–85.

Colby, B. N. and Pierre van den Berghe, "Ethnic Relations in Southeastern Mexico," *American Anthropologist,* 63, (1961), 772–92.

Coleman, James S., "Current Political Movements in Africa," *The Annals,* 358, (1955), 95–108.

———, "Conclusions: The Political Systems of Developing Areas" in Almond and Coleman (eds.), *The Politics of Developing Areas,* 532–76.

Collins, B. A. N., "Racial Imbalance in Public Services and Security Forces," *Race,* 3, (1966), 235–53.

Cowan, L. Gray, "Guinea" in Gwendolen M. Carter (ed.), *African One-Party States,* 149–236.

Crowley, D. J., "Plural and Differential Acculturation in Trinidad," *American Anthropologist,* 59, (1957), 817–24.

Despres, Leo A., "The Implications of Nationalist Politics in British Guiana for The Development of Cultural Theory," *American Anthropologist,* 66, (1964), 1051–1077.

Fallers, Lloyd A., "Ideology and Culture in Uganda Nationalism," *American Anthropologist,* 63, (1961), 677–86.

Farley, R., "The Rise of The Peasantry in British Guiana," *Social and Economic Studies,* 2, (1954).

———, "The Unification of British Guiana," *Social and Economic Studies,* 4, (1955).

Firth, Raymond, "Social Organization and Social Change," *Journal of The Royal Anthropological Institute of Great Britain and Ireland,* 84, (1954), 1–21.

Fortes, M., "Introduction" in Jack Goody (ed.), *The Developmental Cycle in Domestic Groups,* 1–14.

Freedman, M., "The Growth of A Plural Society in Malaya," *Pacific Affairs,* 33, (1960), 158–68.

Freeman, L. A., "Land Tenure in British Guiana" in *Caribbean Land Tenure Symposium*. A publication of the Caribbean Research Council, Port of Spain, Trinidad, B.W.I., (1946), 357–66.

Freilich, M., "Serial Polygyny, Negro Peasants, and Model Analysis," *American Anthropologist,* 63, (1961), 955–75.

Fried, M., "The Chinese in British Guiana," *Social and Economic Studies,* 5, (1956), 54–73.

Gillen, John, "Tribes of the Guianas" in Julian H. Steward (ed.), *Handbook of South American Indians,* 3, (1948), 799–860.

Gouldner, Alvin W., "Reciprocity and Autonomy in Functional Theory" in Llewellyn Gross (ed.), *Symposium on Sociological Theory,* 241–70.

Haynes, J. A., "The Economic Importance of the Sugar Industry to British Guiana" in *Bookers Sugar*. Report of the Booker Brothers, McConnell & Company, Ltd., (1954), 18–20.

Hoselitz, Bert F., "Nationalism, Economic Development, and Democracy," *The Annals,* 305, (1956), 1–11.

Jagan, Cheddi, "Address to the 1956 Congress of The Peoples Progressive Party." Published in the December 22, 1956, issue of *The Daily Chronicle,* Georgetown, B.G.

Jayawardena, Chandra, "Religious Belief and Social Change: Aspects of the Development of Hinduism in British Guiana," *Comparative Studies in Society and History,* 8, (1966), 211–40.

Lens, Sidney, "American Labor Abroad: Lovestone Diplomacy," *The Nation,* July 5, 1965, 10–ff.

Lockwood, David, "Social Integration and System Integration" in George K. Zollschan and Walter Hirsch (eds.), *Explorations in Social Change,* 244–57.

Luckhoo, J. A., "The East Indian in British Guiana," *Timehri* (The Journal of the Royal Agricultural and Commercial Society of British Guiana), 6, (1919), 53–65.

McArthur, J. Sydney, "Our People," *Timehri* (The Journal of the Royal Agricultural and Commercial Society of British Guiana), 7, (1921), 20–28.

McKenzie, H. I., "The Plural Society Debate, Some Comments on a Recent Contribution," *Social and Economic Studies,* 15, (1966), 53–60.

Mintz, Sidney W., "The Plantation as a Socio-Cultural Type" in *Plantation Systems of The New World,* Social Science Monographs VII, Pan American Union, (1959), 42–49.

Morris, Stephen, "Indians in East Africa: A Study in a Plural Society," *British Journal of Sociology,* 7, (1956), 194–211.

Nash, M., "The Multiple Society in Economic Development," *American Anthropologist,* 59, (1957), 825–33.

Newman, Peter, "The Economic Future of British Guiana," *Social and*

*Economic Studies,* 9, (1960), 263–96.

Nyerere, J., "Will Democracy Work in Africa?" in Peter R. Gould (ed.), *Africa: Continent of Change,* 52–55.

O'Loughlin, Carleen, "The Economy of British Guiana, 1952–56: A National Accounts Study," *Social and Economic Studies,* 8, (1959), 1–104.

Parsons, Talcott, "The Position of Sociological Theory," *American Sociological Review,* 13, (1948), 155–64.

Pocock, David F., "Notes on Jajmani Relationships," *Contributions to Indian Sociology,* 6, (1962), 78–95.

Reno, Philip, "The Ordeal of British Guiana," *Monthly Review,* 16, (1964), 1–132.

Rex, John, "The Plural Society in Sociological Theory," *British Journal of Sociology,* 10, (1959), 114–24.

Rubin, Vera, "Cultural Perspectives in Caribbean Research" in Vera Rubin (ed.), *Caribbean Studies: A Symposium,* 110–22.

———, "Introduction" in *Plantation Systems of The New World,* Social Science Monographs VII, Pan American Union, (1959), 1–4.

———, "Discussion of M. G. Smith's Social and Cultural Pluralism" in Vera Rubin (ed.), *Social and Cultural Pluralism in the Caribbean,* 780–85.

Shils, Edward, "On the Comparative Study of New States" in Clifford Geertz (ed.), *Old Societies and New States,* 1–26.

Simpson, G. E., "The Ras Tafari Movement in Jamaica: A Study of Race and Class Conflict," *Social Forces,* 34, (1955), 167–70.

Skinner, E. P., "Group Dynamics and Social Stratification in British Guiana" in Vera Rubin (ed.), *Social and Cultural Pluralism in The Caribbean,* 904–12.

Smith, M. G., "Social and Cultural Pluralism" in Vera Rubin (ed.), *Social and Cultural Pluralism in The Caribbean,* 763–77.

———, "A Structural Approach to Comparative Politics" in David Easton (ed.), *Varieties of Political Theory,* 113–28.

Smith, Raymond T. and Chandra Jayawardena, "Hindu Marriage Customs in British Guiana," *Social and Economic Studies,* 7, (1958), 178–94.

——— and Chandra Jayawardena, "Marriage and the Family Amongst East Indians in British Guiana," *Social and Economic Studies,* 8, (1959), 321–76.

Smith, Raymond T., "Review of Social and Cultural Pluralism in the Caribbean," *American Anthropologist,* 63, (1961), 155–57.

Steward, Julian H., "Culture Areas of the Tropical Forests" in Julian H. Steward (ed.), *Handbook of South American Indians,* 3, (1948), 883–99.

Wagley, C., "Plantation America: A Culture Sphere" in Vera Rubin (ed.), *Caribbean Studies: A Symposium,* 3–13.

## REPORTS

The Constitution, Suspension Ordered on October 8, 1953. *A White Paper Issued by Her Majesty's Government,* October, 1953.

Development Programme 1956–1960. *British Guiana Legislative Council Paper No. 8/1956.*

Development Programme 1960–1964. *British Guiana Legislative Council Paper No. 5/1959.*

Local Government Ordinance of 1953. *The Law of British Guiana,* Chapter 150. London: Waterlow & Sons, Ltd., 1954.

*Report of the British Guiana Constitutional Commission* (Sir E. J. Waddington, Chairman), London: H.M.S.O. Colonial No. 280, 1950–51.

*Report of the British Guiana Constitutional Commission* (Sir James Robertson, Chairman), London: H.M.S.O. Report Cmd. 9274, 1954.

*Report of A Commission of Inquiry into the Sugar Industry of British Guiana* (J. A. Venn, Chairman), London: H.M.S.O. Colonial No. 249, 1949.

*Report of the Land Tenure and Registration of Titles Committee,* 1954–1955.

*Report to the Government of British Guiana on Employment, Unemployment and Underemployment in the Colony in 1956.* Geneva: International Labour Office, 1957.

Sessional Paper No. 5/1959. *Paper of the Second Legislative Council on British Guiana's 1960–64 Development Programme.* Georgetown, B.G.: The B. G. Lithographic Company, Ltd., 1959.

"We're No Pawn of East or West." Pamphlet issued by the Peoples National Congress, 1960.

# INDEX

Printed in the U.S.A.